# THE PERVERSION OF SUBMISION

## IDOLS IN THE CHRISTIAN CHURCH

Joan Erickson

THE PERVERSION OF SUBMISSION
Idols in the Christian Church

Library of Congress Catalog Number: 98-93449
ISBN Number: 0-9665846-0-0


Published by Miracle of Love Ministries
Mr & Mrs Curtis Erickson
4365 Elmwood Lane
Hermantown, MN   55811




Printed in the U.S.A. by
Morris Publishing
3212 E. Hwy 30
Kearney, NE 68847
1-800-650-7888

## INTRODUCTION

**This book is a prophetic, end time warning for the body of Christ.** My mandate from the Lord is Jeremiah 1:10. I am to uproot, tear down, destroy and overthrow Satan's work of darkness by exposing false doctrines and the resulting idol worship in the Church. Then, build and plant truth to replace what is torn down.

The Lord said He was returning for a church without spot, wrinkle or any such thing. Idols in the church, unrighteousness that abounds because of false teaching on "grace", "eternal security", and false submission are interrelated parts of the apostasy of the latter days church.

Idols are produced by false teachings of headship, submission of wives to husbands, congregations to pastors, divorce and remarriage. Because we are dealing with the perversion of submission of women to men, you may feel the book is biased, unbalanced and presents only the feminine side of the story. However, **rarely, if ever, are men told to go home and submit to wives.** Therefore the book must seem biased out of necessity. My intentions are NOT to tear down men and elevate women above men, they are to tear down idols and elevate God. Please do not get angry and stop reading before you get to the Truth. You must read the whole book to get a complete picture. A truth from one chapter builds on a truth from the proceeding chapter. Please read them in order. Many chapters contain startling truths that have been distorted or hidden until now. This is end time revelation knowledge that will clean up the spots and wrinkles in the Body. Those false teachings of submission are Satan's preparation plan for the reign of Anti-Christ.

The perversion of submission has destroyed the beautiful blessing of headship that God intended for the marriage relationship. I am blessed and I cherish the true form of headship my husband practices in our marriage.

May God use this book to bring insight, repentance, healing and freedom to all His people, men, women, and pastors.

## DEDICATION

This book is dedicated to: Christian women who have been wounded by perverse teachings on submission. Deceived Christian men who carry a much heavier burden as "heads of their homes" than God ever intended. All Christians who have had their freedom in Christ taken away by perverse submission to false "coverings" of pastors, church boards and denominations. Pastors, who need to be set free from deception.

*******

THANK YOU TO:
The women who shared their testimonies.
Jean Priest, Erika Laven and Julie Balmer.
Precious daughters, Lynn-Marie, Mary, Renee and Lori for allowing me to share a part of their lives. Special thanks to my sister Beverly, and her late husband, Earl Finke for financial assistance in publishing the book, prayers and encouragement.
Most of all, humble thanks to my beloved husband, Curtis, for showing me what real love and headship is, for his inspiration, for all the many ways he sacrificed, helped and loved me through the $5\frac{1}{2}$ years of writing the book.

THOU SHALL HAVE NO OTHER GOD'S BEFORE ME
Exodus 20:3


THOU SHALL NOT BOW DOWN THYSELF TO THEM,
NOR SERVE THEM; FOR I, THE LORD THY GOD
AM A JEALOUS GOD.
Exodus 20-5


FOR THOU SHALT WORSHIP NO OTHER GOD: FOR
THE LORD, WHOSE NAME IS JEALOUS, IS A
JEALOUS GOD.
Exodus 34:14


FOR THE LORD THY GOD IS A CONSUMING FIRE,
EVEN A JEALOUS GOD.
Deuteronomy 4:24


LITTLE CHILDREN, KEEP YOURSELVES FROM IDOLS.
I John 5:21


DO WE PROVOKE THE LORD TO JEALOUSY?---
I Corinthians 10:22


I believe the church is provoking the LORD to
jealousy.  This is the reason for this book.

Joan Erickson

# PERVERSION OF SUBMISSION

# CHAPTER ONE
## TESTIMONIES

The following testimonies are graphic and explicit examples of how serious the perversion of submission is. Women are being told to stay in these kinds of situations and worse. They are told that "submit to your husband in everything" means they must endure all manner of abuse. Sexual abuse in marriage is a big issue. I apologize if I offend you with these examples. Note how Scripture is twisted in order to accommodate "submit to your husband in everything".

*\*\*\*\*\*\*\*\**

Ann, a godly young woman sat in church next to her husband. The pastor stood in his pulpit preaching. After the service, the pastor approached Ann and said, "You are a very bad witness for Christ". Ann was stunned and asked what she had done to provoke such a reprimand. The pastor replied that she had given her husband very hateful looks during the service. Ann explained, "Pastor, my husband was making very inappropriate sexual advances to me right here during the church service. He does this often. I have repeatedly told him that his behavior is inappropriate, it embarrasses and upsets me very much. But he won't stop it. Unless I make a scene during the service, my only recourse is to communicate my feelings to him through these looks."

The pastor's comment was that it was still wrong of her to look at him like that. The pastor never confronted the husband about his ungodly obsessive behavior in church. Nor did he say anything about the husband's disrespect for his wife, for anyone observing what he was doing, and most of all, his disrespect to God. There was only reproof and condemnation for the woman. There was no apology from the pastor for adding insult to the indignation and humiliation that Ann was already suffering. She was very right to be upset. Her husband was displaying sinful behavior in God's house, where they had both gone to revere and honor God. The man's problem was not acknowledged or addressed and the woman went away condemned and wounded. The only thing confronted was the presumed fault in her!

One Scripture violated here is I Tim.3:15. "You may know how you ought to behave yourself in the house of God which is the church of the living God, the pillar and ground of the truth" (KJV). This verse is not just speaking about how all believers are to act as part of the body of Christ. The word house literally means churches, (plural), of God, the called out assemblies or popular meetings, such as in a synagogue or a congregation. The passage is an instruction on how to act when one is in the meeting of the congregation. Covert sexual conduct with ones wife is definitely inappropriate conduct in the assembly of the believers or church.

********

Joan, whose husband was a pastor, left him because of his anger, violence, verbal and emotional abuse, and his perversions of transvestism and transsexualism. She was gone for five days. Another pastor/counselor friend told her she needed to go back to her husband because her absence was ruining her husband's ministry!! Joan took that advice and admonition, went back to her husband, and in so doing, aborted what God wanted to do in the man's life through that separation. God himself removed her husband from the ministry, but Joan had false guilt to work through because she was so wrongfully accused of ruining his ministry. The pastor/counselor worked extensively with Joan and her husband, but to no avail. In the course of counseling for so much perversion, though, the pastor told Joan more than once, "You are judging him and you have no right to judge".

Again, there was false guilt for her to work through.

One Scripture violation here is I Cor. 5:1-13. Especially verses 3, 5, and 10-13. Paul says he has judged the sin of this one called a brother, just as we are all to judge the sin of one called brother. He said to separate yourself from this one and turn him over to Satan for the burning of the flesh, so that he will repent and be saved in the day of the Lord. Another Scripture is I Tim. 5:17-22. This "elder" should have been openly rebuked so that people would learn to fear God, but instead his sin was hidden because he was a preacher. This was partiality based on position, which is thoroughly condemned by God himself in Malachi.

********

Carol suffered through the painful experience of her husband's adulterous affair when she was about to give birth to their first child. She worked through the pain of it and stayed with him. But some years later, after much sexual and physical abuse from her husband, he had other affairs. Carol went to the pastor for counsel. The pastor quoted the verse about forgiving seventy times seven, and told her to go home and submit to her husband. The husband was never confronted about his immorality. He was allowed to continue in his sin, and was encouraged to continue to come to church, even while living in sin. He was a good tither.

Some Scriptures violated were I Cor. 5:1-13 and I Cor. 6:13-20. Carol was violated and betrayed, both by her husband and by her pastor. The church was violated because the immorality that the pastor knew about was allowed to remain to leaven the whole church.

********

Adam refused to cut the ties with his parents. He was very dependent on them for everything. He refused to take the responsibility of making

3

decisions in his own home. Then he went to the other wrong extreme. He took full control of their finances, among other things. His wife, Diane, was stranded several times because the car was out of gas. She had no money for gas because he wouldn't give her money, and he didn't want her to work to earn any. The relationship deteriorated to the point of physical abuse, including choking. They went for counseling. The Christian counselor's advice to Diane was to go home and submit to her husband, who was the head of the house. Diane was wounded again, but her final word to the counselor was, "I'm supposed to submit to my husband, but if he doesn't treat his wife right his prayers will not be heard." (I Pet. 3:7)

There was a violation of I Pet. 3:7 as well as Gen. 1:24, which commands the man to leave the father and mother and to cleave to his wife. This verse means he is to cut the ties with the parents and establish a new family unit with the wife. It does not mean he should be her dictator.

*********

Evelyn spoke to her husband about the feelings she experienced from verbal and visual sexual harassment from her father-in-law. Her daughter was exposed to the same thing. Her husband excused his father, saying, "He doesn't mean anything by it. That's just the way he is." Evelyn felt that she and her daughter were vulnerable and unprotected but her feelings were dismissed without a second thought. The father-in-law was never confronted about his behavior. Evelyn and her daughter were left defenseless. She went to the pastor for counsel, but his advice to her was to just ignore the harassment. He never spoke to the husband about the matter. It was never explained to him that he needed to protect his wife, not his father. Both of these men were professing Christians and church-goers.

4

TESTIMONIES

I refer again to I Cor. 5 where one who calls himself a brother, and yet does these things, should be disciplined. Matthew 5:28 says, "He who looks on a woman with lust has already committed adultery with her in his heart." Job made a covenant with his eyes not to look at a woman with lust because that would open up his wife to fornication. For Job, the act of looking with lust was the same as doing it, just as Jesus said in Matthew. Evelyn was experiencing in her spirit what was going on in the man's heart. This can be as damaging as an actual encounter. How many women have felt dirty, defiled and used just from a man's lustful look? The husband and the pastor were saying in effect, it was all right for the father-in-law and grandfather to rape his daughter-in-law and granddaughter with his eyes. And with his mouth. Ignore it! It is just his way!!

\*\*\*\*\*\*\*\*

A young, unmarried couple went too far, resulting in a pregnancy. Both Fran and Gene went to the same church, although neither were born again at the time. The pastor told Fran that it would be better for her to leave town. Gene was not confronted at all. Fran was condemned, while Gene went scott-free. Her sin was judged worthy of condemnation, but his part in the same sin was not even mentioned. The pastor did not counsel either of them with the need for repentance, forgiveness of sin, or salvation.

The partiality of this judgment was a violation of James 2:4 "Are ye not then partial in yourselves and are become judges with evil thoughts?"(KJV). Judging sin is not evil, but judging it with partiality is evil. The man's sin should have been judged as well as the woman's. The pastor was negligent by not counseling them with their need of repentance and salvation.

\*\*\*\*\*\*\*\*

Gladys had several children. Tom, her husband,

5

was a genius, but also a sloth. He forced her to sign papers that constituted welfare fraud. He used the verse, "Wives submit to your husbands in everything". He was not a Christian, but his wife was, and he knew that she had been taught that kind of submission all her life, and that she wanted to be obedient to God's Word. He used the Scripture like a club over her head. Tom and Gladys were prosecuted for welfare fraud. Although Tom admitted that he had coerced Gladys into signing the papers, she went to jail also. How much psychological and spiritual damage was done to Gladys and the children? How do they see God and Scripture now?

This was obviously a violation of Eph. 5:24, abusing the Scripture as an excuse to manipulate and abuse the wife.

********

Helen went to her pastor for counsel, relating horrendous examples of her husband Greg's sexual abuse. This deviant behavior would be judged as marital rape. She couldn't even go to the bathroom in private, as he had followed her there and forced oral sex on her. Greg had severe sexual addictions. The pastor told her that the Bible says a man has the right to expect his sexual due from his wife and not to defraud one another of sex. He said there's nothing wrong with sex and she needed to go home and submit to her husband. He did not believe that such a thing as marital rape existed, since sex was a God-ordained part of marriage. Greg's sexual sins and perversions were never addressed.

This is abuse of Heb. 13:4 which says the marriage bed is undefiled. This was used as an excuse for unclean, filthy practices that God condemns elsewhere in His Word, as a justification of the man's immoral behavior.

********

Glen left his house on a business trip. As

6

soon as he left, the phone rang. His wife, India, answered it. It seemed to be a sexual harassment call, since she heard nothing but heavy breathing. She was frightened because she thought someone evil was watching their house to see when she was alone. This happened often. She finally discovered that it was her mother-in-law who was using this cruel tactic to intimidate India into submitting to the mother and her manipulations of her son. India had recently left her husband's family church, which was a liberal church whose pastor was affiliated with a satanically associated organization. Most Christian leaders, including India's new pastor, knew this fact about this organization. Upon seeking advice from this new pastor, concerning her mother-in-law's intimidation, she was told to submit to her mother-in-law because one needs to honor the mother and father. The pastor stressed the importance of having the parental blessing for the marriage to work. He quoted her the verses about Ruth and Naomi, "Whither thou goest, I will go. Thy people shall be my people and THY GOD SHALL BE MY GOD." He said she needed to go back to her husband's church. India took that advice, thinking it was God's Word and wanting God's blessing. She became the mother-in-law's doormat for years. That pastor not only sent her back to years of abuse, but he literally threw a sheep, who had come to him for counsel, back to the wolves when he sent her back to a godless church whose pastor was associated with an organization that practices satanic rituals.

The Scriptures "Honor thy father and mother", and "Obey your parents in the Lord", have been violated and abused. Especially violated is the Scripture from Ruth. Ruth was following THE GOD, but this woman was told to follow a false god. There was also the abuse of the Scripture about the man leaving the mother and father and cleaving to the wife. The mother would not let go of the

control of her son.   But the pastor was condoning
this sin also.

********

Janice was the mother of many children.   Her
husband was an alcoholic and the family was dysfunctional.   She left her husband, but after a
couple of years, she thought maybe God would have
her go back to him.   She consulted her pastor,
who told her he didn't think that would be good
under the circumstances.   The pastor talked to
Janice's husband, who received salvation through
that counsel.   His life changed.   The family got
back together.   The couple stayed together until
he died.

Although this does not fit with the other
testimonies, I relay it for the purpose of relief.
There are pastors who give correct teaching.   Their
counsel is according to the balanced Word and it
produces good fruit.

Praise God that there were no Scriptures
violated here.

********

Joan, whose pastor husband was caught in the
perversions of transvestism and transsexualism,
told another Christian psychologist that what her
husband required her to do was like a role reversal.
Basically, if they were a homosexual couple,  she
would be in the role of the man  and he would be
in the role of the woman, sexually.   What he
demanded of her was to act like a lesbian and it
made her feel like one.   She felt like she was
making love to another woman.   In the course of
counseling with this Christian psychologist, she
too, was told to go home and submit to her husband's
perversions,  because he said a couple needed to
stroke each other in ways that brought emotional
satisfaction to them.   When she told the counselor
that this behavior opened the husband up to demonic
invasion, his sarcastic reply was that "God is
bigger than any old demons".

8

This husband used Scripture to justify his behavior and to force or manipulate Joan into doing his bidding. The Scripture he used was Heb. 13:4, "The marriage bed is undefiled"(KJV). When Joan came to the point where she was totally shut down to him and could not relate to him any longer sexually, he used I Cor. 7:5 about withholding or defrauding the spouse of sex. He tried to manipulate her with false guilt by saying, "How can you be a Christian and want to live according to the Word so much, but you don't live by THIS verse?"

There were many Scriptures violated and abused here. Especially all of the verses that deal with the enemy, "Resist the devil", "Put on the whole armor of God", "Flee youthful lusts," and "Touch not the unclean thing", "crucify the flesh", etc. and those about putting away all filthiness and immorality and impurity of all kinds. Many Scriptures were violated in order to pamper the flesh rather than to crucify it and to die to sinful self.

********

Kristin was separated from her husband and began to attend a new church. She believed that this was the church God wanted her to attend and so inquired about membership. The pastor informed her that she needed to be baptized in order to become a member. She told him that she had already been baptized since she had become a believer, and asked why it was necessary for her to do that again. The pastor told her that since she was separated from her husband and had no spiritual head, this would signify her acceptance of <u>his</u> spiritual authority over her. This would confirm her submission to him. He told her she should allow her make-up to run and her hair to get wet. (What significance this had for him, I don't know, unless it was supposed to show humility.) In addition to all of that, he said she should be rebaptized simply because he asked her to do it.

This is a graphic illustration of how some men in the pastorate have perverted the verse, "Obey your leaders and submit to their authority. They keep watch over you as men who must give account." (Heb. 13:17). Baptism is a precious means of identifying oneself with Him alone. It's a symbol of death to self, the new birth, and new life, in Christ. The pastor perverted Heb. 13:17 in order to use the preciousness of baptism as a means of forcing a woman's submission to a mere man's authority! What idolatry! Baptism is an obedience to God only and not a way of demonstrating obedience to any man!

********

These testimonies are from real women. Two of them are my own. They are not made up stories. Some are so extreme in nature, one would think that I had to search far to find these examples. The pain and woundedness from the perversion of submission is so prevalent that one does not have to search for it at all. I have been in one meeting of mixed genders when the subject of submission came up inadvertently. Within minutes, seven out of ten women present were having a hard time controlling their emotions and were revealing raw pain. No one had done anything to provoke these strong emotions, it was just there, right under the surface. The pain is so much a part of their lives. It is like a boil that is ready to break open, the slightest touch of it causes exquisite pain immediately. That's the way a majority of Christian women feel when the subject of submission comes up. They cringe inside at the sound of the word "submission". Though I do not know thousands of women, I have lived in various parts of the country, attended quite a few different evangelical congregations and I have recognized a certain degree of this phenomena in all of them. It is more predominant in certain

10

geographical areas and denominations. But it has been in every church, Bible college, and denomination that I have come in contact with. I have sat under the teachings of some of the most prominent Bible teachers of our day and have heard the same kinds of teachings from almost every one of them.

I have recognized the error in this teaching for years, but I did not realize HOW wrong and HOW damaging it was until the last five or six years. When I heard Ann's testimony, something ignited inside of me. I was sharing my anger about this with my husband, Curtis. I said I was so angry, but I didn't know what to do with my anger. He wisely reminded me that the thing that makes me most angry is when God's Word is perverted and that the root of this is a perversion of God's Word. I said, "That's true. But what do I do about it? When Jesus got angry about how the temple of God had been made into a den of thieves, He whipped the money changers and overturned their tables. What can I do?" He said, "Write a book".

In a way, the women, and all of those affected by spiritual abuse of church authorities, are also temples of God that have been defiled. There are books out now dealing with spiritual abuse. I feel that God is saying to me, He wants this book written to deal with the abuse of submission to husbands, pastors, church boards, and denominations.

I do not claim to be a great theologian. I have not attended Bible school or seminary. I have taken some correspondent courses in the Bible. During ten years as a pastor's wife, I studied and taught a lot of classes, from children to adults. In addition to attending countless seminars and teachings, I have listened to multitudes of tapes by varied speakers and I've read hundreds of books by varied authors. I have an extensive library that many pastors would envy. I do not know Greek or Hebrew, but I do rely heavily on the concordance and expository dictionaries. Most of all, I rely on the Bible and the promise of God that the Holy Spirit would be my teacher and would reveal the deep things of God to me. I also believe in His promise that if I lack wisdom, I can ask of Him and He will give it freely.

As I said, all of the testimonies given, are actual accounts. Even though these women tried to go along with "submission", the fact is, their situations did not improve, but rather deteriorated. All but one ended in divorce. Usually there were years of counseling, in some cases as much as eight to ten years of it, before the women finally gave up on the marriage. In every one of these cases there has been at least one or more basic biblical principles that have been set aside in order to accommodate, "Submit to your husband in **everything**". This erroneous teaching on submission is producing a crop of it's own rotten fruit as evidenced by the ever increasing number of divorces in Christian marriages. If the teaching of submission, that is so prevalent, is according to the Word of God, it should be healing marriages and bringing harmony into them instead of destroying them.

Though it's taught by many, these teachings are espoused yearly at certain seminars for male pastors only, of every denomination. The seminars are held all over the country and are well attended. The pastors take it back to their churches, teach it, practice it, and use the manuals as a counseling resource. There is much truth in the teachings, but the subtle seeds of distorted truth are being fed into every denomination, like mainlining drugs. It's a diabolical scheme of the devil to make further in-roads into the family to destroy it through perverted submission.

Though I want to protect those who shared their testimonies by using fictitious names, I boldly use these examples as illustrations to expose what I know to be false teaching.

The false teaching on submission to church authorities that has crept into the church of today has the same basis as the false teachings of women submitting to their husbands. Instead of "Submit to your husband in everything", it comes under "Obey those who have been given authority over you in the Lord". It has brought people under the domination and control of the pastor or denomination.

This book is not an indictment against all men, pastors or denominations. It is not my intention to bring condemnation upon anyone or to cause doubt about those honest pastors who are true shepherds of the sheep. Like the pastor who advised Janice not to go back to her alcoholic husband. Instead, he confronted her husband with his sin. The man dealt with it and he let God change him, resulting in the fruit of reconciliation. There are many, many such pastors. Thank God for them. And there are many, many good husbands who are walking after the spirit and are producing good fruit in their families. God bless them, too. But there are also many good pastors and good husbands who are caught in this web of deception. They are truly trying to live God's Word, but they are being deceived about what the Word really says. I pray for these people, that this book might open their eyes and set them free from the bondage of this deception.

Pastors, and Christian counselors, if you recognize yourself in some of these testimonies, please allow God to reveal more truth to you. Satan has captivated you with this deception and you are leading others astray with it. The way you use the Word to lead others, whether it is right or wrong, is what you will give account to God for.

My intent is to expose the schemes of the devil and to show how he is working through God's people to destroy the family. I want to reveal

13

those schemes which keep many of God's children from doing and being all that God intended them to do and to be for Him.

Through the false teaching of submission to the pastor, the devil effectively stops the Holy Spirit from bringing men and women alike into full maturity in Christ and from accomplishing what God wants to do in the Body through them. Many times, a godly person will go to a pastor, saying, "I believe this is what God wants me to do in the Body, using the gifts and the calling of God". But the pastor and the board says "NO". The person submits to them and God's work is left undone. The Body is cheated, the person is cheated, and God is cheated. Christianity is perpetuated as a spectator sport, rather than promoting the participation by all with the gifts of the Holy Spirit as God intended. When the pastor is the only player on the field, he is trying to cover all the player's positions. He experiences burn-out, because God never intended a pastor to be a one-man player, coach, and referee all by himself with the rest of the body acting as fans and cheerleaders.

It is time for the body of Christ to recognize this deception, the damage it is doing, repent of it and move on to maturity.

# CHAPTER TWO
## IN THE BEGINNING


In the beginning God created all the heavens and the earth and every living thing. Then He said, "Let US make man in OUR image". So God created man in His own image, in the image of God He created him; male and female He created THEM. God blessed THEM and said to THEM "Be fruitful and multiply and fill the earth and subdue it. Have dominion over the fish and birds and all living things." After each act of creation God said that what He had created was "good", but it was only after He created Eve that He said it was VERY good. (Gen. 1:26-31). It pleased the triune God to make BOTH male and female in their image and likeness.

God formed the man from the dust of the ground, breathed life into him, then placed him in the Garden of Eden. He gave Adam the command not to eat of the tree of knowledge of good and evil, because if he ate of that tree, he would die. God said that man had no one to be his "help", so He would make one suitable for Adam. He put the man to sleep, took out a part of the man's side, formed a woman out of it, and brought her to the man. Adam called her woman because she was flesh of his flesh and bone of his bone. She was built out of man. Adam's statement indicates that he seemed to be awed by this precious equal counterpart of himself.

God said, as He created every living thing, that they should reproduce their own kind, so He created them in pairs. Adam had no one, thus God said, "It is NOT good that man should be ALONE." Adam's aloneness was the only thing in all of creation that God said was not good. He needed to have a "help" suitable to him. The word help means an aid. Not an aid as in a helper. For instance, a nurse's "aid" is an assistant, one of a lesser or subordinate position who is assigned to help one of a greater position. The word "help" here is the same word that is used of God as a "help" (Ezer) in Ps. 33:20, 70:5, and 121:1,2. It is describing one who comes to the rescue of man. It denotes a superior strength, because it has the power or ability to rescue one who is in trouble. The word "help" also means to protect, surround, and succor. So the purpose of the mate for Adam was not just to procreate, like animals, but a mate who could relate to him in every way. One who would rescue him from his aloneness. I believe there was to be a mutual surrounding, protecting, and succoring that would benefit both.

The Septuagint says the word "suitable" means "according to him", which was the pattern God used when He created pairs of mates of other living things. But the word "alone" distinguishes man from animals in a significant way. Alone means properly, a separation; by implication it means a part of the body, "by self" and "each alike". God created a male and female animal. But for man, He created the man first, then He separated out a part of the man's body and created a woman out of that separated part, so that each was exactly like the other in all ways. They were compatible in mind, body, soul and spirit. She was not inferior to him in any way. Adam was formed out of the dust of the ground, but Eve was formed out of flesh and bone from the man. Had she been made out of dust also, one could say that she might be inferior, but since she was made out the man, there was no possibility of her being inferior. She was his other self, just like him, a part of his own body. He was her source of origin, because of that, he was her head. The source of origin does not entail any kind of authoritarian qualities.

God did not pronounce His creation VERY good until after Eve was created. The word VERY means that God said, "vehemently, NOW it was EXCEEDINGLY

WHOLE". God called all of His creation good but it was not completely whole until Eve was created. Eve was the final creation that made it all exceedingly whole. Remember this point. God said, "VEHEMENTLY, NOW IT WAS EXCEEDINGLY WHOLE". Vehement means fervent, passionate, intense feeling!

God blessed BOTH of his humans and gave THEM dominion over the earth and the living creatures. They were both told to subdue them. These creatures were distinguished from humans because they were not created in God's image. They did not have a will and a spirit like that of humans.

Genesis 3:16 says, "He shall rule over you". To interpret that to mean that God was giving the man the RIGHT of rule and dominion over the woman, is to classify her in the same category as the animals. It is to say that God, who created her in His image, was now lowering His image bearer to the status of the animals. One who needed to have someone rule over her and subdue her like the animals needed to be ruled over and subdued. Is that what God really meant when He said "he shall rule over you"? If that is what He meant, then He would have to take away that part of her that was like Him, her will and her spirit, thus removing His image from her. If He did that, His own VEHEMENT statement, "NOW it was exceedingly whole" would be meaningless. He would be taking away that part that made all of His creation exceedingly whole, thus it would no longer be exceedingly whole. It would again be incomplete. The woman would no longer be a suitable "help" for the man. Therefore, there must be another explanation that is more compatible with God's just and Holy nature.

Having said that, I will attempt to give what I believe is a valid explanation of what He meant.

To do that, we will begin by going to the fall of mankind, where we see that Eve was beguiled by the serpent. The serpent asked Eve, "Did God say?". In Gen. 3:4, she says, "God did say 'you must not eat of the tree in the middle of the garden'." This is different from Gen. 2:16 where it says specifically, "God COMMANDED the man".That difference is important. The woman was repeating what she had been told, whereas, the man had been given a direct command by God.

There is no record that God ever commanded Eve, personally, concerning the tree of knowledge of good and evil. Yet in her conversation with the serpent we know that she was aware of the commandment. Since God did give the command to Adam BEFORE Eve was created, I believe that God had established a certain kind of headship of man. The headship was not authoritarian, it had nothing to do with the woman submitting her will to his or with him being the decision maker. It was a responsibility to SPEAK spiritual things to the woman. Because in I Pet. 3:7, woman is called the weaker vessel, I believe that there was a physically protective assignment inherent in the headship that goes beyond the mutual protection, and succoring that comes from the word "help". But more important than that, according to Strong's Concordance, **the major meaning of "weaker vessel" is that the man, MUST follow through with spiritual actions, which would confirm, authenticate and establish the Word he spoke.** That headship did not include the right of dominion over her, the right to control her mind, her will, or her right of decision in any matter. God gave them the right, the responsibility, and the will, to think and act independently of each other. That included the responsibility to bear the consequences of their own actions and choices. There is nowhere in Scripture where God gives anyone the right to control someone's mind or will. He does not do it Himself! That kind of domination and control is witchcraft and God forbids it in other Scripture. If He forbids it elsewhere, is it likely that He

18

would go against His own Word by giving the right of dominion over the woman to the man?

Eve was beguiled, she made a bad choice while her mind and will were bewitched and befuddled by Satan. God did not make the choice for her. He did not control her will. Adam made a bad choice in his own will. God did not control his will either. Even in the fall, the serpent, Adam and Eve were each one responsible for their own individual decisions and actions. Eve did not bear the consequences for being disobedient to Adam, but for being disobedient to God. In God's discourse with her, He never mentioned or condemned her for making a decision on her own without consulting Adam. Nor did He say she was responsible for leading Adam astray. Adam and the serpent bore their own consequences for their disobedience to God.

Eve was deceived and sinned. ADAM WAS NOT DECEIVED WHEN HE SINNED. Throughout the ages, mankind has said that because the woman was so easily deceived, she cannot be trusted in spiritual matters, or any other matter. Because she was so easily led astray, her mind must somehow be inferior to man's. There is a vast difference between Eve's being deceived and Adam's making a deliberate decision to sin without being deceived!

All people can become a victim of deception. The very nature of deception is that something is presented as helpful, beautiful, fulfilling, good etc. but it is really evil or harmful. It is done deliberately, like a trap set for a victim. If one knew it was a bad thing, or that it would be hurtful in some way, one would not be enticed by it. The essence of deception is to present something differently from what it really is with the intent of leading the victim into the trap.

We are told in Rev. 12:3-4; Rom. 16:20; II Cor. 11:3, 14 that the serpent was only Satan's mouthpiece. Serpent means a snake, and it comes

19

from a root word that has among it's meanings to
hiss, that is, whisper a magic spell, enchanter,
use enchantment. So when Eve was beguiled by the
serpent, this was not an ordinary temptation! Satan
used all of his sinister powers against her. I
believe that Satan came to her much like he came
to tempt Christ in the wilderness, it was that
powerful. After all, Satan had much at stake when
he beguiled her! If he could trick her into eating
the forbidden fruit, he would have the whole human
race under his dominion. She was the victim of
the serpent, who was the embodiment of Satan, the
most powerful, cunning, crafty, deceiver that ever
existed. She was not evil nor did she have any
evil intent toward Adam. She was a victim!! She
was held accountable for her own disobedience,
but she was tricked, deceived, bewitched by the
master of all masters of deception. Satan's power
of cunning craftiness is important to understand
and is emphasized in Gen. 3:1. I believe God's
intention is to make us aware of what a formidable
foe Satan is and to make us aware of his schemes.
Satan, this most cunning creature, this master
of deceit, is what Eve was confronted with. She
became a victim of his beguiling deception. The
fact that she was beguiled is passed off lightly
and glossed over as though it wasn't any big deal.
The attitude, if it is thought about at all, is
"ho-hum, so she was beguiled--so what? She's an
evil creature who tempted innocent Adam. She was
weak and let herself be deceived. She deserves
to be dominated and controlled. In fact she is
so weak, she NEEDS to be controlled. God said
so in Gen. 3:16." That is the mentality that has
been handed down through the ages.

I do not explain the victimization of Eve
in order to excuse her, but rather to show that
there was an enormous difference in the way that
Adam and Eve fell. It is a pivotal point that
is overlooked. It is very important for us to

see that difference because so much teaching and doctrine has been influenced either by ignorance of, or the ignoring of, that truth. Through it, Satan has perpetuated the war of genders from that time to this, but he has diverted the focus away from himself as the perpetrator, and fixed the blame on the woman.

The distortion of Scripture begins in Genesis. Eve was beguiled and she was disobedient to God because of it. Adam was NOT deceived (I Tim. 2:14). There was nothing distorting his thinking when he made a decision to be disobedient! He rationally chose to sin! Since the Word gives no reason for his disobedience, we have no way of knowing why Adam chose to disobey. The Word simply says, "She gave also to her husband, who was with her, and he did eat."

Because I Tim.2:14 says that the woman was deceived and not the man, woman has been looked upon as inferior to man through the ages. It has been taught emphatically, even by the early church fathers, that woman was not only inferior, because she allowed herself to be deceived, but that she was downright evil. A question that I would like to pose for the reader's consideration is this: If the woman was DECEIVED and thus cannot be trusted in spiritual things, then how much LESS should man be trusted when he deliberately chose to sin without being deceived? Is the rationale and judgment of one who deliberately sins more reliable and trustworthy than the rationale and judgment of one who sins because they were deceived? Is one who is deceived into sinning more evil than one who deliberately sins?

In my opinion the opposite is true. I would rather trust someone's judgment, who was so loyal that they had to be tricked into sinning, than one's judgment who knew something was a sin, but deliberately chose to sin. Why didn't Satan choose to beguile the man instead of the woman? It is

21

often said that God commanded Adam personally, so he had first-hand spiritual knowledge, which made him less vulnerable than the woman, who had only second-hand knowledge. Many say the man was too strong to be deceived, so Satan chose the weaker one because he knew he had a better chance of deceiving her. **I believe that Satan knew the woman would NOT sin without being deceived into doing it, but the man would. Therefore, he had to beguile the more loyal one. When the loyal one was deceived into sinning, the other would follow by their own choice. In true fact, this is exactly what happened!! Eve sinned because she was beguiled, Adam sinned because he wanted to.** IF the man had more spiritual knowledge, thus was less vulnerable than the woman, and **IF** he was too strong to be deceived, why did he not employ that strength and spiritual knowledge to resist sinning when he **wasn't** deceived? I do not say these things to discredit man, but to show how unjust and biased these unreasonable teachings have been throughout history.

Even though Eve was deceived and transgressed, Scripture says that death came to mankind by one man, Adam (Rom. 5:12-21). Why does it say death came by one man instead of one woman? Gen. 3:6 is the key passage that holds that answer. "She took of the fruit thereof and did eat and **gave also to her husband WITH HER, and he did eat.**" The following will explain this verse.

There is so little in the Word about the fall. There are simple statements of what the serpent said and what Eve responded with. What she did and then how she gave to Adam and he ate. It **appears** as though Eve spoke to Adam, because God said to Adam, "Because you hearkened to your wife's voice." But what she said to him, or **if** she said anything directly to him, can only be imagination and conjecture since there is no Scripture for a basis. Some theories are:

22

# IN THE BEGINING

1.  All sinners want to entice others to sin with them, so Eve enticed Adam to sin with her.

2.  She ate and nothing happened to her, so this was a powerful argument that she used to convince him that it was okay for him to eat too.

But I have another point of view that I would like to submit here. For centuries, it has been ASSUMED **that Adam was not literally with Eve at the time of the temptation.** That assumption is so ingrained, very few people even give it a thought. It is just taken for granted he was not with her. The Word does NOT say that Adam was NOT with Eve all the time the serpent was conversing with her!! The Word does NOT say that she ate, she left that place and went to find Adam, wherever he was, brought him the fruit, spoke to him and persuaded him to eat it. Nor does it say that he was elsewhere, he happened to come upon the scene just after she ate, then she spoke and convinced him and he ate.

What it does say is this: "She took some and ate. She also gave some to her husband, **who was with her,** and he did eat." By using "with her" as a prepositional phrase, men say that "with her" meant that at a subsequent point in time he came to be with her. Another theory is that "with her" doesn't literally mean that he was with her in person, at that moment, but that they were merely one in the flesh.

Strong's Concordance says that the word "with" means accompanied or beside. In light of that I don't see how it can be stated that Adam absolutely was not with her during the temptation. In fact, if one is to take the Word for what it says, and not add or take away anything to prove a pet theory, it could very well mean that he WAS LITERALLY WITH HER all the time. I believe he was with her all the time because if she had been alone, eaten of the fruit alone and then took some to Adam, her eyes would have been opened before his. She would have known she was naked before he did and she would have been ashamed to let him see her nakedness. Would it seem likely that she ate, but God did not open her eyes to her nakedness until Adam could be tricked into eating and sinning also? The Word indicates that their eyes opened at the same time, simultaneously, and they both knew they were naked and were ashamed. It is more likely, then, that they ate almost at the same time, one immediately after the other because they were literally together at the time. The word "also" is key. In most versions it is misplaced. The Septuagint reads "she gave to her husband, ALSO with her, and THEY did eat." It is a contraction of an unused Hebrew word ,gam, that means **to gather in an assemblage. One cannot gather in an assembly by oneself!!** Notice, too, the plural "they" rather than "he" that most versions recite.

God said to Adam, "Because you have hearkened unto your wife's voice." Hearkened has among it's meanings in Vine's dictionary of New Testament Words, "give audience to---with the idea of stillness or attention". In Strong's the word is a primary root that means "to hear intelligently". In the long list of possible meanings, there are some very interesting ones that stood out to me. They are "call (gather) together, consent, witness". Because of these meanings, I believe that it is probable that:

1. Adam WAS with Eve all the time.

2. He heard the entire conversation between the serpent and Eve. This is when he heard and hearkened to her voice.

3. He understood with his intelligence. He was not ignorant of what was happening.

4. He consented to what she was doing by not voicing an objection to it.

5. He was a silent witness to it all.

6. All Eve had to do was hand him the fruit and he ate also.

In that case, there would be no need to SURMISE what she said to him or why he was so easily convinced to eat the fruit. No one would have to SPECULATE where he was, or when he came upon the scene, or that she took the fruit and went to find him. There would be no ASSUMPTION that she wanted him to sin with her because sin loves company. There would be no SUPPOSITION that Adam loved Eve more than he loved God, that he nobly chose to sin so that she would not have to suffer the consequences of sin alone. That would mean sin has nobility. Others say he could not bear the separation from her if she were to die and he did not, and so he ate. Another THEORY is that after she ate, she was sinful, but he was still holy, thus they could not have intercourse. He HAD to eat also so he could come down to her fallen level so they could have sex, thus providing a way for the Messiah to come through the woman. This absurd theory means that with out intercourse of man and woman, a Messiah could NOT come. The birth of the Messiah did not depend on a man. All of these CONJECTURES, and more, have been presented. They ALL have to be IMAGINED because they are based on the ASSUMPTION that Adam was not with her during the temptation!! The theory that she convinced him to eat because nothing happened to her when she ate would also be put to rest. Inherent in that theory is the fact I mentioned before. It infers that God was cruel and withheld the opening of her eyes to her nakedness and shame until AFTER Adam could be found and be convinced to eat. Otherwise Adam would have known something HAD happened to her as a result of eating and she wouldn't have been able to use that argument. Adam's being with Eve at the time of the temptation would explain why their eyes were opened and both knew shame because of their nakedness at the same time. All of these biased, unscriptural, vain imaginings would be done away with.

One last thought, how many times have you seen three people standing together, but only two are conversing, while the third person just listens and observes without saying a word? I believe this was the scenario at the time of the temptation.

The answer to the question, "Why DOESN'T the Bible say that sin and death came through one woman?" hinges upon the question, "Where was Adam at the time of the temptation?" If Adam was literally with her all the time of the temptation, and everything happened just as I stated, then there would be good reason for Adam to be considered the first to sin, because God gave the man spiritual headship by giving the command not to eat of the tree directly to Adam, which he relayed to Eve. Is it possible then, that he sinned first BECAUSE he did not exercise the **action** part of headship that would confirm and authenticate God's command by saying something to Eve to remind, warn, or caution her about the command? By his silence did he allow her to be deceived? Should he have protected her in some way from the serpent? Was this neglect of headship and responsibility only the beginning of his sin which culminated with his ultimate disobedience to God's direct command not to eat? Thus he brought sin and death to mankind?

These questions are no more "far out" or "off base" than all of the theories I mentioned before, or than the commentaries I've read concerning the matter. In fact, to me, they are legitimate, they make far more sense and they are more compatible with the rest of Scripture. I find NO Scripture anywhere to support the assumption that Adam was NOT with Eve at the time of the temptation. In fact, a pastor who did not like my questions, stated that IF there was such a Scripture to prove that he WAS with her, then much theology would have to be changed!! THAT IS THE

CRUX OF THE MATTER!!
    Much theology and doctrine is based on the ASSUMPTION that he was NOT with her. The only Scripture that I know of concerning the matter at all is Gen. 3:6, "She ate, and gave to her husband also with her, and he did eat". Many translations say "who was with her". There is NO Scripture, **NOT ONE VERSE,** that states or even indicates, that he was not there all the time. The rules of Bible interpretation are that you cannot build doctrine on one verse, and yet, a whole doctrine has been built on an ASSUMPTION that has NO verse for a basis. This false doctrine is the foundation for many other destructive false doctrines!! I present these thoughts as serious things for the reader to ponder.
    Truly, we do not know why God allowed the temptation to happen at all since Adam and Eve had no knowledge of good or evil and did not know what deception or discernment was. But this is no excuse for them. They had the command: "Do not eat". They knew the consequences: "You will die". All they had to do was be obedient to God.
    The Word says it was Adam's disobedience that brought death and sin to mankind, not the woman's! The fact that Eve was the first to be deceived has been twisted to portray women as evil, weak minded, and inferior to men. But this is not an issue of man superior/woman inferior at all.
    Gen. 3:16 is THE major area of misinterpretation, conjecture, and mistranslation that has caused so much trouble for women since time began. "Thy desire (teshuwqah) shall be for thy husband and he shall rule (mashal) over you." The liberties taken by men in interpreting this passage is a grief to women and something I believe men will have to answer to God for. Though I do not have access to them, other researchers discovered that the word "desire" in ten out of twelve ancient versions is translated as

27

"turning" rather than desire. My source of reference is the Septuagint. In it, the word "desire" in the original language is "turning". This word "turning" has the same usage as the word "turning" in Lev. 19:4. It means to turn to idols, turn to face, go away, turn aside, turn away. Most interpretations of Gen. 3:16 will say that "rule" means the right of dominion. Dominion is what Adam and Eve were given over the animals. The word there is "radah", and it means to tread down, to subjugate, to prevail against, to reign over. This is entirely different from the word for rule in Gen. 3:16. That word is "mashal" and it actually means "make to have dominion, or CAUSE to have rule or have power over". Gen. 3:16 should actually read, "Your turning will be to your husband and that will cause him to have dominion, or power to reign, over you." Eve will turn to her husband, away from God. God warns her that if she does this, she will come under Adam's dominion. Her dependence on her husband, rather than on God, and her tenderness, affection and devotion to him would enable him to dominate her and keep her under his subjection.

Though the word "desire" is a wrong translation, the way it is used in Gen. 3:16 means to stretch out after, to long for. It comes from a root word that means to run after. Our modern definition of desire embraces the aspects of longing for companionship and affection as well as sexual satisfaction. A woman can devote herself to her husband to such a degree that she will turn from God to the man, allowing herself to be dominated by him in order to gain and to keep his favor and approval. The favor and approval of man becomes more important than the favor and approval of God.

In this same passage God said to the serpent that the woman's seed "shalt" bruise his head and thou "shalt" bruise his heel. This was prophetic of what would happen in the future, not a punishment

28

or penalty that was handed down. The word "shall" in "your turning shall be for thy husband and he shall rule over you", is more correctly interpreted to be taken as part of a prophecy rather than part of a penalty also. It is a prophetic warning that her new carnal nature would cause her to turn to her husband, away from God, which would cause his new carnal nature to bring her into subjection to him. Jesus exemplified his love of the Father by his obedience to Him. If a woman loves a man, she will want to be obedient to him, but in her fallen, carnal state, it can be a wrong kind of obedience that turns her from God to man. Then his carnal state will dominate her.

This passage has been misinterpreted to mean that a woman's innate desire would be to dominate and control the husband. Some say that she had already demonstrated this by the control Eve had over Adam to make him eat the forbidden fruit. Those who hold to that theory, say that God was putting her in her proper place by giving the man an IMPERATIVE COMMAND to rule or have dominion over the woman. The theory is, God decreed that this penalty and punishment of subjection to the man would be visited upon all women for all time, making them inferior people, to be lorded over, dominated by, and treated like a slave or second class citizen forever by men. In Gen. 2:16, and in many other Scriptures, it says "and God commanded" and He gave a direct command concerning something. This is not the case in Gen. 3:16. **THE REAL FACT, AND THE REAL TRUTH IS, GOD WAS SPEAKING TO THE WOMAN, NOT TO THE MAN!! SO HOW COULD HE BE GIVING THE MAN A COMMAND TO "RULE" OVER HIS WIFE?!! NEITHER WAS GOD GIVING THE WOMAN A COMMAND THAT SHE MUST SUBMIT TO THE MAN!!!** It was a prophetic warning to her that now that she knew good from evil, she would experience the evil of turning from God and turning to the man, who would in turn dominate her. **No one EVER claims** that what God said directly to Adam was a command to Eve or the serpent. No one EVER claims that what God said to the serpent (and to Satan) was a command to Adam or Eve. Yet what God said directly to the woman is ALWAYS touted as an IMPERATIVE COMMAND to the man to rule and to the woman to submit to that rule!! God's proclamations were given to each specific individual. Though they would eventually affect future generations of genders, **they were not transferable, then or now, to the other gender or to the serpent.**

Another interpretation of the passage concerns the idea that even though there will be much pain in childbearing, the woman will have an overwhelming sexual desire for her husband. The very ancient beliefs that all women were evil seducers and nymphomaniacs came from this interpretation.

Here we will take a little side trip into the Scriptures, in order to demonstrate how the false interpretation of Gen. 3:16 is the basis for many other false doctrines.

The mistranslations and misinterpretations of Gen. 3:16 that God gave man the right to control and dominate his wife, is the basis for the misinterpretations of Paul's writings. For instance, in I Cor. 14:32, Paul is speaking about women being silent in church and he says, "As also saith the law". Most study Bibles will cross reference this to Gen. 3:16. Many Bible expositors say that God's pronouncement in Gen. 3:16 is the "law" that Paul was referring to. But women being silent in church had nothing to do with Gen. 3:16, or even the Mosaic law. It is a part of the Jewish traditional law, composed by religious leaders. It was based on traditions of men, not on God's law. Christ Himself had conflicts with "traditional" religious leaders of His day as evidenced in Mark 7:13 when he said to them, "You have made the Word of God of no effect through your traditions". Their traditions actually changed the meaning and

the power of God's Word. This mistranslation or
misinterpretation of Gen. 3:16 has also made God's
Word to be of no effect and has altered the
meaning and power of it so that a great many
God-gifted women have been silenced. This is in
spite of the fact that Paul had just written much
in I Cor., saying that God gives gifts to every
one of his children and how important every one
in the body is and how they are all necessary for
the proper functioning of the body. In this
passage, and others concerning the gifts, there
is no distinction made between male and female
in the distribution of these gifts or in their
operation. The fact that Paul was dealing with
a cultural issue for that time is completely
overlooked or ignored. For the first time people
were being integrated into the Body and the freedom
of Christ. They had to be taught to learn in
decency and in order so as not to disturb the
whole congregation's process of learning. This
was NOT an edict for all time, that women were
to be silent in church and be subject only to men.
Those who hold to this biased interpretation and
refer to Gen. 3:16 as the proof for Paul's writing,
refuse to admit this was a cultural issue of the
time.

Another point that is overlooked in this
passage is that Paul says, "Learn from your husband
at home". Up until this time, few men had taught
their wives spiritual things at all. So this was
a directive to men that they SHOULD teach their
wives. Again, Paul was not laying down an edict
for all time that women were to learn ONLY from
their husbands at home. This verse has been
misused to mean that Paul was saying that a wife
should not go to someone else, pastor or anyone,
to learn spiritual things. She should learn only
from her husband because he is her spiritual head.
It is taught that even if he is unsaved, she should
learn only from him because, supposedly, God will

31

speak through him. I wonder what one does with
I Cor. 2:14 that says Spiritual things are
spiritually discerned. The natural man cannot
discern spiritual things, neither can he understand
them? How can a woman learn spiritual things from
a man who the Word declares cannot understand them?
How can he teach what he does not know or
understand? In those days of the Old Testament,
it was mostly only men who knew the Word, but
after Christ, the written Word was completed for
all. The Holy Spirit was given as the Teacher
and Revealer of all truth to all Christians. Again,
this was an issue in Paul's day that he was
addressing for that time. He was telling the
women to ask their questions at home rather than
to be interrupting the whole congregation with
their questions. Now we know it's not polite to
ask a question in the middle of the preacher's
sermon because that would interrupt the message.
If we have a question, we know we can ask it later.
But they did not know that then. As I said before,
it was also the instruction for men to teach their
wives. Paul was not laying down a foundational
doctrine that must be adhered to throughout the
church age! The proponents of "the man was given
the right of domination or rule in Gen. 3:16" is
the basis for believing that a woman can only learn
from her husband.

These are only a couple of illustration to
show how the mistranslations of Gen. 3:16 are the
basis for many other false teachings. It is only
when we understand the Gen. 3:16 passage
correctly, that we will be able to unravel the
other false teachings.

After that little side trip, let us go back
to the fall of mankind.

In studying what God did and said to each
of the players in this real life drama of the fall,
I found some other very interesting things to
contemplate, such as, God asked Adam and Eve

questions. He asked nothing of the serpent. His question to Adam was, "How did you know that you were naked unless you ate of the tree **that I commanded you** not to eat?" God's question confronts Adam with His command. Adam's response was, "the woman you gave to be with me--she gave me and I did eat." It has been said by many that Adam's response is an attempt to shift blame, first to God because He gave him this woman, and second, to the woman because she gave him the fruit. He does not want to admit his own guilt. This indicates to me that he has been infected with the major sin of Satan, PRIDE. Pride says it's somebody elses fault, I am not guilty.

God's question to Eve did not mention the command to her. In the Septuagint, His question to her was, "WHY have you done this?" The answer Eve gives is more consistent with the Septuagint question of why than it is with other translations that ask, "WHAT have you done?" She states, "The serpent beguiled me and I did eat". The question "why" rather than "what" is important. To answer "why", she is stating a fact, to answer "what" means that she is shifting blame. I don't believe she was trying to shift blame, but by translating the question "what" instead of "why" it makes it appear as though she was following Adam's lead in shifting blame. By doing that, it substantiates the unfounded, bias teachings that say women are evil and inferior. It keeps Adam from standing alone in his accusation, because then it can be said, "see, Eve shifted blame, too. She was just as dishonest as Adam was". If they both did it--it is somehow supposed to make what he did less wrong. Just as when she was deceived first and sinned, that is supposed to make his deliberate sin more acceptable and less offensive then her sin.

Although God speaks to the serpent, He actually deals with two creatures, the serpent and Satan.

The pronouncements that God makes to each of

the three (actually four) are also very interesting. To the serpent He says, **you** are cursed--you will go on your belly and eat dust all the days of your life". The creature itself was cursed, the consequences were immediate and they would last for the length of time the creature was on the earth. The consequences seem to have no eternal importance.

We know that the next statement is to Satan, because the serpent could have no seed that could have enmity with the woman's seed. Some say that the fear of snakes that people have is the "enmity" referred to, but the word enmity means hostility and hatred. Although we have deadly poisonous snakes, serpents cannot experience the emotions of hostility or hatred. The pronouncement to Satan was a prophecy of a future event that had eternal consequences. It was the first prophecy of a Messiah, that out of the woman, whom Satan had deceived, would come a Seed, who would crush Satan's head. God did not say to Satan that he was cursed.

To Eve, God said He would multiply her sorrow and her conception. In sorrow she would bring forth children. "Your turning shall be for your husband and that will cause him to rule over you." Notice, God did not say Eve was cursed. God did not confront Eve with the command not to eat, as He had done with Adam. He did not mention anything about, or condemn her for, convincing Adam to eat. He did not say anything to chastise her for making the decision to eat without consulting Adam. He never convicted her of making a bad decision. He never told her that He considered her too inferior to make a decision and therefore, she must submit her will to her husband. Yet man still holds her in an unrelenting bondage of condemnation for leading Adam astray and for making a decision on her own. The consequences of the multiplied sorrow of conception and in bringing forth children does not seem to have eternal importance either.

34

They are for as long as life is on this earth. Her turning to her husband would have earthly consequences, but it could very well have serious eternal consequences for her too. It could make the man her idol and thus prevent her relationship with God from coming to a saving faith.

God does not say to her, "Because you have done this" as He did to the serpent and to Adam. This is why I believe the Septuagint question of "why" is more correct than the question "what". I believe that God was taking into consideration the fact that Eve was beguiled and did not purposely choose to rebel against God as the serpent and Adam had done. He accepted her statement as a fact, rather than shifting of blame. He knew each of their hearts and their reasons for doing what they did.

God does not say to any of them why He chose the consequences that He did. The favorite one, conceived in the minds of men, concerning women, is the one I mentioned before. They say the woman had proven herself to be incapable of handling spiritual things because she yielded to Satan's beguiling. Therefore, God had to put the woman in a proper place of subjection, so He gave the man the command to rule over her. I've heard that hundreds of times. A few times I have heard that the serpent was put in a place of humiliation as a consequence of his sin. I don't believe I have heard anyone try to explain why God told Adam what He did. The major focus has **always** been on the woman and her unworthiness!! Never mind that Adam sinned willingly. He is still regarded as the only one having the superior ability to handle spiritual things!! Again, the reason for that is to substantiate the bias against women and to justify male dominance. However, it is all conjecture and imagination and has no scriptural basis.

To Adam, God said, "Because you have eaten

of the tree that **I commanded you** not to eat, cursed is the ground for your sake". He did not curse Adam, He cursed the ground. He said that in sorrow Adam would eat of it all the days of his life—by the sweat of his brow would he eat from the earth." "Sorrow" means an earthen vessel, painful toil, grievous, idol, labor. When Adam was told to tend the garden, it was not grievous, painful toil for him and yet it yielded it's fruit to him. Adam's earthly consequences were that he would have to work hard for a living. This implies that he would provide the essentials of living. The consequences seem to have no eternal value, it would last for as long as man was on earth. It is interesting that the words "earthen vessel" and "idol" are in the list of meanings of sorrow. Adam was taken from the earth, therefore he was an earthen vessel. And now the painful toil of tilling the earth that he was taken from, would become his idol.

Eve would have more pain and sorrow in childbirth. Since the name Eve is literally Life, her consequence of more pain in childbearing has to do with the process of bringing forth life. This word "sorrow" is a little different from Adam's "sorrow". This one means to fashion or fabricate in labor and toil and pain. For Adam, making the earth yield it's fruit would be the sorrow. For Eve, fashioning and fabricating a child in the womb and then the labor and pain to bring it into the world would be her sorrow. Their physical strengths would be taxed in both of these processes. These were both prophetic. Now that they had learned the difference between good and evil, they would experience the evil as a result of that knowledge.

Her carnal nature would seek emotional and physical satisfaction from her husband and his carnal nature would take advantage of that and dominate her in order to satisfy his pride and ego.

# IN THE BEGINING

There was the pronouncement by God that Adam would return to the dust of the ground from which he was taken. Then God drove the man out of the Garden. Eve was sent out of the garden also. They were put out of the garden so that they could not eat of the tree of life. There is not much mentioned about this tree of life but there is no recorded command that they should not eat of it. Whatever it's implications were, they were now prevented from eating it so that they would not "live forever". God said that man would now return to the dust from which he was taken. Therefore, there is significant eternal consequences connected with this pronouncement from God. "Living forever" implies eternal life and "in the garden" implies the delights of the sweet fellowship with God that they had enjoyed there. So being put out of the garden also implies that there would now be an end to the physical life that God had not intended mankind to know originally. It also implies separation from Him in spiritual fellowship that was a spiritual death. These, then, seem to have eternal consequences. Sending them away from the tree of life was God's protection over them, so that they would not live forever in their new sinful state. In His prophetic pronouncement of the Redeemer, we know that when He protected them by sending them away from the tree of life, He already had a plan to restore mankind to fellowship with Him and the eternal life that had been lost.

The reason I believe most of what God said was prophetic pronouncements, rather than a handing down of punishments is because of the word "cursed". Cursed means to call down evil upon someone or something, to loath, detest, abominate, and abhor. God DID NOT CURSE ADAM OR EVE!! He never loathed, detested, or abhored them. He did not call evil down upon them. It would come to them as a result of their own disobedience, but He did not call

37

it down on them. The Word simply does not say God cursed them. Yet it is very specific about what He did curse. He cursed the serpent and the ground.

In all of what God said to Adam, there is not one word that speaks of his rulership over Eve!! What He said to Adam and to Eve was an individual prophetic warning of what the results of knowing evil would be in each of their lives in the future. God never said a word that would indicate that the man was superior at making decisions, therefore, the woman should defer to the husband. There is nothing in God's word to substantiate that!!!

One last comment concerning the things God prophesied that Adam and Eve would come to know. Adam's source of origin was the ground because he came from the dust of the ground-his consequence is directly related to the source of his origin. I believe that is significant because God said that by the sweat of his brow he would till the ground. In our day there are very few who till the ground. That has been replaced with jobs and careers. It is a well known fact that men are often consumed with the driving need to be successful in their jobs or professions. I believe that force within the man can, and does, bring him under the control and dominance of his job. That obsession with his job or career becomes the man's idol. As the job consumes his time and energy, it turns him away from God. This is the thing that men have to fight against. The job or career is the thing that dominates and controls him--rules over him. So what God was warning Adam about was really prophetic of what would turn him away from God-the drive to succeed in the job. The tilling of the ground, so to speak.

Eve's consequence is also directly related to her source of origin. She was formed out of a part of the man. Her turning would be toward that man. Because her time and energy would be consumed with pleasing him, he would become her idol. He would then be able to control and dominate her.

So both the man and the woman would be faced with the desire to turn to their source of biological origin for fulfillment. They would both turn away from God and be dominated by their respective origins. Unless they recognize that fact and fight against those desires, they will be dominated and controlled by them. God's edicts were not really punishments but were prophecies of what would be the dominating factors that would separate the man and the woman from Him. Now, in their new fallen state they would always struggle with these things in order to maintain their fellowship with Him.

The real punishment is the struggle that each would have to keep the right perspectives, to keep from allowing jobs and husbands to become the idols that are worshipped, instead of God. Before they sinned, there was sweet fellowship with God without a struggle on their part. Now they would struggle every day to get and to maintain that fellowship, that oneness with God. Even though the Messiah did come, believers in Him still struggle with the old Adamic nature and they struggle to subject that old nature to the new Christ-like nature. Satan does everything in his power to keep the truth hidden and to keep men in bondage to jobs and careers and to keep women in bondage to men.

It is time the Body of Christ wakes up, and rejects the false concepts and teachings concerning Genesis 3:16. These false concepts have a malignant affect on the whole Body, not just the women!!!

In all of this Genesis account there is nothing to indicate that the woman was inferior to the man because he was created first. Rather it shows her equality with him. Nothing in this Genesis account indicates that the woman was EVER required by God to seek the man's advice before making a decision. Nothing in this Genesis account indicates that God thought her judgments were inferior to the man's. Nothing even hints that she is to be subservient to the man in anything. It is only men who have interjected these ideas into the Old Testament life. Then, in spite of Christ, those old traditions have been carried over into the New Testament age.

In all of this Genesis account there are only two forms of man's headship established. 1) She was formed out of him. He is her source of origin, as such, he is her head. 2) He was given the responsibility to **speak** the commandment of God to her and then to **affirm** that by **HIS** spiritual action of warning her when she was faced with the serpent's beguiling. Neither of these encompasses authority, rulership, or dominion of the man. That headship did not make him accountable for what Eve DID. God held him accountable only for his own disobedience, not hers. God held her accountable for her own sin, regardless of how it happened.

I pray that you will pray about these things and that God will reveal truth to you. Repent of the false teachings you have labored under so that God can set you free from them. You will know a new freedom in your relationship to Christ, to your spouse, and to others in the body of Christ.

## CHAPTER THREE
## THE COVERING


Isaiah 30:1-3 says, "Woe to the rebellious children, saith the Lord, who take counsel, but not of me; and who COVER WITH A COVERING, but not of my Spirit, that they may add sin to sin; who walk to go down to Egypt and have not asked at my mouth; to strengthen themselves in the strength of Pharaoh and to trust in the shadow of Egypt! Therefore shall the strength of Pharaoh be your shame, and the trust in the shadow of Egypt, your confusion." (KJV) This key passage will be explained later in the chapter.

The basic misinterpretation, or mistranslation of Gen. 3:16, is the basis for the misunderstandings of Paul's words throughout church history. The perverted Word mixes some truth with error, producing unbiblical teaching that sounds biblically correct. For instance, in the last chapter we learned that God's provision of headship is that man would teach his wife spiritual things. He would provide a physical protection for her because she is the weaker vessel physically, but the greater meaning of "weaker vessel" is that he would confirm and authenticate the spiritual truth that he spoke to her by his actions. Living his life as a spiritual example would strengthen the spiritual knowledge that he shares with her. That provides her with a spiritual protection. However, the protection of "headship" has been carried to such wrong extremes in these latter days, that it is not what God intended it to be at all. In all branches of Evangelical Christianity, this teaching is known as "the covering" or the "umbrella of protection".

This "covering" or "umbrella of protection" theory says that man is "the federal head", or

41

an authoritarian head of the house, as such, he has ALL responsibility to make ALL decisions for the family. I have heard it preached by more than one preacher/teacher on marriage that if you hate yellow and you look awful in it, but your husband likes it, you should have a closet full of yellow clothes that you wear. It is also taught that your husband has the right to choose your hair style and if it is unbecoming to you, submit to that and explain to people that you are being submissive to your authority! This kind of submission is said to be an honor to God so that His Word is not maligned, and that as others observe your obedience, they will be drawn to Christ. The Scripture base is, "Be subject to your husband in **everything**". (Eph.5:24) These are only two examples of the extremes of this teaching. They are minor compared to matters of more serious nature.

In this teaching, since the man has all right, authority, and responsibility to make all decisions for the family, the wife cannot "usurp his authority" in any matter. If she has a different opinion from her husband's, she can appeal to him, give him her reason for disagreeing, and then bow to his authority and his decision. She is to abide by his decisions even if he makes an ungodly, selfish, or wrong decision that will bring harm to her or to the children. If she does not submit to this, she is said to be in rebellion against her husband and is out of God's divine order, out from under her "covering", her "umbrella of protection". Therefore, since she has rejected her God ordained covering, she is subject to all sorts of demonic attacks or attacks from Satan, just as Eve was. God cannot protect her because she is in rebellion against His established order. That is the theory. Sometimes, in reality though, this umbrella or covering is the reason she is being attacked. Her husband is the source of the attack because of his own disobedience and rebellion to God.  In such a case, when she is obedient to the man, rather than to God, she is even more open to attack.  It is taught that IF she does not disagree with her husband's authority, THEN she can pray to God and He WILL change the husband. It is as though any act of disagreement or disobedience to the man is synonymous with rebellion against God, so God will not answer her prayers. Also, it seems as though her act of "rebellion" prevents God from working in the man.  In this theory, it seems as though Christ has no power to protect the woman and she has no right, responsibility, or authority in Christ for herself as an individual in Christ.  It is as though even God himself will not lift a finger to protect her, no matter what the circumstances might be, if she has rebelled against this kind of domination or "submission".  It seems as though "submission" to the husband in EVERYthing  is all a woman must do  to be godly  in Christ.

I, personally, have heard it spoken from many pulpits, by different preachers from different denominations, that even if a woman comes to church and does good works for the Lord, when her unsaved or backslidden husband forbids her to, then she is in rebellion to her husband's authority.  She needs to go home, stop coming to church, stop doing those good works, submit to the husband and wait on God to change him.  This tradition of submission in everything then takes precedence over other Scripture, such as Heb.10:25.  This says "Do not forsake the assembling of yourselves together, as is the manner of some, but exhort one another, and even more so as the day of the Lord approaches".  Is this only for the male brothers in Christ? A woman with an unsaved or backslidden husband needs the encouragement and exhortation of the brethren as much or more than any one else!!  Which Scripture should she abide by?  The one that bows

to ungodly authority? Or the one that bows to
the Almighty God, the one that brings her inner
strength and maturity as she is edified by the
brethren?

The following Scriptures are for all believers.
They show that God has His own purpose for each
woman. His purpose for them is NOT JUST to serve
the man.

Rom. 8:28, "Those who love God are called
according to His purpose". That's ALL who love
Him, not just men. This "called" means that those
who love Him are saints who are invited, appointed,
urged on, and incited by His Word, ordered or
commanded by Him, to do what His will is for each
individual to do. Among the meanings of "according"
are the words, among them, concerning, pertaining
to, and **covered.** It frequently denotes opposition,
distribution, or intensity. It is interesting
that the word "covered" is amongst the meanings.
A possible meaning of that is the saints are covered
with His presence, His power, His protection, His
provision, His giftings, and His anointings to
DO what ever is His will (purpose) for a saint
to do. There is nothing that indicates that these
things are only for men, or for women who are
in complete subjection to their husbands first!
The only qualification for any gender is that they
love God! I see the words that it denotes this
way. God is intense as He distributes gifts and
anointings to who-so-ever He wills. As individuals
operate in those gifts, there will be opposition
to them that they must overcome with an intense
sense of God's calling or purpose for giving those
gifts to them specifically. God's calling overrules
the husband's desire to be served.

I Cor. 7:22,23, "For he that is called in the
Lord, being a servant, is the Lord's freeman;
likewise also he that is called being free is
Christ's servant. "YE ARE BOUGHT WITH A PRICE,
BE YE NOT SERVANTS OF MEN". Women were bought

with the price of Christ's shed blood, not their husband's blood. Because of that, their servanthood is to Christ first. That servanthood to Christ may sometimes conflict with the servanthood to husbands.

Eph. 4:1, "I beseech you that you walk worthy of the vocation to which you are called". Vocation, call and called here does not mean an earthly vocation, profession or job. It means the origin, nature and destiny that are heavenly. Every Christian has a destiny, or a purpose for being, that is eternal, that they must fulfill while they are here on earth. This verse does not pertain to men only! Vocation especially means God's invitation to mankind to accept the benefits of salvation. Salvation includes the freedom from domination and slavery to anyone other than Christ.

II Tim. 1:9, "Who hath saved us and called us with a holy calling, not according to our works, but according to His own purpose and grace which was given us in Christ Jesus before the world began." This is a holy thing, not a thing of merely catering to a man's flesh. Though a woman who loves her husband wants to serve him, her eternal purpose or destiny must be fulfilled also. That eternal purpose takes priority!

Rom. 12:1, "We are called to submit ourselves to Him because this is our reasonable service to Him".

**Submitting to the husband alone is not all that a woman is called to do by God!!! Submitting to Christ has a higher priority!!!** However, in many Christian circles, there is no room for God's holy calling on the woman's life in this perverted kind of submission. Through this kind of teaching, men become idols to their wives. In this false teaching, the woman is to put submission to the man FIRST, in all things, because God made him the "federal" head, God ALWAYS works through the head, God cannot, and will not ever, bypass His

45

own established authority system. If the woman feels God has called her to do something for Him, supposedly, the woman's husband will be told by God that she is to do it. If he does not hear from God, then either the woman is hearing wrong or she must wait upon God to get through to her man. Unfortunately, often God cannot get through to the man, and the purpose that God wanted to accomplish through that woman is never realized. If she goes ahead and does what she believes God has called her to do against her husband's wishes, she is considered to be out from under his authority --her covering-- and is in rebellion. But, truly, if she does not do what God has called her to do and is obedient to her husband instead, who is she in rebellion against? James 4:17 says, "Therefore, to him that knoweth to do good, and doeth it not, to him it is sin." This is just one more Scripture made void for the woman. It is sacrificed on the alter of "submit in everything".

Women are taught that godliness in a woman is represented by her submission to her husband. If she differs from her husband in any way, for any reason, it is synonymous with being in rebellion to God!

Submission to the man takes precedence over all other biblical principles. Preservation of marriage at all costs also becomes an idol. Although it is not said in so many words, the essence of the teaching is, "be more submissive, with the right attitudes and your marriage will be preserved. Even if you have to compromise your own Christian convictions in order to preserve the marriage, that's what you do in the name of submission". Proverbs 14:1 is used as the proof text, "A wise woman builds her house and a foolish one tears it down with her own hands." This is interpreted to mean that disagreeing with one's husband in any way or for any reason, and doing differently from what he says to do, tears down her house. Regardless of what the man does, what his motives are, what his character is, whether he's saved or not, or whether or not he's in right fellowship with God, it is made to appear as though all the problems in the marriage are caused by the woman's unsubmissiveness to the man. The cure all for every problem seems to be: "Lady, submit more to your husband, your God given "covering", and the problem will get better. It is YOUR attitude that is making things so hard for you. Your husband senses your rebellion to him. That is what is making him so stubborn. As he sees the rebellion in you, a Christian woman, that drives him away from God. Your submission, with godly attitudes, will draw him to Christ."

John and Sue were getting along well in their marriage. Sue was a bright bubbly woman, very attractive and vibrant and doing good works in the church for God. She was happy with her church work and it was a joy to her. John was not active in church at all. Then, John was taught this concept of headship and covering, meaning the man has the right to demand complete obedience from his wife, no matter where he's at spiritually and no matter what his motives are. As this principle was applied, it eventually reached into all facets of her life. It resulted in Sue's losing her sense of individuality, independence, esteem for who she was in Christ, and who she was as a person. Her worth as a person was slowly being eroded. As John controlled more and more of her life, she began to feel like she was in prison. Though she was still attractive and bright, the bubbliness and the vibrancy began to fade. Her work in the church became a burden for her rather than a joy to her. She tried to live up to what a "godly" woman was supposed to be, according to her husband's new knowledge about headship, but there was conflict in her spirit and her soul. The more John learned

47

and implemented this wrong concept of headship, the more conflict there was in the marriage. The more Sue tried to be "godly" by submitting, the more her spirit shriveled up as her Christian freedoms and her personhood were taken away from her. They finally ended up seeking pastoral counseling for their marital problems. There she was told, "You are in rebellion against your husband's authority. You need to repent and ask God's forgiveness for your sin of rebellion. You need to learn how to submit and you need to come back under your husband's umbrella of protection and covering and God's divine order of things." John went away justified in his behavior of domination and control, which seems to have been a latent quality in his nature. Sue went away feeling like a failure in her Christian walk, and a failure in her marriage. She carried away guilt, condemnation, and hopelessness because she had already tried so hard to be "godly" in submission and yet things got worse. Now, she even questions if she's saved. Her countenance changed from the vivacious bubbliness to the dead look of one subdued and controlled by others. I don't believe she does any work in the church anymore.

Adam said, "God that woman you gave me--it's her fault that I ate". Man is still saying, through this kind of teaching, "God, it's that woman you gave me-- she causes my bad behavior because she won't demonstrate obedience to me". How Satan has deceived men into thinking this concept of headship and covering is of God!! This false teaching on submission for the woman has brought deep spiritual and emotional woundedness to Christian women by the thousands. It reaches far beyond marriage into the realms of ministry, where Paul's teachings have been misunderstood and misused to successfully stop the ministry of many godly women. How this must wound and grieve God! It has successfully brought women into a bondage of soul and spirit. This teaching seems to say that Christ's blood set only men free from the bondage of "law". It has promoted the very thing that God prophesied would happen. As the woman submits more and more to the man, he becomes her idol. Marriage becomes an idol. The woman forsakes other Scripture to fulfill this distorted one. In so doing, she turns away from God to the man, just as God said she would. In doing that, she forfeits her rightful freedom in Christ and the door is wide open for more domination by man. Again, just as God said it would be.

Eve was deceived by Satan in the garden of Eden and women are deceived by Satan today. Except Satan comes through teachings by prominent religious leaders, ministers who are supposed to be looking out for the souls of women as well the souls of men. They do not even ask, "Hath God said?" as Satan asked Eve. They boldly say, "God hath said".

Part of Gal. 3:1 says, "O, foolish Galatians, who hath bewitched you, that you should not obey the truth?" The whole chapter speaks of freedom in Christ apart from the law. It talks about bondages. Verses 26-29 state, "For ALL are sons of God by faith in Christ Jesus. For as many of you as have been baptized into Christ have put on Christ. There is neither Jew nor Greek, there is neither bond not free, there is neither MALE OR FEMALE, for ye are ALL one in Christ Jesus. If ye be Christ's, then are ye Abraham's seed, and heirs according to the promise".

God said to Eve, "Why have you done this?" Eve said, "The serpent beguiled me." Paul said, "Who has bewitched you?" I say, women of God, reborn through faith in Christ, who has bewitched you? Who has said to you that your freedom in Christ is different from that of men? Who has brought you into bondage, under the guise of "godly" submission? Who has taken away your freedom in

49

Christ? Please read the book of Galatians for yourself. Ask the Holy Spirit to reveal His truth concerning submission to men, how the epistle related to the Galatians, and what it means to you. The book of Colossians is also a book of warning against deception. Read it too, asking God to reveal to you how you are being deceived and by whom.

I must give you a word of caution here. Later in this book you will learn what real Godly submission is. Until then, don't get angry and react by doing something rash. Wait quietly until you get the whole picture. Then you won't react in anger, but will act according to God's way of truth and love.

Remember in chapter two, the definition of serpent was to hiss, whisper a magic spell, enchanter or use enchantment. "Beguile" is a stronger word than deceive and is the best rendering for what the serpent did to Eve. It means to thoroughly deceive. A word study shows that serpent, guile, beguile, craft, craftiness, cunning, deceive and bewitch are all connected. Many of them refer to the creeping or "working into", or "enveloping in" something. Creeping means insinuating oneself, onto or into, something. Insinuating means to introduce by windings and turnings to get into, or to push in indirectly and skillfully where something is not wanted. Creeping comes from the same root word as serpent. That takes us back to enchanter, magic spell, enchantment. Whispering (hissing) has an evil sense, like the muttering of an enchanter or sorcerer. Bewitch has the meaning of bringing evil on a person by false praise, or to mislead by an evil eye, and so to charm. An evil eye means to mesmerize with a fixed gaze. In Galatians 3:1 it means to lead into an evil doctrine. Magic spells, enchantment and bewitched clearly speak of witchcraft. When someone cannot make their

50

own decisions about anything, but yields that right of decision up to another, that is domination and control. When one gives up the right of decision, it is actually giving up their will. The will is subverted and submerged into someone else's will. That is witchcraft. The result of witchcraft is that the bewitched person's mind is befuddled and is not operating rationally. The purpose of witchcraft is to control someone else's mind so that they will do whatever the controller wants them to do for the controller's benefit. God forbids it. When we look at how many Christian women are dominated and controlled, it is the same thing. The women have given over their will to the husband, he controls every facet of their lives, they do whatever he wants for his own benefit. It is evil doctrine!!

Acts 8:9-11 talks about Simon the sorcerer. This man bewitched all the people from the least to the greatest. THEY ALL THOUGHT HE WAS A POWERFUL MAN OF GOD. They gave "heed" to him. The word "heed" means to hold the mind towards, to pay attention to. It comes from a word that has amongst it's meanings, to hold or to possess. He held or possessed their minds because he had bewitched them for a very long time. HE HAD FASCINATED THEM BY FALSE REPRESENTATION. That is what bewitched means. This is the most graphic biblical example of someone holding another's mind in order to control and dominate them. He possessed their wills.

When a man holds such control over his wife that she cannot make a decision or act on her own, even to the details of her own grooming, he is then possessing her mind and her will. It is witchcraft. He is doing that for his own benefit, not hers. It is to bolster his own pride and ego, because he has power to dictate to someone and they will obey. This is done in the name of "submit to your husband in everything". It has the sanction of almost all of Christendom! Men and women alike are held by the cunning fascination of false representation of God's Word concerning what headship means. They follow an evil doctrine of headship, submission and covering!

The same thing is true of pastors who use "obey them that have rule over you in the Lord" (Heb. 13:17, KJV) to control the minds and wills of the people in their congregations to do their bidding. They hold people's minds in a bondage of obedience to them, for their own gain. It is evil doctrine.

Gal. 5:1 in the NIV says, "It is for freedom that Christ has set us free. Stand firm, then, and DO NOT LET YOURSELVES BE BURDENED AGAIN WITH A YOKE OF SLAVERY." I Cor. 7:23 in the NIV says "You are bought with a price, DO NOT BECOME SLAVES OF MEN." There are no exception clauses in these verses, such as, "Don't become slaves of men, unless of course, it's to your husband or your pastor. That is God's will for you to become burdened with a yoke of obedience to them, because they are your God ordained covering."

Some verses describing satanic deception at the end of the age are Mt. 24:4,5,11,24; Mk.13:6; II Thes. 2:8-11; I John 2:18-26 and 4:1-6; II John 7; Rev. 13:4, 19:20, 20:7-10.

The false teachings about submission today are seducing and controlling people's minds so that they are deceived into following other gods, the idols of men, husbands, clergy, and marriage. They are seduced away from the true ways of God. They are seduced into error. It is witchcraft when anyone has as much influence and control over someone else's mind, like we see in the teachings on submission today.

In II Kings 23:24-26 we see that King Josiah did away with all the mediums, wizards, witches, idols, and abominations in the land SO THAT he could perform the words of the law of Moses. Those things had to be gotten rid of in order to turn back to God. Vs. 25 says that there was never,

before or after him, a king who turned to the Lord
with all his heart, soul, and strength. But vs.
26 says that in spite of that, the Lord's wrath
burned against Judah because of all their following
after other gods. Many believe that under grace,
God's wrath does not burn against His people.
But since God is holy, He never changes, and His
principles never change, God's wrath still burns
against those who control other people's minds,
causing them to follow other gods today, too.
The idols of today must be gotten rid of SO THAT
the blood bought believers can perform the true
submission that pleases God.

Gal.4:5-9 says, "We are redeemed from the law
that we might receive the adoption of sons. And
because ye are sons, God hath sent forth the Spirit
of His Son into your hearts, crying Abba! Father!
Wherefore, thou art no more a servant, but a son;
and if a son, then an heir of God through Christ.
Nevertheless, then, when you knew not God, YOU
DID SERVICE UNTO THEM WHICH BY NATURE ARE NOT
GODS. But now, after ye have known God, or rather
are known by God, how then turn you again to weak
and beggarly elements, unto which you desire again
to be in bondage?" Remember God's prophesy to
Eve that she would turn to her husband, but the
word "turning" was mistranslated as "desire"?
That "desire" meant to stretch out after or run
after. Here the word desire means to passively
acquiesce, to willingly choose, to prefer to,
turn back to the things that had previously held
them in bondage. Please remember the verses in
Isaiah that says the people took a covering not
of God. They chose to willingly submit themselves
to Pharoah and they were brought into bondage.

Here in Galatians the word "beggarly elements"
are those worthless principles of religion that
create a yoke of bondage. Women, you have been
set free from the yoke of bondage to ANY man, just
as men have been set free. Christ's blood did

that for you. Why are you "turning" again to the beggarly elements of trusting in a man rather than God? Why are you "turning" again to the yoke of bondage that you have been set free from by obeying a false concept of headship that is a religious tradition? God said, "Your turning will be to your husband and he shall rule over you". When women turn in blind, obedient submission to a man, they are "turning" again to those who are not gods by nature and will come into the bondage of being lorded over by the man.

A study in Eze. 28: 1-19 will shed a great deal of light on why this false doctrine of the "covering", which involves false submission and false headship, in both marriage and the church, is so prevalent in our churches today, and why it has such devastating effects. We will come to understand who is the perpetrator of this false doctrine and why.

The passage begins by God referring to the prince or king of Tyre. However, vs. 11-17 and also Isa.14:12-17 show that this human had an unseen ruler, who is Satan. Vs. 12 says that Lucifer (Satan) "sealed up the sum" which meant he was perfect and complete and he had the power to destroy utterly. He was full of wisdom and perfect in beauty. Vs. 13 says he was in the garden of Eden. Adam and Eve were expelled from the garden and the garden is guarded by angels with flaming swords so that no one could enter it. The king of Tyre came into existence long after that. So we know he could never have been in the garden of Eden. But we know that Lucifer was there with Adam and Eve. Vs. 13 also describes the beauty of all the precious stones and musical instruments that were embedded in Lucifer's body. No human was ever created with such things embedded in their body. Vs. 14 said that Lucifer was a very special angel who had a special anointing from God. He had a special job to do. He was the "CHERUB THAT

54

COVERETH". "Covereth" means to entwine like a screen, to fence in, cover over, to protect or defend. Vs. 2 tells us he was to cover the seat of God, which means the abode, dwelling, or inhabited place, population or assembly. This indicates a place and a group of beings who inhabitated that place. So he was to protect and defend this dwelling place of God. He had power to utterly destroy any enemies of this place. We are not told who or what these enemies might be. This place is further described in Vs. 14 as God's Holy mountain and the stones of fire. Besides the job of protecting this place, it is believed that the other major part of his job was to cover God with worship and to lead the assembly of angels in worship of God. That was the purpose of the musical instruments. So to seal up the sum means he was God's greatest angel, full of wisdom, beauty, power to destroy and power and anointing to worship. Vs. 15 says that God considered him perfect in all his ways until iniquity was found in him. Vs. 16 says that then he was filled with violence, and sinned, that God cast him out of the mountain of God and from amongst the stones of fire as profane. The word profane means to dissolve, break one's word, defile, pollute, and prostitute. Also listed in the meanings is play the flute, pipe, and player of instruments. This seems to substantiate his ministry of worship. Vs. 17 & 18 says his heart was lifted up because he was so beautiful, his wisdom was corrupted because of his brightness, and he defiled his sanctuaries with his iniquities. His sanctuaries are the holy places and the hosts of angels that he was to cover with protection and worship of God. He was cast out from those holy places to the earth. God took away his job of "covering" the holy place with protection and worship. But He did not take away all of his beauty, thus he can come to us as angel of light. He did not take away his abundant, but corrupted wisdom, thus he has the ability to reign over this earthly domain with a superhuman cunning. He did not take away the power to utterly destroy, thus he can kill, steal, and destroy (John 10:10) and he can seek to devour, (I Pet. 5:8). This is why Christians need the armor of God and why they need to be aware of his schemes.

With all of his corrupted beauty, wisdom and power still intact, he was relieved of his position in heaven. Earth became his new domain. All of his ability to "cover" is still intact also. But what can he do with it here on earth? Where is the dwelling of God here on earth? Romans 8:9,1; II Cor. 6:16; Eph.3:17; I John 4:13 all say that Christians, believers in Christ, are that dwelling place. Living sanctuaries. Satan's main goal was to win the worship that was due to God. That is still his main goal. But a Christian would not knowingly bow to worship him. So how can he employ his ability to "cover", which he was specifically designed for, to defile the living sanctuaries? If he could devise and promote a false teaching that would make faithful Christians bow to the idols of husbands and pastors it would accomplish his purpose!!! The Christian would bow to that "covering", thinking they were worshipping and being obedient to God, when in fact it is a corrupted thing that brings them into idol worship. Thus, he subtly and skillfully penetrates the armor and has again successfully defiled God's holy sanctuaries. They do not have a clue that anything has even happened. They go blindly on their merry way thinking all is well. They are being obediently submissive to their "covering" authority. The "cherub that covereth" is still "covering", but he does it to defile the living sanctuaries of God!!.

As I said, this false teaching on submission makes men idols. An idol takes the worship that is due to God only. Idol worship brings anyone into a bondage to the idol. The unbalanced teaching can make idols and because it sounds right, it can make people think they are serving God when, in fact, they are serving the idols. They are seduced, deceived, or bewitched into performing what they think is godly obedience. But they are obeying the wrong command and the wrong commander. Who is the perpetrator of this false teaching? When the church is obedient to it, why are the effects so devastating?

The word idol has already been mentioned many times in this book. It will be mentioned many more times. I have used the word idol in reference to husbands.

Am I being too bold, too harsh, too critical? Is it biblically correct to say men have become idols to their wives and that women have become idol worshipers? Or that men have become idols to themselves?

Let me share some information I found in Vine's Complete Expository Dictionary of Old and New Testament Words, by W.E.Vine, Merrill F. Unger and William White Jr, Page 12. Published by Thomas Nelson Inc. Copyright 1985.

Under the word "Baal, Master": "In Akkadian, the noun 'belu' (lord) gave rise to the verb 'belu' (to rule). The Hebrew word 'Baal' seems to have been related to these homonyms. The word 'baal' has the meaning of 'HUSBAND' 15 times in the Old Testament and 50 times it refers to a deity. The primary meaning of 'baal' is 'possessor'. In Ex. 21:3, man may be the owner of a wife.

A secondary meaning, 'husband', is clearly indicated by the phrase 'ball ha-issah' (literally, owner of the woman) in Ex. 21:22. The meaning of baal is closely related to 'is' (man) in II Sam. 11:26.

Thirdly the word may denote any deity other than the God of Israel.

Hosea pictured Israel as turning to the baals and only returning to the Lord after a time of despair (Hosea 2:13,17).

In the Septuagint the word baal is not uniformly translated. 'Kurios' (lord, owner); aner (man, husband); and baal. The KJV has these translations, Baal, man, owner, husband, master'.

Much of this book was already written before I discovered this information. Although I had used the word "idol" many times in connection with the husband and the position of idol that he is being elevated to through these false teachings, the idol never had a name. It was just "idol". One day, I felt the prompting of the Lord to look up the word "idol" and then "Baal". I was shocked at what I read, for I had never looked that up before. I just assumed that I knew what idol meant and that Baal was an ancient god or gods. The word "idol" means a household god. The amazing thing was that 'baal' can and does mean husband and owner/master of the woman. It was even more astonishing how this correlates with the false teachings on headship and submission and how the enemy has used the mistranslation of that tiny portion of Gen. 3:16 on which to build a whole network of false doctrine. Good Christians have been duped into thinking they are being obedient to God, but in fact, it is Baal worship. Only it has the sanction of almost all of Christendom's leaders! What a cunning deceiver our enemy is!! This is why Christian marriages are being destroyed as people practice these false and perverse teachings!!

The same evil principle is at work when pastors are elevated to a position of idol through the submission that is taught, based on "obey them who have authority over you as those who must give account for your souls". (Heb.13:17)

Let's go back to the beginning of this chapter, to the passage in Isaiah 30. We need to look at it very carefully because it is quite relevant for us today. This is my commentary.

The people took for themselves a "covering" that was not of God. What was that "covering" and how did they take it upon themselves? THE PEOPLE HAD WILLINGLY CHOSEN TO SUBMIT THEMSELVES TO SOMEONE OTHER THAN GOD. God called that sin. He said the people did not ask for His advice, His plan, or His purpose for them. They turned from God, to Pharaoh, thinking there was more safety and security in Pharaoh and his provision than there was in God. They trusted that Pharaoh could take better care of them than God could. They trusted in a man and a nation because Pharaoh was strong and so was Egypt. But God said, (paraphrasing) "since you trusted in Pharaoh and Egypt more than in me, the strength of Pharaoh will be your shame." In other words, the strength of Pharaoh that they trusted to protect and provide for them, would be the very tool Pharaoh would use against them to bring them into shameful slavery. Because they willingly submitted themselves to Pharaoh's power, and they wanted to trust and dwell in the shadow of Egypt, they would live in disgrace, dishonor, confusion and reproach.

Isaiah 30:12 says that they were despising His word, BECAUSE THEY CHOSE TO TRUST IN OPPRESSION AND PERVERSENESS AND TO RELY ON MEN RATHER THAN ON GOD.

Verses 13-14 say it was an iniquity that would break them down suddenly like a broken down wall and a smashed potter's vessel. A vessel smashed so thoroughly, that not one piece could be found big enough to hold a drop of water or to take a spark of fire out of the hearth with.

Verse 15 says that if they returned to Him and would rest in Him, rather than in Pharaoh and Egypt, they would be saved. He would give them quietness and confidence as their strength. Quietness means a settled, still rest. Confidence means a place of refuge, security, trust, assurance, hope, and safety. But the people did not want that. In verses 9-12 it says they were rebellious children who did not want to hear the truth. They did not want the prophets to tell them right things, they only wanted to hear smooth things. They wanted to hear deceitful things. Things that would make them feel good. They wanted the Holy Spirit of God to leave them alone. They despised the true word of God. They trusted in the oppression and perverseness of their chosen "covering" and they relied on them. They wanted it that way.

Verses 18-19 are the beautiful promises of God. How He waited patiently for them to return to Him. How He would be exalted to show them mercy. How He would hear their cries and when He did, they would weep no more.

Verse 20 says that because they chose to stay under their "covering" and refused to return to Him, God would give them the bread of adversity to eat and the water of affliction to drink.

Verses 20-21 says that if they would return to Him, he would let them see their teachers. He would let them hear a voice that would tell them the way to walk. It would keep them from going astray again, either to the right or to the left.

Verse 22 says that when they returned to Him, when they chose to come out from the false coverings that were not of His Spirit, they would defile those coverings and throw them away like unclean rags. Unclean rags are not merely dirty rags that one would use to mop up the floor with perhaps. This is talking about the unclean rags that are called menstruous. In the KJV it says "you will say to it (the idols that are like unclean menstruous rags), Get thee hence!!"

So what am I saying? I know that there is wisdom in the counsel of many. I am not negating the influence of godly peers. I know the Bible says submit to one another. But in submitting one to another, there is neither an "over you" nor an "under you" position. The teaching today about the "covering" or "umbrella of protection" of husband, pastor, and denominations is a false teaching from the devil. It places women under the covering of the husband. It places Christians under the covering of pastors and boards of churches. It places churches under the covering of denominations. Denominations foster the party spirit that Paul condemned in I Corinthians. These coverings are not of God's Spirit for they inhibit His plan and purposes for His people.

This is how the passage relates to women and what is happening in Christian marriages today. The man and the woman listen to the perverted teachings on headship and submission. The woman turns from God as her true source of everything. She is brought into a place where she trusts her husband for his guidance, his provision, his protection, his will in every area of life. She trusts that God will ALWAYS work through the man before He can work through her. She submits her total self willingly to someone other than God. He becomes her source for everything as she believes that he is God's appointed covering over her. The more she does this the less she trusts that, she too, can hear from God. Finally she believes that she does not hear from God at all. He only speaks to her husband "head". As she totally yields herself over to her husband and his will, she dwells in his shadow, just as the Israelites dwelt in Pharaoh's shadow. She is no longer a real person. She is just the shadow of the man. A shadow has no real substance. Then, as God said, the man's strength rules over her and brings her into a bondage of soul and spirit. Exactly the way Pharaoh brought the Israelites into bondage. She feels disgraced, dishonored, and hopeless. She is crushed in spirit, like a smashed potter's vessel. There

isn't enough of her left to hold the living water
of the Holy Spirit anymore. And there isn't enough
of her left to hold a spark of the Holy Spirit
Fire. She doubts, and then discounts everything
she hears from God.

She wonders why she never seems to hear from
God, and why she has no joy, and why God isn't
using her in a powerful way. After all, she is
being submissively obedient in EVERYthing, just
as she has been taught.

But God says that kind of trust and reliance
on any man is a sin. It is not of Him. It brings
her the bread of adversity and the water of
affliction. That is why she feels wounded, full
of pain, and full of hopeless despair, a prisoner.
She is eating this bread of adversity and drinking
this water of affliction because she has turned
from God to man and has made the man her idol.

Her false covering has become her idol. She
willingly submits to him. She is now guilty of
Baal worship. Now her husband dominates her. Didn't
God say to Eve, "your turning will be to your
husband and that will cause him to rule over you"?

God says that the only way to come out of this
desperate place, into a place of quietness, a place
of refuge from the pain and conflict, is to cast
off this false teaching of submission and practice
of "coverings" like you would throw away a
menstruous rag!! Can you imagine cherishing and
holding on to that kind of a cloth? God says this
false submission should be just as abhorrent
as that kind of a cloth is to you. It needs to
be discarded in the same manner that you would
discard that kind of a cloth. Women, go back
to trusting God and relying on God and believing
you hear from God yourself!! Go back to believing
that God will guide you, God will direct you, God
will tell you which way to go!! He is the one
who will keep you from straying to the right or

to the left, not your husband. Because he is human, your husband can go astray and he will take you right along with him. God is Jehovah-Jireh, your provider. The Holy Spirit is the guide, and the teacher that you will hear and see.

Do you want that place of quiet rest and refuge? Then see how God is trying to teach you truth through Isaiah. See how the coverings of men are not coverings from God. Renounce them and turn back to your God who wants to be exalted in His loving mercy for you. He wants to bring you to the quiet, restful, refuge of His strength. Then you can again hear his voice. You will again be whole enough to be able to hold the fire and the water of the Holy Spirit.

Have you wondered why so many pastors today are so discouraged and wounded that they are giving up their pulpits and are walking away from their callings? Reader, are you one of those men?

When Christians willingly submit to men as pastors, because he is the so-called "anointed of God" who was sent to RULE over his particular church, the results are the same. The people are also trusting in a Pharaoh and Egypt. The "church" is so sick today, it's condition is almost terminal. The fruit of trusting and relying on a man/pastor to hear from God for you, is slavery. The burden for the pastor to be the eyes and ears for everyone is also overwhelming slavery. It was never meant to be so. Pastor, God will hold you accountable for people's souls BECAUSE OF THE WORD, THE LOGOS, THAT YOU TEACH, **NOT** FOR WHAT OTHER PEOPLE DO!! He will hold you accountable for how you used that Word to persuade others to follow Him. If you used the Word to persuade others to follow you, woe be it to you, for He will hold you accountable for that too!! When the false teachings of "coverings" is cast off, your work will then be the joy to you that it is supposed to be. The heavy burden will be rolled off your back. You will know a new depth of freedom and a new, refreshing power in ministry.

The same is true of denominations. Pastors, boards, churches willingly submit to them, but they, too, are only men.

Am I promoting rebellion against husbands, pastors, and denominations? <u>INDEED NOT!!!!!</u> But I am most definitely promoting the renouncing of false teachings, the tearing down of idols, that we have been deceived into building into our Christian lives. I am promoting the turning back to God and exalting and elevating Him as the one true "Covering". I am promoting the vigorous marching out from under the shadow of the idols we have built. I am promoting the turning back to God in obedience to Him, first, foremost, and above all. The fruit of this will not be division, hurt, pain, and confusion. The fruit will be a peaceable, quiet, resting in the refuge of God for women, for men, and for pastors. There will be restoration for sick marriages and restoration for the sick church. That is what I am promoting.

Repent of these false teachings that you have labored under. Cast off those "coverings" that are not of God's Spirit. Let God be exalted as He displays his mercy to you and wipes away your tears and brings you into that place of quiet, refuge and rest. He will lift you up in His strength and you will no longer dwell in the shadow of the "Pharaohs" and the "Egypts" in your life. Then you will no longer eat the bread of adversity, nor drink the water of affliction, that has come to you because of the sin of idol worship. Have you lived long enough in a time of despair? Isn't it time to return to the Lord? Do you want to hear the words of the prophet that speaks truth? Or, like the Israelites, do you want to continue to let the false teachings tickle your ears? Teachings that build such pride and ego in men that they willingly take the place of God and become idols to their wives. Teachings that make the women shirk their own responsibilities in Christ by deferring to their idol husbands. Renounce these false teachings of the "covering". Renounce your allegiance to the false "coverings" in your life. Reounce the opression and perverseness that you have willingly accepted. Rebuke Satan for perpetrating this ungodly teaching of the "covering" which he has devised so that he can continue defiling the living sanctuaries of God. Take back the ground you have given him by following those teachings. Forbid him to defile you anymore with it. Walk out from under the shadows into the tender mercies of God and the rest and refuge that He is patiently waiting to give you. Return to God and let Him be your only true covering.

# CHAPTER FOUR
## HEADSHIP AND DIVINE ORDER

Where does the term "Divine Order" come from? Does it have a biblical basis? What is this doctrine that is so promoted by almost all of Christendom? Why is it so accepted that most Christians do not even question it or it's origins? It is assumed, or taken for granted, by most to be a true Bible doctrine. For years, I myself taught it as such. Divine order is also known as "the chain of command", meaning someone must be the boss, someone must be in control or be in charge.

Some of the Scriptures already referred to are part of the basis for this teaching. There are many more of them. Other than an order of creation, there is no real basis for "Divine Order", as we know it, in the Bible. I base this rash statement on many Scriptures, especially I Cor.11:3-16. This passage deals with what "head" means and what head coverings represent. This long, detailed study dispels the false doctrine of "divine order".

"Divine Order" is really a carry-over from medieval history. In those years of 700 A.D. to 1500 A.D., the church was the most powerful organization in existence, both politically and religiously. Their belief was that every person was destined or ordained by God to fill a particular station in life. It was a caste system, that separated people by social class, gender, race, etc. They did everything possible to keep that order, since they believed that God had set people in the caste system positions into which they were born. As political and religious leaders, they thought it was their God-given duty to keep everyone in that position. People who disagreed or tried to upset their established "divine order" where tortured and executed.

Part of the caste system was that since man was created before woman, then her place in the "divine order" was to be under the subjection of man. In those days, and actually almost since the beginning of time, the traditions of men taught that women were inferior, because they were created second, and evil because Eve was deceived and tempted Adam to sin.

Because men could not control their own lustful, sexual desires, they blamed women for being evil. Thus the women had to wear veils and coverings to the feet so that no man could see any part of them. In some cases the coverings were so extreme, the only visible part of a woman was one eye. Everything else was covered. The inability of the man to control his own lust was the woman's fault. Women were to be kept in their proper place, which was that of being inferior chattels of men. Just as slaves were chattels and had to be kept in their place.

Today there are cultures in existence who will throw baby girls on garbage dumps to die or will actually kill them, because only males are valued enough to live. In India, mothers are trained to believe that it is their duty to kill their baby girls, simply because they are girls and do not have the importance in life that males do. In China, pregnant women are given ultra-sound and though many males are aborted, there are far more female babies aborted. Also in China there are orphanages where thousands of abandoned little girls live in horrible conditions. The parents abandon them so that the one child they are allowed to keep can be a boy.

There is such disdain for women that from ancient times until today, Jewish men thank God that they were not born a woman. Is that Jewish saying far removed from our own Western Christian culture? In some ways yes, but in many ways the principle is very much alive here. Today it comes

67

in the form of twisted Scripture that commands a woman to submit to her husband in everything. Even as a Christian, she is not truly esteemed as an equal partaker of Christ and is not on the same level with the man, in the home or in the church.

In 1985, I attended a Sunday church service in a town in Florida. The preacher, who was also the founder, president and main teacher of a small Bible college, blatantly and boldly preached that he, too, was glad that he was not a woman, because a woman's position in life was no better than that of a slave or a child. I got up and walked out. Several others did too. I was told that the man consistently preached this way, this was not an isolated sermon. The tragedy is that this man teaches his students, graduates them from his Bible college and sends them out with this mentality to establish new churches. Obviously, not all of his students will emulate their teacher. The teacher himself may not even practice what he preaches in his personal life, but the Word says that out of the mouth comes the abundance of the heart. I can only judge the words that my ears heard. I attended a women's gathering of that same group and was dismayed at the downtrodden demeanor of these women. Some of their demeanor could be explained by the fact that there were many stresses while their husbands attended college and most had families and very low incomes. But still, that does not account for their low self esteem.

This is an extreme example, but it is true. More often though, the keeping of the woman in her "proper" place of subjection is far more subtle than that. It is couched in fine sounding words so it appears to be a blessing and very biblically correct.

Headship and divine order are interrelated in today's teaching. Gen.3:16, I Corinthians

11:3-16; Ephesians 5:22; Titus 2:5 and I Peter 3:1 are Scriptures that are quoted as proof of headship and are the basis for the "divine order" teaching. The major verse for headship is I Cor. 11:3 "The head of every man is Christ, the head of the woman is the man; and the head of Christ is God". According to Vine's Expository Dictionary, "head" means, "metaphorically, the authority or direction of God in relation to Christ, of Christ in relation to believing men (the church), of the husband in relation to the wife."

"Head" has nothing to do with the man being given the right to dominate and control, to make all decisions, to rule over the woman with an iron fist. It does not give him the right to dictate to her what she can and cannot say, what kinds of crafts and hobbies and work she will do, what she will wear and how she will wear her hair, what groceries she can buy and how much money she can spend, and when, etc. For many, these are the extremes of what "headship" means in our day.

As the Head of Christ, how did God demonstrate authority over Christ? How did God treat, or act toward, His Son? In Gen. 1:26, God involved the Son in the creation of mankind. He said, "let US make man in OUR image." In that statement He is saying that His Son has the exact same image as Himself. In other words, even though God was the Head, He considered the Son to be equal with Him. Phil. 2:6 says, "The Son was in the form of God and thought it not robbery to be equal with God." The Son was not inferior to God just because God was the "head". God did not take all right of decision from the Son. Even in the decision to die on the cross, God did not take away the choice Christ had, even though He came for that purpose. In the garden of Gethsemane Christ cried out three times, "Father, if there be any other way, take this cup from me." In paraphrase, He's saying "This is too hard for me, Father. Can't

there be another way to do this?" But then He makes
the choice and says, "Not my will, but thine."
God did not DEMAND that the Son's will be yielded
to His. The Son chose to yield His will to the
Father. But it was a voluntary choice.

What was the overall picture of the behavioral
relationship between Father and Son? Because the
Son loved the Father there was a desire to be
obedient to the Father, as shown by the many
Scriptures where Jesus says, "I don't do this of
myself, I do it of the Father's will in me." It
was not commanded of Him by the Father. The Father
was not, and is not, a dictator as He fulfills
the role of "head". Did God enforce dictatorial
authority? How did God direct Christ to relate
to man? Did Christ come as a dictator, ruling and
lording it over man? NO!! He forbade that kind
of domination and lordship! He came teaching,
giving, loving, nurturing, and caring for those
who would follow Him. He did not command obedience
from them. He presented Himself, a promise of
eternal life and an astonishing new way of life
in freedom from old covenant laws of sacrifices
and offerings for sin, and freedom from all
traditions and all bondages. He did not give an
invitation to men alone to come out from that
bondage as they followed Him. It was for women
as well. He broke with the old traditions openly
when He talked to the Samaritan woman at the well,
and other incidents when He dealt directly with
women. He left it up to the people to accept or
reject Him and His teachings. It was their
individual choice to be obedient or not. He taught
His followers that the head was the servant. He
was the same kind of "head" over the church as
God was "head" over Him.

In contrast to the world system, the Biblical
"head" is a guide and leader who demonstrates
headship by loving example of service. In the
context of I Cor. 11:3, the headship of the husband

70

in relation to the wife must be consistent with the headship of Christ in relation to the church, and of God the Father in relation to the Son. We cannot say that the headship of Father and Son means one thing but it means something entirely different when it comes to the headship of the husband and wife.

The controversy over the word "head" rages. I have at least six commentaries on I Corinthians on my shelves. The interpretations of 11:3 are very different, but one thing is clear. Some interpretations are consistent with the bias and prejudice toward women of today's teachings. There are some who interpret according to the true meaning of the original words. Christ as head of the church, man as head of the woman, and God as the head of Christ all use the same word, kephale, for head. I found that some interpret the word to mean source of origin. Others, however, interpret it to mean ruler or governor, depending on their own bias. To me, I Cor 11:3 is used in context with verses 11 and 12. The word says that just as, or in the same way, that the source of man is Christ, the Creator, the man is the source of the woman, because originally she was made from his side and came out of man. In the same way, God is the source of Christ because Christ is God's only BEGOTTEN Son.

Dr. Gilbert Bilezikian, in his book, "Beyond Sex Roles", states that there is a Hebrew word, ROS, that means "authority". 170 times in the Hebrew Bible, the word was NOT translated as "kephale" in the Greek, when it meant authority. He says that on the contrary, the authors of the Septuagint rejected the use of kephale as an equivalent for ROS/authority. They meticulously translated ROS 170 times with words other than kephale when ROS meant authority. In spite of that truth, there are those who adamantly hold to the view that God cannot be the source of origin

71

of Christ, because Christ is part of the eternal Godhead. He always existed, therefore He could not have a source of origin. Because of that they conclude that "head" can ONLY mean "authority". Those who dare to say that God is the source of origin of Christ are labeled as heretics and evangelical feminists.

But is that heretical? Does it have anything to do with evangelical or any kind of feminism? We have to dig deep for the answer.

Why did God Himself call Christ His only begotten Son?

According to Strong's Concordance, the word study for begotten utilizes four Greek words. The first one means the only born, the sole or only child. The second word means to remain in that position of only child. The third one is like it, that is to dwell or abide in that state of relationship. The fourth one is the most interesting and the most key word. It is a middle form of a primary verb that means to cause to be, (generate), to become or come into being. These are the main meanings of these words.

Altogether they are indicating that there was a birth of a child. The child was caused to come into being by someone. It would be the only child and it would remain in the place of only child. This is what it means for Christ to be the only begotten Son of God.

So how does this correlate with Christ having always existed?

Theologians make it so complicated, when it is really so simple. As part of the Godhead, Christ did always exist. But He did not always exist in a human body. He had to acquire a human body. Therefore, He had to be born like every other human being except Adam and Eve. How did God do that?

Luke 1:35 says that the angel said to Mary, "The Holy Spirit shall come upon thee, and power of the Highest shall overshadow thee; therefore, also that holy thing which shall be born of thee shall be called the Son of God." (KJV) Notice, the Holy Spirit would be the vehicle that conveys the power, but the power comes from God. The child is not called the Son of the Holy Spirit, but the Son of God. It is THIS human Son of God who had his source of origin from the power of the Highest, God. The word overshadow here means to superimpose with a brilliant haze. The words "upon", "power" and "overshadow" combined means that there would be a superimposition of miraculous power that would envelope Mary in a haze of brilliance, causing her to be pregnant with this holy, but also human, child. Thus the method of becoming pregnant would diverge from the common method of becoming pregnant, but the rest of the pregnancy and birth would be within the natural bounds of order for every pregnancy and birth. Since Christ was without sin, it was not even a human egg that was fertilized by the Father, it had to be a Holy embryo that was placed in the virgin womb to be nurtured into a human form. Though the conception was not ordinary, the rest of the process for Christ to become a human was ordinary. Mt.1:25 and Luke 2:7 calls Him the first born Son. Therefore, God IS the irrefutable source of origin of Christ, the human. This will be explained more later.

It was not the eternally existent part of Christ that died on the cross, it was the human Christ in bodily form. It was the human form that cried out, "My God, My God why have you forsaken me?" The shed blood of that human sacrifice became the source of origin of the church.

There is another set of passages that unfolds the magnificent truth concerning the only begotten Son. As the Lord unfolded this truth to me, I could do nothing but stand in awe of the spectacular God, Father and Son.

Heb. 1:13 "Who, Christ, **being in the brightenss of His** (God's) **glory, and the express image of**

73

His (God's) **person,** and upholding all things by the word of His (Christ's) power, when He (Christ) had by himself purged our sins, sat down on the right hand of the Majesty (God) on high."

Heb. 1:5 "For unto which of the angels said he at any time, **'Thou art my son, this day have I begotten thee?.** And again, 'I will be to him a Father and he shall be to me a Son?'". This does not speak of the eternally co-existent relationship! It is a Father/Son relationship.

Heb.1:6 "And again **when he** (God) **bringeth the first begotten** (Christ) **into the world,** he saith, 'And let all of the angels worship him'."

Heb. 1:8 "But unto the Son he (God) saith, 'Thy throne, O God, is forever and ever; a scepter of righteousness is the scepter of thy kingdom'." (All verses from KJV).

For me, this is a most magnificent passage. It was awesome in it's power as I comprehended with my spirit what it truly meant. I will try to explain it in a way that you can appreciate how awesome it is.

We have already seen what begotten means. Now we will jump around in the Scriptures a bit to see what this passage in Hebrews means.

Col. 1:15 and 18 says Jesus is the IMAGE of the invisible God, the firstborn of all creation", and, "He is the head of the body, the church, who is the beginning, the first-born from the dead, that in all things he might have pre-eminence". Image here means likeness, as in a statue or profile. The word visible means to gaze at, capable of being seen, to stare at, to behold, to appear, to perceive, to see. Invisible is the opposite, meaning something that cannot be gazed upon because it is incapable of being seen or perceived. God himself is not someone we can see but what we are dealing with here is a PART of Him that IS seen!

In Heb. 1:3, we saw the words "express image of His person". This image is slightly different from the above meaning. It means an exact copy or representation. The words express and image have the exact same meaning. Two words used together like that emphasizes their importance. What is being emphasized is the exactness of the copy or the representation. Vine's Expository Dictionary enlarges on this by saying that it's compared to a die used to impress a coin. The coin bears the exact impress or image of the die and is an exact copy. But, he states, Christ is not merely an exact image of God's character, he is an impress of God's very substance and essence.

First-born comes from a word that means foremost in time, place, order or importance. It also means the chiefest, first, in front of, or prior. So as the first born, Jesus was before, He was the beginning, He was the chiefest, the first of all. He was prior to anything else that ever existed. This bears witness with John 8:58 and Ex. 3:14, where Jesus and God are both called "I AM" and in Rev. 1:8, 17, 18, where Jesus' existence is proclaimed as **"who is"**, (eternal pre-existence) **"who was,"** (earthly existence), **and "who is to come"** (present eternal existence). In this one word we see the aspects of His eternal pre-existence, the first-born of his human existence, the first born of the resurrection, and the first born of the church.

The word "brightness" in Heb 1:3 is the most fascinating word of all and it explains the word "invisible". The word brightness comes from two words. One of them is "apo" and it means OFF-FLESH (effulgence), that is, away from something near in various senses such as place, time, or relation. In composition, it is a prefix that usually denotes, separation, departure, cessation, completion, reversal. The word "effulgence" means radiance and splendor. The other part of the word "brightness" means to shine forth, to beam forth. Remember, the meaning of "overshadow" was to

75

envelope in a haze of brilliancy? Now, combine that with this meaning of brightness.

So what all of this means is that Jesus always existed in the form of God. The "form" of God means the adjustment of parts, the shape, the nature of God. But God is so incredibly awesome, there is no way a human mind could comprehend Him. God chose to send Jesus into the world as a human being. Jesus was that radiant, splendorous part of God, that separated itself from God's form, departed from God, to come to earth, to shine forth like a brilliant, radiant beam of light, so that mankind could see the invisible God as a visible being. Thus, He was an exact copy, an exact representation of God that our finite minds could grasp and understand.

In the one little three letter prefix "apo", the whole magnificent story of redemption is revealed.

The verses in Hebrews, combined with the prefix "apo", all together says that there was an adjustment of God's parts so that a radiant, particular section or part of God SEPARATED itself from God's form and then DEPARTED from Him. The word "form" also means an adjustment of parts, a section, division, or particular parts. That particular part was separated from God in time, place, and relationship. That part was invested into Mary's body when she was overshadowed by a brilliant haze, impregnating her, so that part then came into the world as Jesus Christ, the human being. Jesus Christ, the human being, died on the cross. His death and resurrection COMPLETED God's plan of redemption for mankind. That COMPLETED His work of RESTORATION. As Christ was that part that left God, that part CEASED to exist WITH God. So there was a CESSATION of that kind. When He died, it was the CESSATION of His human life. But as Christ ascended and sat at the right hand of God in Majesty, it demonstrated the CESSATION of the power held by Satan and all principalities and powers, both on earth and in heaven. That REVERSED the curse of sin and death. It REVERSED the fallen state of mankind and made it possible for those who believe to be RESTORED to the original state of glory and image of God. Jesus brought back the righteousness to mankind that was lost in the fall. Christ is God's stick or rod that broke the back of all unrighteousness. The righteousness of Christ is the royal banner of His kingdom. Those who believe in Him are the royal banner bearers, who are to represent His righteousness to the world. His ascension to sit on the throne REVERSED the human aspect of Christ, also, and RESTORED Him to the eternal Godhead. This is so beautifully portrayed by God, when He said in Heb. 1:8 "Thy throne ,O God, is forever and ever." God the Father calls the Son, "O God"! In all of this we see the various forms of RELATION between God the Father and Jesus the Son. We see so clearly how Christ could be the eternally existent one and yet have God as His Father, when He was in human form. We can also see very clearly how God is the source of origin for Christ the Son, the human Christ.

Is it an evil feminist spirit or is it heresy to say that God is the source of origin of Christ? I don't believe so. Rather, it is heresy and arrogant male chauvinism to DENY that God is the source of origin of Christ, the human, in order to substantiate dictatorial "headship" doctrine! God said there is a Father and Son relationship between them, even though Jesus always existed.

Let us draw some comparisons and conclusions here.

(A)Jesus was a part of God that left God, was invested into Mary's body, and there took on the form of a man.

(B)Woman was a part of man that God seperated out of man, and formed into a woman.

77

(C)The flesh and blood of Christ was the part of Him that was seperated from Him in sacrifice so that a new body could be formed from it, the living Body of Christ, the Church.

All three were a part of something else before they became what God wanted them to be. Christ was a part of God, woman was a part of man and the church is a part of Christ.

God is the "kephale", the head of Christ. Man is the "kephale", head of woman. Christ is the "kephale", the head, of the church. They are all the same word and they all mean the same thing. Each one is the source of origin of what they are the head of.

A related passage of how Christ is the source of origin of the church is Col. 1:15-18. It explains that He is the source or origin of all things, and as such He became the "head', the "kephale', the source of origin of the church.

The mistranslation of "head" is the basis for the perversion of what submission means. It is unfortunate indeed, and a tool of the devil, that early Bible translators and early church fathers, as well as many modern expositors, theologians, and ministers etc. have used terms concerning headship and submission that are not correct according to the original languages.

There is a Greek word, "meta=change +onoma, onyma=name". It is our modern word metonym. What it means is that a word is substituted for another word, or the use of the NAME of one thing is substituted for that of another associated with or suggested by it. This is the case in I Corinthians 11:10 where it says that a woman ought to have authority on her head because of the angels. According to Vine's this means "that in connection with the context, the word 'authority' probably stands, by metonym, for a 'sign of authority', the angels being witnesses of the pre-eminent relationship as established by God in the creation of man as mentioned with the spiritual significance regarding the position of Christ in relationship to the church". I believe this definition can lead to error.

The context of I Cor. 11:3-16, is talking about an actual covering or veil or something over the head that has the primary function of distinguishing or demonstrating something to the angels concerning the spiritual position of Christ over the church. It is for the benefit of the angels, and has little to do with demonstrating anything for man's benefit. But this phrase, 'sign of authority' has been substituted for the word "power" (exousia) in Scofield's Reference Bible, as well as others, so that it says, rather, that the veil or covering on the woman's head is a symbol of her **SUBORDINATION** to her husband and then cross references to Gen. 3:16---"he shall rule over you". Read the passage in the Amplified Bible.

I find the words "subject" and "submit" in many places in the Word such as Rom. 8:20, I Cor. 15:25, Phil 3:21, Heb. 2:7-8, I Pet. 3:22, and Eph. 1:22. They do have the meaning of "to place under or to subordinate". However, I did not find the actual word "subordination" in the Bible in any context, and certainly not in the context of men and women. I did not find the word in Strong's Concordance or Vine's Expository dictionary either. So I looked it up in Webster's Dictionary to see what it means. The meaning is as follows:

A. Inferior to or placed below another in rank, power, importance; secondary.

B. Under the power or authority of another.

C. Subservient or submissive.

The word "subordinating" means:

A. To place in a subordinate position; treat as an inferior or less important.

B. To make obedient or subservient; to control; to subdue.

Subservient means:

A. That which is useful, helpful, or of service, especially in an inferior or subordinate capacity.

B. Submissive; obsequious. Synonym: servile,

a. A slave or like that of a slave or characteristic of a slave.

b. Held in slavery, not free. Suggests the cringing behavior of a slave.

Finally, the word obsequious means:

A. Excessively compliant or willing to obey, overly submissive; implies a servile, fawning attitude toward someone regarded as one's superior. Antonyms: domineering, imperious.

All of these are very negative words. So when "a sign of subordination" is substituted for "a sign of authority" and then cross referenced to Gen. 3:16, "--he shall rule over you", it implies that a woman is inferior, a slave to be controlled. It presumes that God gave the man the right to dominate and control the woman, like a master over a slave. It is a gross altering of God's Word with the express purpose of promoting this false teaching of headship and divine order. No matter how nice any preacher tries to make it sound, the basis of the word subordinate has a totally negative conotation and he cannot make it sound positive. In actuality, the word "authority" is not even the correct word. It is really "power". According to Strong's, the word for power in this verse is "exousia". It means, "in the sense of ability, privilege, that is, subjectively, force, capacity, competence, freedom, or objectively, mastery, delegated influence ;authority, juris- diction, liberty, power, right, and strength." The base of exousia is another word, "exon", which is a neuter, present tense word. Neuter means genderless, neither male nor female, and present tense means an on-going thing. So this power that is on the woman is a genderless power, that is, it is not bound by gender. It is an on-going power that does not cease to exist with time and it

80

is to continue to function in public.

How do these meanings correlate with the meanings of subordination? They do not. They are opposites!! Taken in context, the meaning of the phrase "the woman ought to have power on her head" would mean that in Christ and the new way of life which He brought into being, the woman has the same ability, privilege, capacity, competency, freedom, delegated influence, authority, jurisdiction, liberty, power, right and strength to pray, prophesy, preach, teach, do miracles, etc. that any Christian man has. Further, she has the right to do that in public assemblies of the congregation. She has been given the same mastery as the man. Christ delegated all of that to her just as He delegated it to man. It does not subordinate her like a slave anymore, as she was in the Old Testament. It elevates her and frees her from the position of slave, which man had forced her into, to a position of Christ's delegated mastery. The passage is supposed to make it clear that the woman was not under the false SUBJECTION of Old Testament law, but man has interpreted it wrongly in order to continue those old biases. Man has focused on this passage as proof text that man has the right of dominion over the woman because Paul said the woman ought to have authority, or a sign of authority, on her head.

Now that we have a correct interpretation of what is meant by "head", Gen. 3:16, and "a sign of authority", we can go on to a better understanding of the whole passage of I Cor.11: 3-16. Some things will be a repeat of what has already been written, but we need to do this so that the passage is seen as a whole, in context.

Many dissect this passage and say that parts of it are speaking to married people only so that they can substantiate female subordination and male supremacy. Let US dissect it to see if they are correct. We must go through the whole passage in order for it to make sense. The way that "man" is used in this entire passage means an individual male person. It is not referring to mankind. The word "head" means source of origin in some places but it also means the literal part of the physical body in other places. In some places the "covering" is a veil or headpiece, in other places it is hair. Vs. 3 says, "The head of EVERY man is Christ". Christ is the head of all men because He was co-creator, the source of origin of all men. He is also the head, source of origin, of the church because the church was formed out of a part of Christ, his shed blood. "Every" means all, any, the whole, everyone.

"THE head of THE woman is THE man." This phrase is referring to one particular woman (singular) and one particular man (singular), Adam and Eve. A part of that man was taken out of him and was formed into the woman, becoming the head, source of origin, of that one woman. "The head of Christ is God" means that the human Christ was a part of God that separated itself from God, departed from Him, was invested into Mary's body, causing her to be pregnant with what became the human baby Jesus. Thus God was the head, source of origin, of Christ the human. Vs. 4 says, "Every man praying or prophesying with his head uncovered, dishonors his head". "Every" man includes married and unmarried male believers who are praying or prophesying in the assembly of believers. There isn't a hint that marital status is a qualifying factor. We know the first "head" here is referring to the literal body part because it should not be covered. The second "head" is referring back to vs. 3 where it says Christ is the head of the man. So the man praying or prophesying with his head covered dishonors Christ, his head. The word dishonors means to shame down, to disgrace, put to blush and confound. Vs. 5 says, "every woman".

82

So this includes ALL women, married or unmarried. They are praying and prophesying in the assembled congregation, just like the men are. They are a part of the body of Christ. As such, Christ is their head as much as He is the head of the men in the church. But it says the women should have their head, literal body part, covered. If she doesn't, it dishonors her head (Christ) as if she were shaved. Vs. 6 talks about how it is a shame for a woman to be uncovered or to have her head shaved. In that culture, moral women wore a veil but a woman with a shaved head was the sign of a pagan temple prostitute. If a woman was praying and prophesying in the assembly it would mean that she was a believer in Christ, her head. IF she was a newly converted temple prostitute with a shaved head, that she didn't cover with a veil, it would dishonor Christ. It would be the same as confessing that she was still a practicing prostitute, even while cofessing to be a believer in Christ. Christ is the head that she would dishonor, not man. But if she covers her head, that would signify that she had submitted herself to Christ, her head. The word "shame" in vs. 6 means a disfigurement or disgrace. It has to do with looks or decorum. Decorum, according to Webster's, is suitable or proper, propriety in good taste in behavior, speech, or dress.

Vs. 7 deals with two important issues, why the man ought NOT have his head covered because he is the image and glory of God, and why the woman is the glory of the man. This has been interpreted by many to mean that Paul was saying man alone is the image and glory of God, because he was created first, but woman is inferior because she is ONLY the glory of the man. Many believe that because she is ONLY the glory of man, her head covering is her symbol of subordination to her husband.

To understand why a man ought not have his

83

covered we need to look at some other Scriptures. Ex.34:29-35 says that when Moses came down from the mountain after talking with God, his face was shining with the glory of God. He veiled his head and face because the people feared him. But when he went in to speak to the Lord again, he removed the veil. This scenario is repeated twice in this passage. It appears as though it was a shame for him to come into God's presence with his head covered. Many believe that Moses' covering his face in front of the people set a precedence, and that is why Jewish men covered their heads. In II Cor. 3:6-18, in the NIV, we find the New testament version of this event. Vs. 6 refers to the new covenant where the Spirit brings life to the whole body of Christ, men and women. Vs. 7-13 confirms that there was a glory on Moses' face that the Israelites could not stand to look at, so he veiled himself. The glory on Moses was of the old covenant, that brought condemnation to the people and faded away. The Holy Spirit's coming would be of the new covenant, it would be far more glorious than the glory that was on Moses, and it would not fade away. That Holy Spirit glory of the new covenant would bring a glorious righteousness to the church, which would far surpass the glory of Moses. The glory of Moses, representing the old covenant, would fade away, but the glory of the new covenant, the church, was greater and would never fade. Since women are a part of this new covenant church body, the same glory that rests on men, rests on the women. Vs. 14 and 15 says that the veil kept the Israelites from being able to understand, and that even today, the veil remains over their understanding when the old covenant is read. Vs. 16 says that only belief in Christ will remove that veil from ANYONE. That includes women who believe. Vs. 17 says that where the Spirit of the Lord is, there is freedom. Women have this freedom as well as men.

Vs. 18 says that ALL who believe in Christ have unveiled faces and reflect His glory. That glory is on women as well as men. It also says that the believer in Christ is being transformed into His IMAGE with ever increasing GLORY. That includes women. II Cor. 4:4-6 says that the light that shines out of darkness and in our hearts, gives us the knowledge of the glory of God in the face of Jesus. The knowledge of this glory is for women too. II Cor. 4:17 says that light and momentary afflictions work an eternal weight of glory for believers. That eternal glory is for women too. In this passage of II Cor. 3:6 through 4:17, the word glorious is used 6 times and the word glory is used 10 times. They are the same Greek word "doxa". It means dignity, honor, praise and worship. Vine's says it signifies an opinion, estimate, hence the honor resulting from a good opinion. This is for the whole body of Christ. Women are not excluded from bearing the image and the glory of God!! All believers are the glory of the Lord because they are formed out of the precious body and blood of Jesus Christ. Without him, there is no glory, for men or women.

Now let us go back to I Cor. 11:7. It says that the man should have his head uncovered because he is the image and glory of God. Even though it does say the woman is the glory of the man, IT DOES NOT SAY THAT THE WOMAN IS NOT THE IMAGE AND GLORY OF GOD ALSO. Notice, she is not the image of the man, only the glory of him. Vs. 8,9 tell us why she is the glory of the man----because she was formed out of him, thus she was a glorious part of him. She rescued him from his aloneness. It is the same glory that the church is to Christ, because the church was formed out of him. He rescued mankind from their aloneness and separation from God that was caused by the fall. For that reason they are His glory.

For the time being, we will skip vs. 10 and

go to vs. 11 & 12 because this continues with the creation account. The woman was made out of the man to rescue him from his aloneness. But since the time of creation, when the one woman was taken out of the one man, all men have been born out of women. Neither can exist without the other. Rather than this passage confirming the superiority of man, it is in fact nullifying the significance of the fact that he was created first. Rather than exalting and promoting a "divine order", verses 8,9,11, and 12 are proclaiming that IN **SPITE** OF THE CREATION ORDER, man and woman are equal in God and Christ.

In verse 13, Paul asks a rhetorical question, is it appropriate for a woman to pray and prophesy with her head uncovered. Notice how his question does not exclude the women from praying and prophesying in the assembly, just like the men do. He uses the same terminology for both. They both have equal right to do the same things publicly. Then he explains in vs. 14 & 15 why it is inappropriate for the women to do those things with her head uncovered. In verse 14, he says it is a shame for a man to have long hair. The word shame here is different from the word shame used for women in vs. 6 and 7, which had to do with looks and appropriateness of dress. Here the word means disgrace, dishonor, reproach, vile. According to Vine's, the word means vile passions or passions of shame. It has to do with character, not looks. The explanation that I have always heard concerning long hair on a man was that it just didn't look appropriate and, at the most, it was a form of rebellion against the established culture. But the word study of it shows that it had a much more significant meaning. A man with long hair was identifying himself to be homosexual (Rom.1:26,27), transvestite (Deut.22:5), transsexual or some other effeminate personality (I Cor. 6:9). He was advertising and flouting his vile and shameful passions. But verse 15 says that the woman's long hair is a glory to her, and it was given to her as a covering, like a veil.

In verse 7, we see that the woman is the glory of the man because she was formed out of him. In verse 15, we see that her hair is a glory to her. In all the other passages we studied about all believers having the glory of God on them, we see that the woman has God's glory on her as well. So what we are learning is that the man has only one glory on him, the glory of God, but the woman has 3 glories on her, the glory from the man, the glory from her hair, and the glory of God.

Now let us go back to I Cor. 11:10. When it says "for this cause", it means that because she has the glory of the man upon her, she should cover up that glory while praying and prophesying in the congregation!!!! There should be no glory in the assembly but the glory of God. Her covering is not to show her subordination to any man. It is just the opposite!! It signifies that she has upon her, and that she is submitted to, a higher glory than that of a man. She is submitted to Christ Jesus, the head of the living body, the church. The passage does not prove her subordination to a man/husband but rather proves her subordination to Christ, which frees her from subordination to man. It is for all women, not just those who are married.

There are other natty problems with the past interpretations of I Cor. 11:10 that we must examine carefully.

First we will look at the word that is translated as "authority" in many bibles when it says "for this cause ought the woman to have authority on her head because of the angels" (KJV). Even though the word "sign" is not a part of the text, most Bibles will actually add it, or add it by way of footnotes, then cross reference

to Gen. 3:16, saying that  the "sign" of authority
means the sign of her subordination to her husband.
We have already seen in earlier chapters how that
interpretation of Gen. 3:16 is in total error.
So let us find out what this phrase really means.

The word "authority" is not a correct rendering
of the word at all. In most Bibles it is a
substitution for the word "power". The substitution
is made so that the theme of male dominance and
female subservience, based on the wrong interpretation of Gen. 3:16, can be substantiated.
The real word is the Greek word "exousia". The
meaning is: in the sense of ability, privilege,
i.e. subjectively, force, capacity, competency,
freedom, or objectively, mastery, magistrate,
superhuman, potentate, token of control, delegated
influence, authority, jurisdiction, liberty, power,
right, strength. These things are not attributes
of a mere man that he can impart to his wife.
Neither are they attributes that are bestowed
on married women only. Christ Jesus bestowes
them on all women who are believers in Him. None
of these words indicate a subordinate position,
in fact they are opposite of subordination. The
word "exousia" comes from two other words. One
of them means 3rd person singular, the other is
a neuter, present participle with the meaning of;
it is right, through the figurative idea of being
out in public, be lawful. It means that it was
lawful for the woman to publicly demonstrate the
ability, the power, the privilege, the force, the
capacity, the competency, the freedom, the mastery,
the magistrate (empowerment to administer and
enforce the law) the superhuman, the potentate
(power to rule, monarch, powerful person) the token
of control, the delegated influence, the authority,
the jurisdiction, the liberty, the power, the right,
and the strength that God has imparted to her
through Christ Jesus. None of this subordinates
her to any man. Neither is any of this subject

to any man's approval. This is all a demonstration of the power of Christ in and on her.

Now that we know what "authority" means, let's look at another word in that verse. In the KJV, in vs. 7 it says the man "ought" not have his head covered. In vs. 10 it says the woman "ought" to have authority on her head. What does the word "ought" mean? It means, through the idea of accruing, to owe (moneywise); figuratively, to be under obligation, must, should, morally to fail in duty; be bound, be debtor, be guilty of indebtedness. Accruing means to be added to as a natural increase. Like interest on a loan. This word comes from a root word that means to heap up, to accumulate benefit, to gain, to have an advantage, profit. When it says the man "ought" NOT--does that mean that he is under no obligation to anyone for anything, he can morally fail in duty, he is not bound, and he can be guilty of indebtedness? Does it mean he is not to have heaped up, accumulated benefit, gain, advantage or profit? In context, is this talking about a human thing for married men only or is it referring to a spiritual thing for all male believers? I believe the context shows it is the latter. When it says that the woman "ought" to have "authority" on her head, does that mean that she owes her husband money, that she is to be under obligation to her husband, that she owes her husband a duty. Many believe this is so. Is she bound to be indebted to him? I have not seen any Scriptures that would indicate those things. In context, is this a human thing between a husband and wife, or is this a spiritual thing for all women believers, married or unmarried? Again, I believe the context shows that it is the latter. I believe it means that she has been given all of the heaped up, accumulated benefit, gain, advantage and profit that the word "power" means. I believe the word "ought" means she is obligated to God to use all of that so that God receives the natural increase from what He has invested in her. If she does not use what He has given her to the fullest, she is derelict in her moral duty to God.

The last hurdle to jump in verse 10 is the phrase "because of the angels". No one knows for sure what that means. I would suggest that it means something had to be demonstrated for the angels sake. I believe it means that now that Christ had ushered in all of this "exousia" power, the Holy Spirit power that came on the whole church at Pentecost, the Old Testament traditions that had distinguished and separated men from women in the congregation were now gone. The angels needed something to distinguish genders, since both men and women were doing the same things in the congregation with the same power. Remember in the definition for the word "dishonors" his head in verse 4, we found the word "confound". It seemed like that was a strange definition for dishonor. But I believe it has a profound use here. I believe the angels were confounded by the power being demonstrated by both genders. Then add to that confusion, the hair coverings of both men and women which was confounding them more. That is why a woman should not be shaved like a man, and she should wear a covering. That is why it was a shame for men to have long hair because that identified them as women, further confusing the angels.

For the angels sake, there had to be something to distinguish male from female in the assemblies of believers. It is only logical that the distinguishing thing would be a head covering for the women and not the men. The men had only the glory of God them, and they shouldn't cover that up. But the women had the glory of the man on her because she was formed out of the man. She had the glory of her hair, as well as the glory of God that was reflected in both genders. There should be no glory in the assembly but the Glory of God, therefore she was the one who needed to blot out the glory of the man and her hair with a covering. So rather than her covering being a sign of her subordination to a man, it was actually a sign that she was rejecting her subordination to man and was submitting to Christ's higher power. That is what she was demonstrating to the angels. She was demonstrating Christ's authority over the church, not man's authority over woman!!

A passage that affirms that to me is I Tim. 5:21. It says "I charge you before God and the Lord Jesus Christ AND THE ELECT ANGELS that you observe these things without preferring one another, doing nothing by partiality" (KJV). The context of this verse is that Paul is giving Timothy instruction concerning church order, discipline of elders and partiality. By definition, an elder is a person, male or female, who presides over or stands before a group, instructing and teaching true doctrine. He says that one who teaches true doctrine well, deserves double pay. Then he says that if such a person is guilty of sin that is confirmed by 2 or 3 witnesses, that person deserves to be openly rebuked, in spite of their ministry position. Their position does not exempt them from rebuke. If they were exempt from discipline, then that would be partiality. He said don't prefer one before another and don't do ANYTHING out of partiality. He said God is watching for partiality, Christ is watching for partiality, and the elect angels are watching for partiality. Do you think this refers to only one type of partiality or do you think it is a principle referring to all types of partiality, which would include gender partiality? Whatever you might believe, the fact remains that the angels are observing and looking for partiality. This helped me to understand what it meant when I Cor.11:10

said "because of the angels". The angels needed to observe something concerning the genders. I believe that Paul went into so much detail about the head coverings and hair coverings so that we would understand how the power of Christ that rested on both men and women equally would confuse the angels. The passage was not so that man could prove his superior right of dominance or the subordination of women. It was to demonstrate for the angels. I further believe that it was not only for the sake of the good angels, but it was also so that the fallen angels could see the demonstration of the united power that Christ had wrought when He died, and rose again, putting all principalities and powers to shame and triumphing over them. The whole thing has a far greater purpose than to prove man's dominion over women and the false concept of headship and divine order!! To use it that way is to belittle God and His Word.

All of this writing is really an explanation of what "head" in verse 3 means. It all has to do with headship and "divine order".

God has never failed in his position as head or source of Christ or of humans. God created mankind with a will, so He is the source of our will. He gave us life and so is the source of life. He gave us the ability to love, because He is love, so He is the source of love. We could go on and on identifying what God is the source of for us humans. He demonstrates headship by loving, giving, and nurturing.

Christ has never failed God in his position to God either, or as head/source of the church. Christ came to serve and to teach and to bring freedom from the death that Adam brought on mankind. He is the source of our life in the Spirit. He is the source of all light and love for those who follow him. God did not fail to bring forth His only begotten Son and He did not fail to bring life to man; Christ did not fail to go to the cross

92

to bring spiritual life back to man.

Man is the head of woman because she was formed out of him. But another aspect of that headship is to affirm the word of God to her by his godly actions. When a man is devoted to Christ, he will not fail to bring a different kind of spiritual life to his wife. As he nurtures her, and loves her by washing her with the water of the Word, he will bring out the best in her spiritually. She will become what God wants her to be. So, as head, he will be a source of spiritual nurturing for her. She will be a glory to him because the inner beauty she develops from being all God has called her to be, will be a reflection of the kind of man he is. In I Thess. 2:19,20 Paul says the Thessalonians are his glory and his joy. He was the pastor/teacher that God had sent to them, just as he had been sent to the Colossians. In Colossians, Paul said that he labored for those people so that they would come to maturity in Christ. He encouraged them, reproved them, exhorted them, and prayed for them. He said the fruit of his labor was his joy. What his labor did in their lives was his glory. His labor on their behalf did not produce an image of Paul in them, but rather a maturity in Christ. The fruit of his investment of labor in their spiritual lives was his glory. So it is with a man and a woman. His labor of love in praying for her, washing her with water of the Word, encouraging her in the Lord, will bring about a maturity of Christ in her. His efforts on her behalf, spiritually, will be his glory before the Lord. The glory comes from the Lord. It is spiritual in nature. It does not come from the subservient subordination of the woman to the man in every physical area of life. The glory that comes to the man for his labors of love to his wife is a bonus for the man. If a woman has a husband who will love her as Christ loved the church, that is a bonus for her. But the fact remains that the glory of God rests on any woman believer whether she is married or not.

In marriage, when a man is not devoted to Christ, when he is being led by his own will, for his own selfish lusts, passions, and desires, when he is seeking to find satisfaction for his "self", has he not already destroyed man's tradition of "divine order"?

Today's teaching on male dominance and female subordination, that supports "divine order", is saying that a woman does not have the capacity or the ability to make good decisions. Her decisions only cause chaos and trouble for the family. But God created the woman with different insights and perspectives from the man's, in many areas. Those differences are to bring balance to the man's decisions and vice versa. If she is not allowed to use those differences, she is not the "help" to her man that God created her to be. He might as well have left the man "alone". If you will remember, back in chapter 2, part of the definition for "help" was to surround, succor and protect. I believe that the man has a stronger role of protecting then the woman does, but at the same time that very definition gives her a responsibility to protect too. Sometimes, that protection might include protecting the man from his own rash decisions by balancing them with her different perspectives.

Having someone to dominate and control produces pride and egotism in the man. Pride was, and is, the sin of Lucifer. A woman who allows herself to be dominated and controlled by her husband will not help build godly character in him. All that does is keep him from being accountable, because it doesn't matter if he's right or wrong, the woman will bow to it. He is allowed to continue in any sin or bad behavior. So she is not a "help" to him in that way either. The man's first responsibility to keep man's tradition of "divine order" intact is to be totally committed to God and His will, as well as being a committed servant of Christ. When he is like that, the "divine order" is in operation. His wife will trust that she is submitting to God through her husband and that he will not take advantage of her or lead her to worship and serve him rather than God. I submit that the first breaking of this so called "divine order" is not the unsubmissive attitude of the wife towards the husband, but is rather the unsubmissiveness of the man to Christ, in most cases.

According to man's teaching of what the "divine order" is, is there any kind of Biblical base for it? No. The only possible divine order was the order of creation. We have seen how Paul brought equality to the man and woman in spite of creation order. So that is not a valid base for divine order. The correct translation of Gen. 3:16 also destroys that base for "divine order". This teaching of "divine order" or "chain of command" has not brought harmony to the Christian home. It has brought destruction instead. If a teaching that is supposed to produce harmony does not do so, then there is a faulty understanding and application. It is time that the church re-examine this doctrine of "divine order" or "chain of command". It is time to renounce and abandon it so that all of Christ's body can be a glory to Him, producing the fruitful increase that is due Him.

In II Cor. 4:7 we are told that we are all compared to jars of clay so that we can see that the all surpassing power comes from God and not from us. Men and women alike are called jars of clay. Power comes from God to each of us individually. It does not come from God to man, then from him to woman. It comes directly from God to the woman. There is no middle man.

I Cor. 11:7 is supposed to be the bed-rock proof

95

of divine order. I pray we have dispelled that myth. Women, you are in Christ. You have the glory of the Lord on you! How sad it is that man has tarnished and robbed you of that sense of awe that comes from knowing that you, too, ARE the glory of God. A woman who is in Christ has the glory of the Lord on her whether she is married or not. It is the power of God that transforms her into the likeness of God and changes her from glory to glory. It is that exousia power, that was imparted to her, that makes her fit for the Master's use. It comes only from the Lord who is Spirit.

Men, repent of usurping God's glory in your wife. Repent of denying Him His right to have His female vessels live out what He has empowered them to do. Whether it is in marriage or in the church, grant them the freedom that has been denied them.

Women, repent of allowing yourself to come under the domination of man, whether it is your husband or church leaders. Ask God to give you holy boldness to come against that false teaching of "divine order" so that you can be all and do all that He has called and anointed you to do.

I pray that this chapter has brought some new insights and a different understanding concerning these erroneously interpreted and overused verses that have held women captive for so long. I pray that it brings freedom to both men and women.

# CHAPTER FIVE
## APOSTASY AND DECEPTION

Why is the false teaching of submission so prevalent today? Why is it that in some churches, it takes precedence over so many other teachings in the Word. Why is it so out of balance? Why is the submission of all Christians to pastors, boards and denominations mentioned so frequently from the pulpit these days? Why are some recognizing that such teachings produce something called spiritual abuse? Some, who are honest with God and themselves, are recognizing the destruction of this false doctrine of submission to authority, whether it's husbands, pastors, or denominations.

The reason for this deceptive teaching is astounding to me!! Satan must get things in order for the big end time finale of the Antichrist. God must allow him to do it and is, in fact, using him to set the stage for it. I believe for Antichrist to rule, people must be programmed to bow to authority.

God is omniscient, omnipotent, and omnipresent, yet He has a hierarchy of angels, a host of lesser angels, and people to do His work. Before time began, God knew, and called, His hand picked people to be trained and placed in strategic places at strategic times to do His work. Though Satan has mighty power, he is not omniscient, omnipotent or omnipresent. But he also has a hierarchy of demons, fallen angels, and people to do his works. He, too, has hand picked people who he programs, trains and places in strategic places at strategic times to accomplish his purposes. His choosing begins in some people before they are born also. These people have ancestors who made a sacrifice to buy his favor. In these sacrifices, they have made a blood covenant with Satan, giving him permission to have dominion over the lives of any of their future generations. So even before they are born, Satan knows whose generations he can

97

pick from, he already has an entrance into their lives. He is the prince of this world and he has a right to rule and reign in it. He rules and reigns over his subjects and he chooses those who will best suit his needs to carry out his plan. He programs their lives and grooms them for the position he wants them to fill. He absolutely must have the power to do this in order to have strategic people in strategic places to govern over strategic areas for the reign of Antichrist. These people have been supernaturally endowed with great power and knowledge. He could never pull off the reign of Antichrist without these people because he is not omniscient, omnipotent or omnipresent like God. He must work through human beings who are dedicated to him, in the same way that God uses human beings who are dedicated to Him.

There are several Bible texts on which I base this belief. II Kings17:35-41. Vs.41 says that even though the Israelites feared God, they also served other gods and so did their children and their children's children. One could say this only shows how sin follows generations, but it also shows the generational claim Satan has to the children of people who serve him, for he is another god. In I Samuel 18:3 and 20:14-17 David and Jonathan made a covenant together. Vs. 15 and 20:42 speaks of the "foreverness" of the covenant that continues from generation to generation forever. This speaks to me that a covenant that someone has made with the devil will continue from generation to generation too. Psalm 106:34-39 speaks of people sacrificing their sons and daughters to demons to appease or to gain favor from their gods. Ex.20:5, 34:7, Nu.14:18, and Deut.5:9 all speak of the iniquities of the fathers that are passed down to future generations. I used to think that only meant the propensity to follow in the father's sins, but I came to know that it means generational demonic curses as well. Thank God for Deut. 23:5 that says God turned the curse into a blessing because He loved them. In the new testament, Matthew27:25, shows how the people called down curses upon their children when they responded to Pilate, "Let the blood of Jesus be on our heads and **on the heads of our children**". God so loved all the world that he gave His only begotten Son to shed His blood so that curses can be overturned. That shed blood can break the power of any generational curse or sin for anyone who loves Him and calls on Him to do so. The covenant made with the shed blood of Jesus is more powerful then any blood covenant made with Satan. Jesus' blood covenant, supersedes and cancels all other covenants, but one must appropriate that blood.

The false teaching in churches of submission to husbands for the women, and submission to pastors in all things for all believers, is preparing the way so that when the time comes for the big deception to happen, people will believe the lie, because they are already programmed. At the time of the tribulation, those who have been religious people will have been trained to accept anything they hear! More than that, they will be trained to believe that their obedience to religious leaders is of God. Those with a strong religious bent, but who have not accepted Christ, will be totally satisfied that they are doing God's will by submitting themselves to their leaders.

What is the Scripture basis for these bold statements? First, God said in Isaiah 66:3b-4, "They have chosen their own ways, and their souls delight in their abominations. **I also will choose their delusions,** and I will bring their fears upon them because when I called, none would answer, and when I spoke, they did not hear; but they did evil before mine eyes, and chose that in which I delighted not."(KJV) The Word warns that there is a way that seems right to man but it is the way of death. God has His prophets working today

to warn people about their personal walk with
Christ, but few will listen because it does not
make them feel good. There are many today who
think they are walking in The Way, but they are
doing evil in God's eyes and He does not delight
Himself in them.

Then there is II Thes. 2:2 where Paul says,
"Do not be soon shaken in mind, or be troubled,
neither by spirit, nor by word, nor by letter as
from us, as the day of the Lord is present".(KJV)
In other words, don't let those things that you
know be unsettled in your mind by spirits or words
or even a letter or speech, supposedly teaching
truth, from a well known person. Don't take it
for granted that everything they say is truth just
because they are well known and respected Bible
teachers. Verse 3, "Let **no man** deceive you **by
any means,** for the day shall not come, except there
be a falling away first". Here the words "no man"
includes spouses, pastors, teachers, or any human
being. The phrase "by any means" describes how
someone can turn a person away from truth with
their style of conversation, their deportment or
character. A speaker with a very charismatic
personality can make anything sound right. Doctrines
of demons are couched in fine sounding words from
any human being who promotes traditions of men,
and upholds them, even when Scripture proves them
wrong. "Any means", includes false signs, wonders,
miracles and prophecies etc.

If the possibility of being deceived did not
exist, there would be no need of a warning. There
cannot be a falling away unless there was first
a belief to fall from. Paul is talking about a
falling away by those who are called "brethren".
This means people who do know Christ but who refuse
to follow in obedience to His every word.

Falling away is the word "apostasia" and it
means a defection or a revolt. It signifies apostasy
**from** the faith. One cannot defect from something

they have not been a part of. As an analogy, I cannot defect from a country unless I have lived in that country. Likewise, one cannot fall away or defect from the faith unless they have been in the faith. This falling away must come before the anti-christ is revealed and before he that restrains is removed. Paul said this mystery of iniquity was already at work in his day. So, this apostasy is the falling away of the church, the called out body of Christ. It is **NOT** a falling away by the world or religious cults. Those kind of people never had a faith in Christ to fall away from. People within the church will defect; they will believe all manner of power and signs and lying wonders, and with all **deceivableness of unrighteousness** in them that perish, because they received not the truth, that they might be saved. Unrighteousness here means moral wrongfulness in character, life, or action. Deceivableness means a delusion or deluded. These are people who are deluded into thinking moral wrongfulness is okay for them to practice. Who are them that perish? Those in the church who have said a prayer to accept Christ but who have not embraced the truth that says that faith in Christ MUST produce good works or it is a dead faith (James 2:14-26). Good works are works of righteousness and obedience. So while knowing, and receiving, the truth that there is salvation in Christ, many live in unrighteousness and disobedience. They are deceived into believing that's okay.

Matthew 7:21-24 and 26 says that not all who call Him Lord would enter heaven. Only those who DO the will of the Father will enter. Many will say that they did mighty works and they cast out demons in His name, yet He will say to them, "I never knew you, depart from me **you who work iniquity.**" Iniquity means a violation of the law, wickedness and unrighteousness. He is speaking to people who thought they would have every right

101

to enter heaven because they thought they knew Him. They had done things in His name, but they also walked in unrighteousness, ignoring His eternal laws of obedience. The will of the Father has always been righteousness and obedience to His word. Then Jesus says that wise men hear and **DO** what God says and they are saved because **their doing proved** that what they said they believed was really in their heart. The foolish ones hear and say they believe but there is something they do not do, which shows that He is not really in their heart, even though they did use His name to do miracles and wonders etc. So what is it they were not doing? They were not doing acts of righteousness and obedience. Luke 6:46-49 is the same story. Only it says, "Why do you call me Lord, but don't **do** as I say. **Whoever comes to me, hears my sayings and DOES them, he is the wise man who will be saved.**" What were the sayings? Throughout the Gospels he spoke of all kinds of things about righteousness and obedience. It seems to me that Jesus is saying that some will come, some will come and hear, and some will come, hear, and do. Only the ones who come, hear, and do are the wise ones who are saved. John 14:15 says if you love me, KEEP my commandments. There are a multitude of verses that speak of keeping His commandments by DOING them.

In Luke 13:23-28, the question was asked, "Lord are there few that be saved?" Jesus answered that they should STRIVE to enter the narrow gate because many will seek to enter but won't be able to. The word "gate" is interesting. It means a wing that unfolds. In other words Jesus was saying it was not just a matter of saying a simple prayer to ask Jesus into your heart that was going to let you enter the narrow gate. Jesus himself said STRIVE to enter it. The word strive encompasses a struggle to compete for a prize, to contend with an adversary, to endeavor to accomplish something,

to fight for it, labor for it fervently. It was
a command to them to strive for this prize of
salvation. He says "the gate is strait", that
is, it is narrow because there are obstacles that
close it in. "Many that seek" means that many will
try to worship God, or will go about desiring,
endeavoring, inquiring, seeking after or seeking
for God. Their seeking does not include seeking
the development of holiness of their own character.
(Read II Tim.3). But He will answer those kind
by saying "I don't know you". Then they will say,
but we ate and drank with you and we listened to
your teachings. Again He will say "depart from
me you **workers of iniquity**". "Iniquity" also means
moral wrongfulness, either in character, life,
or actions. It means unjust, unrighteousness and
wrong. Notice, the **deceivablness of unrighteousness**,
the stumbling block to those who know Christ, is
defined as **the working of iniquity by those who
believe!!!** Though I have always heard it taught
that the gate is narrow because Jesus is the only
way, and that Jesus is the gate, I see a different
picture here. What I see is that there are those
who accept Christ and then strive to overcome the
obstacles that the adversary puts in their path
so that their life becomes one of righteous
character and actions. These are the doers of
righteousness and obedience to God's every word.
Then there are those who accept Christ, who use
His name to do miracles and cast out demons, but
their life is a life that does not include striving
for moral righteousness of character and actions.
These are the ones that Jesus said He won't know.
He says they were deceived into thinking that their
seeking after him and using his name was enough,
but it doesn't qualify them to enter heaven. He
said there would be weeping and gnashing of teeth,
because even after eating and drinking with him
and listening to his teachings, going to church,
doing things in His name, etc. He did not know

103

them and He thrust them away from Him. They were unable to unfold the wing of the gate because they would not strive for righteousness as He had commanded them.

Matthew 25:31-46 is another story about how Jesus will separate the goats from the sheep. The sheep are docile obedient animals, but the goats are obstinate, stubborn creatures. The sheep will follow the shepherd but the goats want to go their own way, even though they are under the shepherd's care. Because the Lord is truly in their heart, the sheep automatically do works of righteousness, without realizing they are doing them. (Matt.25:36-38). They have the shepherd's character. His law is written in their hearts. But the goats, while under the shepherd's care, will not do the works of righteousness, because they think that all they need is to be under the shepherd. They think that nothing is required of them. They do not strive to acquire the shepherd's character. His law is not in their hearts. But those kind of goats will be sent to eternal punishment. The doers of the word, the ones who have cultivated the righteousness of Christ within themselves so that they produce the fruit of righteousness, they are the ones who will go into eternal life, with Jesus. Jesus IS the narrow gate in one sense, because He is the ONLY way. But there are many Scriptures that indicate the fruit of righteousness must be developed in people through exercising themselves in godliness before they can enter. So Christ is the only way, but works of righteousness is the fruit of being in the Way. There must be fruit. One must strive to get the fruit. Only through Christ, can the Holy Spirit indwell and impart the necessary power to overcome the adversary and to grow fruit of righteousness.

These are the doctrines of righteousness, spoken of in Heb. 5:13 that are strong meat for mature believers.

APOSTASY AND DECEPTION

The easy believism, that promotes the deception that all you have to do is say a prayer to accept Christ and you will go to heaven, is part of the apostasy of the last days. It is cheap grace. It is what I Tim.4:1 calls doctrines of demons that causes one to fall away from the faith. They have faith that Jesus saves, but there is no substance to their faith because they are deceived into thinking that all they ever have to do is believe. So when the contending or striving for the faith begins, they depart from it. They prefer to believe the things that tickle their ears because that is easy for them. They know the truth, but live in unrighteousness and disobedience. Their salvation is a delusion because it has produced no change in them. This is the parable of the sower of Matthew and Mark in action.

Now, with that background, we can understand what II Thess.2:11 means when it says "for this cause **God shall send strong delusion,** that they should believe the lie, and that they all might be damned who believed not the truth, but had **pleasure in unrighteousness.** This is why I say God is using satan to prepare the way for the reign of anti-christ. It says GOD will SEND the delusion.

The iniquity that was already at work **in the church** in Paul's day was the beginning of the apostasy that must come to it's fullness in the church before the anti-christ can be revealed. This iniquity that started way back in Paul's day is the preparation for that evil reign.

It has been preached for so many years that believing on Jesus is all that is needed for one to be saved. It has been said that Jesus paid it all, there is no work involved in salvation. Jesus paid the price and no one can add anything to that. They say that the apostasy that Paul was talking about was that the Judaizers were adding works to salvation. What they were adding was that one must be circumcised and must follow old Jewish traditions. Their fear resulted in a belief in the opposite extreme. Today, many are deceived into thinking that all it takes is a prayer and then they can go on living like the devil. They think that their sins are forgiven and every sin they commit after their prayer is forgiven. Grace covers it all. There are many who are going to hell because they believed the prayer was all that was required of them. There was no change in their life, no fruit of the Spirit, no obedience to God's word. They are not taught that once one has said the prayer, and the Holy Spirit takes up residence in that person, He empowers them to strive to obtain the righteous character of Christ. Everyone who truly believes will begin changing. Everyone is in a different stage of development. Some are like newborns and others are like old mature folk. But they are forever changing into His image. If there was never any change, then those people are deceived by the lie that all you have to do is say this prayer. These are the ones who will be told, "I never knew you. Depart from me you evil doers".

II Peter 2 is a strong indictment against these false teachers who sneak in with their damnable heresies that deny the Lord who bought them. Many say the heresy is that some were adding works to salvation. But what the heresy really is, is that The Lord bought them, but they **deny him by living a life unchanged by His power.** They walk in the destructive ways of **unrighteousness** that blasphemes the way of truth. We know that Peter is talking about their unrighteousness because verse 4 speaks of the angels that were cast out of heaven because of their **unrighteousness.** Verse 5 says that Noah was saved out of the world because he was a preacher of **righteousness.** Verse 7-8 says Lot was saved because of his **righteous** soul. Verse 9 says that the Lord knows how to deliver the godly out of temptation. This power is what is denied. Instead of accessing that power to deliver them out of their sinful ways, these people rely on the "grace" that all sins are forgiven anyway and so verse 10 says they walk after their own flesh in **lust of uncleaness** and they **despise the dominion (Lordship) of God.** Despising the dominion of God means that they refuse to allow God to be their supreme governing master, their LORD. They refuse to allow Him to transform them into His image. It says these people are presumptuous and self willed. They do not DO the will of the Father. Verse 12 says they speak evil of things they don't understand. So anyone who says that one must strive to attain righteousness, and must access the power of God to do that as proof of the salvation experience, is called an heretic. But the verse says that **those who don't understand about righteousness** are the ones who are like brute beasts and they will perish in their own corruption. Verse 13 says they will **receive the reward of unrighteousness, because they took pleasure in unrighteousness.** They are spots and blemishes and they are deceived, even while they fellowship with the righteous. If they did not believe they were righteous because they said a prayer to accept Christ, they would not be fellowshipping with those who are. Read Eph. 5:25-27. Christ is coming back for a Church that is without spot and blemish because the people have sanctified and cleansed themselves by the washing with the Word. Note, it does not say the blood of Jesus sanctifies and cleanses in this passage, it is the work each must do for themselves by the washing with the Word. Back in II Pet.2, verse 14 says they have eyes full of adultery, they can't stop sinning, and they beguile unstable souls to follow them. Verse 15 says they have forsaken the right way and have gone astray like Balaam, who loved the **wages of unrighteousness.** Verse 17 calls these people wells without water and clouds that are blown about by every wind. Their end will be the darkness forever. Verse 18 says they speak wonderful sounding words that are just vanity, and THEY LURE YOUNG CONVERTS WHO HAVE JUST ESCAPED HELL, INTO FOLLOWING IN THEIR ERROR. Who are these newly converted people who have escaped hell? They are truly born again, saved people because they have escaped the penalty of sin which is hell. They join a church to be nurtured in the word, trusting the teachers and preachers to teach them truth. But instead, these trusted people draw them back into sin with their damnable teachings. In verse 19 they promise these new recruits that they are free at last from obeying, because all is forgiven, and so they feel safe to continue in the lusts of the flesh. Then they are brought back into bondage of the flesh. Verse 20-21 are the most powerful ones. "For if, after they have escaped the pollutions of the world through the knowledge of the Lord and Savior, Jesus Christ, they are **again** entangled in it, and overcome, the latter end is worse with them the beginning. For it had been better for them not to have known the **way of righteousness** than, after they have known it, to turn from the holy commandment delivered unto them". What was the holy commandment? To follow after righteousness. To be conformed to the image of Christ, the righteous one. To strive to attain the excellency of righteousness in their own lives.

What is that iniquity that would cause people to be deceived into thinking they are following God, when in reality they are falling into apostasy? It has to be the leaders and teachers inside the church and the false doctrines they teach. Although there are many false teachings, the two areas that I recognize most as major problems are the false teaching on submission to men, husbands, pastors, and denominations, and the false teachings on grace, that allows unrighteousness to reign in believer's lives.

Read all of Jude. Jude 3 says, "Beloved, when
I gave all diligence to write unto you of the common
salvation, it was **needful** for me to write unto
you, and **exhort** you that you should **earnestly
contend for the faith** which was once delivered
unto the saints." Notice the strong action words,
diligence, needful, exhort, earnestly contend.
Jude calls them saints, so these are people who
have received Christ. These saints are to fight
hard to maintain or guard their faith. Why? "For
there are certain men crept in unawares". Crept
in unawares where? Into the church! If people
were aware, they would not accept the teachings
of these certain men. It is their subtle teaching,
that sounds so good to the ears, that makes the
people unaware. "Who were before of old ordained
to this condemnation, ungodly men, turning the
**grace** of our God into lasciviousness, and denying
the only Lord God, and our Lord Jesus Christ."
Remember what the word "creep" means from chapter
three? In an evil sense it means to envelope
something, to enchant, to bewitch, and in Gal.
3:1 it means to lead into evil doctrine. This
"crept in" is the same thing. Evil doctrine has
crept **into the Church!**

Who ordained that these men should creep in
unawares, causing the people to believe a lie?
**God ordained them to this.** Why? So that the way
would be prepared for anti-christ and the strong
delusion God will send at that time. How do these
men turn the grace of God and the Lord Jesus Christ
into lasciviousness? What is lasciviousness? It
denotes excess, licentiousness, indecency, **absence
of restraint,** wantonness. Many will say, with
indignation, that those things are not in the
church. Most churches preach against those kinds
of things. Yes, preachers may preach against it,
but they will allow members in the congregations
to live in gross moral sin of all kinds and never

use church discipline to stop it. Gossipers, malicious slanderers, and backbiters abound in the churches, sometimes the pastor is amongst the greatest offenders. The list goes on. Preachers preach that we are under grace and grace covers the people's sin. They preach that we are not obliged to live by the law, or the commandments any more. By the false teaching of what grace really is, believers are allowed to do sinful things without restraint. Notice in this verse it says the LORD God and LORD Jesus Christ. Men preach the grace of salvation but they deny the grace that accesses the power so that one will come under the Lordship part of salvation.

There is very little, or no, church discipline today, such as Paul demanded that the church of Corinth exercise in the case of the man who was having an incestuous relationship with his father's wife. I Cor. 5 says that the church ought to put that man out of the congregation because of his sin. Paul said the man's sin would contaminate the whole church. He said they should have nothing to do with that kind of person who called themselves a brother. He said he was not talking about people of the world, but people in the church. He said they were to judge the sin of the brother and deal with it. It was their responsibility to do that. He did not tell them to ignore the sinning brother and his sin, because he was under grace. Nor did he tell them that they could not judge the sin or the sinner lest they be judged. In fact, in II Cor. 2:9, Paul says that GOD HAD GIVEN THE CORINTHIANS A TEST to see if they would stand for obedience to the laws of God or if they would choose to please the man by not judging his sin and not disciplining him. Today, no one wants to judge, no one wants to discipline because they don't want to embarrass the person who is sinning. They do not want to invade anyone's privacy or interfere in their lives. So the church is contaminated and polluted by sin that is allowed to

110

go unchecked because they would rather please man
than be obedient to God.

Do you see how the grace of God has been perverted today in our churches?  For instance, even
though God destroyed Sodom and Gamorrah for  the
sin of homosexuality, today Bible believing churches
will hire a man who is an avowed, active homosexual
as their leader. Many ministers are being caught
in all kinds of sexual immorality, but the congregation hangs on to them as their leaders. There
are many pastors whose personal life does not
qualify them to be an elder in a church and yet
they are protected as "God's anointed ones"  by
the body!  Instead, the body should be obeying
I Tim.5:17-22. We know that the grace of God can
bring erring ones to repentance and restore them
to ministry, but they ought not to be in the pulpit
while engaging in such lifestyles. Unless they
demonstrate their repentance by humility and a
changed life, they should never be allowed back
in the pulpit.

There are many men in the pulpit who have
a spirit of Diotrophes. (III John 9-11). Rather
than equipping the saints and encouraging  them
to minister with their gifts from God, they refuse
to allow anyone  to do righteous ministry in their
church. They want the pre-eminance. Their sin
is pride, but they stay in the pulpit in spite
of that. Worse yet, congregations encourage and
uphold them. They idolize these men and will
ostracize anyone who dares to question their pastor.

Jude 12-13 says that anyone doing any of these
ungodly things are "spots in the love feasts when
they feast with you, feeding themselves without
fear. Clouds they are without water, carried about
by winds; trees whose fruit withers, without fruit,
twice dead, plucked up by the roots. Raging waves
of the sea, foaming out their own shame; wandering
stars, to whom is reserved the blackness of darkness

forever." These men do not fear God nor man. They are smug and arrogant because of their calling. They have no fear because they are resting in the assurance that they said a prayer and now they are going to heaven with all sins forgiven. But "twice dead" means they were once dead in sins and trespasses, they found the way and became born again, but now they have died **again.** That is what twice dead means!! **DEAD AGAIN!!**

Is Jude referring to ministers? He is especially referring to those who are leaders in the church. Jude 15 says their hard speeches are ungodly and against Him. "Hard" means dry, (there's no life in them) harsh, tough, severe, fierce. "Speeches" means fine sounding, elegance of language. It can be reverential or it can bring condemnation. Jude says these are harsh words that sound good but they are against God because they are promoting condemnation. Hard speeches are when the words are used to manipulate and control people by twisting the Word to bring about shame-based performance from the congregation for the pastor's advantage. Jude 15 is an indictment against the preacher because he's speaking against God, not for Him. Verse 16 says their mouths speak great swelling words, tickling people's ears with good sounding words and using flattery to get their own way. They preach nice words that people want to hear, words that flatter people so that they will admire the pastor. He does this in order to manipulate the people for his own gain or to accomplish his own agenda. That's what "having men's persons in admiration because of advantage" means. One pastor that I know personally, brokenly and penitently, confessed to the whole church that he had been taught **IN SEMINARY** how to "cultivate" people in the congregation so that he could manipulate them into being agreeable to his agendas, whatever they might be. Have you heard the statement, recently, that the purpose of the congregation is to work toward fulfilling the pastor's vision for that church? I truly believe in working together for a common goal, but I thought the opposite was true. I thought the purpose of the leadership was to train and equip people to do the ministry that God called **them** to do. The men Jude is talking about are men in "authority" positions in the church. People are more apt to listen to pastors or teachers. Jude 18 says there would be mockers who come in the last time who would walk after their own lusts.

Jude 19 says, "They who separate themselves, sensual, having not the Spirit". Who is more separated than a pastor who says that because he is THE pastor one needs to submit to him, because God has placed him in authority over you? He is separating himself into a position that does not represent what God intended when He set pastors and teachers amongst the people to teach, to guide, to serve, to equip the saints. The power that comes from dictating to others and from having that kind of authority over others is heady wine that appeals to the sensual ego of a man. Who is more of a mocker of God than one who uses the place God has put him in to take the place **of God** in ruling over the body? Jesus himself said that kind of ruling and lording it over others was forbidden. Who is more separate than the elite society of pastors who feel it is their duty to discuss, and sometimes slander, members of their congregations as part of their local ministerial association meetings? I have personally heard the statement made that it is their **duty** to warn their colleagues about the congregational trouble-makers who have left their church and have gone to another. Sometimes the people they are warning others about are innocent of the accusation!! I am reminded of Paul and Barnabas and John Mark. Paul had a personal distrust of John Mark and would not work with him, but Barnabas had no such personal distrust so he took John Mark and worked well with him. It was a matter of a personality clash between Paul and Mark. So it is with many pastors who must "warn colleagues about the trouble makers" today. Sometimes, the person is not a troublemaker, it is just a personal issue of the pastor that causes the problem. Many times, pastors will cover each other's mistakes and uphold one another, right or wrong, simply because they are "fellow pastors". Isn't that mocking God and His hatred of partiality? Again I refer to I Tim.5:17-22 and Mal. 2.

Do you see how headship and submission have been perverted in the church? Do you see how the teaching of "grace" has been perverted and how subtly it is done? The Word says these things are not of the Spirit.

I respect the pastoral call on a person's life. I respect a godly pastor/teacher. But, I am diligent to judge the content of any message. I am also diligent to inspect the fruit that is displayed in the deliverer, as well as the delivery of, that message. Even though I feel I was blessed with a gift of discernment between true and false teachings, for years I did follow some wrong teachings because the gift was undeveloped. Much of the time I was able to discern the good in a teaching, apply that to my life, and discard the part that was not good teaching. Not all believers are so blessed, thus many are led astray by these wrong teachings. For that reason I hate false teaching. Therefore, I won't condemn a man or his ministry, but I will expose the false teachings.

Jeremiah 7 talks about God's anger and wrath toward people who do all manner of evil and yet come to the temple to worship Him. God says, (paraphrasing and partly quoting from the NIV) "Reform your ways and I will let you live in this temple. Really change your ways and your actions and do not follow after other gods to your own

114

harm.  Then I will let you live in this place.
But you are trusting in **deceptive words** that are
worthless.  Will you steal, murder, commit adultery
and perjury, burn incense to Baal and follow other
gods you have not known, and then come and stand
before me in this house which bears my Name and
say, 'We are safe',  to do these detestable things.
Has this house become a den of robbers to you?
But I have been watching", declares the Lord.
He says, "Go to Shiloh and see what I did to the
place I first called my dwelling for my Name.
I did that because of the wickedness of my people
Israel." He says, "While you were in these sins
I talked to you again and again, but you did not
listen.  I called you but you would not answer.
And because of that which I did to Shiloh, I will
now do to the house that bears my Name.  The temple
you trust in, that place I gave you and your
fathers.  I will thrust you from my presence, just
as I did all your brothers, the people of Ephraim.
So do not pray for this people  nor offer any plea
or petition for them, do not plead with me for
I will not listen."

What does that mean to us today?  In I John
5, it says that we are the children of God if we
love God.  That love is to be expressed by carrying
out his commandments.  Through faith in Christ,
we are His children and that faith will overcome
the temptation to **continue** in sin.  That faith
will make us want to obey His commandments.  It
will not be difficult to keep them, because our
love for Him makes us feel grieved when we  sin.
But I John 5:16 says the same thing that Jer. 7:16
says.  "If anyone sees his brother commit a sin
that does not lead to death, he should pray and
God will give him life.  I refer to those whose
sin does not lead to death.  **There is a sin that
leads to death,** I am not saying that he should
pray for that."  Many say the sin that leads to
death here is the sin of not accepting Christ.

But this cannot be, because we are admonished to pray for people to repent and to accept or receive Christ. We are never told to stop praying for that. Before one comes to saving faith in Jesus Christ, are we told anywhere in the Word that there are any sins that are too big or too bad for God to forgive? In Mark 3:14,15 Jesus gives the disciples power to heal sicknesses and to cast out demons. But in Mark 3:22-30 the Scribes say that Jesus' power to cast out demons came from Satan. Jesus himself says that if one attributes the work of the Holy Spirit to Satan, that is blasphemy and it is a sin which will never be forgiven. I believe this speaks to saved and, perhaps, unsaved people. (See Heb. 6:4-6 and Heb. 10:26) But here John is referring to the sin that leads to death in a "brother". John goes on to say, "All unrighteousness is sin and there is sin that does not lead to death. We know that anyone born of God does not **continue** in sin; the one born of God keeps himself and the wicked one touches him not." Notice, it is the one who keeps HIMSELF from continuing in sin who is immune to the wicked ones attacks. The converse is true. A Christian needs the Eph. 6 armor of God because the wicked one will attack one who is not walking in the righteous principles that constitutes the armor! He has every right to do it if one chooses to live in continued sin.

What I see in this passage in I John is that there are those who do not believe that one who is born again has to keep the commandments of God. They say, "Even if we sin and do detestable things, we are under the grace of God. He will not send us to eternal death, because Christ paid for this sin." They steal, kill, commit adultery, lie and follow all kinds of gods of materialism, sex, or whatever their gods might be. They say, "We are safe, we are safe, we ARE the temple of the Holy Spirit because we have accepted Christ and His

blood covers our sin". They are people who do all
manner of evil and yet come to the house of God,
the local church, to worship. They call themselves
by Christ's Name. While they are doing all these
evil things, they are trusting in deceptive words.
Words that say, "God is not dealing with His people
in wrath and anger in this day of grace". They
say, "He has promised eternal life to those who
name His Name. He cannot go back on His promise".

But God says, "While you are doing these
detestable things, I have spoken to you again and
again. But you would not listen. I have called
you again and again, but you would not answer."
He says that what he did to the temple in Shiloh,
He would do to this people, because of their
disobedience. Are the people who are called by
the name of Jesus Christ better than those people?
Will our God, who never changes, not thrust away
from Him those who walk in disobedience, claiming
safety in Christ all the while they do their evil
sins? Will they, too, come to the place where
God declares, "This is blasphemy, it is a sin unto
death. Do not pray for these people anymore.
I will not listen to your pleas for them anymore."?
Is this why Jesus said, "Depart from me you evil
doers, I never knew you" in all of the passages
that I quoted earlier?

Ephesians 5:3-5 describes the behavior of
God's children. There's a long list of evil things
that one who knows God through Christ are forbidden
to do. The list includes an idolater. He says
anyone doing these things will NOT have any part
in the kingdom of Christ or of God. I see the
millennial reign as the Kingdom of Christ and
eternal life after that as the Kingdom of God.
Those who are destined to reign with Christ in
his kingdom must prove themselves worthy of
reigning in this life. They do that by conquering
sin in their own lives and by standing for what
is just and right, and hating evil. If they cannot

conquer their own sin now, if they cannot judge
between good and evil now, and if they cannot make
a righteous judgment and stand by it now, how will
they know how to rule with integrity and justice
then?

Ephesians 5:6 says, "Let **NO** man **deceive** you
with vain words because the **wrath** of God will
come upon those who do them". This refers to the
list in Eph. 5:3-5. The vain words are words
that say you can do these things because now you
are under "grace" and all sins are under the blood
of Jesus. It is flippantly said that even though
we are saved, while we live on this earth we are
only human and we will sin. Though that is partially
true, that philosophy makes no distinction between
the occasional sin that we all commit after we
are saved, and the habitual sin that some willingly
live in as a part of their life. It is the
habitual, continually living in sin that is being
referred to here. If the sins listed are the
pattern of your lifestyle, don't let anyone deceive
you into thinking that it's okay, because the wrath
of God will come on you. Pastors and husbands
are men, part of the human race. They are not
perfected yet. They can deceive and be deceived.
And what is this other word in this verse?? WRATH!?
In the New Testament!? And it says it will come
to those who do evil!? The wrath of God came upon
Sapphira and Ananias at the very beginning of the
church age of grace. The grace and blood of Jesus
did not cover their sin. Because of God's wrath
they both bore the consequences for their own sin,
even under grace. God's wrath and consequences
were not delayed, those two died immediately for
lying to the Holy Spirit. Great fear came upon
the church, and on many outside the church, who
heard about it. They were awestruck at the power
and holiness of God. They knew that salvation
was not a trifling thing. It was a very serious
matter and it demanded obedience. Everybody knew

it. Does everyone know that salvation demands obedience from the one saved today?

In the phrase "of those who deceive with vain words" in Eph. 5:6 the word deceive is the verb listed under deceit, deceitful in Vines Dictionary. It is the Greek word, apalao, and it means to **belittle the true character of the sins.** Vs.7 says, don't do those things, Vs. 8 says, because when you were in darkness you did them, but NOW that you are in the light, walk in the light. Vs. 9 says because the fruit of the spirit is in goodness, righteousness, and truth. Vs. 10 says, by walking in these things of the light you **prove** what is acceptable to the Lord. The opposite is also true then, if one is not walking in those things of the light, then that is not acceptable to the Lord. That person is not proving themselves to be in the light. Vs. 11 says that not only do YOU not do those things mentioned, but REPROVE, EXPOSE AND CONFRONT those who do them. Vs.17 says understand and be wise about these things because **they** are the will of the **Lord.**

Do you see how many of these passages refer to righteousness and holy living that MUST accompany salvation? This is what it means to put on the righteousness of Christ. He is all righteousness, but it is not ours just because we say a prayer. We have to strive to put on that righteousness that emulates Him. Contrary to what most believe, in Rev. 19:8 the garments of fine white linen are not the righteousness of Christ that is automatically given to believers. The garments are the righteous **acts** of those who believe. Rev. 22:11-14 says that the unjust and filthy, will remain unjust and filthy. They do not receive the robes of righteousness just because they said "Jesus come into my heart" at some point in time. Just saying that and then living unjust and filthy lives, means they are still unjust and filthy and they deserve the reward of the unjust and filthy.

Those who live righteous and holy lives will remain righteous and holy. Both of these descriptions have to do with people's action. Jesus says He is the Alpha and Omega, the beginning and the end and He will bring His reward  with him. The reward will be distributed according  to every man's works. The word reward here is  a singular word, not the plural "rewards", and it means pay for  service, good or bad, wages. Remember, the wages of sin is death. Likewise, the wages for righteousness is life.  Verse 14 says, blessed are the ones who **did His commandments so that** they would have the right to the  tree of Life, and they may enter the gates into the city.  These are the ones who unfolded the wing of the entrance.  They overcame the obstacles. Those who have accepted Christ, but who have not lived by His commandments will not be able to enter the gate.  They do not have the right to the tree of life. It was disobedience to God's command that sent Adam and Eve away  from the tree of life.  Is it wise to believe that man can now live in sin and disobedience and yet have a right to that same tree of life?  I think not. The grace of God cancels the debt of sin, but it does not cancel the need for obedience and righteousness on the part of  the believer. **Through Christ they were given the power to overcome the obstacles, but they did not avail themselves of that grace. They have not unfolded the wing of the entrance.** Christ will say I never knew you. Depart from me you workers of iniquity. There will be a great weeping and gnashing of teeth as the incredible truth dawns on them that they have believed a deceptive lie.  In believing the lie, they have laid up for themselves the wrath of a holy God.

These principles that  say grace covers it all, thus minimizing the character of sin and the need to live in righteous obedience, is a lie that is part of the apostasy of the last days.  The

other part is the false teaching of submission
to husbands, pastors, and denominations that makes
them idols.

   As I go into chapters 6 & 9-11 please know
that I do not condemn these pastors or teachers
as persons. I do not judge or condemn them or
their ministries. What I do judge is **part** of the
messages they bring. I believe that is scriptural
because we are not to be blown about by every wind
of doctrine. We are not to believe every spirit,
we are to test them. Heb. 5:14 says that we are
to become skillful in the Word so we can discern
good from evil. No one on earth is above being
deceived. I use the following examples to show
how good teachers and preachers can be deceived
into teaching false doctrine. I use many of their
own words in the examples in an effort not to
distort their messages through brief quotes taken
out of context. I am trying to be fair by quoting
so much, so please pardon the length of these
chapters.

   I also challenge the reader to examine all
Scriptures I use. Pray about them and ask for
discernment and wisdom from God, that He would
reveal to you if what I write is truth or not.
My prayer is that you will know truth and that
this truth will set you free from some very hurtful
things in your life. My prayer is that the wiles
of the devil will be exposed. My prayer is that
preachers and teachers will take an honest look
at what is happening in the church today and will
seek the Lord to see if they are caught in some
of these deceptions. My motives are:

   1. My love of God and a desire to be obedient
to what I believe He wants me to write. I believe
He wants it to be written in order to reprove,
expose, and confront false teaching.

   2. My love for the brethren, especially the
ones who are most wounded by these false teachings.

   3. My love for the ministers and teachers who

are deceived, for they will be held accountable by God for what they teach.

My motive is not vindictive, I do not want to cause harm to anyone, or to anyone's ministry. My desire is to bring repentance and restoration to the Body of Christ, laymen and pastors, alike, who are caught in deceptions of the devil that make men idols.

Romans 16:17-18b says, "Mark those who cause divisions and offenses contrary to the doctrines which ye have learned and avoid them....for by good words and fair speeches they deceive the hearts of the innocent." (KJV) I have always heard it preached that those who caused division and offenses were members of the congregation who differed from the pastor. By voicing their different opinion, they were supposedly undermining the pastor's authority. I have rarely heard it taught that the preacher himself may be the cause of the division by his false teaching and his demand that people submit blindly to his authority. The words here are specifically speaking about those whose major gift is speaking, such as a teacher or pastor. Good words means words that sound very plausible, they sound useful, they are easy and gracious words. Fair speeches means elegant language, like a eulogy, a benediction or a blessing. While any laymen can speak these things, usually it is one who gives a public speech who is most listened to and who has the most opportunity to subvert innocent hearts. I am not negating the fact that many laymen DO cause divisions with gossip etc. that sounds plausible and good. But the laymen are not the primary ones who are teaching doctrines that deceive. The more our churches are a one man show, taught predominately by one person, the greater the possibility for deception.

Let me explain that through Eph.2:1-12. Christ is the uniting force for His body. There can be a difference of opinion amongst the brethren, but that does not cause division or destroy unity.

What destroys unity is the pride and arrogance
in some that makes them feel that they are set
apart, set above, or better than others. They
feel they have the greater knowledge, they are
always right and they have all the answers. They
feel they have the right to censor what "their"
congregation hears. They are vain and conceited
and operate out of selfish ambition. Husbands exalt
themselves over their wives because they have been
named "head" over the wife. Today, pastors have
come to the place where they exalt themselves as
an elite separated group. Though I fail to find
a Scripture that says the church has a head other
than Christ, they call themselves "head" of the
local church because they say, "Someone has to
be in charge. God has appointed me as pastor over
this church. I am responsible for what goes on
in this church. So this won't happen here, or
this is what will happen here in my church. Since
God placed ME over this church and not YOU, if
you cannot abide by MY authority as the leader
of this church, than you are free to leave and
to find a church where you will be happier. Nobody
will do anything here without my permission and
approval." They forget that all Christians are
called and it is God who works in everyone as an
individual to bring their wills into agreement
with His will, and to act according to His purpose
for each one. God is the one who gives gifts and
callings to all Christians. He sets them where
He wants them. So, the pastor should be saying,
"I am the undershepherd whom God has sent to
minister **amongst** you in this church. Let me help
you find God's will and purpose for you. Let
me help you develop your gifts, so that you can
use them here to bless the brethren. If you make
a mistake, we'll work it out together to get it
right. Your gifts are different from mine, but
I am no different from you. I just have a different
gift, or a different calling, but that does not

mean I am more important than you. Your gift and your calling are for my benefit because I am part of the Body of Christ also. Let us help one another to understand the Word and help one another to walk in the light." The pastor is not called to be "over" others, but to minister as a servant to them.

I do not know of a doctrine that is being taught today that causes more division, offense and destruction than the false doctrines that are preached concerning headship, submission, coverings and authority. False teachings on "grace" are equally destructive to the whole body of Christ. Those two false doctrines are the root of the problem because they promote idol worship, pride, and disobedience. It is a disease that permeates the church. It is the falling away, the apostasy, that is coming to it's fullness in the Church. False teachers and teachings have crept in unawares and are deceiving the innocent, causing them to depart from the faith and to follow after idols. It is all preparation for the reign of anti-Christ. Who are you being prepared to follow? Who are you following, even now?

# CHAPTER SIX
## GOD ,THAT WOMAN YOU GAVE TO BE WITH ME

Adam said, "That woman you gave to be with me, she gave to me and I did eat". First, it seems Adam blames God for giving him this woman. Then it seems that when she gave him the fruit, he had **no choice** but to eat it. So he blames Eve for his disobedience to God's command.

This is the beginning of the carnal man who wants to blame woman for his own sin. It is the beginning of the perverse thought that women are evil and are bent on destroying the man. It is the basis of Satan's work of creating division by destroying the unity that God had put between Adam and Eve. Throughout history, focusing on the instability of the woman for allowing herself to be deceived, has diverted the focus from the evilness and power of the deceiver. He was, and is, the person of evil, not Eve!! And not women in general!!!!!

Satan's plan was to start the conflict between the man and the woman who were so close to one another and to God. He would separate them from God first, and then from each other. He would start up competition between them through shifting of blame. This was the first wedge to be driven in Satan's long range plan to destroy the family unit, and society, through the principle of divide and conquer. Then, twist the word to keep the wedge driving ever deeper into the unity that God had intended for the husband and wife to know. Keep the deception going by having preachers of God teach things that sound good, but are entirely different from what God actually said!!!! Keep their attention riveted on the blaming issue and they will be diverted from the worship of God!!!! Keep their eyes focused on who is superior and who is inferior and God's men will go off the track in carnal pride of man. God's women will go off the track by turning to man, trying to

125

gain his approval and trying to please him. When she can't please him, then she will rebel against him and his control!! Use Scripture but subtly distort it's meaning!!

All of this was Satan's plan, and it is working beautifully in these last days to destroy the foundations of Christianity from the inside. Satan is using this method to wound, hurt and destroy women within the church. He is using the feminist movement in the secular world. He is using man's pride in himself in both arenas.

How truly cunning and crafty Satan is!! How Christian leaders and laymen alike are ignorant of the wiles of the devil as he gleefully promotes his division with such finesse!!! While the war against each other rages between men and women of God, their united effort to war against Satan is diverted. A house divided cannot stand.

In the next few chapters I use some examples to expose the kind of preaching that promotes and perpetuates the war between the Christian husband and wife.

I have a taped message by a man who preaches on TV, his gospel goes out to any who will listen all over the world. I have appreciated some of his sermons. His preaching is powerful. But one day I took time to listen very carefully to what he was really saying on this tape. I took the time to write down in long hand everything he said. I won't write all of it for you, but in order to be fair and not take things out of context of the message, I will quote much of it. My own thoughts and comments will be in parenthesis.

After an introduction, in which he explains that the feminist movement wants to take over the country by using witchcraft methods of intimidation, manipulation and domination, he started his message by saying, "Let the redeemed of the Lord say so! It is time for the church of Jesus Christ to come to order and to express their Bible convictions.

# GOD, THAT WOMAN YOU GAVE TO BE WITH ME

To say 'I believe in the Father, Son and Holy Spirit and that Jesus is Lord!! The Bible is the truth and I stand on the authority of God's Word. I will not be intimidated, I will not be manipulated, I will not be dominated!!! I am a child of God!!" ( I thought, "YES!! This is great!")

Then he began to explain about witchcraft and how Satan is using witchcraft, through the feminist movement, to destroy God's plan for the home. He quotes from a feminist author showing how the feminist attack is on both the political and domestic front. He said the book stated that religion that centers on the worship of the male creates moods and motivations that keep women in a state of psychological dependence on men and male authority.

(My comments: I am quoting the man, not the book, since I have not read the book. As I have already stated, the false teachings of today, in the church, about submission and headship do make the male or the husband an idol to the wife. This kind of teaching creates idols under the guise of "submission and headship". While I do not now, nor would I ever, subscribe to feminist tactics, I have to agree with the woman author. The kind of submission and headship taught in churches today clearly does create the mood and motivation that keeps women psychologically and in every way dependent on their husbands and male pastoral authority in the church. This is exactly what God said would happen in Gen.3:16. As the woman turns to the man, away from God, he would be given the opportunity to dominate her.)

The preacher goes on to say that the author is saying that religion that gives patriarchy it's place, and God the Father his place of leadership, has upon it the psychological power that legitimizes masculine leadership in the home and in the nation.

He then goes into detail on how the feminist movement had intruded itself into religious and political arenas. He called the Anita Hill/Thomas incident a prime example of feminist witchcraft workings.

(My comments: I do believe that the feminist movement **and** witchcraft are playing a vital role in Satan's plan of destruction. I, in no way, would lend credence to such ungodliness. But what the woman author sees is accurate. She, and people like her, gain fuel for their fires by listening to preachers preach this kind of message and by watching what has happened in much of the Christian community concerning the perversion of submission. Many Christian sisters are in far greater bondage to men then their secular contemporaries are.)

The preacher then gets into Scripture. He starts with Gen. 1:6, "Let THEM have dominion, saying God's plan was for co-regency. Gen 2:18, The Lord said it's not good for man to be alone, I'll make a helpmeet for him. Co-regency, companion, not competitor. Gen.3 the serpent seduced Eve, attacked the Word of God. The curse happened because the woman Eve began to take the spiritual lead in decision making. She made some big decisions without taking her husband into consideration and these decisions led in rebellion against the will of God. All Eve would have had to do was to say to the snake,'I don't talk to strange snakes without consulting my husband'. He says women should follow the same policy to save herself a lot of trouble.

(My Comments: Praise God that Mary did not say to the angel, "I do not talk to strange angels without consulting my fiancee or father". This is the kind of teaching that infers that from the beginning of time, **even before the fall,** God NEVER intended for woman to make a decision for herself. We have already seen that Scripture does not support the belief that a woman must defer all decisions to the male.)

The next statement by the preacher was that the curse happened because the woman took the lead.

(My comment: I truly do not believe Eve was trying to take any lead. I do not believe there was any thought of controlling her husband. I believe that she was faced with the most powerful of all deceivers. Since most of us have not been face to face with Satan himself, how can we understand the depth of the power he employed to beguile her? This was no ordinary temptation!! I believe that her husband, being with her, witnessed it all and ate the fruit when she handed it to him.)

The preacher says, **"Adam's sin was that he submitted to Eve's lead,** not to Eve's need. Look at the Bible record of the trouble that started when the husband submitted to the wife's lead. Adam submitted to Eve's lead and the punishment was that man had to work hard for every crumb of bread that went into his mouth". He says he will kick Adam in the shins for that when he gets to heaven.

(My comments: I would say that it was not that Eve took the lead that was the problem. Where was Adam's loyalty and love for God? Was he not given a strong will that he could have employed to refuse the fruit? Was he not given the command by God himself not to eat the fruit of that tree? Where was his superior mind? Where was the accountability for his own actions? I can offer you a piece of candy, but I cannot open your mouth and make you swallow it. I cannot even open your hand and make you take it from me if you do not WANT to take it from me in your own free will!! It was Adam's own desire for the fruit, not Eve's lead that caused him to be disobedient to God. The word says that sin and death came by Adam's sin of disobedience to God's direct command, not Eve's lead.)

The second husband the preacher uses as an example is Abraham. He says Abraham followed his wife's lead when she said for him to have a child by Hagar. The preacher gives a little laugh and says "Abraham says 'that sounds like the will of God to me!'. Ishmael is born. Now when Ishmael is about 12 years old, Sarah is unhappy with this son being there with Hagar and she tells Abraham to throw them out. **Then Isaac is born**". (This is incorrect Bible sequence which changes the meaning.) "The point is that Ishmael was the father of the Arab nations and Isaac was the father of the Jewish nation-so now we have Jews and Arabs going at each other. This family feud started because the husband followed the wife's lead and **not the lead of the Almighty God.** Don't ever say that a little family dispute has no effect on anybody but yourselves--this one affected the planet earth."

(My comments: Here I would like to give my understanding of the order of events in this story. In Genesis 12:4-7,13:14, God gave Abraham the promise of offspring. In Genesis 15:24, Abraham reminds God that he had no children yet as heir. God says that there will be an heir from his own body. In Genesis 16:1-2 Sarah suggests that maybe they can build a family through the maidservant, which was an acceptable practice in those days. Abraham agrees and the child is conceived. The maidservant despises Sarah and flaunts her ability to conceive a child and Sarah suffers from this. She tells Abraham and asks that the Lord judge between herself and Abraham. Was Sarah accusing Abraham of being responsible for the disrespect and taunts from Hagar? Why did she not ask the Lord to judge between herself and Hagar rather than Abraham and herself? Is it possible that Sarah suggested Abraham lay with Hagar only to conceive a child as heir, but that Abraham developed a deeper relationship with her than he should have? Was he showing a greater preference for Hagar than he was for his wife and that is why Sarah said "the Lord judge between you and me"? Was he guilty

in God's eyes for laying with Hagar at all?
These are just my own musings, they are not facts.
Abraham tells her to do what she wants with the
maidservant. Sarah treats the maidservant so badly
that she runs away. Contrary to the preacher's
accusation that Sarah caused this feud, it was
in God's sovereign mind for Ishmael to be born
and for him to be a rebel. GOD told Hagar to go
back, pronouncing that her son would be a rebel
who would fight everybody and would live in
hostility toward everyone. She goes back and in
Gen. 16:15-16 Ishmael is born. In Gen. 17:1-2,
God again tells Abraham that he would be the father
of nations (pl.). The very first time that it is
recorded that Abraham would have a son through
Sarah is Gen.17:16. God said He would bless Sarah
with a son. She would be the mother of nations
(pl.) Kings of people would come from her. It
is ironic that we ALWAYS hear about Abraham being
the father of nations, but how often is it mentioned
that Sarah is the mother of nations? In God's eyes,
she had an equally important part in producing
nations and Kings, otherwise Hagar's son would
have sufficed as an heir for Abraham. Sarah was
God's chosen vessel to be the mother of that heir.
When Abraham heard Sarah was to have a child, he
laughed, because she was 90 years old. He said
to God, "If only Ishmael could have your blessing".
His mind seems to be on his own plan, not God's.
But God said, "It's your wife Sarah's son whom
you will call Isaac that I will establish my
kingdom. I will bless Ishmael too, but it is Isaac
whom I will establish the covenant with. Sarah
will have the child this time next year." Up until
this time Abraham had no promise that the heir
would come from Sarah. So what he did with Hagar
was more from his own hopes and desires for an
heir than it was Sarah's suggestion. Sarah did
not know until she hears it the first time in Gen.
18:10 that she will have a child. The following

is the correct biblical sequence concerning Sarah's demand that Hagar and Ishmael leave. Sarah has Isaac and in Gen. 21:9-13 when he is about 12 years old, she sees Ishmael mocking Isaac and she said to Abraham that Ishmael would not be an heir with her child. Abraham is distressed over this because of his love for Ishmael, but God said, "Don't be distressed. DO AS SARAH SAYS, because it is through Isaac that the promise will come." **So it was a direct command to Abraham from Almighty God,** to do as Sarah said and to send the woman and child away. Because of Abraham, God would make Ishmael into a nation (sing.). God had to remind Abraham twice that it was through Isaac that He would establish His covenant and would make nations. It was Abraham's desire to keep Ishmael with him in spite of the promise of God. It was Sarah who was speaking the will of God, even though her motives might have been wrong. So even though Sarah suggested to Abraham that he have a child by Hagar, it was his own decision to act in a carnal way that produced the child. Sarah could not impregnate Hagar, only Abraham could do that. God's sovereignty and His plan for the ages was accomplished through this, but, deliberately, all the preacher's rhetoric is focused on how wrong it was for Abraham to listen to his wife. Through the preacher's distorted words, Sarah is depicted as a temperamental, selfish, controlling woman. She caused this feud by her suggestion. Abraham is depicted as a poor innocent who could not go against his wife's suggestion. The fact of the matter was that he was concerned for himself that there was no offspring to be his heir and he was the one who took matters into his own hands. I believe they both did what would ultimately bring about God's sovereign plan for the ages, but the incident is used as an occasion to discredit the woman. Abraham talked to God and heard from God, it was his own lust and desire for an heir that made him do as Sarah suggested, not her suggestion. Sarah was a godly woman. When Hagar was so disrespectful, and Sarah asked Abraham to go to the Lord to judge between herself and Abraham, it indicates that there was something amiss between herself and Abraham. God needed to judge which party had committed wrong in His sight. It appears as though Abraham felt convicted because he told Sarah to do what she wanted with Hagar. I've never heard a sermon that condemns Abraham for what he did, the focus is always on how wrong Sarah was to suggest what she did. It is always her fault.)

The preacher goes to his next example saying Isaac is deceived by Rebekah concerning Jacob and the birthright blessing. As a result of this, Jacob went into exile and Isaac never saw him again. Rebekah died under a divine curse. Esau and his descendants became slaves forever. ( My comments: Rebekah was a woman of faith who talked with God. In Gen.25:22 she talked to the Lord about the struggling of the babes in the womb. God **told her** that there were two nations in her womb and the elder would serve the younger. **She did not plan anything!! God's plan of the ages was in her womb.** He told Rebekah what was planned. It was the man, Jacob, who bartered and cheated the man, Esau, out of his birthright. It was the man, Esau, who sold his birthright for a pot of stew long before Rebekah suggested that the man, Jacob, deceive Isaac. It was the man, Jacob, who did the act of deceiving the father. One could say he deceived his father for his own sinful motives. I have been obvious to stress "the man" in all of this because I wanted to emphasize how little a part Rebekah played in this whole scenario and how much the men did on their own without any suggestions from her.

Gen. 27:7 says that Esau was Isaac's favorite son because of the stew. In Gen. 25:28 God had told Rebekah His plan for the two sons, but Isaac was willing to give the birthright to the godless, Esau. All he wanted was a venison stew himself!! He was following the traditions of men by giving the birthright to the first born son regardless of what God wanted. What about Malachi 1:2-3 where God said that he hated Esau? Who was discerning and following the will of God?? Rebekah or Isaac? It does not say why Rebekah loved Jacob more or why he was her favorite son. But maybe it was for the same reason that God loved him.

In this whole account, too, the preacher's motive is to show how controlling and conniving women are, rather than to see God's sovereign hand in it all. He wants to show how much trouble a woman causes by taking the lead and making a decision. It isn't even true that Rebekah deceived Isaac! She told Jacob what to do, and she helped him, but it was Jacob who did the act of deceiving. The truth is distorted to discredit the woman only. The real truth is in Romans 9:11, "The children being not yet born, neither having done any good or evil that **the purpose of God,** according to election might stand, not of works, but of Him that calleth". [Read Romans 9:8-13]. God spoke to Rebekah. God wanted both Isaac and Ishmael to be born and He wanted both Jacob and Esau to be born. Just as God chose Isaac over Ishmael, so He chose Jacob over Esau. All four were born for God's purpose!!

I do not know what the preacher was referring to when he said that "Rebekah died under a divine curse". Maybe he was referring to Gen.27:12-13 where Jacob says, "If perhaps my father feel me and I shall seem to him a deceiver, and I shall bring a curse upon me and not a blessing" and Rebekah replies, "upon me be thy curse". But there was no curse that came to Jacob from his father. Therefore, there was no curse on Rebekah. Even though it is not true that she caused these things to happen, perhaps the motive for the preacher saying such a thing was to demonstrate that because SHE deceived Isaac, SHE caused Jacob to go into exile, and Isaac never saw him again, and SHE caused her other son to be a slave forever, SHE caused God's judgment to come against her as a curse. Perhaps he meant this as a warning that God will curse any woman who makes a decision or suggestion.

One other distortion here is that the preacher said that Isaac never saw Jacob again, but he did. In Gen.35:27-29, Isaac and Jacob are reunited and then Isaac dies. Esau and Jacob had already been reunited and together they bury their father.

The only purpose for this kind of distorted teaching is to discredit the woman!)

The next example from the preacher is: "King Ahab listened to Jezebel and brought Baal worship into Israel. She killed the prophets, she controlled the church and she manipulated the government through her husband and put together a mother-child cult that is called Baal worship. It is called the mother-god cult throughout the universe that was born through the woman Semiramis in Gen. 10 **who controlled Nimrod**". (My comments: Jezebel-- the name is synonymous with wicked women. She was every bit as wicked as the preacher says. She was a godless idol worshiper. There was no good in her. Yet, by what the preacher says, if one did not know the story, one would think that King Ahab was an innocent, God-fearing man who was led astray by this woman. That is the inference. However, Ahab was a king over Israel who did evil in the sight of God, as he walked in the sins of his fathers before him. HE was a wicked, weak-willed man who defied God and married that evil creature. HE brought Baal worship in and set up altars for Baal. He made an idol and provoked God more than all the kings of Israel before him who were sinful enough in themselves. According to I Kings 16:29-33, he just added to their sins.

His own corruptness brought Jezebel into the place and position where she could exert her ungodly power. It wasn't that Ahab LISTENED to his wife that brought all the trouble. He himself was evil before he ever met her, just as his fathers were evil before him!! Again, this preacher takes the truth of Jezebel's wickedness to imply that every man who listens to his wife is weak-willed and will be led astray. It also implies that any woman making a suggestion or decision of any kind has an evil, controlling, Jezebel spirit, who does nothing but cause trouble and problems with her control.

The preacher tries to strengthen his indictment by bringing in another woman's name to reinforce how evil they are. He says both of these women are the cause of this mother-child cult and this mother-god cult. The preacher says that Nimrod was **controlled** by this woman, Semiramis, inferring that is why he went wrong. Though she is not mentioned in Gen. 10 or 11 where Nimrod is mentioned, she was his wife. But the inference here is that she was a bad, controlling influence on Nimrod and caused his downfall. In my research, I found that the name Nimrod means "let us rebel". Since his father, Cush named him that, some believe that his father trained him from childhood to be a leader in a planned and organized rebellion against God's purposes for mankind. **He was named and grew up in rebellion against God before his wife ever came into the picture.** Though she may have been an evil person, she was not responsible for what was already in the man's heart, no matter whether her influence on him was good or bad.

Both of these women are mentioned in order to promote the idea that women are basically evil controllers. They should not be allowed to make decisions because they will lead good men astray.)

The preacher goes on to say the Old Testament is a sad story of **"one man after the other who**

**capitulates responsibility to the wife.** Listen
men, the Bible said you fathers train up your child
in fear and admonition of the Lord. We are still
doing the same thing today. We have assigned the
spiritual growth of our children over to the
mothers. You take them to Sunday School and church!
Not, 'I'll go golfing and fishing'. God places
the spiritual well-being of your children squarely
on your shoulders, not your wife or your grandmother. You! You take them to the house of God,
you teach them the Word of God. Whatever comes
out of your mouth, let it be Christ exalting and
God-edifying and then America will know a new
destiny." (My comments: Thank God, Timothy did
not refuse instruction from his godly mother and
grandmother. I agree that fathers are given a
responsibility to bring up their children in fear
and admonition of the Lord. But that does not
negate the mother's teaching and influence on the
child's spiritual life. Prov.6:20-21 shows the
mother teaching the law, too. In Prov. 31, King
Lemuel's mother instructs him. Eph. 6:1-3 and
Col.3:20 talks about obeying parents, plural, mother
and father. These are only a few verses that refer
to mutual responsibility for both parents to teach
their children.)

The preacher goes on. He says, "He shall rule
over thee." He inserts, "Those with a feminist
spirit will want to cut THAT out of the Bible
tonight!!" (My Comments: To be wounded and
offended by the perversion of the Word and the
cutting, sarcastic way it is presented, seems to
be equal to having an ungodly feminist spirit.)

He goes on to say, "God says the curse for
Eve's part in the rebellion against God would be
pain in childbirth and your desire shall be for
your husband. The word desire has nothing to do
with sexual desire, sexual desire is not a curse
from God. It is God's plan. It means "teshqua"
which means rule or dominate". (My comments:

Not by the furthest stretch of imagination can that word mean rule or dominate. The original meaning is to stretch out after, to long for and that comes from a root word that means to run after. As we have already seen, the Septuagint says the actual word is "turning", not "desire". God said there would be consequences for her actions, but he did not curse her!!!) The preacher says, **"The curse is this, women will seek to dominate the man but will not, because the husband shall rule over her.** Why did Paul say, 'I permit not the woman to usurp authority over the man?' Because he knew it was the carnal instinct of the woman to do that very thing. A fallen woman seeks to dominate". (My comments: God did not call down a curse on Eve, or on Adam. What God cursed was the serpent and the ground. Is a born again woman still a fallen woman? Are all women fallen women? Did Christ bring restoration for men only? In the preacher's reference to Paul's teaching, can you see how distorted preaching is an outgrowth of the distorted understanding of God's Word as was demonstrated in previous chapters? What Paul meant will be explained in future chapters.)

The preacher says. "The father has the **God given assignment to rule the house.** Today the feminist movement is trying to throw off and rebel against God's pattern for the family. God's plan for the wife is to submit to a loving husband, but when the husband tries to rule without love you have the ingredients for a perpetual dog fight". (My comments: Notice the ingredient here for the dog fight is when the husband tries to rule without love. Also, notice how the word "rule" is used here!) "But the lady says I can't submit. But if you are spirit filled, it is no problem. However, if you are controlled by the spirit of rebellion and the spirit of witchcraft and the spirit of carnality, you are right. Get ready for the fight, call your lawyer and get the boxing gloves, it's not going to get any better. Satan's plan for the WIFE, from Genesis to this moment is one of conflict with masculine leadership". (My comments: If the lady cannot submit to an **unloving** husband, SHE is not spirit filled, SHE has a spirit of rebellion. SHE has a spirit of witchcraft. SHE has a spirit of carnality. SHE will cause a divorce, SHE is following Satan's plan. He is blatantly saying that Satan only works through the woman! I would say that Satan's plan is for both the man and the woman. The man perverts what God intended. He is the first to go against God's plan because he does not love his wife as he should. Then she rebels at the perversion. So the conflict rages on, but the preacher says it is all her fault that these evil spirits are in the marriage.)

The preacher says, "In Genesis 3 we see man versus woman. Genesis 4 is polygamy". (My Comments: Genesis 4 is the story of Cain's grandson, Lemech, who took two wives. Women did not have many husbands, it was men who took many wives. Does this illustrate the woman's weakness of trying to control and dominate or does it illustrate the man's sexual, lustful, carnal desire and his rebellion against God, who made only one woman for the man and said to cleave unto her?? Is this a demonstration of man capitulating his authority to his wife?)

Next he says, "Genesis 9 is pornography-lustful looking." (My comments: This is the account of Noah and his son Ham who looked at his father's nakedness. There was no woman involved here at all!! Who demanded that women cover up to the eyeballs because seeing any part of the woman caused men to lust after her? A lust that he could not control. That wasn't caused by a woman trying to dominate and rule over the man, but it was man's own lust of the eye and lust of the flesh. Who are the ones so demonically hooked on

pornography today? Who are the main producers
and purveyors of that filth? The overwhelming
majority of them are men. Not women. Women do
not control men into seeking after such pornography
or voyeurism. If they could, they would control
their men into NOT indulging themselves in it.
I'm sorry, but I cannot see where pornography is
caused by women's desire to rule their husbands
or their rebellion against God's plan of submission.
Job 31:1,7,9,12 says, "I made a covenant with my
eyes not to look upon a woman with lust; if my
steps have turned from the path, if my heart has
been led by my eyes; if my heart is enticed by
a woman; it opens my wife up for fornication; it's
a sin to be judged and a fire that burns to
destruction and will destroy his harvest." Job
understood his own personal responsibility to
conquer lust of the eyes before it became a lust
of the heart, and he understood the defilement
that would come to himself and to his wife if he
didn't take that responsibility. Many women and
many marriages are defiled by the husband's
addictions to pornography. Men would do well to
follow Job's example, rather than say women cause
pornography because it is their carnal nature to
dominate.)

"Genesis 16 is adultery" (My comments: This
is Abraham and Hagar. Though Sarah suggested it,
Abraham is the one who committed the adultery with
Hagar. Hagar, a woman, was a party to it.)

"Genesis 19 is homosexuality" (My comments:
These are the MEN of Sodom who lusted after the
angels that had come to Lot's home, not the women.
Women were not controlling anyone here. In fact,
those men even refused Lot's two daughters when
he offered them to the men to be defiled as they
chose.)

"Genesis 34 is fornication". (My comments:
A man rapes a woman here. Did the carnal instinct
of woman to dominate the man cause this?)

140

# GOD, THAT WOMAN YOU GAVE TO BE WITH ME

"Genesis 38 is incest and prostitution". (My comments: This is the account of the dishonesty on the part of the man, Judah, first and then the trickery by Tamar, the woman, to get what was lawfully hers. God killed her first husband, Judah's son, because of his wickedness. Then He killed the second son because he defrauded her. Judah said that she was more righteous than he was, even though she tricked him into conceiving a child. Tamar was not a prostitute and this was not incest since she was not married to any of the sons at the time. One of the twins she bore from this was in the genealogy of Christ. Again, God's sovereign hand was in this, but facts are ignored so the preacher can blame incest and prostitution on the woman's desire to dominate and control.)

"Genesis 39 is seduction". (My comments: This one WAS a woman. It is the story of Joseph and Potipher's wife.)

(My comments: These were all supposed to be examples of the results of the wife's conflicts with masculine leadership and the results of man capitulating his spiritual responsibility to his wife!!! Are all of these the result of women's dominating and controlling their husbands and their disobedience to God's plan of submission? I think not. The facts in the message are inaccurate, distorted, slanderous, untruths, designed to bring dishonor, shame, and blame to women.)

The preacher then says, "Why this conflict against marriage? Because if Satan can destroy the family, he can destroy the church and if he can destroy the church, he can destroy the purpose of God.

Because the man and the wife in 1992 live in a demonic society saturated by pornography, adultery, fornication, homosexuality, incest, prostitution, drugs, drinking, divorce, all destroy the fabric of marriage, the fabric of the home.

# PERVERSION OF SUBMISSION

Viruses that kill the marriage. Books, movies, television, all mock what is pure and holy in marriage, and exult the spirit of rebellion against the will of God." (My comments: Again I say, who are the majority of authors and media producers? Who are the majority of those responsible for this stuff being on TV. Who has control over what goes over the air waves? Mostly men.)

He then mentions TV and Norman Lear and says, sarcastically, "You (meaning women) hear a smart cutting line that comes out of the mouth of some woman about her husband and something in you says, 'that's what I need to say to old meathead next time he gets out of line'. And that goes into your computer bank and you kind of rehearse the lines. Some of you are looking at me like, 'Well, I never.' But let's get real! How many of you get into a little tete-e-tete at home and you rehearsed lines you were going to say when he opened his mouth and said thus and so? And, man, you said, 'whenever she says this, I'm going to come back with this', and she's coming back with this.--You (meaning women) listen to the lines and rehearse them and you wait for your husband to foul up, and he will because he's a human being, and then when he does---whoooosh. I mean he's devoured before he knows the fight is on. When he realizes world war three has broke out he counter attacks and the marriage becomes a war zone and the devil is over there feeding your mind (meaning women again) with bitter, vicious, mean things to say. Let me tell you something, words have power, they have a life within themselves and they can rip and devour a relationship, even the relationship of Spirit filled Christians. And when you speak those words, he will remember them for a decade. The strategy is to tear down your partner, rip him apart. What does that? It only brings glory to Satan himself. See how far you (meaning women again) are from God's plan of mutual submission to each others

142

needs? **God is fighting back with Eph. 5:21,** Submit
one to another in the fear of the God and wives
submit unto your husbands as unto the Lord, for
the husband is the head of the wife, even as Christ
is the head of the church and God is the head
of Christ. Be subject unto their husbands in
**everything. (with emphasis) Ah!! say it AGAIN--
in EVERYTHING.** Husbands love your wives even as
Christ loved the church and gave himself for it.
Cleanse with the washing of the water by the Word.
Do you have a hard time reading the Word together?
You shouldn't. So ought men to love their wives.
God's plan is for wives to submit to their
husbands. Wife, quit taking direction from another
man about anything! Husband, if you have a problem
that involves another woman, you go to her husband,
don't you EVER go to her. You solve the problem
through him, not around him. If you have a
controversy with someone, you do not send your
wife to solve the controversy, whimp. You go solve
it. I know husbands who are too chicken to stand
up and face the music and so send the wife to take
the heat and then say something like, 'Well, I
don't know how this controversy ever got started.'
It got started because you are such a chicken!

Colossians 3:18, **I LOVE this! says wives submit
yourselves to your husband as is fit in the Lord.**
This translates, submit because it is fitting in
all ages. It works because it is God's plan.
What does it mean? Like gears that fit together.
When they don't mesh, there's a grinding
noise--.When there's no submission in the home,
that's what God hears in his ears, but when there
is submission, the gears fit together

(My comments: He skips over the mutual
submission and dwells on explaining the submission
of the women only. He implies that the lack of
submission in the wife is the only thing that causes
the gears not to fit and to be a horrible sound
in God's ears. He does not go on to Col. 3:19

143

that says, "Husbands, love your wives and be not bitter against them." He forgets the instruction of Col. 3:5 that says, "Mortify your members: fornication, uncleanness, inordinate affection, evil concupiscence or desire and covetousness which is idolatry." A person who craves to be a dominating controller over someone else has an evil desire. They have an inordinate affection for themselves. They covet a place of higher honor for themselves. They set themselves up as idols. Col. 3:8 says, "Put off all anger, and wrath, blasphemy and filthy communication out of your mouth." Col. 3:12 says, "Put on, therefore, as the elect of God, holy and beloved, tender mercies, kindness, humbleness of mind, meekness, and longsuffering". Verse 14, "Above all these things, put on love, which is the bond of perfectness (unity)." So far in this "sermon", I hear anger, wrath, malice, malicious slander, and even blasphemy as God's Word is perverted. Satan said to Eve, "Hath God said?" But this man boldly adds all kinds of things to God's Word and God's intentions and brazenly declares, **"God hath said!".** I do not hear tender mercies, kindness, humbleness of mind or meekness. I do not hear Love. With this kind of preaching, how can there ever be a bond of perfectness? That bond of perfectness, that unity, comes from both parties submitting to God and from exhibiting tender mercies, kindness, humbleness of mind and meekness to one another. There must be a mutual submission to one another in these things. It does not come from the man dominating and controlling the wife into submission. When the man acts in a dominating, controlling way, it is he who is causing the gears not to mesh, because he is not loving his wife as Christ loved the church. He is being bitter against her. Bitter here is a word that conveys the idea of piercing or sharpness. The preacher is preaching the piercing, sharpness of bitterness against all women. Col. 3:15 says, "Let the peace

144

of God **rule** in your hearts to which you are called in one body; and be thankful". This word rule means an award of arbitration, a prize in a public game. It also means to govern, to prevail. What all of that means is that the peace of God is a prize. It will prevail and govern your heart. That peace that is awarded as a prize comes from practicing the things of verses 12 and 14 in **mutual** submission. It's talking about the peace of God that rules, not the man. Finally, Col. 3:16 says, "Let the Word of Christ dwell in you richly; in all wisdom, teaching and admonishing **one another** in hymns, psalms, and spiritual songs, singing with grace in your hearts to the Lord". These are the things that bring the sounds of gears meshing perfectly in God's ears. No matter how loudly the submission of women is preached as the cure-all for all the world's ills, the harshness such as this sermon shouts, can never promote love or the bond of perfectness (unity). There is nothing that would enrich the soul in this sermon. There is no wisdom and there is no grace in it. There is no love. This is an example of what was called "hard speeches against God" in the last chapter. The delivery style was fine sounding speech, but it brings condemnation.

The preacher goes on to another derogatory part of the sermon that concerns I Tim. 2:9. He says, "The nature of the submitted wife is modest apparel. Treat your womanhood with love and respect." (My comments: This is the nature of all godly woman, rather than just a submitted wife. Otherwise, I agree with those statements). But then he says, "Dress should be modest, not to advertise. When you walk down the street in clothes, the sum of which would not make a man's necktie, you're advertising. When you drag your moving billboard by a man who has two hormones that are working and he looks at you, don't drag yourself up and say, 'well, I did not expect him to look

at me like that!'. Yes you did. He's looking
and you like it!!" (My comments: I hate immodest
dress because it causes good men to be tempted.
I have taught other women about immodest dress.
I have heard other pastors teach it, too. But
it is done in a loving way that promotes change
in the woman who is dressing provocatively and
it is palatable to any woman hearing it. It does
not condemn the innocent along with the guilty.
It does not assume that all women are determined
to be seductive. A word spoken in love covers
a multitude of sin, but insults like this only
trigger angry defenses because of it's disrespect.
Furthermore, this sermon was being preached to
a church packed full of Christian women who, I
could see, were very modestly dressed. It was
meant to be crudely funny, but it was insulting,
wounding and inappropriate.)

The preacher goes on to I Tim. 2:11-12. "Let
the woman learn in silence with all subjection.
But, I permit not a woman to teach, nor usurp
authority over the man, but to be in silence."
He explains the custom of the order of worship
in the orthodox synagogue. He explains that the
forbidding to teach has been misappropriated.
He admits that women have gifts from God and may
use them, but that they may not have spiritual
authority over men. They may not pastor a church.
(My comments: I will go into this in another
chapter.)

Then he gives some really edifying words.
He says, "A woman says, 'I can't submit to my
husband's lead, he's stupid.' Yes, look who he
married! 'I can't submit because he is so full
of sound advice--99% sound and 1% advice!! I
married him for life only to discover he doesn't
have any'." (My comments: When I heard this tape
for the first time, I laughed at some of his
sayings. But when I took time to study it, the
true character of the message came through. The

stupidity of the man for marrying his wife is a
slam against women.  The remark about the man and
advice certainly does not inspire respect or
reverence for the husband.  Coarse jokes that wound
and tear  people down have no place in a Christian's
speech, let alone in a sermon.  I love humor and
I love to laugh and I like jokes, but I hate it
when someone is being hurt by it.  Even in jokes,
the mouth reveals what is in the heart.)

Then he goes into historical accounts of how
women wanted  to be equal with men. He says, "Their
motto was 'live  your own  life'. The same as we
hear now from the feminist movement.  It started
in  Gen. 3:6, it was alive in Paul's day and it
lives in our day.   You (women) will have to choose
to be in rebellion to God's plan or submission
to God's plan. If you rebel against God's plan
you then have given your marriage over to the spirit
of witchcraft. "(My comments: These intimidations,
accusations and threats  instill fear in the heart
of every woman that if she does anything,  in any
way, contrary to her husband's wishes or demands,
she will cause a spirit of  witchcraft  to come
into the marriage. She does not dare to retain
her individual personhood. I will discuss this
in detail in another chapter. The Word says that
rebellion is like the sin of witchcraft.  But it
also says stubbornness is like the sin of idolatry.
A man who dominates and control his wife is a
stubborn man who wants idol worship from his wife!
For a Christian woman to  have a differing opinion
from her  husband's is not witchcraft!!)  He says,
"If you submit to God's plan you will have peace,
love, joy, and the Holy Spirit." (MY comments:
If I do not submit to my husband's every whim and
wish, does that mean I do not have the Holy Spirit
or that I cannot have the fruit of the Spirit in
my life?)

Next he goes to I Cor.5, he says, but he is
actually in I Tim. 5.  He talks about the provisions

for widows, and how younger women become busybodies. I Tim. 5:14 says that women under 60 are to marry, have children and take care of the home. He says, "Compare this to Titus 2:3-5. Older women teach younger women to love their husbands and children and to keep house. No one in or out of the churches teaches young women how to do these things. They have no knowledge of what God wants them to do. So, they go into marriages knowing only secular humanism and not knowing how to keep a marriage together. **No wonder the American home is falling apart.**" (My comments: I know that there has been a lack in the church in this area. But the implication is that older women either do not know how to do it themselves, or they are in rebellion against their husband and God and so cannot or will not do it. Or they are just falling down on the job, and are not doing it. Whatever the reason for failing to teach the younger women, the American home is falling apart because the woman is not in proper submission and is not teaching proper submission. So, the ills of society are the woman's fault).

He says, "The woman's place is to stand by her husband and for the husband to stand by the wife for life, loving her as Christ loved the church. Satan will come to you, lady, just as he came to Eve. 'Would you like to live your own life? Would you like to be like God? Let me appeal to your ego'. He'll do anything he can to seduce you to get away from your husband's authority. God is calling to the women of the world to be submitted to a loving husband, to be Spirit filled, to be a helpmate, to be godly, to be pure, to be chaste, to be loving, to love children and parents and widows and orphans and to show hospitality to all. That's what God plans, but the radical feminist movement says, 'we want to tear up the nation and we want to control it.' The Church of Jesus Christ must commit self to absolute

ruthless obedience to the Word of God. If you
can be manipulated and intimidated by threats or
lies, you will be.  If your commitment to Christ
is so feeble that you look for a way to escape
controversy anytime there is a conflict between
the kingdom of God and the kingdom of darkness,
you won't make it to heaven.  Because between
now and the rapture of the church will be a
spiritual street fight.  Put on the whole armor
of God and get ready for battle."

    This was the end of the preacher's sermon.
The rest of the chapter is my thoughts and comments.

    The preacher opened his sermon with, "I will
not be intimidated. I will not be manipulated.
I will not be dominated. I am a child of God."
Women are also children of God.  They are not to
be intimidated, they are not to be manipulated,
they are not to be dominated either.  The Word
is full of instruction for the joint heirs of
Christ, that brings them out from domination and
control of man and sets them free in Christ.  No
where is woman commanded to be transformed or
conformed to the image of her husband.  Yet in
preaching like this, that is exactly what she is
told to do.  When a woman does not dare to express
an opinion different from her husband's because
she fears she's being rebellious and is bringing
a spirit of witchcraft into her marriage, that
is intimidation.  When she cannot make a decision
without first submitting it to her husband, because
that would usurp his authority, that is control,
manipulation, and domination.  Under Christ, why
does the preacher have the right not to be
intimidated, dominated, manipulated or controlled,
but the woman in Christ is to be denied the same
freedom from those things?  Why does the preacher
say that those things are witchcraft and he won't
submit to them as a child of God, but that the
woman is to submit to them when it comes from her
husband?  Why is it called witchcraft in one

instance, but it is called God's plan in the other?

Notice that the preacher said the ingredient for the dogfight was when the husband tries to rule without love. **But the woman was to submit anyway.** If she cannot submit to unloving control, then he says she is a fallen woman, she is not spirit filled, she has a spirit of rebellion, a spirit of witchcraft and a spirit of carnality. The magnitude of these accusations is frightening. The intimidation is monumental and it is designed to manipulate the woman with so much fear that she will become a clone of her husband. She won't have a thought in her head or a feeling in her heart, that is her own. She won't trust anything about herself. Worse yet, she won't trust God's working in and through her. She gives up her individuality to be transformed into the image of her husband. She fears that if she doesn't do this, she is the cause for all the pornography, adultery, fornication, homosexuality, incest, prostitution, drugs, drinking and divorce that is in our society because she is going against God's plan for marriage. What a guilt trip!! A great, heavy, false, burden is dumped on her!! God's pattern for the home supposedly is submission of the wife to the husband in everything. Rather than that perverted kind of submission being God's plan, it is intimidation, manipulation, domination and control. These are all Satan's plan--not God's.

If the kind of words spoken in this sermon were used in context of races, it would be called out and out discrimination, prejudice and bigotry. It would be called inflammatory and would incite riots. But because it is said by a well known preacher about women and what he presumes is their position in the family, one is not supposed to become incensed by his inaccurate, insensitive words. If a woman cannot accept them, she is in rebellion, she is a fallen woman, she is in witchcraft, she is not Spirit filled. The man's

GOD, THAT WOMAN YOU GAVE TO BE WITH ME

audience for this message was a congregation of
thousands of Spirit filled, Bible believing people.

The preacher spoke truth about words. They
do have a power of their own. They do have a life
within themselves. They can rip and devour a
relationship. Even a Christian relationship. When
the preacher spoke all those hurtful words, they
too, will be remembered for a decade. The strategy
is to tear women apart, and to keep the conflict
that Satan started going. The words wound and
hurt and destroy the spirit of the woman. They
destroy the unity of the marriage and they destroy
the unity of the church.

His words go out over the airwaves all over
the world. How many are being wounded by them?
How much damage are they doing to the Body of
Christ? **How many women refuse to come to Christ
because they fear that being a Christian would
require them to submit to this kind of domination?**
How many preachers think his rhetoric and crude
jokes are cute and funny and so copy it, thereby
multiplying the destruction even more? I have heard
some of them repeated from pulpits myself! Go
back to Col. 3:8. Paul said to put off filthy
communication. Filthy communication does not mean
just gutter language. It is also foolish jesting
that wounds and tears down. It is words that heap
defilement and condemnation on a person as this
sermon does.

Mary Stewart VanLeeuwen makes a startling
statement in her book "Gender and Grace", Copyright
1990. She writes, "In recent years we have
discovered that although eighty percent of sexual
abuse and family violence occurs in alcoholic
families, **the next highest incidence of both incest
and physical abuse takes place in intact, highly
religious homes.** The offending fathers in such
families, (for it is overwhelmingly men, rather
than women, who practice child abuse), often espouse
'old fashioned values' to the point of rigidity

151

and stuffiness. They **emphasize the subordination of women,** sometimes to the point of believing they 'own' their wives and daughters. In addition, they believe so strongly in individual self sufficiency that the family often lacks close contact with other adults who can dilute the father's possessiveness."

This is the kind of subordination our preacher was teaching. If the kind of submission he promotes is a godly biblical teaching, why is it producing such rotten fruit?

The disturbing statements I just quoted are really very mild and are already out of date. Primarily, that dealt with the abuse of children who are brought up in homes where females are subordinate. But just a few years later, look at the kind of rotten fruit that has been brought to light concerning the abuse of Christian women in our Western Christianity.

In Charisma and Christian Life Magazine, March 1995, there is an article that I wish every Christian could read. It gives an accurate view of what is really taking place in churches today as a result of distorted Scriptures pertaining to marriage and submission. It reveals some shocking statements and statistics. The article, written by Marcia Ford, Religious News Editor for Charisma Magazine, is "The Silent Shame". "Christian women who are abused by their husbands don't always find help in the church."

Some of the statistics quoted from the article are:
NATIONAL COUNCIL AGAINST DOMESTIC VIOLENCE
1. A woman is battered every 15 seconds in the U.S.
2. Each year 4 million women are severely assaulted by their current or former spouse.
3. One third of all women who seek medical care have suffered domestic violence.
4. It is said to be the number one crime in America

but is the least reported.

5. **The most shameful statistic:** Many of it's victims and perpetrators are Christians.

DON SAPAUGH, PRESIDENT OF RAPHA TREATMENT CENTERS, DALLAS TEXAS

1. Reluctance to share information is especially characteristic of pastor's wives who suffer some form of abuse.

2. Many of the calls to Rapha's Confidential minister's hotline are from women who are being abused by their minister husbands.

3. Some calls are from pastors who want to confess they've been abusing their wives.

ELIZABETH STELLAS TIPPENS OF THE SEATTLE BASED CENTER FOR PREVENTION OF SEXUAL AND DOMESTIC VIOLENCE--A NON-PROFIT GROUP THAT FOCUSES ON **ABUSIVE CLERGY.**

1. There's no evidence that the incidence of domestic violence in clergy marriages is any less than the national average.

2. The problem is that it's much more hidden.

EXPERTS SAY

1. About half of the abuse committed by Christian men is physical or sexual. **The rest is emotional abuse involving mental manipulation.**

2. Emotional abuse is taken less seriously by the church, trapping many Christian women in an emotional prison, where thoughts of suicide are prevalent.

JIMMY EVANS, PASTOR AND MARRIAGE COUNSELOR, AMARILLO TEXAS

1. Pastors don't know how to counsel an abused woman. His opinion is confirmed by a survey of battered women who successfully escaped their abusers. These victims ranked clergy last in helpfulness.

The article states: "Why aren't women finding more safety in their churches? At least part of the problem, experts say, can be traced to misinterpretations of Scripture about marriage.

The Bible passage most often used to justify abusive behavior is Eph.5:22-24, 'Wives submit to your husband as to the Lord. For the husband is head of the wife, as also Christ is the head of the Church and He is the savior of the Body. Therefore, just as the church is subject to Christ, so let the wives be to husbands in everything'." (NKJV)

Sapaugh says that some pastors "set up man-made criteria for what is and what isn't submission and end up throwing spousal abuse in the middle of it. I am confident that is not the intent of the Scriptures". Evans agrees and says, "Biblical submission does not include physical violence or the violation of personal sovereignty".

This chapter and many others in my book were written at least ten months before I read this article. As I read this article from Charisma, my mind jumped back to the sound of the preacher's voice in the sermon I just shared with you. I can hear him say, after stating that the carnal instinct of woman was to dominate the man but she wouldn't **"because GOD is fighting back with Eph. 5:21"**. While quoting the passage of 5:22-24, he used special emphasis as he said, "be subject unto your husbands in everything-**AH!! say it AGAIN!! in EVERYthing!!**". And again, the special inflections of his voice as he said in reference to Col. 3:18, **"I love this!! wives submit** yourselves to your husbands as is fit in the Lord". My mind cringes at the thought that my God is fighting against women. My heart aches as he infers that the weapons God uses to fight against women are husbands and a right of dominion! That is exactly what this preacher says!! The sad part is, he is not alone in his assessment because many others preach it too.

My mind recalls the hundreds of times I've heard the same thing taught in the same way, by so many pastors, and I weep for the women. I weep especially for the abused wives of clergy, for

GOD, THAT WOMAN YOU GAVE TO BE WITH ME

I was one of them myself. Even after hearing it
so many times, and even after knowing the truth,
I still feel daggers of pain piercing my soul every
time I hear this kind of preaching. How much worse
it is for my Christian sisters who do not understand
the truth of God's precious Word. They think this
is what God assigned to them because of the sin
of Eve in the Garden of Eden!!

The article in Charisma ends with the story
of one man who conquered his abusiveness. He states
that what reversed his abusive behavior was
exposure. He says the cure is exposure to the
light and accountability.

I believe the preaching and teaching by clergy
that promotes this kind of rotten fruit also needs
to be exposed. I believe that is why it is God's
agenda for this book to be written. More and more
facts and statistics demonstrating the fruit of
this perversion of submission are being published.
This kind of corrupt teaching must be exposed to
the light of true Bible interpretation in order
for it to stop. Those who misinterpret and misquote
Scriptures need to be held accountable by the church
for the destruction, woundedness and hurt they
are producing in the church.

A loose meaning of prophet is a person who
either foretells something or who speaks forth
a revelation from the Word. Scripture says that
a prophet is subject to the prophets, meaning that
a message given is to be examined by other prophets
to make sure that error does not creep into the
church. For centuries, it appears as though no
one would dare challenge a preacher/teacher/
prophet's message on the issue of submission,
so serious error has crept into the church. It
is God's timing to expose it and deal with it.

The Shulamite Girl of the Song of Solomon says
in chapter 5, verse 7, "The watchmen that went
about the city found me; they smote me, they wounded
me; the keepers of the walls took away my veil

from me." (KJV) The words she spoke are so relative
for today. The watchmen or the keepers of the
wall were men who were supposed to protect her,
carefully attend to her needs, and take care of
her. But instead they smote her, they wounded
her, they took away her veil. The words "smote"
and "wound" both mean to strike and even to murder,
to split. The word veil means a sense of spreading
and it comes from the primary word that means to
tread to pieces, to conquer, specifically to over-
lay, spend and subdue. Some have considered that
rape might even be suggested by those definitions.

I identify with the Shulamite because the
watchmen over women are the husbands. Also, pastors
are supposed to protect them and watch over them
as part of the flock. But the husbands abuse in
every way and then the pastors become accessories
to the abuse by upholding the husband's deeds with
twisted Scripture. When abused women come to them
for counsel, the pastor tells them the Bible says
it is their Christian duty to go back and submit
to their "head" in everything, even abuse. The
pastors themselves perpetrate more abuse by
preaching things that strike at women's dignity
and worth, both as persons and as part of the
Body of Christ. Their words murder the spirit
of the women. They tread her to pieces emotionally.
Their words and actions have overlayed her with
intimidation, manipulation, and domination until
she is conquered and subdued in body, soul, and
spirit.

I have been healed of my wounds that were
inflicted by my ex-husband and by pastors. But
many of my Christian sisters have not been set
free or healed from the wounds of the watchmen
in their lives. That is why this book is being
written. I feel their pain. Much more than that,
God knows their pain. He wants to bring the
watchmen to account.

As bad as the emotional damage is to women,

there is a far more serious reason why God wants to bring the watchmen to account. It has to do with the veil that they have taken away from the women and what the veil represents. I must use several Scriptures to explain what I mean.

II Cor.3:13-16 is the passage that refers to the veil that Moses covered his face with after he had been in God's presence on Mt. Sinai. He covered his face because the people feared the glory of the Lord that was upon him and because the glory was fading away. Because of the fear, the people's minds were made dull. Even to this day, the veil of the old covenant covers the hearts of those who do not believe in Christ. Because they do not believe in the Messiah, for them, the veil was never rent or taken away. But when ANYONE comes to the Lord, for them the veil is taken away. When that veil is removed, they take on a new veil or mantle, which is Christ Jesus. He overlays them with Himself as their covering. We are changed into the same image, from glory to glory, as by the Spirit of the Lord. (II Cor.3:18).

Next we'll look at the word "veil" in Heb. 10:20. This word for veil means the body of Christ, His flesh, which he gave up to be crucified, thus giving everyone who believes a new and living access into the presence of God. The veil IS the flesh of Christ that covers, or is the mantle around the body of each individual believer. It is because of that veil that God can look upon a believer as righteous.

The flesh of Christ IS the new covering, the new veil that replaced the rent veil of the Temple. It is the access to God for women as well as men. The new veil has overlayed women believers as well as men believers.

In I Cor. 11:10 the power that is on the woman's head is the "veil" of all of His delegated power and privilege that He has bestowed on her. It includes the freedom to do all and to be all

that He wills her to do and to be, in her private
and public life.

But the watchmen, the husbands, the pastors,
and theologians, have taken away her veil and
have trodden it underfoot. They have tread it
to pieces with the doctrines of men. They have
taken God's beautiful power that is on her and
have made it an evil tool of subordination to a
mere man. In essence, what they have actually
done is to deny the efficacy of Christ's flesh
and blood as the cover of the woman. They have
replaced HIM, the Christ, with a husband.
Therefore, they are treading under foot, like so
much dirt, the flesh of Christ that is the mantle
of the woman.

They have taken away her veil in another way
that is even worse for them, as the watchmen.
When they deny her the right to minister in ANY
way, which God has gifted and called her to
minister, they are again taking God's place and
they are treading underfoot Christ and God's gifts
in her. Over and over again, I have heard it stated
and proclaimed, adamantly, vehemently, and loudly,
that any woman who wants to administer her gifts
in the congregational body, is usurping the man's
authority. They refer especially to those who
have the calling of apostle, prophet, pastor,
teacher, or evangelist, and even the gift of
administrations. First, they deny that a woman
can have most of these callings and then they say
she has a Jezebel spirit that wants to take over,
if she tries to exercise those gifts. They say
the Jezebel spirit is a demon spirit from the devil.
In reality, what they are doing is attributing
the gifts and callings of God in her to the devil.
That is getting dangerously close to blaspheming
the Holy Spirit, according to Math. 12:31,32 and
Luke 12:10. In Paul's dissertation on coverings
in I Cor.11:3-16, he does not deny or forbid the
woman the right to minister her gifts in the

congregation, he only says that she should put
something on her head for the  sake of the angels
when she does it.

The article in Charisma Magazine referred
to the misinterpretation of Eph. 5:22-24 as the
basis for justifying abuse of women. Sapaugh and
Evans agree that the misinterpretations of that
passage is the problem, but they gave no solid
alternative interpretation for it. As far as I
know, **no one has ever done that.** All they ever
say is that they are  certain God never meant it
to include abuse. A later chapter in this book
is devoted to what Eph. 5:22-24 REALLY says.  I
believe it is God's answer. When many read that
chapter, there will be a mixture of joyful release,
pain and anger. Joyful because it is God's key
to the release from their prison of abuse. Pain
because of what has been perpetrated on them all
these years. Anger because of  unnecessary suffering
that is a direct result of deliberate misinterpretation and misapplication of that Scripture.

My prayer for the people who read this chapter
of the book is that it will take away the veil
that is over the eyes of the perpetrators and that
those who suffer will be released from their
suffering. I pray that it will bring deep
conviction and repentance to the preacher of this
chapter and to those who have preached the kind
of message I shared with you. I pray that there
will be a healing and restoration for all.

I stand with Paul, who says in II Cor.4:1-2,
since we carry this image of Christ we have this
ministry, "But have renounced the hidden things
of dishonesty, not walking in craftiness, nor
handling the Word of God deceitfully, but by
manifestation of the truth commending ourselves
to every man's conscience in the sight of God."(KJV)

CHAPTER SEVEN
GOD'S CHOSEN WOMEN

The sermon of the last chapter brings up the
following questions. Are women chosen by God to
be in leadership positions and to do mighty works
of valor? Does God listen to women as individuals,
apart from their husbands? Has God ever told men
to listen to their wives or other women? Does
He honor women's decisions? Is there any kind of
biblical foundation for the belief that women are
to defer to their husbands in every decision, or
that men are to have the last word on any decision?

SARAH

In the last chapter we saw how Sarah was
discredited even though God spoke to Abraham and
told him that Sarah was right. Isaac would have
the blessing of God. Abraham was to do as Sarah
said and send Ishmael and his mother away. (Gen.
21:12) After hearing God's instruction, Abraham
listened to his wife and did as she said.

ZELOPHED'S DAUGHTERS

In Numbers 26:33 a man named Zelophed had
five daughters but no sons. In Numbers 27:1-7 the
father died, the five daughters went to the Tent
of Meeting, stood before Moses, the Priest Eleazer,
the leaders and the whole assembly. They said their
father had died leaving no sons as heir. They
wanted to know why their father's name should
disappear from the clan just because he had no
sons. They said, "Give us property from amongst
our father's relatives." So Moses took their case
before the Lord and the Lord said, **"What Zelophed's
daughters are saying is right.** You must certainly
give them property as an inheritance among their
father's relatives **and** turn their father's inheritance over to them." Apparently they did not receive
their inheritance immediately. Because Joshua 17:3,4
says the five daughters again went to Eleazer the
Priest, Joshua, and the leaders and said, "The
Lord commanded Moses to give us an inheritance

among our brothers". So Joshua gave them an inheritance, along with their uncles, according to the Lord's command. Nu.36:7 says the five women eventually married men within their father's clan, so their inheritance remained within the tribe. But that was not a condition for them to receive their rightful inheritance. God said it belonged to them.

In this account God said to the men, "These women are right. Do as they say". Moses, Joshua, Eleazer the Priest, the leaders and the whole assembly knew that God said the women were right and to do as they said. They listened and they did it.

This account is very important. Apparently, Jewish tradition said that only sons could be heirs, because there was so much emphasis on the male gender. But when the leaders of the nation took it to the Lord, **no such partiality was found in the heart of God.** Those women were entitled to their father's inheritance, according to God. The significance of this account is that it established the fact that traditions of men were often imposed as the biblical standard, rather than God's standards. As it was then, so it is now. The kind of partiality practiced in many Christian churches today is based on traditions of men, rather than on God's heart.

I do not want to take away from, or deny men anything. All I want to do is to present this to the "elders". If they take it to God, they too will hear God say, "Women are joint heirs in Christ, give the women their inheritance, it is certainly right".

## HULDAH

Huldah was a prophetess. She must have been well known for speaking the Word of the Lord, because in 2 Kings 22:13, after King Josiah read the recovered Book of the Law, he sent the priest, the scribe and others to "Go and inquire **of the**

**Lord** for me, and all the people and for all of Judah about what is written in the book that was found." Why didn't the king seek this information from the priest, scribe and men leaders? Why did he tell them "Go and inquire"? How is it they knew where to go and who to go to, to hear from the Lord? The priest and scribe and others went to Huldah, who lived in the second quarter. Why is it mentioned where she lived? I think there is some significance in that. On some maps the second quarter is the place in front of the temple. The second quarter, in the Septuagint and in the KJV, is "the college". Jewish history says she was a teacher in the college. The college was a public school. Quite likely she was a teacher of mostly men and boys. Whether she was a teacher or not, the fact remains that she was a prophetess of God of such reliable reputation and renown, that the priest, scribe and company went directly to her to inquire of the Lord.

They went to her to have the book they had found authenticated. So she must have had a highly developed knowledge of the language and the Word, as well as being able to hear from God directly. Then the King acted on that word that came from the Lord through the woman.

A woman spoke the Word of the Lord and a king listened to her. Of all the people of God at the time, it was a woman who was most in touch with God. It was a woman whom the king could trust to get a true word from God.

Huldah and her ministry have been discredited by men who say she was not a real prophet, like men prophets. They say she was briefly mentioned **only** once in the Word, so it could not have been a significantly valid ministry. They say she ministered to the men ONLY because THEY went to her and **invited** her to minister to them. They went to her in private-so this was not a public ministry like that of men prophets. Because of these manufactured facts, they say she was not a real prophet so she cannot be used as an example for today's women to follow in the ministry of prophet.

## MICHAL
In I Sam.19:11,12 Michal, David's wife, speaks a warning that Saul was seeking to kill him. Though it was a fact she had heard and not a word from the Lord, David listened to her and she helped him escape.

## ABIGAIL
We will read a great deal more about Abigail in another chapter. But for now I want to mention her briefly. In I Sam.25:24-31 Abigail speaks to David. Much of what she says to him is a prophetic message for him from God. David listened and praised God for sending her to him.

God used women in David's life. He trusted them and listened to them.

## ESTHER
The beautiful Esther who became the Queen of Xerxes. Her name means "heroine". When the decree was issued for all of the Jews in that kingdom to be annihilated, it was Esther who told Mordecai, a cousin who had raised her, to tell every Jew to fast for three days and nights. He listened to her and carried out her instructions. Everyone listened to her and did as she said. It was Esther, a woman, whom God put in that place at that time. She engineered the plan to entrap the evil Haman, who had sent out the fateful decrees. It was Esther, the woman, who put her life on the line to carry out the plan. The king listened to her. It was through her that Haman was executed. His estate was given to Esther, who put Mordecai in charge over the estate. She then told the King how she was related to Mordecai. The king gave Mordecai his signet ring, which meant he was second to the king in power. Esther pleaded with the king to overrule the decrees to annihilate her

people. The king listened to her again. Since the previous decrees could not be revoked even by the king himself, he gave Mordecai unlimited power to write new decrees that would override the first ones. The new decrees were written, sealed with the signet ring by Mordecai. This saved the Jews for that day. Then Esther again spoke to the king. Again he listened. He granted her petition to have the same decrees invoked for one more day. This saved the Jews completely and set them free. Every time Esther spoke to the king, she was taking her life in her hands, because if what she said displeased him, he could have her killed.

When it was all over, Mordecai, in a place of power, wrote new decrees for the people on how to observe feast days to celebrate the victory. Esther 9:29 says that Esther and Mordecai wrote "with full authority" concerning these things. 9:32 says **Esther's** decrees confirmed the regulations for the feast days.

So God sent a woman to save her nation. A king listened, a nation listened. A woman helped write the important documents concerning regulations of the new religious feast day, documents that became part of permanent Jewish records. A whole book is devoted to this heroine.

## DEBORAH

Deborah was a prophetess, which means she spoke and sang by the inspiration of God. Prophetess is the exact same word as prophet, except one is female, one is male. They do the exact same thing. The Word specifically called her a prophetess. There were many judges who were not given that distinction when their reign was recorded in the Word.

Deborah was a judge over the entire nation of Israel.

Deborah is found in Judges 4. I'll give you a little running commentary, starting in Judges 4:5.

V.5  As judge she held court and the Israelites came to her to have  their disputes settled.

V.6   She  was  the  commander-in-chief  of  the military.

V.7  God gives her the battle plan.

V.8  She gives God's command to Barak, but he refuses  to  go  to  battle  without  her.  In  the Septuagint,  he  says  he  refuses  to  go  because .SHE knows  the  right  plan  and  time  from  God,  but  he does  not.  (To  me,  this  does  not  mean  that  Barak is  a  weak  man.  It  signifies  that  he  recognized the  spiritual  condition  of  Deborah  and  himself and  he  wisely  chose  to  submit  himself  to  her spiritual  authority.  That  submission  to  her authority was  for  his  own  good  as  well  as  the  good of  his  nation.  To  me,  this  shows  the  strength  of the  man,  not  his  weakness.  His  weakness  was  in his  faith  in  himself,  not  a  weakness  in  character. He  had  faith  in  God  and  faith  in  Deborah,  but  he was  weak  in  the  faith  of  his  own  ability  to  hear God.  This  is  confirmed  in  the  faith  chapter  of Heb.11.  In  verses  32,  34  it  says  "out  of  weakness was  made  strong,  valiant  in  fight,  turned  to  flight the  armies  of  the  alien.)

V.9  Deborah  agrees  to  lead  them  in  battle, but  she  prophesies  that  the  honor  of  the  victory over  the  enemy,  Sisera,  will  belong  to  a  woman.

Men  say  that  the  honor  was  given  to  a  woman because  that  was  God's  judgment  against  Barak  for deferring  leadership  to  a  woman!  They  say  God will  **ALWAYS**  bring  judgment  against  a  man  who  defers his  leadership  to  a  woman.  I  ask,  why  is  he mentioned  in  the  Hebrews  chapter  of  heroes  of  the faith  if  God  had  a  negative  judgment  against  him? Why  did  God  tell  Deborah  the  **honor**  for  killing Sisera  would  go  to  a  woman  instead  of  to  another man,  if  deferring  to  a  woman  was  the  cause  of judgment?  Why  would  God  honor  a  woman  if  He  was judging  the  man  for  honoring  a  woman  by  deferring to  her  leadership?

V.10  She went with Barak, to lead 10,000 men.

V.14  Deborah gives battle instructions and encouragement to Barak that the Lord has gone before them.

V.15,16  As Barak advances, the Lord routs all of Sisera's troops, killing every man.

V.17  Sisera is the only one who lives. He flees. He goes to Jael, the wife of a friendly clan leader.

V.18-21  She invites him into her tent, gives him milk to drink, covers him up when he lays down to sleep. While he sleeps she kills him.

V. 24  The Israelites grew stronger and stronger until they destroyed Jabin, the king of the Canaanites, the oppressors.

Chapter 5 Deborah and Barak sing a song of inspiration, a song of praise, glorifying God.

Even Deborah's name has been misinterpreted. The dictionary says her name means "bee" or "honey bee". In Hebrew, it does mean bee, with the sense of orderly motion and the systematic instincts of the bee. But there is a more important meaning which comes from a primary root word. Among it's meanings are these: to arrange, to speak, subdue, appoint, bid, command, commune, declare, talk, teach, think and use entreaties. It also means: a cause, act, advice, business, chronicles, counsel, decree, eloquent, glory, judgment, oracle, power, promise, provision, song, and speech. These are far more accurate to describe who she was and what she did.

I believe Deborah employed all of those things as a judge over the nation of Israel. As judge, she fulfilled all the duties of that position, just like every other judge over Israel. Like them, she dealt with all civil, political, military, financial and religious matters. She held court where she settled peoples disputes, counseled people, appointed people to offices, taught, led them in military pursuits etc., etc.

She was a prophetess. The word says that in old times, God spoke to his people through the prophets (prophetess, in this case). They alone heard the Word of God. So God spoke to her directly, giving her messages for His people. She gave them to the people and the people listened to her.

When the armies of Israel shrank in fear from the powerful giant Goliath, David slew him in the name of the Lord. When men leaders of the armies of Israel shrank in fear from the powerful Sisera with his 900 iron chariots, Deborah led them in battle in the Name of the Lord. Judges 4:6 says that the honor for slaying Sisera went to a Canaanite woman, Jael, who killed him with her own hands. Jael means valuable, useful, do good. She is a woman who was certainly a valuable person whom God used in a very heroic way. Jael has also been criticized. Men hold her up as an example of a betrayer. If a man had done what she did to an enemy leader, he would be held up as a brave hero, who had accomplished the Lord's work. God said the "honor" would go to a woman, yet man does not "honor" her, but rather condemns her as a betrayer.

When the men of Israel faltered in their leadership, it was a woman who trusted God, heard from God, prophesied to the people what God would do, led them in battle, and denounced the men leaders of the tribes of Israel for not fighting for God. Then she sang the song of praise and worship to God, just like David did.

Deborah ruled Israel and they had peace under her leadership for forty years. In spite of this, it has been said that Deborah was not a real judge, because a real judge was a military leader. They say Deborah was NOT the military leader, Barak was. They sight Heb. 11:32 as proof, saying it was Barak who was mentioned as a military hero, not Deborah. Therefore, she was not the leader, she was only a supporter of the man. Never mind the fact that Deborah's faith was strong and she was NOT the one whose faith needed to be made strong through weakness! It has also been said that Deborah was not the official judge, because she held court under a tree in a secluded place rather than in a public place where the other real judges sat. It is looked upon with as much respect as if she had a picnic under the trees one day and settled a few issues for a few people. The fact that she held court there for forty years is ignored.

Deborah had a husband. There is nothing recorded about him in these two chapters of Judges except that his name was Lapadoth. There is no indication that Deborah consulted her husband about any of the decisions she made while judge of Israel. There is no indication that she had his permission or approval to be judge over Israel. Nor is there any reason to believe that she was acting under his "headship" and authority. God called her to be judge, she obeyed that call. God gave her authority over her husband and over all men of Israel. She was under no headship but God's.

When the word says that a woman is not to usurp authority over her husband, the key word is "usurp". "Usurp" means to cease or take authority out of one's own free will, for one's own benefit, and on their own, with no authorization to do it. It is NOT usurping authority when that authority is given to a person by God's calling and God's gifting!! It was not usurping authority in Deborah's case and it is not usurping authority in our day when God gives a woman a call to high places of leadership. Like Barak, men of today need to recognize God given authority in women and submit to that authority. Not because it is a woman, but because the authority is given by God. To refuse to submit to the authority God gives to women, is to fight against God. I am reminded of the warning Gamaliel gave to the Pharisees concerning

Jesus and the Apostles in Acts 5:34-39. I liken
it to women in leadership. If the woman's authority
is not of God, it will fade away and come to
nothing, but if it is of God, then to fight against
it is to fight against God.

I have heard it stated and I have seen it
written by many men, that Deborah was a judge **ONLY**
because there was no man to be found for the job.
**And it ONLY happened ONCE!!** Today we have the
same kind of reasoning when a woman answers a
call to the mission field or a pulpit ministry
where men won't go. Men themselves say a woman
is going because a man won't go and that is the
only reason she is **allowed** to go. The essence
of this reasoning is that a man is **always** better
qualified and the better person for the job. A
man is **always** God's first choice for any job.
But since the man won't go, then God has to use
second best and so He sends a woman. It is
demeaning and derogatory toward women and an
abasement of their calling.

In the case of Deborah's being chosen by God
to be a judge over all Israel, the men were found
lacking. There was not one man in all of Israel
that had a heart toward God. God did not find
one man worthy of leading His people. Not one man
was willing to be obedient to God. **Surely, our
omnipotent God could have raised up a worthy man
if He had chosen to do so!!** But God chose to
raise up a woman for the job. It was a woman whose
heart was toward God. It was a woman who had
the courage to be obedient to God. Rather than
emphasizing that Deborah was God's second choice
because He couldn't find a man for the job, I
believe that God purposely called a woman to show
that He chooses his leaders. He is not partial
to genders. He calls, He gifts, and He qualifies,
male or female to accomplish His purposes and plans.
It is only in the minds of men that there is a
distinction between genders. It comes from pride

169

and arrogance and a stubborn refusal to see how God chooses and entrusts women, as well as men, to do all facets of His work in this world. Stubbornness and idolatry go hand in hand.

If it is as men say, that God's only reason for making Deborah a judge, was that there was no qualified man to do it, is that not a shame and an indictment against men rather then negative judgment against women??!! Shouldn't it be a praise for women that one was found to be worthy of God's appointment? With their own mouths, men condemn themselves, yet justify themselves by denigrating the role of the woman.

It seems to me that the Word is a most powerful commentary on genders. Even though Deborah was a woman, the Word has only positive things to say about her. She ruled well and there was peace for forty years. There are no such negative words concerning her, like there is for so many of the male kings and judges that ruled over Israel. Many, many of them have words in them that say "and HE did evil in the sight of the Lord", "HE did evil in the sight of the Lord, even more than his fathers did before him". They brought pain, sorrow, slavery, and captivity to the people. They did not bring peace and freedom from slavery to their people as Deborah did.

What a sad commentary it is for men, when this heroine of the faith is looked upon by many men as God's second-best choice, rather than seeing her as God's first and choicest vessel, chosen to accomplish His purpose. The honor and dignity that is afforded to men who were chosen by God to be prophets and judges is denied to women. Flimsy arguments are used to say she wasn't really a judge in the true sense of the word. It doesn't matter that she was chosen by God, she did a superb job that exceeded most men's accomplishments, and she brought peace to the land for forty years. Men say that women ought not to hold her up as

an example to follow today, because she wasn't
a real judge or prophet!! We ought not to think
that just because God used this one woman, this
one time in that way, that it means we should
consider that as God's ordination of women in
high ministry positions.

## RUTH

Our next woman of God is Ruth. The name Ruth
means a female associate, an additional one, to
tend a flock, to rule, by extension, to associate
with (as a friend), pastor. This definition comes
from four words in Strong's Concordance. #4327,
7468, 7462 & 7453.

Ruth is the epitome of faithfulness and
loyalty. The key to understand Ruth's character
is her statement in Ruth 1:16. When she chose to
go with her mother-in-law, she was not just following a woman. She had chosen Naomi's God! She said,
"Thy God shall be my God". Her trust in, and
faithfulness to, the woman Naomi, was a picture
of her trust and faithfulness to God Almighty,
Naomi's God.

Naomi and Ruth were led by the Lord every
step of their way. Because of what God had done
through Ruth, to bless Naomi, the women of the
village recognized that Ruth was better for Naomi
then seven sons (Ruth 4:15). God could not have
blessed her in such a way through any man.

God had a larger purpose in blessing Naomi.
God filled Ruth with the qualities of devotion
and loyalty, because He had chosen Ruth, a Moabite
woman, to have the honor of becoming the great-
grandmother of David! Again, our God displays
His total lack of partiality, by choosing a woman
from the Moabites, to be an ancestor of Christ.

The hero of the story is Boaz. But the book
was written in honor of the woman Ruth. It's
significance is twofold. 1.) God chooses to use
whomever, regardless of race, gender, economic
or social status, to fulfill His purpose. Those

things mean nothing to Him.   2.)  The book uses Boaz as a portrait of how Christ is the kinsmen redeemer.  Ruth, though she came  from a clan that was the product of the incestuous relationship of Lot and his daughter,  is mentioned in the genealogies of Christ in Matthew 1:5.

God has beautiful ways of honoring women that are very special.  They are not second class to Him.

## LEAH AND RACHEL

Gen. 30 and 31 says some interesting things about women.  Gen. 30:17 says that God heard Leah's petitions for a son and he "hearkened" unto her and she bore a fifth son  to Jacob.

Gen. 30:22 says God remembered Rachel and "hearkened" unto her and opened her womb.  She bore Jacob's favorite son, Joseph, who would play such an important part in history.

Contrary to our modern day theology that says men will make all decisions, we see in Gen. 31:4-16 where Jacob sent for his wives, Leah and Rachel, to come out to the field where he was watching his flocks.  He explained to them what God had said to him concerning taking his flocks and herds and his wives and children and going back to his father's land.  In other words, he sent for them specifically  to ask his wives for their insights and their advice.  The women knew of their father's deceitfulness and assessed the situation correctly.  They advised Jacob to do what God  had told him to do.

So Jacob sought and listened to his wives' counsel.

God listened and answered these women.  They prayed to God personally.  These sons were born in answer to their prayers,  not Jacob's prayers.

## TAMAR

In chapter 6, the preacher accused her of dominating and controlling men by prostitution and incest.  Gen. 38  portrays her as a woman who fought for God's plan for her to be fulfilled. Tamar was the wife of Judah's first born son, Er. But Er was a wicked man in God's sight and God killed him. It was the custom of the day for a brother of the deceased man to take the widow to be his wife so that a child could be conceived to carry on his brother's name. So the second son of Judah, Onan took her, but refused to impregnate her. God was so displeased with that, He killed him too. Judah's third son Shelah, was too young to marry so Judah sent Tamar to her father's house to wait until he grew up. He promised that he would send this third son to her when the time came. But he did not keep his promise, because he feared that this son would die also.

Tamar had a right to expect that her father-in-law would fulfill his promise. This was her rightful due. So she thought up and carried out a plan that tricked Judah himself into conceiving a child with her. She had his signet, his bracelets and his staff to prove the child was his. When Judah found out she was pregnant, he thought it was a child of harlotry, he was disgraced and wanted her to be killed. When she produced his belongings to prove that he himself was the father of the child, he acknowledged that the signet, bracelets and staff were his. His reaction to these events is rather startling to me. In spite of the fact that she had tricked him, he said, **"She hath been more righteous than I, because that I gave her not to Shelah, my son .**

What did God think of this? The Word says that God killed her two husbands because they were evil and defrauded her. Since God is the author of all life, and no child can be conceived unless He does it, He must have felt she was more righteous also. At any rate, God chose this woman to have a child, one of twins, whose name was Perez, who was also in the genealogy of Christ. God wanted this child to be born of this woman and He went to great lengths to do it!!

In the book of Matthew, in the first chapter, three women are specifically mentioned in the genealogy of Christ. They are Tamar, this one who fought for her rights, whom God honored. Rahab, a harlot, who was the mother of Boaz. And Ruth, the Moabite. These women were choice vessels of God, that He chose himself to fulfill his purposes. We see again, that He is not partial when it comes to genders, races, or social status.

## REBEKAH

There was much written in the last chapter about Isaac, Rebekah, Esau and Jacob. But I will mention Rebekah in this chapter also, because she was a chosen vessel of God .

Rebekah was Isaac's wife. She was barren. Her husband prayed for her and God answered his prayers and she conceived. But Rebekah was a woman of God. In Gen. 25:22 she went to the Lord herself to inquire why there was such a struggle in her womb. Verse 23 says the Lord spoke to her that there were twins in the womb. They were two nations and two kinds of people. One would be stronger than the other and the elder would serve the younger. All of this was revealed to Rebekah, not to Isaac.

God had his own purposes for Jacob and Esau. God did not adhere to the traditions of men that said the first born should inherit the blessing. God had spoken his intentions for those two before they were born. He chose their temperaments and their destinies. God fulfilled those things in their lives according to His plan. Though there was trickery involved, the blessing went to the one God had chosen. Rebekah was used of God to fulfill His word, when Isaac would have given the blessing to Esau for a venison stew, and because of his partiality toward one son. Isaac would have gone against the will of God. Like his father before him, he would have chosen the wrong son rather than to abide by the Father's will. Both Abraham and Isaac loved their sons and would have put that love of sons before God's will. Both Sarah and Rebekah heard from God. Both saw to it that God's plan was accomplished.

Mal. 1:3 and Romans. 9:13 are very clear that Jacob was God's choice. He was the child of promise that was counted as seed through which the purposes of God would stand. God told Rebekah that. Rebekah acted according to the will of God. She was a godly woman who listened to God.

The preacher of the last chapter portrayed both Rebekah and Sarah as trouble makers and meddlesome women **who interfered with God's plans, causing trouble that has lasted throughout history.** The real truth is, God told both of those women what His plans were for their sons. What purpose is there for that kind of preaching? Why do so many preachers insist on tearing down these women of God? Why is it that, even though the women may have had wrong attitudes or methods, according to man, yet they were God's instruments to counteract the error of the men, in order for His plans for the ages to unfold. Men cannot see and admit the sin of these men, they can only blame a woman. I am not belittling Abraham or Isaac. I am just stating Bible truth. When Bible truth is spoken, neither man nor woman has reason to exalt their gender. It is only God who is exalted. Who has deceived good men into thinking male is better than female in God's sight and that all actions of men must be defended and all actions of women must be condemned? Do they do this to substantiate the belief that God does not use women in leadership? What are men afraid of? Inferior feelings cause people to down grade others.

## HANNAH

Elkanah was a man who had two wives. He was a godly man, who took his wives and children to the temple at Shiloh every year to make required sacrifices. One wife had born him children, but Hannah had not. Hannah was grieved over this, but Elkanah seemed to be content to have his children by his other wife. He asked Hannah why she couldn't be happy that they had each other, for he loved her. It was Hannah who prayed and begged and pleaded with God for a son. God did not act through prayers of the husband, but through the petitions of the woman. God acted because of the woman's own relationship to Him. I Sam.1:11 says she identified herself as a "handmaiden" of the Lord. I believe this showed her humbleness before God, her submission and dependence on God. This submission and dependence was to God himself, not to her husband. She took matters into her own hands and went to God himself. She expected to have God work in her, as she prayed on her own behalf. Her prayers, actions, and the answer to her prayers were entirely independent of Elkanah.

Eli, the priest, when he saw her lips moving, but heard no voice, thought she was drunk. Her prayer was the travail of the heart as she poured out her grief to the Lord. Eli then pronounced that she should go in peace, God would grant her petition.

There is no record that Elkanah prayed or interceded for Hannah to have a child. The child was a direct answer to Hannah's prayer and vow. We have no record that once the child was conceived, that Hannah and Elkanah discussed whether or not the child would be dedicated to God's service in such a dramatic way. It was Hannah's request to God for a child and it was her vow, alone, that the child would be dedicated to God for His service. These were her decisions, alone, and God was pleased to honor them. I Sam. 1:23 says that when it came time for the next year's trip to make the sacrifices at the temple, Hannah declined to go. She didn't ask her husband what she should do, she told him what she would do. Elkanah said "Do what seems good to you, wait to go to Shiloh until he is weaned, **only let the Lord establish His word.**" Elkanah listened to his wife, he trusted her to do what the Lord told her to do. Inherent in his trust was the fact that he trusted that she would hear her instructions from the Lord herself.

It was Hannah who gave her son in dedication to the Lord. It was Hannah who exalted God in her prayer, as she gave her son back to God. (I Sam. 2:110)

Elkanah was the father, but it was through the prayers of Hannah that the prophet Samuel was born. It was **her** faith and God's working directly through her, not through her husband, that brought about Samuel's birth. God had Samuel and His plans for him in His mind, but the birth came about because of the faith of the woman, Hannah. God answered her cry to Him for a son that she could dedicate to God. Hannah acted on her own decisions, apart from her husband. God's purposes were accomplished through her.

Though there are many more great women in the Old Testament, we will move on to New Testament women.

### ANNA

Luke 2:36-38 is the very brief story of a woman prophetess. This was Anna. She spent 84 years of her life ministering to God, rendering religious homage and worship to God through fasting and prayer, night and day. The word says she departed not from the Temple. The word "departed not" means that she lived there, she never left it, she lived there permanently. The Temple means a sacred or holy place--that is the entire precincts of the Temple at Jerusalem. The word prophetess means a female foreteller or an inspired woman speaker. A person who spoke by the inspiration of God. Obviously, to be a foreteller, to be an inspired speaker, means that one would have to speak these things aloud to someone. Since she never left the Temple, she spoke them aloud in the Temple. She is the bridge between the Old Testament and the New Testament women prophets. It is interesting that in Luke 2:25-38, two old people who were looking for the coming of Jesus, the redeemer, are mentioned. If you were to ask the question, who confirmed that Jesus was the looked for redeemer when He was brought to the Temple to be circumcised, most of the time it would be answered with the name Simeon. We hear of the man much more often than we do of the woman. Though he spoke in a prophetic manner, the man is called only a devout and righteous man. His service to God is not mentioned. God's personal promise to him was fulfilled, now he could die in peace. He confirmed who Jesus was to those who were there at the time, but he was not called a prophet. Anna, on the other hand, in the KJV is called a prophetess who served God with fasting and prayers day and night for 84 years in the Temple. She proclaimed Jesus' birth to any who would listen, indicating it was an on going witness. The description of Anna is far more impressive than that of Simeon. Why is Simeon mentioned in sermons far more than Anna is? Why is Simeon included so often in the Christmas story, but Anna is omitted just as often?

## THIS WOMAN

Luke 7:36-37 and 44-47 is the account of a nameless woman. The account, as related by John in John 11:2, identifies her as Mary the sister of Lazarus. But she was chosen by God for a special assignment. She has been honored throughout history because of devotion she lavished on Jesus, when no man did. We have no record of any man ever demonstrating such love to the Lord. This woman washed Jesus' feet with her tears, dried them with her hair, kissed his feet and anointed them with costly perfume. The men rebuked her for doing that. But Jesus rebuked the men because none of them had extended the common courtesy of the day by providing for the washing of his feet. The account in Matt.26:7-13 says she anointed him for his burial. What an honor the Lord bestowed on this woman! He could have chosen a man to do this, but he did not. He put it in the heart of a woman to do it. Then Jesus declared "that wherever this gospel is preached in the whole world there shall also be this, that this woman hath done, be told for a memorial of her". It was very significant that it was a woman whom God chose to anoint His Son for His burial, not a man. Women applied ointments and spices to dead bodies, but in the Old Testament the ministry of anointing live people was the function of the male elders, prophets, and priests. Here, again, Jesus himself acknowledged and approved the right of a woman to perform the ministry of anointing. He was ushering in the new rights of ministry for women under the new covenant. He rebuked the men, not the woman.

MARY

There are several Marys that I want to mention here.

We have Mary the sister of Martha and Lazarus. This Mary sat at Jesus feet to learn from him. When Martha complained that Mary was not helping her, Jesus rebuked Martha, not Mary. Even though Mary was a woman, Jesus said she had chosen the better thing (which was to learn from Him) and He would not take that away from her. Jesus honored her desire for Him above her position as a woman. He did not deny her, in favor of the traditional role for women. He was doing away with the old traditions. Again, we see that Jesus was approving, acknowledging, and teaching what the rights of women would be under the new covenant. Women had to learn these new rights.

One Mary was the first to see the resurrected Christ. He chose to reveal Himself to a woman

179

first, rather than to a man. He chose this Mary to be the first person to see Him and the first to receive His evangelistic commission to "Go and tell". She was the first person to carry out the new commission as she carried the news to the male apostles. The man, Peter did not have the faith to believe Jesus was resurrected even when he saw the empty tomb. The woman Mary was given the honor of seeing Him first because of her faith and devotion.

Mary, the mother of Jesus. There was no man who could ever be found worthy enough to be the father of Jesus. But there was a woman who found enough favor in God's eyes to be His mother!! Even in this, man has said that Mary had no special qualities, it was just that God randomly chose to gift her with the honor of being the mother of His Son. However, the word study I did on some words in Luke 1:28,30 said something different to me. Vs. 28 says she was highly favored and blessed. "Highly" means **lofty in character** and highly esteemed. "Favored" here means grace, indued with special honor, but it comes from another word, Charis, which means to be gracious of manner or action; the divine influence upon the heart and it's reflection in the life. "Blessed" means to speak well of religiously, to praise. The "favor" in verse 30 is only the word Charis, with the same meaning as above. The word "found" means to get, obtain, perceive, see. What all of that says to me is that God perceived that she had a lofty or high quality of character that He highly esteemed. He saw that she had obtained a graciousness in manner and action that came from His divine influence on her heart, which was reflected in her life. Why is it that it can be said of a man that "he was a man after God's own heart" and it is accepted that the man had a character quality that God highly esteemed, but the same cannot be accepted about Mary, the mother of Jesus?

Because God created man first, man uses that
as a basis for his claim that God chose man to
be first in all things. Man has also boasted that
God gave the superior function of procreation to
man, because only a man carries the "seed". Therefore, the man is God's favored gender. However,
in Gen.3:15 God said, "I will put enmity between
thee and the woman, and between thy seed and HER
SEED; he shall bruise thy head, and thou shall
bruise his heel." The word seed here is the same
as the word that speaks of Abraham's seed etc.
The word, in connection with humans, means posterity, child, offspring, (including male sperm).
The words, posterity, child and offspring include
women as well as men. Women were not excluded
as carriers of the seed. The seed spoken of here
in Gen. was Jesus Christ himself. This "seed"
would come through the woman only!!! No man would
ever carry the seed that was Jesus into a woman.
He was nurtured in her body as her "seed" alone.
Jesus would bring back the spiritual life that
was lost to mankind in the fall and He would come
through a woman.

One could say that man was the father of living
mankind, because he was created first. But woman
was the mother of the One who brought spiritual
life back to mankind. So through the woman's body
came the restorer of spiritual life. It was a
woman whom God honored by having His Son come
through her. Satan deceived Eve, a woman, but the
means of restoration also came through a woman,
Mary.

God could have made humans in a different
way, so that males could bear children, but he
did not choose to do that. Could it be that, in
his wisdom, he knew that man would need something
to hold back the tide of arrogant pride in being
a man and so He sent His Precious Seed through
woman only, so there would be no grounds for man
to boast?

Even though we know that Jesus was not conceived from a union of the woman and God, but was a holy embryo, placed in her womb by God, He still said that her seed would have enmity with Satan's seed. Doesn't the fact that God found a woman pure enough to be the mother of His Son counter balance the fact that man was created first? Shouldn't that fact remove man's tendency for arrogant boasting of male superiority?

Neither male nor female has anything to boast in, except Jesus Christ.

There is an argument that Christ established the exclusion of women in leadership roles in the church because He chose only men as his twelve apostles. While Jesus lived on earth, He abided by the Law and the old covenant. He even told the disciples to do as the Pharisees **said** because they sat in the seat of Moses and what they taught was right. But He said, don't do as they do. (Math.22:23) Because He abided by the Old Covenant, He chose only men as His twelve Apostles. After Judas Iscariot killed himself, the eleven apostles chose one man to replace him so that the number again would be twelve. However, after Jesus' resurrection, the New Covenant was established. **As the twelve Apostles died off, the others did not select a new one to take his place. Thus the tradition of twelve men would not continue. When they died off, that ended that era, the Old Covenant tradition died with them. From the time of the death and resurrection of Christ on, the new Covenant was established. There was no longer Jew or Gentile, male or female and there was no longer only twelve.** Pentecost brought the fullness of power to all believers including both male and female.

One other fact about the twelve apostles, was that they were all Jews. If we want to cling to the tradition that they were all men, and for that reason a woman cannot be an apostle, shouldn't we be consistent and cling to the fact that they were all Jews too? Therefore no one but a Jew can be an Apostle today. Everyone recognizes and agrees that the old tradition of Jew only has been done away with, because under Christ there is no longer Jew or Gentile. Why can't everyone recognize and admit the same thing holds true concerning male and female, that is, that under Christ there is no male or female? Scripture says the same thing about both, there is neither Jew nor Gentile, male nor female.

Though women were not included as patriarchs and the original twelve apostles, there is sufficient evidence that they are chosen by God in ways that are just as important. Some in leadership positions, like Deborah and Junia and Phoebe and the daughters of Phillip, and others in other ways, no less significant.

God listened to women. Husbands, kings, and nations listened to them. All did as the woman said when she spoke in the power of the Lord. Are men today fighting against feminists or are they fighting against God when they refuse to give godly women places of leadership in churches and places of equal honor with the man in the home? God hates partiality in any form.

JUNIA

Junia is in Romans 16:7. Paul called this woman and Andronicus "of note among the apostles". The word "note" means remarkable and eminent. The name Junia was a common feminine Greek name. Up until the 13th century, most Bible commentators understood this to be a woman apostle. But in the 13th century a man substituted the name "Juliam" which is also a feminine name, but he pronounced this person to be a man. In the English versions of the Bible of today the identity of this person is masculine. So over the centuries male commentators have tried to carry out the tradition in order to substantiate that leadership ministries

183

were only for men. Paul acknowledged this woman, Junia, as an authority in the early church. He respected her. She and Andronicus were fellow prisoners and companions of Paul. They were Christians before Paul was. In Strong's, when one looks under the name Junias it says to look under Junia, which is a strong indication that the correct name is Junia.

I have read in a number of books that speak about the ancient fathers of the church of how one man named Chrysostom, promoted the idea that women were evil. One remark attributed to him was that among the wild beasts, there was none more harmful than a woman. Yet this same man is also attributed with a very positive saying that affirms that Junia was a woman who was worthy of the title of apostle. It is even more credible to believe he spoke the truth because of the time in which he lived, and because of the fact he was so anti-woman. She would have had to be outstanding for him to concede that she was an apostle. Given his abhorrence of women, he never would have said such a thing if it had not been absolute truth. He never would have attributed that honor to a woman, unless there was complete truth in the fact she was a woman and he couldn't deny it.

## PHOEBE

Paul called this lady "diakonos". There is an obscure word "diako" which means to run errands and to do menial things, like wait on tables. Many would have us believe that this is what Phoebe was. In many translations, in Romans 16:1 where Paul says , "I commend unto you Phoebe, our sister, who is a servant of the church of Cenchreae, "the word "servant" is deliberately substituted for the original "deaconess" because servant sounds like a lesser position. It demeans the office that she really held. Strong's says that the word "diakonos" means specifically a Christian teacher and pastor, minister, and servant. It includes male deacons and female deaconesses.

The word "diakonos" does not give a gender qualification. Paul's use of the word in reference to this lady, demonstrates that it does not have a gender qualification. Paul says she was the deaconess at the church in Cenchreae. In other words, she was the minister there, the pastor, the teacher. He has sent her as an official ambassador to the church of Rome. He wasn't sending her only as a messenger, a mere "diako", to deliver a message for him, because he said for the people in Rome to assist her in whatever business she had to do there. In other words she had other affairs of the church to attend to other than to just deliver a message from Paul. He gave her a favorable recommendation and introduction to them, saying she was a succourer of many. Again, in many translations, the word "helper" has been substituted for the word "succourer". Helper denotes a more menial job, whereas, a succourer in this case, is the feminine of the word proistemi which means to stand before, to preside, to maintain, to be over, and to rule. It is the same word that is used in connection with the word elders in I Tim 5:17. The feminine word is prostatis, it means patroness and assistant. Paul said that Phoebe had been a succourer of many and himself also. Since the word church in Rom. 16:1 is really plural, it appears as though Phoebe was the minister or pastor of the particular church in Cenchreae, but that she was an overseer who assisted in other churches and assisted Paul in his work as an apostle and overseer also. In the early church, diakonos meant the office of minister, later it took on a lesser meaning, such as we have today.

As I said, most translations say "Phoebe--a servant" rather than minister. It is the only place where the word has been translated this way. Every other time the person referred to as diakonos has been given the proper recognition afforded the office.

There is one other place where the mistranslation of a word takes away the right of women to be deaconesses. That is I Tim. 3:11 where many translations will say "so must the **wives be**". It should be, "so must **women** be" or "likewise must **women** be". This passage deals with the qualifications of deacons. Verse 11 is included in them. But by calling these women wives, instead of women, it means that they are only wives of deacons. They are not actually deacons themselves. By calling them women, it means they themselves hold the office of deacon apart from their husband. They must have the same qualifications as men. Verse 12 is the verse that is used to justify saying "wives" instead of "women". This verse is used to say that women can't be deacons in the same way a man can because it says a deacon has to be the **husband** of one wife. They say, "There is no way a woman could be the husband of one wife, therefore only men are deacons. This proves that God chooses only men to fill that leadership position. Paul said so." But this verse is not excluding women as deacons. It is an instruction for men only **because women did not need that instruction. Women did not have more than one husband! Only men practiced polygamy!!** Polygamy was not of God!! If the man wanted to be a deacon, he could have only one wife, he could not be practicing polygamy. That is in accordance with God's original pattern of marriage, because He only made one woman for the man. It is emphasizing that under the New Covenant, polygamy was no longer allowed. In the New Testament there is not one case of men in leadership having more than one wife such as is found in the Old Testament! Men adamantly deny that I Tim. 3:2,12 is referring to polygamy, but if one looks under that word in Nave's Topical Bible, it is listed under "polygamy forbidden", along with Titus 1:6 and Mark 10:2-8.

Some men who have done important scholarly works agree that it does refer to polygamy.

I Tim. 3:13 says "they" who serve in the office of deacon well, purchase for themselves a good degree and great boldness in the faith which is in Christ Jesus. The Amplified Bible says," For 'those' who perform well as deacons acquire a good standing for themselves and also gain confidence and freedom and boldness in the faith which is founded and centered in Christ Jesus." The words "they" and "those" does not distinguish male from female. "They" and "those" are neuter, neither male nor female. They are all inclusive. How is it that the words, "they" and "those", have been changed to mean "men only"?

If a woman is called, and gifted by God to be a deaconess in the fullest meaning of the word, as it was in the early church, meaning a minister, can man deny her the benefits and blessings that would come to her from serving well in that office? Is God and the church to be denied what He has ordained her to do? Is there deliberate misunderstanding of Scripture in order to support the partiality of gender distinctions concerning leadership roles in the church?

THE FOUR DAUGHTERS OF PHILLIP

Acts 21:9. In the first century church, prophecy was a ministry of preaching, teaching, or proclaiming the word to all of the believers. The prophet ministered to men and women alike to build up and edify all of the body. The body was no longer a separated group. Acts 2:41-47 is the picture of what the early church was like. Verse 44 seemed rather benign to me for years, but one day I did a word study on that verse and discovered something very significant hidden in it. The verse says that all that believed were together. The word "together" is a combination word. The first word means a superimposition of time, place, order etc. The second word simply means the feminine. Another spelling of it means neuter. The third word means a baffling wind + personal pronouns of her, she, other persons, him, self, etc. In grammar, a feminine word pertains to women. It's usage here is of great importance because it is indicating that the new order of things, under Christ, has been superimposed over the old order of things. For the first time women have been given the privilege of being together as participants with the men in the assembly of believers. There were no more distinctions made between male and female. They were all one in Christ. The wind of the Holy Spirit had fallen on men and women alike with all of His power and all of His gifts. Henceforth, **all** would worship, fellowship, pray, prophesy and participate in the assembly of believers for the benefit of all.

Acts 13:1,2 shows that the prophets and teachers had ministerial duties that included prayer, fasting, worshipping, receiving instruction from the Holy Spirit, laying on of hands, and commissioning others for ministry. The prophet was to receive and interpret divine revelation from God, and then to proclaim it to the believers. Prophecy is the understanding of knowledge and mysteries that are hidden from others. To be valid, other prophets must agree with every prophecy given, it must be in accordance with the Word, and it must lift up Jesus as Lord. The function of the teacher was to maintain the integrity of the Word as well as to understand and explain it to believers.

As prophets, these four daughters of Phillip were recognized as these kinds of ministers in their community. In this we see that God did choose women to serve in leadership roles. They did not minister to just women, but to all of the body. God did not exclude women, in deference to men, when He distributed His gifts. Forced deference to men was part of the old order. We are still under the book of Acts new order. God still chooses women to be apostles, prophets, teachers, ministers and evangelists. Some will teach that a woman can be a teacher. They will even admit that she can teach men, **IF** she has the permission of, and is under the leadership of, a man. Some admit that women can be evangelists, with a male "covering", so those two are allowed, with conditions. But the other three are denied her.

These are seven of the women God chose to fill leadership roles in the New Testament. There are others. But this is sufficient to establish the impartiality of the new covenant.

## CHAPTER EIGHT
## CALLED BY GOD, DENIED BY MAN

The church is so far from it's powerful beginnings because of the misinterpretations and misapplications of the Word. Men have altered the Word of God and have made it of no effect and powerless. Because of their misuse, the blessings of the Lord cannot be poured out in abundance on the church, just as the blessings could not be poured out on the Israelites.

I am just a woman, who has never been to Bible school, college or seminary. I have not studied Greek or Hebrew. Yet I was able to discover many of these distortions just by looking up the words in a concordance or a Bible dictionary. There are principles of grammar that I don't know. Even without knowing them, I was applying them because of what the Scripture and word studies were showing. It was clear. Many chapters of this book were written out of sequence. Most of it was already written before I had the following grammar lesson. A pastor clarified the underlying grammar principle that I was seeing and applying, but didn't know it existed. This principle has been ignored through the ages so that these passages on submission have been freely distorted. He explained that in the English grammar there are what is known as the active voice and the passive voice. The active voice means that the subject is the one doing the action. The passive voice means that the subject is the receiver of the action. Our English grammar has only these two voices. However, the Greek language has a third voice which is known as the middle voice. It means that the subject is the receiver of the action, but they also participate in the action. The most graphic example of this is found in chapter nine, where the word "hindered" from I Pet.3:7 is explained. Chapter Nine was written many months before I had this important little grammar lesson.

In all of these troublesome passages, concerning women's submission to husbands, the middle voice is used. This means the woman willingly submits to her husband **in response** to his actions of loving his wife like Christ, the head, loved the church. He initiates the action but she participates in it by willingly submitting to his action. Chapter 16, "Submit In Everything", clearly outlines what it is she is to submit to. Surprisingly, it is NOT what we have been taught that it means!

Highly educated theologians, Bible translators, commentators, and scholars have had this information and knowledge throughout the ages. They have studied Greek and Hebrew extensively. They have known the true meanings. Yet they have consistently hidden and distorted the truth of the Word down through the centuries in order to make these passages say that God issued an **imperative command** to the man to rule and for the women to submit to their husbands, in everything, with no qualifications, and with no exceptions to the rule. In these latter days, the distortion has been extended to mean that if a woman is not married, she should submit to her pastor as her spiritual head, in the same way she would submit to a husband. Not sexually, of course. My heart is deeply grieved that men who have been entrusted with knowledge and the Word have deliberately kept the truth of the Word hidden for centuries. The purpose is to substantiate and perpetuate false doctrine concerning the equality of genders and the subordination of women. It is a diabolical scheme of Satan to keep the division going that he started in the garden of Eden. By doing this, he fosters his own sin of arrogant pride in the male gender and keeps women from doing God's will.

The Old Testament ended with Malachi and God's condemnation of the priests, who He had entrusted with the Word, because they had perverted it by teaching partiality. I wonder what God is saying today about ministers, pastors and teachers who have perpetrated this same evil that permeates the beloved, blood bought, Church of Christ??!! The indwelling Holy Spirit teaches us, guides us in all truth, and empowers us to walk in that truth. The priests of old did not have the indwelling presence of the Holy Spirit like church leaders of today have. Because of that fact, I believe those who are responsible for this evil being promoted amongst us will be held doubly accountable for their teaching of partiality.

The misuse of the following terms has hindered God's work on earth because they have been altered too. The words are pastor, elder, deacon, bishop, overseer, and teacher.

To understand some of these distortions, we need to understand something about male and female. In most places in the Old Testament the word male is "zakar". It means "as being the most noteworthy sex". It also means mankind. In the New Testament, the word is "arrhen" or "arsen." It means "as stronger for lifting". By these meanings, one can see how the men of the Old Testament might presume that they were superior. But there is a drastic difference of meaning in the New Testament. Now there is only a superior physical strength. It shows clearly that the direction of the new covenant is neither male nor female in Christ. There is only a physical difference left. In Vine's, under the word "male" it refers to Gal. 3:28 where it says, "there can be no male or female, meaning there is no sex barrier to salvation nor to the development of Christian graces or gifts". I will add, there are no distinctions made concerning which gifts go to which gender either. All graces, and all gifts, are for all Christians. Not all Christians have every gift, but each one has the gift or gifts that God wants them to have according to His will, not according to gender.

We have just seen how the word "male" was

192

changed in meaning from the Old and New Testament. Now let's see what else it changed.

As far as I know, there were no verses in the Old Testament that gave women instructions to submit!! The words "submit" and "subject", as it pertains to women submitting in marriage, are New Testament words only!! The words, subject, subjected, submit, submitting, submitted are found 48 times in the Bible. 38 of those times are in the New Testament.

The old tradition of men being the most noteworthy sex prevailed in the Old Testament. Women were subservient to them as part of the tradition. There was no need for instruction on submission. Though I do not believe God ever intended it to be so, submission became the only option for women. But now, under Christ, it is clear that the new meaning of "male", brought a renewed meaning for submission. Because a male/female distinction no longer exists in Christ, and all old traditions had passed away, now there was a need for instruction for women and submission. These instructions are based on the grammar principle of the middle voice. The woman will voluntarily submit **because** of the man's godly, righteous behavior. THE FORCED INVOLUNTARY SUBSERVIENCE OF WOMEN IN THE OLD TESTAMENT TRADITION WAS NOW SUBJECT TO OPTIONS. The woman has the choice of submitting or not submitting according to the man's behavior. This is the principle of the middle voice. The principle is the same as how we all have a choice of submitting to Christ in spiritual things or not. If one is a Christian they will voluntarily subject themselves to His love and His righteousness. In the same way, a wife will voluntarily subject herself to the spiritual righteousness and love of Christ in her husband. **Submission for the woman is a whole new dynamic in the New Testament. Christ brought back the equality of genders like God intended it to be before the corruption of the**

**fall.** This truth is a supremely significant factor in understanding these abused passages concerning the submission of women.

Man is the word Anthropos. It refers to a human being, male or female, without reference to gender or nationality. There are many uses of the word "man" throughout the Word where man means any person. Man can be, and is, used to include female. It often has a generic meaning throughout the Word.

The word female cannot be used to refer to mankind because it means breast or one who suckles. That is a unique function of the female that cannot be duplicated by the male. Therefore, female cannot include the male gender like "man" can include the female gender as part of mankind.

With that clarification of terms, let us go on to find out what pastor, elder, deacon, bishop, overseer, and teacher means.

As far as I can see in my studies of the words bishop or overseer, and elders, there is no indications that these are masculine only. I find the emphasis in not on gender at all. The emphasis is on persons who are being raised up and qualified by the work of the Holy Spirit in them to do what God has appointed them to do. That is, caring for and exercising oversight over local bodies of believers.

The words bishop and overseer is the word episkopoi, indicating the nature of the work they are called to do. There is no gender qualification.

Elders is the word epeskopeo. These were people who were appointed when they demonstrated that their lifestyle was fulfilling God's qualifications. None of these specific qualifications were based on gender.

The word presbyter comes from the word presbuteroi which refers to spiritual maturity, not gender. It is evident in Scripture that there were to be more than one of these in a local body. All of these words indicate the kind of work to

194

be done. A godly lifestyle and spiritual maturity are the qualifying factors necessary to do the work, not gender.

Pastor or shepherd is the word poimen. It means one who feeds the flock spiritual food. More importantly, it means one who gives them careful and vigilant care. Acts 20:17, 28, indicates that a Christian pastor was called to do the same work that elders (bishops or overseers) were called to do. The actual word poimen has no gender distinctions either.

Teacher is didaktikos, meaning a person skilled in teaching. To teach is the word didasko and it means simply to give instruction. Neither word has any gender distinctions.

Deacon is diakonos, which was already explained in the last chapter, where we looked at Phoebe of Rom. 16:1. It primarily means a servant of the Lord doing the work of teaching and preaching in the church. Two synonymous words are, leitourgos, meaning one who performs public duties, and therapon, one who serves with freedom and dignity. None of these terms are gender distinctive.

These are the simple definitions of the words in question. To see how they have been distorted, we must go deeper yet.

In Vines, under the word Bishop-overseer there are several very interesting facts. A note says presbuteros, an elder, is another term for bishop or overseer. There is a reference to Acts 20:17, 28 and says the term elder indicates the mature spiritual experience and understanding of those so described. The term bishop or overseer indicates the character of the work they do.

Under the word episkope, Vine's refers to I Tim.3:1 where it says, "If a man desires the office of bishop" should literally be "If **anyone** seeketh overseership", because there is no word in the original language that represents the word "office". It is disturbing to me that most translations of the Bible do say "if a **man** desires the office of overseer". Man, referring to gender, is substituted for the word anyone which is neither masculine nor feminine. By substituting man, it indicates that this is for the male gender only. By calling it "the office of", it is set apart as a very distinctive leadership service that can be performed by men only. This kind of tampering with the Word is the basis of forming a hierarchy that did not exist in the earliest New Testament Church, and it excludes women from acting as presbyters or overseers, which they did in the early church.

Remember what we learned about Phoebe in the last chapter where the word "prostatis" was the feminine of the masculine word "proestemi" and how it is the same word used for elder in I Tim. 5:17? Because of that, I believe it has been clearly shown that Phoebe had oversight of at least one church and that she assisted other pastors, including the Apostle Paul, in the oversight of other churches as well. She, too, can be called a bishop, overseer, and elder in every sense of the word.

Another troublesome word is Elder, used in Tit.2:1,3. Tit.2:1 speaks of old or aged men. The term presbutes, comes from the word presbuteros which is a noun that means a senior. There is no gender associated with senior. In the Old Testament, it meant an Israelite member of the Sanhedrin, which was all men. In the New Testament, for the Christian, it means a presbyter. Though there is no gender distinction in this word, we shall see how man has made that distinction.

Tit.2:3 is speaking of older women. The term is presbutis. It means old or aged women. However, in the definition given, there is no reference to the fact that it's origin is also presbuteros.

So presbutes and presbutis have the exact same meaning. Yet it is said that the masculine word comes from presbuteros, meaning the presbyter for Christians. But by omitting the word presbuteros, from the feminine meaning, women can be prevented from functioning as presbyters. The facts are, if one looks under the word "woman" in Vine's, they would find that the word presbuteros is used there for older women, exactly as it is used for older men. Does the word have different meanings then, one for men and one for women? I find no differing definition!! It appears as though there has been a deliberate and treacherous attempt by men to continue the Old Testament traditions of keeping women subservient to men, especially in leadership in the church.

In context, both of these verses are giving qualifications for a bishop or overseer and what leaders should teach, each in their specific realms. It also gives qualifications for their personal life and character. Yet even though it is in the same context, men are given the dignity of acting as presbyters, but women are excluded from being presbyters. Even though they are called by God to be presbyters, they are denied that dignity and that calling by man.

Another point we must consider here is the word "likewise" in Titus 2:3. It comes from the word hosautos, which comes from two words. One means in the same manner or the like manner. It means, the way men are to be or to do, the women are to be and to do in that same way. The same duties, character and spiritual maturity, apply to both. The other part of the word is one we have come across before. It has the meaning of a baffling wind, coupled with the pronouns of self, she, her, itself, the other, him them, they. etc. Remember this was part of the word "together" in Acts 2:44. This is where the Wind of the Holy Spirit had fallen on men and women alike in all of His power and all of His gifts as a part of the new order of things that had been superimposed over the old order. The old order excluded women, but the new order includes them. It is very significant that this word is used here. It confirms that in the same manner that men took their place as presbyters, teaching younger men, so women were to take their place as presbyters, teaching younger women.

**There is a hidden truth here that men ought to recognize.** When the Lord gives gifts to whom so ever He chooses, He gives them to the those who can most effectively minister to His people. He gives men and women certain callings, but men have denied women the opportunity to use the callings God gives them. In denying the women that right, they have usurped the authority that was given to women. To "usurp" is to take a self appointed authority to minister where they were not appointed or anointed by God to do that job. In other words, they have put themselves in the place of teaching women, on their own authority, not the authority given them by God. They are appointed and anointed to teach the word to all, **but there are many women's issues, that they have not been called by God to deal with.** Women are to be pastors, elders, deacons and presbyters, who care for other women. **As a result of usurping the women's role and doing most of the teaching and counseling of women, men have put themselves in a most vulnerable spot. God has a built in protective plan, when He distributes His gifts. I believe that much of the immorality that happens between pastors and female congregation members, is a direct result of men overstepping the boundaries by taking leadership roles where women are supposed to be. They have usurped the authority and the functions of women that God ordained women to do. The women are called of God, but denied by men. By denying the women's callings, they have stepped out from God's protective plan, to their own harm.**

Even though some of this material will be a repeat of thoughts presented elsewhere in the book, to further illustrate how the perversion of submission has made shipwreck of the Church, let's look at Math. 20:25-28. The context is that the mother of James and John wants a special place of recognition for her sons. Jesus explains how the Gentile princes practiced "dominion and authority" over the people. It would not be like that in His Church. He said that whosoever (no gender) will be great among you, let him be your minister (diakonos). Whosoever, (no gender) will be chief among you, will be your servant (diakonos). Jesus did not come to be served or ministered to, he came to serve and minister to others, even to the point of dying for them.

What did He mean when he said the Gentile princes used dominion and authority over the people?

The word authority comes from the word autos meaning self and the word hentes, which means to work to exercise authority on one's own account, to domineer over, to have dominion. So authority means one who acts on their own to exercise authority or dominion over others. In other words, they lord it over others.

The authority to carry out any of the duties of elder, pastor, deacon, overseer, teacher, etc. comes only from God, never from man. (IICor.1:21) Therefore, in I Tim.2:12, Paul is not excluding women from teaching or pastoring or doing anything that God gives her the authority to do. The key word is "usurp", meaning one who takes it upon themselves to do these things without the appointment or anointing of God. This is what Paul is forbidding. He is not forbidding women to minister, he is forbidding them to do it without God's appointment and anointing!! The "usurping" is what he is forbidding.

Another key word in I Tim.2:12 is the word "permit" which means "entrust". Paul is not saying that woman is so inferior that he can't allow her to teach. That would be contrary to the rest of the Word. He was not putting forth a doctrine for the church to follow forever after. What he was saying is, in that new, infant church period, he could not entrust that responsibility to a woman, because up to that point, under the old order of things, women had been kept ignorant of the Word. They had been kept segregated and were non-participants in religious gatherings. For the first time they were being given the opportunity to learn. If they were just learning, how could he entrust them to teach at that time? As an analogy, we could not trust a first grader to teach a college class. But when he grew up and learned enough he would be entrusted to teach it. Because he was too young to know anything at one time, doesn't mean he would never be able to teach. This is what Paul was saying. He was not setting up a church doctrine. But that is how this Scripture has been misunderstood. Because of it, the church has been robbed of much fine teaching from women who have been given the knowledge, wisdom and authority to teach by God, but have been denied the opportunity to teach by man.

Another part of the passage in I Tim.2:11 is that women are to learn in silence and all subjection. This has also been distorted to mean that a woman shall never teach, she is only permitted to learn. Silence means a quietness or a tranquillity that comes from inside a person. Subjection means that they should quietly allow themselves to be persuaded about Christ and the Word of God and to learn what the men had to teach them. This subjection is in the middle voice that says the subject is a participant in the action. She is to quietly submit herself to his teaching. Paul was not laying down a decree that women should never teach if she is given the appointment by God to teach. Nor was he saying that her God given appointment to teach would always be subject to a man's permission, a man's approval, and only under a man's leadership.

By denying women the right to use their God given gifts, particularly leadership gifts, the churches have not only wounded their women, but they have robbed God of what is rightfully His. They have weakened the church and have taken another step into apostasy and powerlessness. It is the male leaders of the churches who have shown such partiality toward men, by discriminating against women in leadership roles. It is the male leaders who have robbed God. God cannot bless what robs Him and what He hates. Thus the church today is more like the oppressive pharisaical time just before Christ than it is the church of Acts.

One last comment on that. The meaning of the word usurp is to exercise authority on one's account to domineer over, to have dominion. This definition is consistent with the correct rendering of Gen. 3:16, where it says the woman's turning will be to her husband and that shall cause him to rule over her. The wife, because of her fallen nature, turns away from God, to the man. The man then begins to exercise authority over her on his own account. **He is not acting on God's authority, but he is acting on his own account because of his fallen nature.** This is what God prophesied would happen. I bring up this point because in so many Bibles there is a cross-reference to Gen. 3:16 as proof of what "subject" supposedly means here in I Tim.2:11.

Going back to the Matthew 20:25-28 passage, let us look at the word "dominion". This is the word kratos, meaning force, strength, might, manifested power. It is derived from a root word that means to perfect, to complete, and is probably connected to creator. It signifies dominion. Synonymous words are "bia", to use oppressive force. Dunamis, is inherent power; energia, power in exercise or operative power; exousia, primarily liberty of action and then either delegated or arbitrary authority; ischus, physical strength, power as an endowment. Kuriotes denotes lordship, power, dominion either human or angelic. The verb kurieuo, to lord over, rule over, have dominion.

These word studies are probably boring to most people, and one would want to jump over them as a meaningless, time consuming waste. But they are very important keys in understanding where the church is today and how it got there.

In the context of Matt. 20:25-28, the essence of what Jesus was saying is bound up in these meanings. He is saying that no one in the position of minister has any right to rule, dominate, have dominion or authority over any other person and their faith. **That is not a part of their calling.** This is firmly established in II Cor.2:21,24. 21 says "Now he who establisheth us with you in Christ, and hath anointed us, is God."(KJV) Paul is referring to himself, Timothy, and Silvanus as preacher/teachers who have been appointed by God to minister to the people at Corinth. Verse 24 says, even though we have been appointed by God to minister to you, **"Not that we have dominion over your faith, but are helpers of your joy; for by faith ye stand".** (KJV). This most definitely shows that no one, regardless of what ministry they have been called to do, has any right of dominion over anyone, each one stands alone in their own faith and walk with God. This is consistent with Malachi 2 where God says that even in the marriage relationship, He retains their spirits as His own.

In the passage in Matthew when Jesus said the Gentile rulers have dominion, he is using the word "katakurieuo, which is to exercise, or gain dominion over, to lord it over. This is the same word that is used in I Pet. 5:3. where Paul has instructed the "elders" that they should feed the flock, taking the overseership of them, not because they are forced to, but because they want to, not for money's sake, and not **"as being lords over God's heritage,** but by being examples to the flock".(KJV) This instruction implies that there is an inherent tendency for elders to think they have an obligation to lord it over, or to dominate, the saints under their spiritual care. Women are also God's heritage, no one has the right to lord it over them either. In Christ's Church, NO ONE is to lord it over, dominate, or dictate to ANYONE else. Jesus said it would NOT be like that in His Church. Two Christians, united in marriage, are a part of that Church. There should be no lording it over, dominating or dictating in that part of the church either.

Both II Cor.1:24 and I Pet.5:3 are saying that a deacon, pastor, elder, shepherd, teacher, etc. has no dominion over your faith. They have no right to dictate anything to you about what you are to do or not to do. They have no license from God to dictate anything. They are helpers only. They are to teach the Word, and what is right and good in God's sight. They are to correct error in doctrine.(James 5:19,20) They are to confront and help a person deal with moral sin (I Cor.5:1-8) etc. But they are never to dictate what a person has to do. The choice remains with the individual. If they choose to remain in sin or error, they must be warned that there are consequences that could include disfellowship. While there is discipline, it does not overrule the person's choice and free will. Each person stands alone in their faith. The leader's job is to inform the person of their sin, that repentance is necessary, what the consequences of their choices are, but they must let the person decide for themselves what they will do with that information. This is dealing strictly with sin, not other aspects of the Christian's life or God's individual giftings or callings.

A leader cannot dictate to anyone "This is how we worship here". "You can't use that gift here". "This is how you can use that gift here". "Women are not allowed to do that here". "You cannot do that ministry without my permission here." "Women cannot minister unless they are under the authority of their husband and pastor." etc. etc. etc. These things are all dealing with God's giftings and callings for an individual. The leader has been given NO authority over these things.

One final word that must be looked at to see how the perversion of submission has been inflicted on the church as a whole, is the word "obey". Today the word "obey", as used in Heb. 13:17, has been perverted to mean that the pastor has the right of dominion, or the right to control what happens with the flock. It is said that he is the one whom God has put in charge of the congregation. This is because the verse says, "obey them that have rule over you and submit yourselves, for they watch for your souls, as they must give account, that they may do it with joy, and not with grief". (KJV) The word "obey" here is the word peitho. The definition means to convince by argument, right or wrong, to assent to authority, to have confidence, persuade, trust, yield. **All of this is in that middle voice again,** that says the leader will speak truth in such a way that his followers will be persuaded to follow his example in following God. Vine's says it does mean to persuade, to win over, to be persuaded, to listen to. We see clearly how the leader is to use truth to persuade, this is the action part. We also see clearly how that action is received by the follower so that they allow themselves to be persuaded to follow. This is following God and his word, not the man. This is the recipient and participant part of the middle voice usage. It, in no way, tells the pastor he has the right of dominion because it says "obey". "As one who must give account", because he "watches over their souls", has been twisted to mean that he will give an account to, or will be held responsible by God, **for what the individuals in the flock under him DO.** Therefore, follow him and obey his every word for you so that his work will not be a grief for him now and when he gives that account to God. The word "account" is the word "logos" which is "The Word". Rather than give an account for what people under his leadership **do,** he will be held accountable for the Word that he teaches. He will be held accountable for the content of what he teaches and for how he uses the word to persuade others to follow God. If he uses it to persuade others to follow him and his dictates because he is their leader, he is perverting the Word for his own benefit. He will be held account- able by God for perverting God's gifts and God's calling for his own personal gain. The people under the teacher are responsible to allow themselves to be persuaded by the truth that he teaches. They are also responsible to discern what **IS** truth and to reject it if is not truth.

These are the distortions of the word that have been passed down through centuries of church history. They have been altered so that God's true Word has become impotent and ineffective and so have His people.

The old Jewish and old covenant traditions have become pre-eminent is His church. The authority that is now on a woman's head is the exousia power, the power that God has delegated to her to do the ministry service that He calls her to do. Women are held in oppressive bondage, and are denied the freedom to use the gifts bestowed upon them by God. So the church operates with a disability or a handicap, like a person who has lost the use of eyes and limbs etc. They can function, but not at full capacity. Many men are denied the use of their gifts also because of how everyone is to bow to the church leader's authority. The leaders have become pre-eminent, like the priests and pharisees of old. Therefore they have become wells without water. They have no springs of living water bubbling up and flowing out to nourish the Church.

Women are called by God to be a functioning part of the body, in all areas of giftings. We saw in the last chapter how men have denigrated the callings of great women of the Bible, denying that they are examples for today's women to follow. In this chapter we see how man has ignored that middle voice principle in order to keep women subservient in the home and in the church. Man resolutely continues to deny the woman her rightful place in Christ. Women are called by God but are denied that calling by man. Thus much of the church is powerless and lifeless because it functions at half capacity or less. Man has gone to great lengths to preserve the Old Testament subservience of women. It is time for men to repent and for women to rise up to do the work they were called to do by God.

CHAPTER NINE
PRINCIPLES THAT DESTROY

I have personally attended 7 seminars, all taught by the same man, that changed my life for the good. Therefore, it grieves me to say that much of what is being taught today concerning submission and headship comes from these seminars and this teacher's seminars for Ministers. A very careful study reveals gross errors in some of the material. I will use selected teachings to show how they undermine the worth and value of women in today's Christian society, how they promote idol worship of the male gender, and how apostasy creeps into the church.

This chapter discloses 12 principles in the teachings that are blatant Scriptural distortions. They were the most grievous to me personally. After I had applied these principles to my life, God revealed how wrong they were by the fruit they produced in my life and through Scripture.

I believe this kind of distorted teaching has caused much woundedness in Christian women and divisions in marriages. If these teachings were only from one man, teaching in his own pulpit, it would be harmful to only a few. Though it is taught by one man, it is reproduced in thousands of pulpits across America because of the way the material is preached in the minister's seminars and is then used for counseling resources by many. The potential for wide spread harm is astronomical. Sadly, that potential is being reached. The affect is the same as mainlining drugs. Drugs are injected into the blood stream so they can rapidly spread throughout the body. In this case, the injection is the seminars. The teachings are taken back and fed directly into the bloodstream of the church body, where it spreads rapidly.

These principles are quoted from the Institute of Basic Youth Conflicts Syllabus, Section Title

"Responsibility", Sub section "Seven Basic Needs of A Husband." Author Bill Gothard, Copyright 1968-1975. Page 1. His direct quotes will be in quotation marks. My comments, explaining my point of view, will be prefaced by, MY COMMENTS:
 "1. A husband needs a wife who respects him as a man.
 A man wants to prove his manliness.
 How does a wife destroy her husband's manliness?
 B. By being financially independent.
 1. Love is killed through self sufficiency.
 2. Whoever controls the money, controls leadership.
 * Center your work and your ministry in your home."
MY COMMENTS: False Principle #1: There were no Scriptures given. Supposedly, if I am self-sufficient and financially independent, that represents my lack of respect for my husband. Thus I am destroying his manliness, and his love for me. Control of money equates with leadership. This says to me that I need to allow him to control me with money in order for him to feel like a man and to feel respected. By being financially independent I usurp his authority as the leader in our home. Is a man's manliness and his love for me based on money? If so, he's on pretty shaky ground, so am I and so is our marriage.
 The Proverbs 31 woman is always held up as an example of a perfect godly wife. I found that was a better foundation for me to build on than a philosophy which has no Scripture.
 The Proverbs 31 woman was a virtuous woman. In the King James Version and the Septuagint she is called "woman". In other versions, she is called "wife". I believe "woman" is more correct because that gives the woman worth,

separate from her husband, it gives her an
individual identity, and it includes single
women as virtuous women.

The passage talks about the virtues of this
woman. First, her husband is blessed because
of her virtues. The Scripture says "Blessed
is he who finds a virtuous woman." The word
find means to appear, to exist, acquire, meet
or be present. She is already virtuous when
he finds her! She does not become virtuous
because he marries her. These virtues are
priceless in any woman, not just a wife. If
a man finds a woman like this, he is indeed
blessed. The word virtue in Hebrew means wealth,
able, activity, might, power, riches, strength,
strong, valiant. She is rich and wealthy, she
is strong in mind and body, she is able and
active in many spheres of life, she has might
and power and she's valiant. So this woman is
considered virtuous **because** of her self
sufficiency! She did not rely on her husband
to make all the decisions for her or to tell
her what to do. Nor did he expect her to.
He did not control the money to show his leadership or his manliness. Leadership, headship,
or manliness has nothing to do with controlling
money!! The heart of this lady's husband trusted
her. Because of her, he will lack no gain.
In other words, her abilities and wise ways with
finances will help to bring him prosperity.
She goes out and makes a real-estate deal on
a field. She takes **her** earnings, that she has
already earned from somewhere, and plants a
vineyard in the field. That's buying and in-
vesting. She provides clothing for the whole
household. She uses her home as a manufacturing
base to make clothing to sell. Then she goes
out and finds a retailer to sell it for her.
That's manufacturing and marketing. She is a
sound business woman. She manages her maid-

servants and oversees all the household chores. She's a domestic engineer. There is no indication that her husband feels that she is showing him disrespect. Nor does it show that her self sufficiency was a cause of his diminished or dying love for her. Rather, there is a cross reference in this passage that indicates that because of her abilities she was a crown to him when he sat in the gates. (Prov. 12:4). Her husband actually loves her more and praises her and tells her she is the most excellent of all women. Her virtues are known for what they are. The fruit of her own personality and productivity. The final verse says ,"Give her the fruit of **her hands** and let **her own works** praise her in the gates." Though her husband is an important man, his wife will be known by important people because of herself and her own accomplishments, not because he is important.

Am I putting too much emphasis on this passage? Is it important for a woman to have an individual self worth, apart from just being somebody's wife? If she is to be a woman of virtue, she must feel good about herself. She must have confidence in herself. Verse 18 says it all. "She perceives that her merchandise is good." She knows that she is being all that God intended her to be. She knows that she is doing all that God gave her the ability to do. She feels good about herself. Her children feel good about her, they praise her. Rather than losing his love for her, her husband feels good about her, he praises her. Her goodness, her reputation and her accomplishments brings her praises from the elders who sit in the gates. Her self sufficiency brings him respect and honor from his peers.

She is a lady of ministry. It starts in the home but it reaches beyond her house to the poor and needy. She opens her mouth and speaks wisdom and kindness. This wisdom she speaks is not only worldly wisdom of how to keep house etc. because this word is the same word that is used in other Proverbs and it is a wisdom that comes from the Lord. She does not sit on the side lines and wait for her husband to speak. She speaks out openly and unreservedly of the wisdom she knows from God. The wisdom and kindness she speaks ministers to people. She is a vibrant lady who is out and about doing the Father's business.

In light of this one passage of Scripture, can you see how the application of this one false principle, a tradition of men, because it has no scriptural basis, can destroy a woman's worth? How it undermines her confidence in all that she would set her hand to do? How it would rob her of all initiative to be or to do anything that God called her to do? Do you see how it would wound and destroy, and bring her into domination by the man? Can you see how God's prophetic word "You will turn to your husband and he shall dominate you" is being fulfilled? Just think of what she is yielding over to the man in obedience to a false philosophy of man. Finally, do you see how it elevates a man to the place of an idol for his wife?

In my own life the control of money was a weapon used to keep me bound. It was a tool of ungodly control and manipulation. I had access to the checkbook and I paid the bills, but at the same time, I was scolded for every penny I spent. I had no financial freedom and no money of my own. I felt guilt when I had to buy necessities for the family. For most of those years my ex-husband did not want me to work. He told me many times, "You could never support yourself", thus reinforcing how inadequate I was and how I needed to depend on him to survive.

While there is no Scripture to base this

philosophy of man on, there is yet another Scripture, besides Prov. 31, that comes to my mind concerning control of money demonstrating headship. The Scripture is , "the love of money is the root of all evil". Controlling money to demonstrate manliness and headship is a demonstration of the love of money. It is the root of evil in a family. It is promoting an ungodly, carnal, system of the world, rather than demonstrating godly headship and manliness. A major cause of marital conflict and divorce is money!!

Another principle to show how a woman supposedly destroys her husband's manliness comes from the same syllabus, same section, subsection and page.

"C. By greater loyalty to outside leadership.
    1. Pastor and church leader.
    2. Men and women Bible teachers.
    3. Relatives and friends.
*Ask your husband your spiritual questions, I Cor.14:35"

MY COMMENTS: False Principle #2: This principle sets up a doctrine of not asking spiritual questions from anyone but one's husband. It is built on one verse that is giving instruction to the new believers, who were ALL to learn the Scripture but only the men had been privileged enough to know the Scripture thus far. So it is a matter concerning that period of time and a custom that was being changed by the new order of Christ. In actuality, men were being told to teach their wives, and the wives were to quietly learn what the men had to teach. This false doctrine ignores Scripture that says spiritual things are spiritually discerned and they cannot be understood by the carnal man. Therefore, a husband who does not have the Holy Spirit, through rebirth in Christ, cannot discern them or know them. How can he teach what he does not know? This doctrine excludes men and women as a source for the teaching and edification of other believers. It is exclusiveness and isolation, perfect breeding ground for error. This doctrine ignores the verses that say pastors and teachers are for All believers. This teaching does not take into account the fact that an infant Christian husband would lack the knowledge of the word and the wisdom to apply it, whereas a pastor/teacher has been equipped by God to do it.

This doctrine sets aside all other Scripture as a means of learning and centers only on a tiny part of a verse that says, "Let her ask her husband at home". If this doctrine is correct, who is to teach the unmarried? Who do they ask? If this is true doctrine, in Luke 10:38-42 Jesus should have told Mary that she should not sit at his feet to learn. She should go to her brother, since she had no husband. Instead he told Martha that Mary had chosen the better thing and He would not take that away from her!!! Jesus himself was doing away with that kind of old tradition. In Acts 18:24-28, Appolos should have refused instruction from Priscilla. Timothy should not have received instruction from his godly mother and grandmother. There are many examples of godly women in the New Testament who taught and were listened to by men. It seems that those Scriptures and the ones saying that God gave pastors, preachers, prophets, and teachers for the whole body are also discredited.

Is a man's manliness so fragile that he can not handle his wife asking a spiritual question from anyone but him? Is he God, that he alone should have all the answers for her? The author's list excludes everyone except the husband that the woman could ask from. How does it show disloyalty to admit that someone else is better equipped to answer her spiritual questions because God, in His wisdom, has equipped them to do so? The one Scripture given as a basis for this principle has a distorted meaning.

God removed my ex-husband from the pulpit because of the perversions in his life and the resultant distorted teaching. If I had relied on my ex-husband to teach me, I would still be lost and walking in the same darkness, deception, and error of his perverted teachings!! God forbid that I should learn only from him and remain loyal to that!!!

Going on to the next principle that will destroy the husband's manliness, in the same syllabus, same section and sub-section, same page we see the following:

"D. By resisting his decisions in your spirit.

1. A wife's spirit controls her husband's ambition.

* Learn how to wisely appeal to your husband."

MY COMMENTS: False Principle #3: NO SCRIPTURE. I agree that a wife's spirit can influence how a man feels. It can be an encouragement or a hindrance. But it does not control the man. He is responsible for what he does himself. It is a proven fact that most men have a competitive drive within themselves to succeed in their jobs and careers that is independent from how their wife motivates them. The man will often sacrifice intimacy of relationship with his wife in order to fulfill that drive.

However, under this kind of teaching, if a man refuses his wife's "appeal", the man can definitely control his wife by his decisions. What effect does it have on the woman's spirit when he makes wrong decisions that she knows are wrong, decisions that have a direct negative or destructive effect on her or the children and yet she has to bow to that wrong decision?

Does that not truly kill her initiatives with hopelessness? Her spirit is just as sensitive as the man's. She is destroyed when her right decisions are thwarted in favor of his wrong ones. She is completely annihilated as a person by this wrong teaching of "submit in everything". There are times when the Holy Spirit in the woman MUST resist the man's evil decisions!

As for learning how to appeal to the husband, there are some men who would listen but there are many who would not listen to an appeal of any kind. Nor would they accept any kind of appeal. There is another chapter concerning this subject of appeals and it's distortions by this author.

Again, since there is no Scripture to base this principle on, it too, is nothing more than traditions of men that promotes division in marriages and hopelessness for women.

As you will see in a later chapter, I applied this principle of submission for 34 years. I will admit that some times I was not able to have the right "spirit". But much of the time I did. That, along with years of applying the right kind of "appeals" proved to be fruitless.

Continuing to quote from the Institute Of Basic Youth Conflicts Syllabus, Section Title, "Responsibility", Sub-section "Seven Basic Needs of A Husband" Page 2. Author Bill Gothard, Copyright 1968-1975. Sub title, "II. A Husband Needs A Wife Who Accepts Him As A Leader And Believes In His God-Given Responsibilities."

"What are the basic needs of a leader?

A. Reassurance that his authority comes from God.

1.Husbands are **commanded to govern** (emphasis mine) their wives.(Gen3:16)

2. Wives are **commanded to submit** to husbands. Eph.5:22; Col.3:18; I Pet.3:1 (Emphasis mine)

3. A wife's submission qualifies her husband

for church leadership. I Tim3:4,5.

4. The headship of the husband is illustrated in Christ and the church. I Cor.11:3.

*Reassure your husband that he is your God-given head."

MY COMMENTS: False Principle #4. Gen. 3:16, God gave the man the COMMAND to govern his wife. We have already studied how the wrong interpretation of the verse is the basis for this wrong teaching. God was speaking to the woman, so it wasn't a command from God to the man for him to govern her or for her to submit to his governing. God never took away the woman's right to make a choice or decision and He never took away her own free will. The author refers to Eph. 5:22 to prove that women are to submit to their husbands, but he ignores Eph. 5:21 which says "Submit to **one another** out of reverence for Christ". It does not say a woman is commanded to submit to her husband because he is her husband, it says submit to ONE ANOTHER out of REVERENCE FOR CHRIST. The submission here in these verses is referring to a voluntary submission to the husband's godliness, not a COMMAND to submit!! As we saw in Chapter 8, the use of the middle voice here is the basis for voluntary submission rather than a command.

Col.3:18 says, "Wives submit to your husbands, as is fitting in the Lord." But the balancing Scripture, which is ignored, is "Husbands love your wives and don't be bitter against them". Col.3:19. Bitter here means sharp and piercing. Chapter 19 in this book tells what kind of submission is fitting in the Lord.

I Pet.3:1-6 gives instruction on how the wife is to dress and act that she might win her husband. It says, "In the same way, be submissive to your husband." In the same way as what? This is referring to the sufferings of Christ spoken of in I Pet. 2:18-25. Here it is being distorted to say that no matter how a woman is treated by her husband, she must suffer anything that he chooses to do to her, just like Christ did. But is that really what it means? Christ did not always suffer, but fled when it was not the Fathers will for him to suffer (John 10:39), Jesus "went forth" from that place of danger. It is my opinion that "in the same way" means what it says in I Pet. 2:23, that He did not retaliate and He made no threats. He entrusted himself to the Lord. This is consistent with the "purity and reverence of your life" in I Pet. 3:2, and "of your inner self, the unfading beauty of a meek and quiet spirit" in verse 3. It is consistent with I Pet.3:8-9 that says "--live in harmony with one another, be sympathetic, love as brothers, be compassionate and humble. Do not repay insult with insult, ----evil with evil, but with blessing, because you were called so that you may inherit a blessing." As I said, Christ endured suffering when it was the Father's will for him to do so. He did it with meekness and without retaliation, but when it was not the Father's will, he was still meek and did not retaliate, **but he did leave the situation.** He did not stay there to suffer whatever anyone wanted to do to him. There was balance. We are not called to stay in a situation that is extremely destructive to us, unless that is God's will for us. We are instructed to be meek and to have a quiet spirit. Some suffer for Christ's sake, and there is reward in that. Some suffer because of their own choices. There is no value in sufferings that one causes oneself to endure because they are following wrong teachings. I Peter 3:17 seems to confirm this because it says, "For it is better **IF THE WILL OF GOD BE SO,** that you suffer for well doing than for evil doing". It is not always His will for one to suffer.

217

The meaning of "if" here is conditional. This passage is not laying down a command that all wives stay in a suffering mode for the rest of their lives. The husband referred to here is unsaved or backslidden. **He is not the norm, he is the exception.** This is teaching how one is to behave IF it is the Lord's will for her to be in that exceptional situation. It is not teaching that this is the norm and that every woman in that situation is commanded to remain in it!! The balancing Scriptures and the leading of the Holy Spirit determine if it's the Lord's will in each individual case.

I Pet.3:7 is the balance to 3:1. It says, "husbands, dwell with them according to knowledge, giving honor to the wife as to the weaker vessel AND as being heirs together of the grace of life, so that your prayers be not hindered". Giving honor has to do with esteem. According to knowledge is referring to the fact that the husband should know his wife so well that he will know what to do to raise her self esteem. He will know what to do and say that will bring her up to her best. The weaker vessel is not inferior in worth or value, and though it is weaker physically, it means he is to demonstrate godly character to her to reinforce spiritual truth that he speaks to her. Why should he treat her with honor? Because they are BOTH heirs of the grace of life. If he doesn't treat her this way his prayers will be hindered. What does the grace of life mean? How does it relate to honor? According to Vine's Expository Dictionary of Old and New Testament words, honor has to do with value. A price that is being paid or received for something. Some of the meaning of honor and the grace of life together is the honor and inestimable value of Christ Himself that is bestowed on those who believe, who are joined together as living stones with

Him as the Corner Stone.  I believe that when
the man is told to give honor to the wife, it
means that he needs to recognize that he has
no more value than she does  and that Christ
is the same in her as He is in him.  Christ's
worth and the price he paid has brought the same
value to the woman that was bestowed upon the
man.  They are joint heirs.  When the man thinks
he is superior to her, and he  has the right
to make all decisions, he is not honoring her.
He is not demonstrating trust in her  or her
value.  Or trust in God either.  He is tearing
her down.  He is denying her value in the Lord.
He is denying Jesus' value in her.  He is
demonstrating that he believes  his  mind  and
his judgments are superior to hers.  He denies
that she, too, has the mind of Christ, and the
mind of Christ in her has been discounted as
null and void, making her inferior to him.

Because these particular instructions are
for the husband, it says that  **his** prayers will
be hindered.  The word hindered here is very
interesting.  In Vine's it is the word EKKOPTO
and it means to cut out, repulse. It says the
"prayers are hindered through low standards of
marital conduct".  So the way a man honors his
wife determines whether she will want to pray
with him, accept his leadership  or whether she
will be repulsed by it. It also means that if
his conduct of honoring his wife is not acceptable
to God, God will be repulsed by his prayers.
The man's marital conduct is the basis for the
submission of the wife!! This again substantiates
the use of  the middle voice in submission of
the woman to the man.

In this false principle, the verses are
taken out of context so that the false teaching
on submission sounds so biblical,  but it is
not biblically sound or correct teaching.  The
biblical truth is that though the verse says

"women submit", it is really the husband who carries the responsibility of motivating his wife to submit by the way he honors her as an equally valuable, blood bought, individual in Christ. She is an heir, equal to him. There is no honor to be found in the domination of the man over the woman.

I Tim.3:4-5 is used here to say "A wife's submission qualifies her husband for church leadership". The verses say "A man rules his own house well, having his CHILDREN in subjection with all gravity, for if a man knows not how to rule his own house, how shall he take care of the church of God?" This verse is not speaking about the woman's submission at all. It is speaking entirely about a man's character. It speaks of the man's ability as a father, to bring up his children in the ways of the Lord. It speaks of disciplining them in a way that they will learn to respect their father with dignity. They would be well behaved children. Their respectful good behavior would demonstrate the man's ability to train and discipline, in love, without causing discouragement, rebellion or wrath in the children. If he can demonstrate this through his children, then he is qualified to be a leader in the church. It is not a demonstration of being the boss, ruling with an iron fist over the wife and children or dominating them. It is, rather, a show of his own godly character. This goes back to what I just wrote. His conduct determines whether the wife and the children will accept his leadership or whether they reject it. This, then, is what determines whether people in the congregation will follow his leadership or if they would reject it. That is what qualifies him for leadership, not his wife's submission!!! One last comment, Prov. 14:26 says that the reverence (or fear) of the Lord gives a man deep strength and his children will have a place of refuge and security. So, the man's closeness to God determines how he rules his house.

A man can dominate his wife and children into outward submission but inwardly he is building resentment and rebellion in them that will surface sooner or later. Unless his leadership is according to God's standards for **HIS** character, he disqualifies himself as an elder.

Again, I ask the question, can you see how this false teaching takes away the woman's dignity as an individual in Christ, makes her into a mere shadow of the man and elevates the man to the place of an idol?

Concerning I Cor.11:3. The focus here is on "the head of woman is man". As in other passages, this one also has a cross reference to Genesis 3:16. It still stands on that same old distorted meaning. The focus should be on how **was** Christ the head of the church and how **was** God the head of Christ. The study in previous chapters about headship clearly demonstrates what headship really means. It certainly was never demonstrated by the Father nor by Jesus that their headship divested anyone of their right of decision and their own free will. Matthew 20:25-28 and Mark 10:42-45 says, "You know the rulers of the Gentiles lord it over them. **Not so with you.** Instead, whoever wants to become great among you, must be your servant, and whoever wants to be first must be your slave, just as the Son of Man did not come to be served, but to serve and to give His life as a ransom for many". Here, Jesus Himself is saying this is how the "chain of command" works **in the world.** The rulers of the world lord it over the people under them. They use their position as a right to dominate. In other words, the higher officials dictate rules and make decisions and expect the people to carry out their dictates. The people have no right of decision. Those under the highest officials, carry out their commands and those under them are expected to do the same. **Chain of command is a system of the world. But Jesus said that believers in Him would not operate that way.** He did away with that kind of "chain of command" entirely. He said, "Not so with you". You will not lord your position over anybody. INSTEAD, the word instead means that one thing is replaced with something else. INSTEAD, anyone, (that includes husbands as heads of families), in order to demonstrate that headship would not dictate to anyone and take away the right of choice or decision from anyone but would become servants to those under their headship. He said the way to be head was to put self last. That simple teaching by Christ Himself did away with the concept of head or ruler or authority in his people as being someone to dictate and take away all right of freedom of choice and decision from anyone under that headship or that authority. But this teaching of Christ Himself is ignored by those teaching the wrong doctrine concerning the headship of husband over the wife!! I agree with Scripture. The headship of the husband should imitate the illustration of Christ and the Church. So let's make sure we are looking at the correct illustration, the one Christ Himself gives us and not the one man wants us to see. The chain of command as taught here, and by many other like-minded teachers, elevates the man to the first place, rather then the last place. A place where everyone in the family bows to him and his decisions. They serve him, whether he is right or wrong. **It is exactly opposite of what Christ said the head should be. It is an exact copy of the system of the world. It is ungodly, false teaching.**

In the same syllabus, same section and

subsection, etc. page 2 and under the subheading:
"What Are The Basic Needs of a Husband:
    B. Confidence that God is working through him.
    1. God works through a **man's** decisions good or bad. (Emphasis mine)
    2. Bad decisions reveal his needs and allows his wife to appeal and demonstrate godly character.
    3. The more the wife trusts her husband, the more careful he will be in giving her direction.
    *When your husband makes a bad decision, explain how God is using it to benefit your spiritual life."
MY COMMENTS: False Principle #5. There are no Scriptures given again. The false principle is that I must abide by every decision my husband makes. Right or wrong. When he makes bad decisions, I can appeal to him and then stand by, hopelessly waiting for him to change his mind. Remember, we are talking here about EVERY DECISION HE MAKES. That includes his decisions about the children, which could prove to be totally destructive for them, emotionally and perhaps physically. It can mean financial ruin, where the wife has to hear irate bill collectors over the phone or at the door. It does no good to say to them, "You have to talk to my husband," because by this time she has already born the brunt of their demeaning harassment. It has already done it's damage to her emotions. I could go on and on. But, knowing that she is helpless to do anything, she must then tell him how God is making her a better person because he is too stubborn or bullheaded to listen to reason. Then, she just bears the consequences of his wrong decisions.
    Though this philosophy has no Scripture, some other Scriptures come to my mind, such as, "come, let us reason together", and "stubbornness is as the sin of idolatry". Proverbs is full of admonitions about foolish and wrong decisions, and how

we should avoid those people who consistently make them. Yet through this philosophy, women are told to embrace this foolishness as a means of spiritual growth. And then they are to commend the husband for giving them this opportunity to grow spiritually. She is to trust him more. Never mind the Scriptures that say, "don't trust in the arm flesh for it will fail you". And others that say not to put your trust in man, but in God. And that "to trust in man is a snare". In my own life, the more I trusted my ex-husband, the more I was taken advantage of. That won't be everyone's experience, but it was mine. A marriage license does not automatically make a man trustworthy! Becoming a Christian does not automatically and instantly make him wise and mature either.

My Bible does not tell me that God will work for me ONLY through my husband or ONLY through a man. My Bible says God works in and through me, too, as one of His children. There is only one mediator between God and me and that is Jesus Christ. God works directly in my life as a believer and as an individual. It is heresy to say God will work in my life ONLY through my obedience to my husband's every decision, right or wrong. I will be held accountable by God for every wrong decision I make, whether it is a wrong decision I've made on my own or a wrong response because of my husband's decision. This is blind obedience to man. It is idolatry. It is condemned by God.

We will go to point C in this same section, same page.

"C. Loyalty when mistakes are made and pressures increase.

1. Loyalty can only be demonstrated in adversity.

2. A husband's trust in his wife is often misinterpreted as taking her for granted.

*Never ask others for counsel without your husband's approval."

MY COMMENTS: False Principle #6. Again there is
no Scripture. The principle is that I can demonstrate loyalty to him only in times when he is
making mistakes and things are going wrong for
him as a result of his bad decisions. No matter
how often this happens and no matter how bad
things get, I should never share my burden with
a counselor or anyone unless he gives me permission
to do so. Loyalty is NOT demonstrated only in
adversity. It does not mean that one upholds
somebody in wrong doing. It does mean that I am
loyal enough to confront him. Proverbs 27:5,6
says, "Open rebuke is better than secret love.
Faithful are the wounds of a friend, but the kisses
of an enemy are deceitful". This says to me that
my loyalty to my husband requires me to confront
him. If I don't, I'm being deceitful to him and
I am like an enemy to him. It means that I love
him, whether he's making mistakes or not. Whether
things are going good or bad for him, I love him.
I forgive him. Everybody makes mistakes. My
dictionary says loyal means to be constant and
faithful in a relationship. But for a teaching
to demand that a woman sit idly by and let her
husband destroy them or their children through
consistently making bad decisions is folly,
foolishness. Scripture says that a man like that
has no self-control and no good reasoning. Proverbs
25:28 says "He that hath no rule over his own spirit
is like a city that is broken down and without
walls." Proverbs 26:1-12 are all about foolish
men. Verse one says "As snow in summer and rain
in harvest, so honor is not fitting for a fool."
Verses 4-5 say that we're not to answer a fool
according to his folly or we'll become like him
and that he will become wise in his own conceit.
To continually allow a husband to make bad
decisions, uphold him and encourage him in them
and then say it's a good way for the wife to grow
spiritually is complete foolishness. She will

become as foolish as he is and she will encourage more of the same behavior. She encourages conceit and PRIDE. She is NOT demonstrating loyalty, she is destroying him. There is a balance that one must reach. One's trust in the Lord will determine what course should be taken in each instance. Sometimes it would mean comforting and consoling. Sometimes it would mean confronting and disagreeing with them. But always loving and always faithful. The author did not state that the mistakes being made were on a consistent on-going basis. But neither did he state any limitations on how often this happens either. Therefore, I took the liberty to give the worst case scenario.

As for seeking counsel, often times a man would never approve of his wife talking to anybody. His pride would forbid it. Most often, desperation drives the wife to seek counsel while he is saying there is no problem. The counseling that women seek, even without the husband's approval, is often what saves the marriage. He is forced to come out of denial, face the issues, and deal with them.

We are still in Basic Youth Conflicts Syllabus, Section Title "Responsibility", Sub section, "Seven Basic Needs of a Husband". Page 3, and cont. on page 4. Author Bill Gothard, Copyright 1968-1975. Sub Title: "III A HUSBAND NEEDS A WIFE WHO WILL CONTINUE TO DEVELOP INWARD AND OUTWARD BEAUTY.

Ephesians 5:24 How Can You Become More of the Wife of Your Husband's Dreams.?

    A. Hair---Symbol of Being Under Authority (I Cor. 11:10)

       1. Hair "is given her for a covering" (I Cor. 11:15)

         2. Hair is a basis for spiritual protection (I Cor.11:11)

         3. Hair is a woman's glory. (I Cor. 11:15)

         4. Hair style MUST reflect the husbands' wishes. (Eph.5:24) (Emphasis mine)

# PRINCIPLES THAT DESTROY

*Extra Time and Effort--Expression of Reverence
*Discover and conform to your husband's real wishes.
* Encourage him to learn principles of hair styling.
EXPLAIN YOUR HAIRSTYLE TO OTHERS ON THE BASIS OF
SUBMISSION TO AUTHORITY."
MY COMMENTS:False principle #7. The principle here
is that I do not have a right to my own personal
tastes or desires concerning my own grooming.
It is based on one lonely little part of a verse,
Eph. 5:24, that says "therefore as the church is
subject unto Christ, so let the wife be to her
husband **in everything.**" (There is a surprise meaning
to the word "everything" in a later chapter devoted
to this verse). This means that even if I feel
like I look horrid in a certain hair style, I MUST
conform to his wishes and wear my hair that way.
Then, it is assumed that everyone who thinks my
hair style is awful too, will ask me about it.
No one in my lifetime has ever approached me and
volunteered the information that my hair looked
awful to them! Neither have I ever been asked why
I was wearing my hair in such an unbecoming style.
But if either event should happen, then I will
have the glorious, golden opportunity to tell them
"I am wearing my hair this way because it is my
husband's favorite style. Even though it is very
unbecoming to me, I want to demonstrate my submission to his authority." Wouldn't this entice you
to follow my example? Wouldn't it entice an
unbeliever to come to Christ? Does it honor Christ
or God? I think not. Truly, it would repulse
believers and unbelievers alike. But more than
that, as far as I know, Christ never dictated to
anyone about those kinds of temporal things!! His
teaching and leadership dealt with things of the
spirit. He condemned the religious leaders for
making traditions of men concerning those kinds
of temporal things more important than the spiritual
things. They would dictate all kinds of these
rules to the people and then demand strict adherence

227

to their traditions. Christ firmly rebuked them for such things. In this passage Paul was answering a specific question about women's hair covering--it was a cultural matter and because of the angels. It was not a directive on how women should submit their hair style to their husbands.

We have covered this in earlier chapters, but for the sake of continuity, we will briefly cover it here too. Concerning I Cor. 11:10,15, the "covering" and "authority" here is NOT a symbol of her subordination to her husband. The covering was for the benefit of the angels. The word authority here is really the word "power" (EXOUSIA) and it means the Lord's authority over the church. It denotes a freedom of action, a right to act. In other words, it conveys to the woman the same rights, privileges and powers that Christ bestowed on the men. Both men and women were given the exact same power in Christ as equal members of the body of Christ. The covering for the women was to demonstrate something to the angels concerning this equal power that was given to both men and women. The interpretation that the covering was a sign of the women's subordination to the husband is one of those erroneous, biased teachings that has been handed down through the centuries and adopted as Bible truth when it is not truth at all.

Concerning point 2, "Hair is basis for spiritual protection". (I Cor. 11:10) There is **nothing** in this verse that remotely relates to giving the husband the right to tell his wife what kind of hair style to wear. It does not remotely relate to spiritual protection. What this teaching is saying is that if a woman does not wear her hair the way her husband wants her to, then God is not obliged to protect her. It makes God's promises of being our refuge and our protector null and void for the woman. The promises of God do not depend on a woman's hair style, whether it is

228

her own or her husband's choice!!!

Point 3 is that hair is a woman's glory. It is HER glory, not her husband's. If she must wear her hair in an unbecoming style, it is not a glory to her but a shame. The word "glory" is Doxa. It means an opinion, an estimate, the honor resulting from a good opinion. If a woman MUST wear her hair in a way that she feels makes her look ugly, it certainly is not an honor to her. It robs her of her good opinion of herself and it robs her of the good opinion and honor from others.

To explain my hair style on the basis of submission to authority, would say to anyone that in Christ I have become a non-entity. I am here only to conform to the wishes of my husband, no matter what he chooses to dictate to me. I have no freedom in Christ to be myself. I have abdicated my self to my husband. This actually would demonstrate an ungodly, blind obedience that is symbolic of idol worship. It represents a dying to self, which is scriptural. But it is not dying to self to become more Christlike, it is dying to self to conform to the will of man. That is NOT scriptural at all.

Continuing on page four of the syllabus.
"B. DRESS IS SYMBOL OF HUSBAND'S TASTE, STANDARDS AND PROVISIONS.
1. Modesty is always in style.
2. Wife should dress to please husband.
3. Dress should draw attention to her countenance.
   *Explain how colors, lines, patterns, and access-ories affect your appearance.
   * Remember that what your husband likes, he enjoys seeing often."
MY COMMENTS: False principle #8. There is no Scripture to base this on either. Personally, I know some Christian women who have refused to wear what their Christian husband's wanted them to wear because what he liked was sexy, provocative,

and sleazy. They felt like he was using them to promote a macho image of a guy who was able to attract a sexy woman for a wife. They felt that he was displaying them like a trophy. It was degrading to them. Being a Christian husband does not automatically make a man give up his own sensual desires. Nor does it make him an expert on clothing tastes or style. He may know what he likes, but if it makes the wife look like a tramp or a refugee from a rag bag, that is not an honor to him. His taste and his standards may be way out of line. His provisions are better represented by the wife's own taste and standards for herself in most cases. If she feels good about how she looks, in both the matter of dress and hair, she will have a happy, confident look that is a far better testimony of her husband's provision for her.

Proverbs 31 says the woman designed and manufactured clothing for the whole family, including her husband's clothes. She was commended for the good job she did. There is no indication that she abdicated her responsibility concerning the family's clothing to her husband. In all of Scripture, I do not find any instruction for the wife to turn that responsibility over to her husband. So this teaching is again the philosophy of man, with no scriptural basis and it robs the woman of one more aspect of her individual personality and diminishes her worth. It assumes that her tastes and standards are inferior to her husband's. His tastes and standards are more important than hers. She is to relinquish this part of her personality on the basis of "submit in EVERYTHING", ignoring all other Scripture.

On page 5 of the same syllabus, same section etc., under the letter F. is the next area in a woman's life that needs to be developed for her husband, because he needs a wife of inward and outward beauty.

"F. A Meek and Quiet Spirit--Basis of a Wife's beauty. (I Pet.3:1-7).
    1. Meekness is yielding rights.
    2. A quiet spirit is conquering fear and worry.
  * Separate your rights from your responsibilities
  * Yield your rights and expectations to God.
  * Visualize how godly character can result from disappointments."

MY COMMENTS: False principle #9. I Pet. 3:1-6 is used in this context as a basis for yielding all rights over to the man. It is saying in essence a woman is not to have any rights and should not expect anything from the man. Give them all over to God and let him work everything out through the man. Give up all your rights, but assume all of your responsibilities. This is equated with meekness and quietness of spirit. At the same time, it ignores the qualifying verse to the husbands, verse 7, that says give honor to the wife as joint heirs together of the grace of life.

A meek and quiet spirit is primarily to be developed because that is precious in God's sight. Though that would be pleasing to a man, it is something we do for God. What is meekness and quietness of spirit? Meekness is not giving up your rights to a man so that God can work in your life through the man. Meekness is a fruit of the spirit. According to Vine's Expository Dictionary "Meekness is an inwrought grace of the soul and the exercises of it are first and primarily **toward God.** It is the temper of spirit in which we accept His dealings with us as good and therefore without disputing or resisting HIM (emphasis mine). It is closely linked with the word tapeinophorsune (humility). It is only the humble heart which is also the meek heart and which as such, does not fight against God and more or less struggle and contend with Him. This meekness to God is also such in the face of men, even evil ones, in the sense that these, with insult and injuries which they may inflict are permitted and employed by God for the chastening and purifying of His elect. Meekness, as manifested by the Lord and commended to believers is the fruit of power". This does not mean that it is ALWAYS God's will. It CAN be what He wants to use sometimes.

A person is not meek because they yield all their rights to another man. Nor does it mean they are helpless and must endure every insult or injury someone wants to inflict upon them.

They are meek because they have the resources of God at their command and they employ them in humility and gentleness. Jesus did not always yield to his oppressors!! He submitted to what the Father wanted him to submit to. But when it was not the Father's will, he took action and rebuked the authorities. Meekness is power that is under self-control.

As for the quiet spirit, this word is an adjective that indicates a tranquillity that arises within, causing no disturbance to others. It is peaceable. It is a steadfast, unmoveable, settled quality in a person's life. There are many Christian women who have yielded up all their rights to their husbands. They have a quiet spirit. But they are beaten, battered and abused by their husbands. They live in terror and fear and worry. Yet their faith in God is steadfast and unmoveable. It is a spiritual quality that comes from yielding to God, not to man. But it does not mean that the God given instincts of fear and danger are extinct in them. A person with a quiet spirit is not required to endure all manner of abuse because they have a quiet spirit. They can do like Jesus did, just quietly remove themselves from the danger without retaliating evil for evil, but keeping their unmoveable faith in God intact. God can work to produce godly character through the sufferings of separation or divorce as well as he can work through the sufferings of abuse.

There are elements of truth in 'meekness is yielding rights' and 'a quiet spirit conquers fear and worry' but it is distorted truth, taken to the extreme. It is the kind of teaching that sends a woman back into anything and everything that a man wants to do to her or to the children. It is a truth out of balance, a word taken out of context and it brings destruction to women and the home. It perpetuates the problems that should be confronted and dealt with. It is the Word, but it is distorted to fit man's philosophy. I repeat, it also ignores the 7th verse in the passage in I Peter 3 that the author uses as his proof text. In his interpretation, there is no honor for the woman or for Christ in her.

The meek and quiet spirit, that is of great value to God because a woman has allowed God to produce that in her, through the work of the Holy Spirit, is attributed to a mere man and his training.

I know that ultimately my expectations are in the Lord. Yet, perhaps because of a fault in me, I found that if I carried all of my responsibilities but could not expect **anything** from my ex-husband, it produced a desperate hopelessness. If I was without any kind of expectations, then how could I have hope? Expectations and hope co-exist. Though I am taking it out of context, I Cor. 9:10 says that he that plows should plow in hope, and he that threshes in hope should be a partaker of that hope. I felt that if I plowed in the marriage with all of my responsibilities, then I should have a hope of partaking of something of what I sowed from the partner.

On the same page 5 of the syllabus the next item is G.

"G. POISE ---SYMBOL OF HUSBAND'S TRAINING.
    1. Basis of poise is contentment.(I Tim.6:6)
    2. Basis of contentment is self-acceptance.

(I Tim.6:6)
        *Be well groomed so you can concentrate
on others.
        3. Poise involves giving something of
importance."
MY COMMENTS: False principle #10. In order to have
poise, I must have a husband to train me to have
poise.

        Again, Scripture is used completely out of
context to support philosophies of man. I Tim.
6:6 is speaking to ALL Christians about being
content with whatever God has provided, whether
it is much or little. That verse has nothing at
all to do with poise nor does it have anything
to do with submission of wives to husbands. There
are many people who are content but who do not
have poise.

        What is poise? It is a state or quality of
being balanced. A composed resting and dignity
of manner, self-possession. Another way of putting
it, it is self-confidence, it is self control with
dignity. Self control is a fruit of the spirit
every Christian develops for themselves. It is
a symbol of the woman's individual walk with the
Lord. It is the character and personality God
has put in her and that she has allowed God to
develop in her. It is a symbol of what she is
inside. A symbol of who she is in Christ. This
one heading "Poise--the symbol of the husband's
training" takes away the woman's worth as an
individual who has been created and molded by
God and attributes everything she is to her husband
and his training!! She is nothing without that
man. This teaching even negates the influence
of the parents on the woman as they raised her.
This one phrase negates God, his creation, His
working in the woman, the woman's character and
personality in herself and the fruit of the Spirit
in her, as well as the parents' influence and
investment in their training of her. All of this

234

is attributed to the man and his training. Has the man not just taken the place of God in this statement?

There are many dignified, self controlled, poised women who have husbands who don't even know the meaning of the word. They are good men, but they could care less about poise and dignity. Those things are not high on their priorities list. Whose training do these women symbolize?

Is poise a quality that is unobtainable for a single woman who has no husband to train her?

My last comment is that I do not understand how poise and giving of something important is connected. Perhaps it's meaning goes back to the previous point of yielding rights. If that is the case, that does not produce poise. It produces a pathetic woman who displays a total lack of self confidence, one who looks and acts like a defeated, helpless, hopeless person with no dignity at all.

The last area of distortion I want to look at in this section begins on page 5 and cont. on page 6, under the heading of:

"IV. A Husband Needs A Wife Who Can Lovingly Appeal To Him When He Is Going Beyond His Limit-ations And Wisely Respond To Those Who Question His Ideas, Goals, Or Motives.

What words, actions, or decisions should you appeal?

D. Help others understand your husband's perspective.

*Build appreciation for your husband's motives, **even if his ideas are wrong.** (Emphasis mine)

*Explain your husband's actions on the basis of his convictions."

MY COMMENTS: False principle #11. No Scriptures! I must assume that **all** of my husband's perspectives, convictions and motives are always right and pure. This cannot be, because no human being still on earth is like that. Often, even for born again Christians, "There is a way that seemeth right

to a man, but the way thereof is death." There
are other proverbs that say the same kind of thing.
(Pro. 12:15,14:12, 16:25, 21:2). Though he thinks
he may be right, it is not always so. This also
puts the responsibility on me to monitor and judge
his actions and motivations in order to know when
he is going beyond his limits. There is a burden
on me to make everything my husband does look right
in the eyes of everyone else, whether he is right
or wrong. If other people are questioning his
ideas, motives and goals, then obviously something
is amiss. The ideas, goals, and motivations might
be wrong, need to be examined, and perhaps changed.

There are many Scriptures about love covering
a multitude of sins etc. But there is also
Scripture that brings the balance to them, like
Pro. 28:13 that says he who covers his sin will
not prosper.

What is wrong with trying to make your man
look good by trying to cover up for his wrong ideas?
Isn't that something everyone would want to do?
One reason for that can be very unhealthy. One's
motive for it could stem from a deep sense of pride.
If someone speaks or thinks badly of our spouse,
we take that as a reflection on our own character
somehow, and we don't want to look bad to anybody

How can anyone build something good on the
basis of something wrong? If a man has wrong ideas,
wrong motives, or wrong convictions, how can a
woman make that look right? To try to do so is
to learn to be deceitful and manipulative. When
one tries to make everything look right to others,
they cover up for the person. This leads to classic
co-dependent behavior. Many, many Christian women
and their children are caught in that kind of
behavior, because they do that very thing. It
is deceitful to the woman herself because she either
goes into denial that there is a problem at all,
she blames herself, or she minimizes the destruct-
iveness of the man's behavior. It is deceitful

236

and destructive to the children. They learn to be dishonest and deceitful, as they see and hear Mom cover up for Dad even when he's wrong. They learn that they do not have to be honest about taking responsibility for their own actions because Dad doesn't have to. It is deceitful and dishonest to others because she is presenting something wrong as though it were right. It is harmful and deceitful to the man because he is not being confronted in love for his wrong doing. This enables him to continue in the wrong doing without suffering the consequences of his own behavior. The Word says when a brother errs, we should confront him in love and gentleness so he can recover himself out of the snare with which the devil has taken him captive. We are always admonished to speak the truth in love. Truth is not justifying a person's wrong ideas, motives, or convictions to other people. I am making such a point of this because the author uses the strong words of "motives" and "convictions". These words give the impression that he is talking about spiritual things or at least, very serious things.

Frankly, it would destroy my husband's self respect if I went about making excuses for his ideas, motives or convictions, right or wrong. That certainly would not build my respect for him, nor would it build anyone else's respect for him. I love to do it and I do speak well of my husband to others. And when there is a goof-up, if it is an error in judgment and I know his motives are right, I do defend that. But I don't cover up for him deceitfully. I do not try to make something wrong seem right to others. He is the same with me.

In the same section is item E.

"E. Don't appease reaction by discrediting your husband.

1. Abigail's appeal to David discredited her husband (I Sam. 25:25)".

MY COMMENTS: These two sentences sound very innocent don't they? What harm is there in them? The next chapter will explain it thoroughly. It is a prime example of the distortion of the Word with the purpose of maligning women. It's a graphic illustration of how the apostasy of the latter days creeps in unawares as well known Bible teachers call evil good and good evil.

Continuing on in the same section, page 9.

"VII. A husband needs a wife who will be praised by other people for her character and her good works.

F. Special cautions.

**\*A wife's good works should demonstrate her husband's sincere motives:** giving to needs of others without expectation of reward. (Luke 14:12-14) (Emphasis mine)

\*A wife should not try to resolve her husband's problems with good works without his consent."

MY COMMENTS: False Principle #12. There is a contradiction here. The woman is to be praised by others for HER character and HER good works. But then it is stated these good works and her good character are only a reflection of her husband's motives! So, her character and her good works are not her own attributes at all. They are her husband's.

In the biblical context, Luke 14:12-14 does talk about giving to others needs without any expectation of reward. However, it does not remotely relate to the wife's good works demonstrating anything at all about the husband or his motives. To apply this Scripture this way, is taking it out of it's biblical context entirely in order to make it say something it does not say. This is an instruction for ALL believers. Any Christian's good works demonstrate their own love for God. Period. It demonstrates their own obedience TO God, FOR God's sake. In fact, the Word says good works are a sign of a believers faith. Without those good works, the faith is dead. What gross arrogance to say the wife's good works demonstrate her husband's motives!! To attribute her good works to her husband's motives is to deny that her faith, and her motives are pure towards God. Her only motivation and her only purpose in life is to please the man and make him look good. She is only a puppet, who demonstrates when he pulls the strings.

There are many men who have good motives, but there are also many men who do not have sincere motives and are very negligent in doing good works themselves. Many times, a woman has far more pure motives than the man has. Many times a man will prevent his wife from doing good works, because of his own selfish motives.

The last statement from the author about not trying to resolve the husband's problems with good works without his consent didn't make much sense to me. And maybe it doesn't make much sense to you either. But what I want to share in the next chapter about Abigail, will shed much light on this statement.

Aside from that, I assume the meaning could be that if the husband has a problem with somebody, she should ask if she can help rectify the situation or compensate for it by doing some good works for the offended person. If he consents, then she may do some good works for them. This is what he demonstrates clearly in the subject of the next chapter. I guess the principle might be that to do something without asking him, in that situation, it would be meddling in his affairs. Also, she would be usurping his authority. I can agree, no one should try to solve some one else's problems with other people. That is always a personal thing everyone has to do in their own way. But I also know there are times when one must intervene in certain instances in order to avoid a severe disaster that would be the result of someone's wrong doing.

I have quoted 12 principles from this material. All of the quotes, by themselves, would only take a page or two to print. Yet I have written pages of explanation. Why? These false teachings have wounded and robbed the woman of her individual motivations for her walk with God. It focuses on doing things only to demonstrate to others what a good man her husband is. It elevates him to the place of an idol. She becomes an idol worshiper. The message is so subtle.

By applying these 12 false principles, what has been taken from the woman? 1. All her financial capabilities and freedoms. 2. All her chances to learn from godly teachers. 3. All right of decision of any kind. 4. All right to her personal choices of hair style, clothing style and color that are reflections of her personality. 5. Her meek and quiet spirit are not hers. 6. Her poise is not hers. 7. Her good works and 8. even her good character are not hers, they are all attributed to her husband. 9. She gives up all her expectations of receiving anything from her husband. 10. She gives up her self. What is left of her? Nothing. She is now a pitiful clone of the man. He is an idol, because, 11. she has given up being obedient to many of God's commands throughout the Word except for, "Submit to your husband in everything". She is no longer obedient to God, but to a man. I am sure you see other things she has given up.

The results of applying these false principles to my life were disastrous to me and to my children. They affected other people's lives negatively also. I refer to people in my ex-husband's congregations, personal friends who trusted us, our extended families and even acquaintances. They are still affecting my daughters, their spouses and the grandchildren in some ways.

In 1976 Wilfred Bockelman wrote a book entitled

"Gothard. The Man and His Ministry: An Evaluation". In his book Mr. Bockelman states "Bill Gothard is one of the most influential figures in the seventies." The book tells about the phenomenal growth of Gothard's ministry. For example, he says in April of 1973, 8,000 people attended the 32 hour Basic Youth Seminar in St. Paul MN. By April, 1974 the attendance had swelled to 27,500 in the same city without the benefit of any great promotional campaign. By the time the author wrote his book, Gothard had already started the Minister's Seminars and had distributed his Basic Church Ministry manuals to senior pastors only. He had formulated a local church training ministry that would provide sermon guides. He developed work-shops for men and women, to thoroughly explain his views on divorce and to show **how the chain of command works in the family, business, and the Church.** Remember I explained earlier that this kind of "chain of command" is an exact copy of the world system that Christ forbade for anyone in His Church to practice!!

I quote Mr. Bockelman, "There is no doubt about it, this more formal program of providing a ministry to congregations will have a multiplying affect on the program that is now already reaching **hundreds of thousands** of people through the basic seminars."

He stated several times in his book that various counselors and therapists had told him their case loads went up every time a Gothard seminar came to town. The presenting complaints of clients were generally condemnation and false guilt because they felt they weren't good enough people.

In the beginning of this chapter, I stated the potential for wide spread harm from these seminars was astronomical and that the potential was being reached. I also stated the affect of them on the Body of Christ was like mainlining

241

drugs. The poison goes through the body rapidly. When I wrote that, I was unaware of Mr. Bockelman's book. But since I've been given the book, the information from it is included to substantiate and impress on the reader's mind how wide spread and influential Gothard's teachings are. I had chosen his works to expose the roots of how so much devastating apostasy has crept into the Church. The work, and the influences of it, have been in operation for almost thirty years!! Many people who have never heard the name of Gothard are experiencing the "benefits" of the teachings without ever knowing it. Many pastors think they have found a gold mine of information with which to help their congregations, so they will share that information with other pastor friends, who then share it with their congregations. Individuals share it with others. Some use it to teach Sunday School classes etc. Currently, there is a program of home school curriculum that is distributed to select families who swear an oath that they and their families will abide by Gothard's rules before they are permitted to buy the curriculum. I have not seen the curriculum, but I am confident that the academic quality is excellent. However, I am also confident that these poisonous principles are interwoven through out the material. So children, who will one day be parents, are being indoctrinated with these kinds of false doctrines.

To what degree have these particular false teachings influenced the Body of Christ today? They are vain philosophies of men, for they have either no, or a distorted, Scriptural basis, yet they are preached as "gospel".

The serpent said, "Yea, hath God said?" He said it to cause doubt about God's Word. And I say, "Yea, hath God said?" I say it to cause doubt about man's word. I say it so that some may doubt and search out what God really did say about some of these things.

Please do not misunderstand me. I do not condemn Bill Gothard or his ministry. He teaches much truth. I commend him on much of his work. But these particular principles are not truth. All of them turn the woman to the man as God said in Gen. 3:16. Relying on man is a snare.

# CHAPTER TEN
## ABIGAIL DISCREDITS HER HUSBAND

The purpose for examining this portion of Gothard's work is not to discredit all of his work or his ministry. Rather, it is to demonstrate how the application of the false principles of the last chapter can bring the Church into apostasy.

The title of this chapter is taken from the last chapter under "E". This is the explanation of those two innocent sounding lines from the syllabus of Basic Youth Conflicts, Sub-Section, IV. A HUSBAND NEEDS A WIFE WHO CAN LOVINGLY APPEAL TO HIM WHEN HE IS GOING BEYOND HIS LIMITATIONS AND WISELY RESPOND TO THOSE WHO QUESTION HIS IDEAS, GOALS, OR MOTIVES, Pg. 6,"E. Don't Appease Reaction By Discrediting Your Husband. 1. Abigail's appeal to David discredits her husband. (I Sam.25:25)."

The following material comes from the "Supplementary Alumni Book," Vol. 4, copyright 1978 Basic Youth Conflicts, Pg.8,9,10. Bill Gothard, Author.

I use this for two reasons. First, the author's own work explains his meaning best. Secondly, but more importantly, is this is an outrageous distortion of Scripture. It's purpose is to discredit women and to show how they supposedly destroy their own household by making a decision and acting on it, instead of appealing to their husbands. It portrays a courageous, godly woman of the Bible, as a rebellious, irresponsible woman who makes a wrong decision, takes matters into her own hands, and causes her husband's death by her actions. The author uses it as an example to prove how wrong it is for a woman to make a decision. It turns the Word of God up side down, in order to substantiate the false philosophies exposed in my last chapter. It promotes the husband to the place of idol. How the author assassinates the character of this woman of God in this twisted account is an affront to every Christian woman. It is an affront to every Christian man, too, because God's appointed man, David is also portrayed as evil. False teaching like this is causing the decay of the home and marriages and even Christian churches. It is latter-day apostasy.

The whole teaching is based on the I Sam. 25 account of David, Abigail, and Nabal.

The biblical account says that David sent his men to watch over Nabal's flocks and men, protecting them from bandits and marauders during the sheering of the sheep. They took nothing from Nabal's men or flocks. When that was finished, they were hungry and there was no food to be found. So David sent some of his servants to Nabal to ask for food in return for what they had done for Nabal. Nabal was a beast of a man. He was not grateful to David and his men. He "railed" at them and refused to give them food. David was so angered by this, that he decided to kill Nabal and every male in the village. One of Nabal's servants heard about this impending doom and went to tell Abigail. Abigail and the servants gathered food, then she went with them to appeal to David not to kill Nabal. David listened to her and did not carry out his plan of revenge.

In the following account, "the author" refers to Bill Gothard, author of the "Supplemental Alumni Book". The distorted account follows:

The author believes that this whole account is a study of a series of appeals. He uses it to demonstrate how the various characters in the account were wrong in their appeals and why he believes they were wrong. He sites attitudes, reactions, and motives. In this study, he judges everyone wrong except Nabal. The author believes he is demonstrating truth through Scripture. What it demonstrates is how the false principles, as discussed in my previous chapter, are put into practice in this one account. The distortions are clear.

The author did not think David's appeal to

Nabal was right because he did not go to Nabal himself, but sent a servant to talk to Nabal. He judged this wrong because Nabal was a rich man and rich men resent dealing with a middle man. As he was sending his men to Nabal, David said, "Thus shall you say to him that liveth in prosperity" (I Sam.25:6) The author says this remark by David communicated disrespect for Nabal which they in turn communicated to Nabal. He concludes that David and his men had bad attitudes. They were also giving evidence of **their** ungratefulness toward Nabal and **their** expectation of reward for well doing. Thus David was wrong in his appeal and so were his servant/messengers. (MY COMMENTS: According to the Septuagint, what David actually said was asking a blessing of seasonal prosperity upon Nabal and his household!! The author's judgment against David is based on the world system of partiality shown to the rich, not on a Scripture that David had violated. The author says that David was displaying evidence of ungratefulness. He is standing on his principle that one must be grateful to the head of the house simply because they are the "head". David was not even a part of Nabal's household. I fail to see what David was supposed to be grateful for. It was David and his men who had done a great favor for Nabal. David could not be grateful for Nabal's generous offer of food! David wasn't really expecting a reward. The fact was, David and his men **needed** food with which to sustain themselves. Nabal is the one who had the ungrateful attitude. The author is also standing on his principle that one should take all their responsibilities, but should never expect anything in return. David had no obligation to Nabal. Perhaps he did what did for the very purpose of obtaining food rather than just asking for a handout. So David's good is called evil and Nabal's evil is called good!)

The author says Nabal's servant is wrong.

He poses the question, "Why didn't Nabal's servant go to Nabal with his report that David was coming to kill him?" He says this man displayed his wrong attitudes, first, by going to Abigail instead of to Nabal, and secondly, by what he said to her. He said, 'David sent messengers out of the wilderness to salute our master and he railed on them--for he is such a son of Belial (son of the devil) that a man cannot speak to him' (I Sam. 25:14,17). The author says "The servant's attitude totally disqualified him from appealing to the right person. It was unfortunate, because he gave a marvelous report of David and his men. (I Sam. 25:15,16). Had the report been given to Nabal in the right spirit it might have caused him to change his mind." (MY COMMENTS: The word salute here means to kneel, to bless man as a benefit, to praise and to thank. This was definitely not a dis-respectful greeting. The author is standing on his principle that God will work through the head of the household, no matter what kind of man he is. By speaking truth about Nabal, the servant is disqualifying himself. According to the author's principles, that truth should have been ignored and excused so the servant could demonstrate loyalty to his master, regardless of what kind of man he was. Here evil Nabal is called the "right" person. Nabal's servant supposedly has a wrong spirit. David's men had a wrong spirit, that is why Nabal railed at them.)

The author poses the question, "Was Abigail's appeal to David right?" He says, "The servant's appeal was quite effective-to the wrong person. He **persuaded Abigail to take matters into her own hands** (emphasis mine). She did what her husband refused to do. She gathered food and rode out to meet David and his men. Her appeal was important enough for God to record it word for word, as well as her actions giving it. 'When Abigail saw David, she hastened, and fell before

David on her face, and bowed to the ground. And fell at his feet.(I Sam. 25:23,24)' (MY COMMENTS: Here the author is standing on several of his principles. Women should not do **anything** without their husband's approval or consent. Women should never, under any circumstance, make a decision on their own. They should never take matters into their own hands. They should never show more loyalty to anyone than what they show to their own husband, no matter who or what the husband is, or who or what the other person is. I find it curious that the author himself states that "her appeal was important enough for **God** to record it word for word" and yet the author deems it "wrong". Isn't it strange that God would do that if what she did was wrong?

So in the author's eyes, Abigail is wrong. She appealed to the wrong person because he was not her husband. Also, she showed more loyalty and honor to David than she did to her husband.)

While Abigail was intercepting David with food and her appeal to him to spare the lives of Nabal and all the males in the village, Nabal is back home getting drunk. In the morning, when he sobered up, Abigail told him what she had done. Then, "his heart died within him".(I Sam. 25:37). The author questions why this should have happened since the danger of being killed by David was over. He suggests it happened because now the wife's actions had exposed him to a greater danger from the king. (My thoughts about that are, had she not intervened, he would have already been dead. There was no greater danger from the king than there had been from David. It doesn't matter whose hand causes it, death by one hand or the other is still death!) The author surmises that Nabal was a wealthy man and as such, knew of what was going on in the land. He had heard that David "had broken away from his master". He knew the king was trying to kill David. He knew that the

248

king had killed many priests because one of them
had given only bread to David. So Nabal figured
that if Saul had killed so many priests for giving
just bread to David, how much more danger was he
in because of all the food his wife had given
to David. (I Sam.25:18,37) I quote the author,
"No wonder he had a heart attack. Why couldn't
she display the same reverence for her husband?
She had the wrong attitude toward him. The first
evidence of this is that she listened to a bad
report and acted on it. The second indication is
the way she referred to her husband to David. 'Let
not, my lord, I pray thee, regard this son of belial
(son of the devil) even Nabal; for as his name
is so is he. Nabal (meaning fool) is his name and
folly is with him. (I Sam. 25:25)'. Her appeal
covers eight verses of Scripture, and it was
effective. **But it could have been just effective
with her husband if she had had the right attitude."**
(Emphasis mine).

(MY COMMENTS: Let us look at what false
principles the author is using to make these
assessments. 1) Cover up for the "head", and
make excuses for the husband's wrong convictions,
motives or ideas. 2) Deny and excuse the man's
wrong doing and it's effect on her and everyone
else. 3) Even if it cost the lives of every male
in the village, she shouldn't have spoken truth,
because that showed bad attitudes of disloyalty.
4) Do not show loyalty to anyone but your husband.
5) The major principle here is that no matter what
God's plans are, if the woman will appeal in the
right way, at the right time, with the right
attitudes and especially with a right spirit, God
will work through that man, regardless of how evil
he is or what is in his heart. The man becomes
the idol in the place of God.)

The author then poses the question, "How do
we know Abigail was wrong? Abigail took matters
into her own hands. Prov. 14:1 warns that a woman

destroys her house by doing this, and that is precisely what happened to Abigail's family. The very death she tried to prevent--- **she occasioned** (Emphasis mine). When her husband found out what she did 'his heart died within him'. Ten days later he died **as the Lord slew him.**"(Emphasis mine).

The author says that further evidence that Abigail was wrong was that she married David, had one son by him whom she named Chileab, but the name was later changed to Daniel which means "God is judge" (II Sam 3:3). More evidence of her error is found in her appeal, he says. "It comes under the heading of 'what might have been'--Abigail wisely predicted that if David killed her husband, it would be a grief to him when he became king. (I Sam 25:31) Her words were true because David had a tender heart." He suggests that had David killed Nabal the consequences he would have had to suffer from that act might have prevented him from killing Bathsheba's husband Uriah. He says, "God often allows man to stumble in the shadows so that he can run the race before watching crowds."

The author says that the right thing that Abigail should have done was to take the servant with her, and together, share the facts with Nabal. But, he says, both of them would have to change their bad attitudes about Nabal so they could go to him in the right spirit. Then if Nabal refused, she could have asked his permission to go to appeal to David without giving him food.

(MY COMMENTS: My question from the last chapter was, what did the author mean when he said the wife should not discredit her husband and should not appease the offended with good works without his permission. This is what he means. God had a purpose for Abigail doing what she did. But in spite of God's purposes, the author stands on **his** principle that no woman should do anything unless she has her husband's permission. Even God's purposes take second place to his principle!!)

ABIGAIL DISCREDITS HER HUSBAND

The author's next question is, "How could Abigail have appealed to David? Scripture says that Abigail was a woman of good understanding and a beautiful countenance (I Sam. 25:13). She had heard reports about David and knew that he was destined to be king (I Sam. 25:30). No doubt she also had heard how David had spared Saul's life when he could have killed him, and how he had purposed not to lift his hand against the Lord's anointed one. Based on these factors, she could have appealed to David to also spare her husband **for the loyalty he was trying to show to the king's command."** (Emphasis mine)

The last question the author poses is "Would David have listened to her appeal?" He follows that by saying "David made a reverse vow. Instead of saying 'So and more also, **do God to me** if I leave Nabal or any of his men alive by the time morning comes.' David actually vowed, 'So, and more also, do God unto the enemies of David if I leave---'(I Sam 25:22). He was saying in effect 'if I let him live, let God kill him'. This is in fact, what happened because Nabal was churlish and evil in his doings. (I Sam. 25:3)" (This ends the author's narrative).

In this last statement the author says it was a reverse vow. But I do not understand that reasoning. David was not asking that God kill him (David) if he did not kill Nabal. That would be asking God to kill him if he failed to take revenge into his own hands. David was saying "God if I don't avenge myself, then you do it." Thanks to Abigail's intervention he returned to his true character, which was to give God His right to avenge the wrong done to him.

Another point of confusion here, is that the author stated earlier that Abigail occasioned Nabal's death by her wrong actions. But here he states that God killed him because of his evil ways. I suppose the confusion might be clarified by saying God did it, but it was the woman's fault He did it, if one wanted to. I am being facetious. Truly, was it her actions or was it his own evilness that caused God to kill him? Was God fulfilling His own plan through this whole scenario? Was God living up to his own Scripture that says "The wages of sin is death" and "Vengeance is mine, I will repay"? How could anyone conclude from the facts given that Abigail "occasioned" her husband's death? It can only be done by adding things to God's Word that aren't there for the purpose of degrading a woman.

A sign of the apostate church is when evil is called good and good is called evil. In the apostate church, the leaders preach and teach that very thing and the people believe it. The false principles and this twisted account are presented to thousands as Bible truth. David, David servants, Nabal's servant and Abigail are all portrayed as wrong but the real evil one has been defended. Evil is called good and good is called evil. All for the sake of proving false principles. This is why I have chosen to use this work. This author is so prominent, so much of his work is excellent, but this is how the church is being led into apostasy!! This is false teaching that has crept in unawares. This is only one example of twisted Scripture, there are many others just as bad.

I do not want to leave it like this. I want to present the truth of this whole account so that you can judge for yourself what is truth. The only way I know of to find out what Scripture really says is to look up the meanings of words. That gives a clear understanding of what a verse or a passage of Scripture means. So please bear with me as we do some word studies here.

What kind of a man was Nabal? Scripture says he was wealthy, churlish, and evil in his doings. Strong's concordance says that churlish means to be severe, cruel, grievous, hard hearted, impudent,

252

obstinate, one who would prevail, rough, stiff
necked, and stubborn. Besides that he was evil.
Among the meanings of evil are these: bad, exceedingly grievous, hurtful, ill favored, mischievous,
misery, trouble, vex, wickedly, wretchedly, and
WRONG. The name Nabal means dolt, foolish, stupid,
wicked (especially impious) and vile. This does
not sound like an ordinary, reasonable man who
could be persuaded by anyone's "appeal" about
anything, whether those appealing had the right
attitudes or spirit or not. He was an exceptionally
vile, ill tempered, unreasonable man. Especially,
he was an impious man. The words "hard hearted"
means devoid of spiritual perception!

The man's character was well known by every
person who knew him. Particularly those in his
household. They knew him for what he was. They
did not have to listen to any "bad reports" about
the man. They lived with him and had experienced
his evilness. No amount of "good attitudes" and
"loyalty" would change his character or his mind.
He was reprobate. No amount of concealing or
denying the truth could change the facts, and
neither could that kind of thing persuade anyone
to respect the man. There is no way anyone can
build respect for a man like that. This is the
truth about this man, according to the Scripture.
He was an ungodly, evil man.

What kind of a person was Abigail? Scripture
says she was beautiful and of good understanding.
We want to see how her character compares with
Nabal's character. So let's look at "good" and
"understanding".

Good means: best, better, bountiful, cheerful,
at ease, gracious, joyful, kindly, kindness, loving,
merry, pleasant, precious, prosperity, sweet, and
well favored.

The meaning of understanding comes from two
words. One means intelligent, success, discretion,
knowledge, prudence, sense, and wisdom. The second

253

word is the primary word and it means to be circumspect, consider, expert, deal prudently, skillful, have good success, teach, wisely, guide, wittingly.

Abigail was beautiful on the outside, but her inner character was even more beautiful. Her character was poised, at ease, and gracious.(Her poise did not represent her husband's training!). She was kind, loving, pleasant, and joyful. This was combined with intelligence, wisdom, discretion, and good common sense. She was probably able to deal with people in a prudent, skillful way. She was probably able to guide and teach people with wisdom. The word circumspect means to give careful attention to all the circumstances that may relate to an action, judgment or conduct etc. It means cautious and careful. Prudent means one is capable of exercising sound judgment in practical matters. It also means discreet in conduct, sensible, not rash. Comparing just these things, who do you think the servant should have gone to prevent a sure disaster?

The names Abigail and Nabal are significant. Abigail is a name that is a compound of two words. Ab which means father (i.e. source) of joy, father in a literal or immediate sense or in a figurative and remote application; chief, (fore) father, patrimony, principal. It is the very same word that is used in Abraham's name. The second word is giyl which means, a revolution (of time, i.e. an age) also joy, exceedingly, gladness, rejoice. A spinning around (under the influence of violent emotion) i.e. usually rejoice or (as cringing) fear-- be glad, joy, be joyful, rejoice.

In the light of all of this, rather than being the action of a foolish woman tearing down her own house, I see what Abigail did as a demonstration of a great many of these godly characteristics and qualities being put into practice. God put those characteristics in her and they were given to her to fulfill God's purpose and plan. Had Abigail been following the false principles we have been exposing here, ALL of these qualities would have been shunted aside in favor of the godless qualities of Nabal, the husband, to which Abigail, supposedly, should have subjected herself. God's plan and purpose would have been left undone!! In your own mind, what is truth here? In obedience to these false teachings, many women do ignore their God given qualties and gifts and bow to evil or ill tempered men.

But let's go on. Was Nabal a man following God? There is not one word in the whole of Scripture that would indicate that he knew God at all. His name means he was especially impious and devoid of spiritual perception.

Was Abigail a woman following God? I Sam. 25:26,28,29,30,31 indicate that she knew God well enough to know His will for David and David's enemies, and God's will for her. She knew David was God's anointed one, and that he fought for God. Actually many of these verses are prophetic utterances, from God to David, through her. She was God's chosen instrument of the hour. We **know** this because in verse 32, David blesses God for SENDING her to him. Had Abigail bowed to the godless Nabal, David would have been denied this blessing. God's history would have had to be rewritten.

What of David? We know he was God's anointed, appointed, obedient servant. David sinned, later, but God knew that David would be obedient to do anything that God asked him to do. His lifestyle was obedience to his God.

The motives of all of these characters were examined by the author and all but Nabal's motives were judged wrong. So let's look at that.

According to the author, Nabal's noble motive for withholding food from David and his men, was that he was trying to be obedient to the king.

I think his motive was simply in accord with his character. He was acting out of ungrateful, stingy, greed. If he had heard about David, he should have known that David was destined to be king. There should have been respect for who David was. There should have been gratefulness for what David and his men had done for him. But instead he ridiculed David and called him a run away slave, and his heart was so hard he did not have enough compassion in his soul to give a starving man food. David said in verse 21, "He requited me evil for good". That sounds like David had expectations that good deeds should produce a hope of good in return. In verses 10 and 11, after the report of what David had done for him, Nabal says, who is this Son of Jesse, this runaway slave, I don't know him. Why should I give MY bread, MY water, MY meat to this one I don't know. His attitudes and motives are very clearly not pure. They are in accordance with his evil, churlish, character. His statement "to this one I don't know" could very well indicate he knew nothing about the priests who had been killed because of David. He might have only known that David was the son of Jesse and a run-away slave. The story does not tell us what he really knew about David.

What was Nabal's servant's motive. I see him as a man who had a great concern for all the people in the village. It was not just Nabal who David was going to kill, because in verse 17 the servant says the evil is determined to be carried out against our master and against all his household. Knowing Abigail's character, he went to the one who had any authority to do something to prevent disaster. He did not "persuade her" to take matters into her own hands as the author stated. He told her the facts and said "consider what you should do". (V. 17) He respected David, he respected Abigail, he correctly assessed the facts concerning Nabal and his character. He correctly assessed what disaster would come upon many people because of Nabal's nasty character. He acted wisely and courageously and according to God's plan. Again, had the servant been following the false principle of "obey those who have rule over you", and "God ALWAYS works through the head of the house", God's plan would not have been carried out.

What about Abigail and her motives? I do not believe that there was any kind of rebellion against her "head" involved. Did she jump into the action she took? I think she summed up all the facts of the situation and made a godly judgment. Then she quickly followed through on that judgment with a course of action that averted certain death for many people. Most of all, it averted something that David would surely have lived to regret had it happened. It would have smitten his conscience in two ways. He would have shed the innocent blood of all those people and he would have gone against his own nature by taking revenge himself and not allowing God to avenge him with his enemies (V.31). Her purpose was to protect the people, but more importantly, her loyalty was to God and to God's anointed one. Her first priority was not to protect her godless husband but to perform what God had appointed her to do. Her motive stemmed from her love of God, her loyalty to God and her loyalty to God's man. How can anyone view these pure motives as wrong? She was so in tune with God that she felt she had wronged David because she did not see or hear his servants the first time they came to ask for food. She asked David's forgiveness for that, even though that was not her fault. Her heart was toward God and his appointed servant. I believe she was following God's will and doing exactly what God wanted her to do to protect David from his own rash reaction. I base that on verse 32 where David said "God sent you to meet me".

In the long list of words under the word "sent"
is the single word "appoint". It is my belief
that David was saying "God appointed you to meet
today." I believe what she did was a divine
appointment by God.

By her actions, did she cause the death of
her husband? NO! The Lord God Almighty himself
avenged David by killing him. It had nothing to
do with Abigail's actions. It was Nabal's churlish,
evil character and actions that caused God to
choose to kill him. It was God's will for him
to die. Only the evil one suffered, no other
innocent people were killed. David's good reputation
and good conscience were left intact.

The word "heart" means the innermost organ.
It is also used to indicate the feelings, the will
and even the intellect of a person. It is the
center of anything. Based on that meaning of
"heart" and knowing Nabal's character, my thoughts
are that when Nabal heard what Abigail had done,
it did not cause a fear of what King Saul might
do to him. What it did was to cause his vile nature
to rise up in an excessively great anger because
some of HIS possessions had been given away, that
he had a stroke that paralyzed him for ten days
before he finally died.

Were Abigail's attitudes towards her husband
wrong? NO!! She discerned the facts accurately
and she acted accordingly. If she had "appealed"
to her husband would it have worked? I think not,
for God's plan was unfolding. It was suggested
that if she and the servant had gone to Nabal with
a "good report" of David, with good attitudes,
in the right spirit, Nabal **might** have changed his
mind and set things right. Or at least, would
have permitted Abigail to go talk to David, without
bringing him food. However, he had already heard
the good report of what David had done for him.
In spite of what the author says, I believe there
was respect in what David told his servants to

say to Nabal, because, as I stated before the
Septuagint says he was giving a blessing. Also,
since his request for food had not yet been so
rudely refused, he had no reason to be disrespectful
to Nabal.    If Abigail had asked her husband's
approval to go to David, would that permission
have been granted? I doubt that, also, because
there is not one shred of evidence that anything
could get through that man's seared conscience.
There is no evidence that his actions were based
on loyalty to the king.   There was nothing noble
or honorable about the man  that would make anyone
believe that he might listen to reason.  His motives
and his attitudes were scripturally proven to be
evil.   To  see  anything  in this man's character
that would portray  him as an innocent, betrayed,
husband is sheer speculation and vain imagination.
       To  even  suggest  that  what Abigail did was
interfering  in  God's   plan  for  David's  life  in
a negative way, is absurd.   I am referring to the
author's  statement  about  "what might have been"
and  then  saying  that  because  she did  not allow
him  to  kill  every  male  in  the  village,  as well
as Nabal, in avenging himself, he did not suffer
the  consequences  of  his  actions.   That  was  the
reason  he  could  so  easily  kill  Uriah  later  on.
Instead  of  "interfering"  in God's plan for David's
life,  the  truth  is,  she  "intervened"  in  David's
life in accordance with God's plan for his life.
I refer again to verse 32 and 33, where David said
"God sent you to me  today".  He blesses her for
her advice,  for keeping him from shedding innocent
blood and avenging himself.  In verse 34 he declares
it is the Lord who kept him from hurting her and
every  male  in  the  household  of  Nabal.   In  verse
35 he tells her to go in peace, because he listened
to her plea and he accepted her person. That means
he held her in high regard as an honorable person.
       Another  proposed  "proof"  of  Abigail's  error,
is  the  matter  of  her  subsequent  marriage  to  David,

the birth of a son and the changing of the son's name from Chileab to Daniel.

Was becoming David's wife a bad thing for her? Some say that it was a shame to become only one of many wives. I view it as God's provision for her because her obedience to God came before her obedience to her ungodly husband. She discerned correctly, acted bravely, God and God's chosen one were honored. Many lives were saved, David was spared from dishonor and from grieving God. And God provided for her through David. Then He gave her the blessing of a son.

The changing of that son's name from Chileab to Daniel was supposed to be proof that what she did was wrong because "Daniel" means "God is judge". Even though there is very little written about the name change, the author concludes that God was judging Abigail for what he considers wrong doing by her. This carries the veiled threat that any woman who makes a decision, and acts on that decision, will be judged and punished by God. Because the name change did not occur until the son was much older, the possibility exists that God judged him worthy of a name change, as He did others in the Old Testament. The truth is, according to Strong's Concordance, the name Chileab literally means "restraint of his father". To me, that would be a positive indication of what Abigail, his mother, did in the life of his father. Her intervention restrained David from doing evil. The name Daniel means, "Judge OF God" NOT "God IS Judge" or "Judged by God" or "Judged of God". Judge OF God means one is given the authority to be a judge for God. Judge here means to rule, to judge (as an umpire), contend, execute, and minister judgment, strength, mighty one, godly power, strong. To me, that indicates both the positive actions Abigail took when she intervened in David's life and also the good character of the son. There can be no negative proof of wrongdoing derived from the name or the name change, either for Abigail or the son. In spite of that, the author adds his own interpretation to the Word in order to substantiate his principles.

What about God in all of this. Nabal is really only a minor character in God's scheme of things. He is neither God's chosen or anointed vessel. He is only mentioned as a part of something that was happening in David's life for God's purposes. God chose to use Abigail in David's life. And God chose to have David marry her. It is shown in verses 28-31 that Nabal is an insignificant person and David is the primary person. Abigail says the Lord will make David's house sure because David fights the Lord's battles and the Lord has not found evil in him all of his days. Even though Saul was pursuing him to kill him "the soul of my lord (David) shall be bound in the bundle of life with the Lord thy God. And the souls of thine enemies shall he sling out, as out of the middle of a sling. And it shall come to pass, when the Lord shall have done for my lord according to all the good that he hath spoken concerning thee, and shall have appointed thee ruler over Israel that this shall be no grief unto thee, nor offense of heart unto my lord, either that thou hast shed blood without cause, or that my lord hath avenged himself; but when the Lord shall have dealt with my lord, then remember thine handmaid." KJV

Why have I chosen this work to use as an example? What is my purpose? Let me preface the answer to those questions with Romans 3:1-5. Paul is speaking about the Jewish circumcision and how that was a valuable thing because those of the circumcision had been entrusted with the word of God. He says that even if some lacked faith, that did not nullify God's faithfulness. He says, "Let God be true and every man a liar. As it is written: 'So that you may be proved right when you speak and prevail when you judge.'" I say that born again Christians have also been entrusted with the Word of God and all are given the Holy Spirit as a teacher. All are admonished to become skilled in the use of the Word, understanding it correctly. All are admonished not to be tossed about by every wind of doctrine. Galatians and Colossians, especially, are full of warnings to mature believers not to be deceived by philosophies of men and false teachers and false teachings. Rom.3:7-8 says, "Someone may argue, 'If my falsehood enhances God's faithfulness and so increases his glory, why am I still condemned as a sinner,' Why not say -as we are being slanderously reported as saying and as some claim that we say- 'Let us do evil that good may result'? Their condemnation is deserved." Paul is saying that no matter how good a teaching sounds, if it is a falsehood, it is condemned. It is condemned even if that falsehood has some good results. When it comes to the Word of God, any man can tell a lie and believe that it brings God glory. But let God be true. Let His Word be true. Let man be called a liar.

My purpose is to expose the lies that are being perpetrated on God's people. This is the stuff that is being fed into ministers by the thousands every year. It has spread throughout the Christian community like evil leaven. Thank God there are thousands of ministers who do not buy into these distortions. But sadly, there are thousands who do. Those who do embrace the lies, pass them on to others in their congregations and to their friends.

The distortions concerning Abigail are out and out heresy that maligns one of God's women, God's Word, and God himself. It's malignant purpose is to discredit all women and to very subtly impress on Christian's minds that women are basically evil and that no matter what the decision is, if a woman acts on it she will tear her house

262

down. She is the cause of all the evil in her marriage.

What is the purpose of all of this biased teaching? It is Satan's way of fostering his own sin of pride in men, to elevate men to the place of an idol and to bring women ever deeper into subjection to man. This fulfills Satan's diabolical schemes that started in the Garden of Eden. And thus fulfilling God's prophetic warning "you shall turn to man and he shall lord it over you".

The careful critique of this small portion of this teacher's work may seem unnecessary to some. But I feel it's purpose is two-fold. 1) It is a lesson, especially for a newer Christian, on how to study the Word. Don't just take a well known teacher's word for anything. At the very least, get a Concordance and do some word studies to discover what things really mean. A teacher may be popular and well known. Their words may sound biblical, and wonderful. There can even be some good results of their words. But they can be wrong words, false doctrine.

2) It is also a significant demonstration of how the Church becomes apostate, even while the people are trying to be godly. Paul said this apostasy had already begun in his day. He warned, "Beware of the false teachers." He was talking to mature believers!! I say, wake-up Christian, discern false teaching and false teachers, lest you fall into apostasy. Those two reasons are why I went to such great lengths to show how the sermon of chapter six and the 3 chapters on the teachings by Bill Gothard are good-sounding words, taught or spoken by popular preachers/teachers, but they are false teachings. Thousands who listen to them are being sucked into apostasy by those teachings, even while being helped and blessed by other teachings of these same men.

I pray that these chapters will alert God's people to the dangerous traps that Satan has set

for them in the mouths of men. Let God's Word
be true and all men liars. To trust in any man
so explicitly, that you never doubt a word they
say, is a snare to you. Study the word they teach.
Retain the good and throw out the bad. Let the
Holy Spirit be your teacher. Like Abigail, your
first loyalty is to God and His purposes, not to
any man, be he husband, pastor, teacher, preacher
or other well known and trusted person. STUDY to
show YOURSELF approved by God.

# CHAPTER ELEVEN
## PERVERSIONS CONCERNING DIVORCE

As I go into this next section, my heart weeps for women who seek counsel from pastors who have had this training and who apply what they have learned. I think of the pain and misery these women are suffering, and how that pain is multiplied when they receive this kind of counsel. They are seeking what they think is God's solution to their problems by going to a pastor for counsel. But the women come away guilt ridden, believing the problems are all their fault because they feel they're inadequate. They feel they are not spiritual enough. They are made to believe that they do not have the right submissive attitudes, they are not doing the right thing in the right spirit, or saying the right thing, at the right time. They want to be obedient to God's will so they take the pastors counsel.

This material comes from Bill Gothard's manual for ministers only, "Basic Church Ministry", the section is under "Marriage Harmony, When The husband Wants a Divorce", page 10-11, under "Questions to ask the wife". These are questions for the pastor to ask a wife who comes to him for counsel when her husband initiates a divorce. As in the other chapters, the author's work will be in quotation marks. I will preface my thoughts with, MY COMMENTS.

"Number 8. Have you developed loyalty and appreciation among your children for their father?

A strong factor in a husband's desire to leave may be a spirit of disloyalty and ungratefulness which he senses in his children.----**If the wife IN ANY WAY resists her husband, SHE forces her children to choose between them, since no man can serve two masters.** (Emphasis mine). The wife can take the following steps to build loyalty and appreciation in the children:
1. Ask her children to forgive her for being a

265

poor example of a submissive wife.
2. Discuss with the children the need for them
to ask forgiveness for an independent or ungrateful
spirit. ----"
MY COMMENTS: There are no Scripture references.
    The father creates the feelings of disloyalty
and ungratefulness in his children by his actions
and attitudes. The Word says **fathers** should not
to provoke their children to wrath because many
fathers do have a tendency to do that with a
harshness that is unfair and demanding. If the
man is displaying bad manners, hurtful behavior,
cruelty, and if he is unjust, dishonest or lies
to his children and wife, he will reap disloyalty
and ungratefulness from them. Unless the man
repents and changes his ways, no matter what the
woman does or says to the children it will not
build loyalty and appreciation in her children
for their father. Notice how it is taken for granted
here that the woman is responsible for the feelings
the children have because she has not been
submissive to her husband! The author doesn't
even give her the benefit of doubt by using a
qualifying "IF". In this case, by taking the blame
for his bad actions, by asking forgiveness from
them for her unsubmissiveness and ungratefulness,
she fosters a host of bad things in the children.
That shows them that to be a Christian means that
you must, and will, take anything from anybody.
Then faun at their feet in abject shame because
you can't endure anymore hurt and abuse from them.
It teaches them that men can act in whatever way
they choose, they are not to be held responsible
or accountable for anything they do. It teaches
boys that they can blame all their bad behavior
on someone else. Girls are subtly taught that
the men's bad behavior is their fault. It teaches
children to be deceitful and dishonest and that
Christians are deceitful and dishonest and truth
must be hidden behind masks. It teaches them

266

that male adults are never wrong. It teaches children not to trust their own God-given instincts, intuitions and feelings. It teaches them unhealthy co-dependency. Co-dependency starts when one begins to make excuses and allowances for the other person's bad behavior,then takes blame on themselves for it. They minimize or deny the hurt they feel. Then they feel guilt because they are made to feel they are being disloyal or ungrateful when they acknowledge the fault in the other person and begin to hold them accountable. Co-dependency is also a form of idol worship, because everything in life centers around that person. Anyone who has been snared in that trap knows what a struggle it is to get out of it. These teachings teach children how to set men up as idols. It promotes irresponsibility in the fathers. Worst of all, it teaches them that God is not a God of justice, but a God of partiality.

Now, concerning loyalty to the father and how the woman can destroy that by resisting her husband in any way. Scripture tells me that father and **mother** are to be equally honored and obeyed. The mother deserves loyalty and obedience from her children also. Honor and loyalty are earned by one's behavior. There is a little more on this subject later.

"Question 10. Have you appealed to your husband to allow you not to violate your conviction of Scripture by getting a divorce? Answers: 1. She should appeal for a further opportunity to learn how to be the wife he wants and to gain the protection against temptation by staying under his authority.

**3. She should also assure him that every time she thinks of the divorce it will remind her of what happens when she tries to run her own life. (if she had a strong will)."** (Emphasis mine).

MY COMMENTS: There is no Scripture! This assumes that the man is all goodness and righteousness and the problem is that the wife has been completely negligent in being a good wife. It does not consider that the wife may have been everything a man could want, but that the man had abnormal expectations that no person could fulfill. It does not allow that the husband may be at fault because he beats her and the children, he's a drunk or sexually immoral, etc. It doesn't matter that he might be the one she needs protection from. No matter what he has done, she is supposed to bow to his majesty, the man, and say, 'I'm not good enough to keep you happy, what else do you want me to do? How else do you want me to degrade myself so that I can cling to you for protection?' And then, 'No matter what you have done or how you have treated me, I'll always remember how I ruined my own house and brought this on myself because I was not submissive to you. Forgive me for not wanting to be beaten and degraded and annihilated as a person by you with my unsubmissive attitude. I will always remember, I drove you away. It is all my fault.' I am being facetious and sarcastic. But believe me, I have encountered women in those kinds of situations, they are real. Their pain and suffering is not facetious. Please forgive my sarcasm, but I write with righteous indignation. I also speak from my own experience.

In the same manual, under SPECIFIC QUESTIONS RELATING TO DIVORCE, there are three categories, 1. Her questions, 2. Her frame of reference in asking the questions, 3. Insights she must realize in answering the questions. Page 13 of Building Marriage Harmony section.

"C. If my husband has left and filed for a divorce but occasionally returns to have a physical relationship, what should I do?
1. Frame of Ref.--She is repulsed at the thought of physical relationship without love or his accompanying responsibility.
Insight: She must see this as a supreme test that

her spirit is not bitter against him.
2. Frame of Ref. **She may fear physical disease
if she suspects he has been with other women.**
( Emphasis mine)
Insights: **She must be willing to bear in her body
the suffering of Christ to heal her husband
spiritually.** (Emphasis mine)
3. Frame of Ref.: She may feel degraded and fear
a bad reputation.
Insight: When the divorce is final, he no longer
has rights to a physical relationship."
MY COMMENTS: There are no Scriptures! Before a
relationship gets to the stage of divorce, extreme
woundedness and suffering has already occurred.
Add to that the rejection one feels when a mate
leaves and takes another woman. Add to that the
fact that it has been proven that a woman who cannot
trust and feel secure in her husband's love and
protection, becomes emotionally and biologically
shut down to him. There is nothing she can do to
generate those sexual feelings. It may not be a
reflection of her bitterness at all. NOBODY wants
to be used sexually by someone who does not want
them, except to use their body as a receptacle
for their sexual urges. It demonstrates the degree
of selfishness in the husband. It shows the measure
of hatred and disrespect the man has for her,
when he would want or demand a physical relationship from someone that he wants nothing else to
do with. It is using her like a cheap prostitute,
because he uses her body without paying her for
her services. The woman who allows herself to be
used like a prostitute by a husband who does not
want her, does not promote respect for her in
him, nor does it promote respect for him in her.
It totally destroys her self-respect. No one can
build harmony on such a faulty foundation.
   The next insight, that she must be willing
to bear suffering in her body to heal her husband
spiritually, is absurd. First of all, Christ has

269

already paid the price of suffering for healing. It is what is in the man's heart that will bring healing to him, not how much his wife suffers for him. If he has a reprobate mind, no amount of suffering in her body will bring him spiritual healing. This theory places a responsibility on her for something that only God and the man can do. Scripture says that adultery is worthy of stoning to death, that an immoral person is unclean and not to touch the unclean thing. Scripture says have nothing to do with one who calls themselves a brother and who does these things. Scripture never tells a Christian to embrace evil to draw another back to Him. No one in their right mind deliberately, knowingly, subjects themselves to sexual diseases, some of which can mean life long suffering. Some can be horribly damaging, if not fatal, to any future children the woman might have. Some, like AIDS, will cause agonizing death. After she submits herself to degradation and disease and has her reputation ruined, her life threatened, her self esteem scrapped, there is no guarantee that it will do anything in her husband except to make him loath and despise her more. Nobody respects a spineless jellyfish who does not respect herself enough to refuse to be used that way. Someone like that is pathetic. A man who would expect sex from a woman he is divorcing is repulsive and reprehensible. I speak from experience. Though there was no potential for sexually transmitted disease during the last eight years of my former marriage, I was willing to, and I did receive suffering in my body, to help my ex-husband get spiritually healed. But it was a fruitless endeavor because his heart was not yielded to God. I was willing to die for him, if it would have brought healing, but it would not. My suffering never made a dent in his armor-clad conscience.

One last comment. If the woman should get pregnant from his "visiting" her, then she will have another child to raise alone. The child will suffer in a home where it probably would not have a father to take care of it and share responsibility for it. So an innocent child is subjected to a life of misery and confusion. Then the woman and a child would bear the suffering for the man's healing, which might not ever take place.

"E. Question: Should I obtain legal counsel in getting a fair settlement?

1. Frame of Ref.: She may be unwilling to go through the suffering that God could use to convict the husband.

2. Her expectation may be on the husband for provision rather than the Lord. 3. She may be unwilling to reduce her standard of living according to the provision which God would provide.

Insights: 1. The more treacherous he is toward his wife the more pressure God will bring to him later **if his wife's spirit is right.** Mal.2:13-15. (Emphasis mine).

2. Even if a good settlement is reached she may expose herself to much bitterness when he fails to make payments or is late in making them.

3. God may be planning to use other people or means to provide her needs. 4. **Christians should go through the husband in providing for the wife.** (Emphasis mine)

5. **Going to a lawyer would only illustrate her demanding attitude and further alienate the husband.** (Emphasis mine).

MY COMMENTS: There is only one twisted Scripture given. Will God not deal with the man's treachery if the woman's spirit is not right? My Bible says nothing about the woman's spirit in that passage in Malachi. It merely states that God hates a man's violence and treachery against his wife and He will deal with it. God holds the man accountable for his actions, not the wife's spirit!!!! As far as other Christians trying to help the wife by going through the husband, he has already

demonstrated his treachery and that he is not to
be trusted for providing for her. It would be
futile to try to help her through him. He would
be just as treacherous with their provision as
he was with his own. Since the husband has already
hired a lawyer to start a divorce, to say that
her going to a lawyer to see that justice is done
is an illustration of her demanding attitude is
ludicrous. What kind of attitudes did her husband
display when he hired a lawyer first? Isn't the
man accountable for anything? If he wants everything and doesn't want to give her an equitable
amount, is that not showing his greedy, unloving,
irresponsibility? My Bible says that a man who
does not provide for his own is worse than an
infidel. God might want to use the enforcement
of an equitable settlement to bring him to a
conviction of his own idolatry and love of money
and his lack of love and caring concern for
someone he made a vow to and also for his children,
if there where any. If she is cheated financially
because she didn't retain a lawyer to protect
herself, couldn't she become bitter over that as
much as if he didn't make payments on time? After
all, she has no choice in the matter since he's
insisting on divorce. In this too, I speak from
experience. At the time of my divorce, my ex-
husband retained a lawyer who was supposed to
expedite a no-contest divorce. I was charged half
of his fee. However, he presented me with a paper
waiving all of my rights to legal council and
everything was geared to favor my husband. I was
desperate to be freed from him, so I signed it.
But I prayed that God would look out for my
interests. Through a series of circumstances,
God set aside those first papers and He provided
me with legal council!! Even though I was, and
still am, grateful for the settlement I did get,
it was not an equitable amount for my part of
34 years of faithfulness. Nor did it compensate

for my sacrifices over all those years to acquire the possessions we had. None of them came easy to us. I was taken advantage of and cheated. I chose to accept that. I did not have the desire or the will to fight for more. Also, I was still very much intimidated by my ex-husband and his threats. Even in a mutual desire for divorce, an attorney is necessary.

One last thought on these "Frame of Reference points. In all of this man's teachings, the woman is taught to be totally financially dependent on the husband. So how would she know that God would be her provider, in this divorce situation? Why wouldn't her expectations be that the man would be the provider? She cannot be trained to believe that she is never to be financially independent, that the husband is the provider, and yet not expect him to be, at the same time. That is not logical.

Remember these were questions from the woman whose husband was initiating the divorce. Yet, the pastor/counselor turns everything around to make her the one who bears all the responsibility, fault and blame, even though the husband left and may be involved in adultery!

The next section in "Building Marriage Harmony" is called "Enlarging The Frame Of Reference Of A Woman Who Wants To Get A Divorce". Page 14. There are two categories. 1. Specific reasons she gives for the divorce. 2. Is she Aware of the following factors. I will abbreviate them as "Specifics" and "Awareness".

"Specifics A. My husband is involved with another woman.

Awareness: 1. Many of the godly women in Scripture had husbands who shared their love with others. (Sarah, Rachel, Hannah, etc.)"

MY COMMENTS: While these men did have other wives, the fact remains that God made only one Eve for Adam. God intended marriage to be monogamous. Man

corrupted God's intentions and practiced polygamy
against God's commands. Because the patriarchs
did it, does not mean that it is right in God's
sight. Nor does it mean that because those men
and women did it, a woman has to accept it. Neither
does it mean that the woman is ungodly if she
cannot and does not accept it. See Deut.17:17;
Lev.18:18; Mal.2:1,4,5. The very basic foundation
of the marriage is destroyed in that one false
teaching. In the New Testament, a godly man was
to be the husband of one wife only. See
Matt.19:4,5; Mark 10:2-8; I Tim.3,12; Tit. 1:6.
 Scripturally, sex with anyone other than the
marriage partner is considered adultery! The
Old and the New Testaments both call adultery sin
worthy of stoning. The New Testament does away
with stoning but it DOES say adultery is grounds
for divorce, no matter how anyone wants to rationalize and explain that away. I do not recall any
incidences in the New Testament of polygamy amongst
the leaders in the Church. Finally, even as ungodly
as our country is, the government of our land
still recognizes that polygamy is wrong. Ungodly
Old Testament practices can never be a basis for
a godly marriage.
2. Awareness: "God is able to work directly on
the husband's conscience as illustrated in Gen.
20".
MY COMMENT: Gen. 20 is held up as the model for
doing whatever your husband says, even if it is
a lie and it will bring you great harm. In this
account Sarah is used as the example that even
though she could have been sexually used by the
king, God protected her because she was obedient
to her husband in everything. God did protect
her, no doubt about that. **But he did not protect
her by working on Abraham's conscience!!!** He did
it by speaking to the king! The king acted out
of a righteous fear of God here. Not Abraham.
Abraham would have let happen to Sarah whatever

the king wanted to happen to her. **It was not a repentant heart or a smitten conscience from Abraham that saved her.** Yet that is exactly what this Awareness says. Sarah's protection came because of her own worship, obedience, and trust in God, not from her worship, obedience and trust in Abraham.

I understand Sarah's obedience to Abraham even though what he asked her to do was wrong. She knew his faults and sins and yet she called him lord and master. That was because she knew from experience that his heart was God's. He had demonstrated his obedience, and his love of God many times. She could trust that in him.

In the New Testament, God said he would not work on the of mind of a person who has a seared conscience. He turns it over to it's own reprobation.!! Heb. 12:16,17. I am not implying that Abraham had a seared conscience or a reprobate mind. We know he was a righteous man called by God. I am referring to other men who do have reprobate minds. Even though they might cry out to Him, He says he will not hear them, it's too late, once He's turned them over to their own reprobation. So God will NOT work directly on the husband's conscience in such a case. To trust that He would on the basis of Gen. 20, is shear folly, for God DID NOT work on Abraham's conscience.

3. Awareness: "Are there needs the other woman is meeting that she must learn to meet, especially in her spirit."

MY COMMENTS: There is no Scripture. This again puts all the responsibility on the woman for not being good enough. The husband assumes no responsibility for breaking his vows, or perhaps for not communicating his needs to his wife. If a woman doesn't meet her husband's needs he is apparently free to disregard his vows and God's commands and is free to find somebody who will meet them. Supposedly, it's his wife's fault that he has to find someone else. His wife's bad spirit excuses him for the sin he blatantly commits against her and God. Never mind the fact that his "needs" may be something that no human could meet. Also, the other woman has an unfair advantage. She has not lived with the man and his faults full time. When she does, she may develop a negative spirit towards him, too, if he has not changed what caused the negative responses in his first wife.

4. Awareness: "Has the wife looked on this as an opportunity to heal her husband through a spirit that is deeply grateful and not easily alarmed? I Pet. 3:6".

MY COMMENTS: Again Scripture is twisted to allow the man total freedom to commit adultery with no consequences for his sin. Where there is no accountability, there is no godly sorrow, that works repentance. To set aside a multitude of other Scriptures, in order to use this passage this way is foolishness. It sends a woman back to endure more shame and heartache, and pays no heed to what this does to the wife and children, emotionally and spiritually.

Specifics B. :"My husband either neglects or is too hard on the children. "Awareness 1. "Can the wife work with the children to remove actions or attitudes that prompt the father's responses?"

MY COMMENTS: Again, there is no Scripture basis. The father is the one who provokes the Children!!! They are responding to his actions. No matter how the mother works with the children, it is his behavior towards them that is the source of the problem and a change in his own attitudes is the only remedy. He must repent, ask forgiveness from his children, and change his ways in order for them to make a lasting change in their responses. As with all of these points, the responsibility to make wrong things right, is shifted to the woman, instead of making the husband be accountable for HIS harshness, HIS neglect that is so bad the woman

276

feels the need to get the children away from him.
Awareness 2. "Is there a clash of will between
the husband and wife? This will cause the children
to take sides. 'He will either hate the one and
love the other or hold to the one and despise the
other'. Matt.6:24"
MY COMMENTS: In other words, if the woman is not
completely dominated by the husband and if she
expresses her desire that he either pay more
attention to the children or requests that he not
be so harsh with them, then SHE is causing them
to hate one or the other of the parents. I know
from experience that children feel wounded and
abandoned, and are sometimes emotionally damaged
beyond repair, when a mother stands by and lets
the husband beat the kids or be unduly harsh with
them or lets him neglect them. That makes them
hate the father (provokes them to wrath) and feel
abandoned by the mother. They feel extremely
vulnerable with no one to protect them. Remember
this is severe enough neglect and hardness to drive
the mother to want a divorce to get the kids away
from him to a place of safety. That Scripture
was never intended to mean that a man is to be
dominant and the woman subservient, so that a child
can have only one master. This would completely
disregard all other Scripture about honoring both
father and mother, and obeying your parents
(plural). That Scripture, in context, says that
one cannot serve God and the world at the same
time. This is an outrageous misinterpretation to
even suggest that it is a proof text for the
domination of the father in the home and that any
opposing expression by the wife will divide the
loyalties of the child and cause them to hate one
parent.
  Specific C. "My husband is attacking the children
morally."
Awareness 1. "Are the children dressing and acting
sensually?"

# PERVERSION OF SUBMISSION

MY COMMENTS: NO SCRIPTURE!! Who is the responsible adult? First, if the child is doing those things, it is the parent's job to provide them with decent clothing and then to teach them how to act so it is not sensual. There is absolutely no excuse for a father to blame his own perverse, pedophile behavior on his children.

Awareness 2: "Has the wife appealed to the proper authority, husband, grandfather, pastor and law?"

MY COMMENTS: Most often, the father will force the child to keep this kind of thing a secret. The woman, in all of these teachings, is taught not to make a decision on her own, never to disagree with her husband in ANY matter, but to bow to his every command. She is taught that she is never to seek outside counsel without her husband's permission. She has been taught to cover up for his wrong doing. Where would she ever get the backbone now to go to an authority against the man????

Awareness 3. "Has she taught the daughter how to build up a resistance to immoral approaches and to cry out to God if they should occur? (Duet. 22:24; Psalm 56:9)".

MY COMMENTS: **OUTRAGEOUS** !!!!!!!No daughter should have to be taught to build up a resistance to her father's molestation!! If the man sexually abuses or rapes his daughter, it is too late for her to cry out to God. The physical, emotional, spiritual damage is already done, no matter how she cries out to God. Often, this kind of abuse is perpetrated on a child so young that they would not know how to cry out to God or to any one else. All the crying out to God did for a woman who was being raped, was to proclaim her innocent of voluntarily participating in the act. It did not prevent the attack from happening!! It is a gross misuse of Deut. 22:24 to apply it to a father molesting a child. Many times this kind of molestation goes on for a long time before the mother ever even suspects that it's happening.

How could she ever tell her daughter to ward off her father, if she does not know about it? A far better Scripture to use here would be I Cor. 5 where it speaks about incest specifically. That was an abomination to God, and should have been to the Church. It should be an abomination to Church teachers today, too. Paul instructed that the man was to be shunned by ALL until he repented!!!! Instead of saying that a mother ought to teach her daughter how to ward off her father's immoral approaches, the woman should be counseled to handle the matter in the same way Paul instructed the Church to deal with the issue!!! Again remember this sexual abuse of the children was bad enough for the woman to want to get the children away from the father to a place of safety!! To say that this is not grounds for divorce and that the woman and children should stay with him, that the woman should appeal to the husband, etc. and teach her daughter how to fight off her dad's advances and to call on God to protect her from her daddy is more than outrageous. It seems that nothing a man does is worthy of any kind of censure according to these teachings. He is put so far above mortal man that he has truly become an idol. The marriage becomes an idol, that must be maintained at all costs!! In many states, by law, the mother would be deemed just as guilty as the father if she did not report this and take those children out of that situation. Morally, if she did not end this in what ever way was necessary, she is as guilty as the man. She becomes an accomplice to his crime. In this "awareness", even the innocent children are made to bear the brunt of the responsibility for the man's sinful actions. The mother is to teach them how to avoid being molested by their father. It's the children who are required to change--not the father. He does not bear the consequences of his sin by losing his wife and children perhaps. Or

of being brought to justice by the law. So he
does not repent. Rather than his wife being a loving
helpmate, she enables him to sin. He is the
spiritual loser.
Specifics D. "My husband gets drunk and then beats
me."
Awareness 1."Is the wife fulfilling the physical
needs of her husband?" Awareness 2. "Are there
attitudes or actions which are irritating him when
he is sober? Often a man will do in drunkenness
what he desired to do in soberness because the
inhibitions are lifted."
Awareness 3. "Has she corrected all past offenses?"
Awareness 4. **"Has she dedicated her body to God
and inwardly purposed to thank God for whatever
happens?"** (Emphasis mine)
Awareness 5. "Was she aware that he drank before
she married him"?
MY COMMENTS: No Scripture!! If the wife does not
meet his physical needs, or does something to
irritate the man, does that give him license to
get drunk and beat her? Or if she has offended
him and hasn't made that right with him with abject
humility and repentance, does that also give him
liberty to get drunk and beat her? The man's vow
is to love and protect his wife. Why should she
dedicate her body to be beaten and assaulted by
him? If we suffer or are martyred for Christ's
sake their is honor and reward. There is no honor
in being beaten, maimed or killed by a drunken
husband, just because of his bad uncontrolled
temper. What has happened to the Scriptures about
long suffering, and forbearing? Doesn't that apply
to a man whose wife has not confessed every deed
that she has done that hasn't pleased the man?
What has happened to the Scriptures that say,
honor the woman as the weaker vessel and as a joint
heir of salvation, and love your wife as Christ
loved the church and gave himself up for her?
What ever happened to the Scriptures that say don't

let the sun go down on your anger, and don't be drunk with wine, and God hates a man who covers his violence towards his wife with a cloak? I guess those and many more apply only to women and have been erased altogether when it comes to men being responsible for their own behavior. The man is allowed to act out his aggression that is an evil in his own heart. It is there when he is sober but he uses drunkenness as an excuse to unleash it on his wife. But she is at fault because she irritated him. Why didn't he talk to her about his irritations and deal them with within himself like a responsible adult "head of the family"?

This kind of teaching is poison and it is polluting the church with ungodly, unbiblical principles of heresy. My heart aches for women who are sent back into homes like this where the man is the idol king who can do no wrong and the woman and the children are the reason for all the man's bad behavior. It is a perversion of biblical submission to say that the wife must submit to any evil thing the man wants to do to her and the children, and to do it in the right spirit. They must endure all manner of pain and suffering and wait upon the Lord for as long as it takes for God to get through to the man. Unfortunately, if the man is not confronted and is not made to see his sin and is not held accountable for it--he never comes to a place where he has to deal with it. This is a perversion of God's word. It is an abomination to Him. A stink in His nostrils. Why am I being so harsh? How do we know this is how God feels? Because Mal.2:7,8 says "For the lips of a priest should preserve knowledge and men should seek instruction from his mouth for he is the messenger of the Lord of hosts. But as for you, you have turned aside from the way; you have caused many to stumble by the

the instruction; you have corrupted the covenant of Levi" says the Lord of hosts. Vs. 9, "So I also have made you despised and abased before all the people, just as you are not keeping My ways but are **showing partiality in the instruction**". Vs. 14, 15 b. says, "Yet you say 'For what reason?' Because the Lord has been a witness between you and the wife of your youth, against whom you have dealt treacherously, though she is your companion and your wife of covenant. ---------So take heed to your spirit, and let no man deal treacherously against the wife of your youth". Vs. 16, "For I hate divorce" says the Lord God of Israel, "AND him who covers his garment with wrong," says the Lord of hosts, "So take heed that you do not deal treacherously". The word garment here is a euphemism that means wife. God hates it when a man covers his wife with wrong. Vs. 17, "You have wearied the Lord with your words. Yet you say, 'How have we wearied him?' In that you say, 'Everyone who does evil is good in the sight of the Lord, and He delights in them'. Or, 'Where is the God of Justice'."(NASB) What this says is that God hates it when a pastor teaches partiality that allows a man to abuse his wife and then twists Scripture to prove it was God's command. God says that kind of teaching wearies Him, He does not approve of it or take delight in it. It is opposite of His just nature. He hates it as much as He hates divorce. He is giving a stern warning to men to be careful how they treat women. He hates and despises preferential treatment given to men by pastors, ministers and teachers of His word, for they have corrupted the covenant of Christ!

Concerning Gothard's point, has the woman dedicated her body to God and inwardly purposed to be thankful for whatever happens, the implication is that whatever she suffers at the hand of her husband, is for the glory of God. My mind keeps going back to the Scriptures of Romans 5:1-11. That explains that we are all justified by faith and we stand in THAT grace. It is an individual stand. The woman cannot do it for the man by suffering his cruelty to her. That Grace is the Hope of Glory. The Grace here is the gift of Christ who died for us. That includes the suffering He did. THAT suffering was for each individual. I am sure that verse 7 is used as a basis for the theory that if we suffer and die for someone it will bring glory to God. It says that **sometimes, someone,** might choose to die for a **good and righteous man.** I take that to mean that sometimes a few very loving and dedicated persons might choose to take the place of a very good and righteous person and die in their stead. The specifics are clear. A righteous person is dying in the place of another righteous person. It is not a matter of a person dedicating their body to be maimed, beaten, or even killed by an unrighteous person, in response to a false teaching on submission. Vs. 8 shows clearly that that kind of thing is not God's plan. He said His love was shown for us in that while we were in the unrighteous state of an evil person, Christ substituted himself for us. His death brought reconciliation to God. To think that a woman should purpose in her heart to suffer every vile and cruel thing a husband wants to do to her, even to the death, for his salvation is really taking Christ's place, because Christ already did that for him. I have heard of rare testimonies where a woman will suffer inhuman treatment at the hands of her spouse for many years and finally the spouse says, because you suffered all of this, I see the witness of Christ in you and I will accept Him. But one needs to be sure that is what God is calling them to do. But how does it bring Glory to God when a professing Christian man demonstrates such cruelty to his Christian wife? That goes against

every Godly principle for marriage. It cannot
be a witness for Christ and God's love. As we have
just read, God hates that kind of abuse of the
wife.

These teachings are propagated throughout the
churches of America every year through the Gothard
minister's seminars. The Minister's Manuals are
used as reference material for marriage counseling
by many pastors across our country. The partiality
in these teachings is glaringly pronounced. To
say the abusiveness of the man is a good means
of building spiritual character in the woman, while
she suffers untold misery at his hands, is what
God calls dealing treacherously and unjustly with
his wife. God hates the violence and injustice
of the man towards his wife as much as he hates
divorce. God is tired of man justifying his bad
behavior against his wife and his children in the
name of "submit to your husband in everything".
That is a gross perversion of His word and His
principles and His plan for the home life of his
people. The Old Testament called the leaders
priests, but God hates it when pastors and teachers
of today show this kind of partiality and favoritism
toward men. He was condemning the leaders for
that specific offense then, and since He never
changes, He condemns it today too. God himself
will deal with teachers who are purveyors of this
kind of perversion of His Word, for He says He
hates those who pervert the Word He has entrusted
to them to teach with purity. They are supposed
to be representatives of God's impartial heart.

Before I leave this chapter, that exposes
the false teaching that a woman must submit to
her husband's cruel and unjust treatment because
he is the authority over her, I'd like to bring
your attention to a couple of other passages.

In Acts 14:2-6 there is a balance to the
teaching that one must submit to all authority
over you and one must always turn the other cheek

to receive more cruelty from one who wants to despitefully use you. This passage relates how Paul and Barnabas were in Iconium and "There was a plot afoot among the Jews and Gentiles **together with their leaders to mistreat them and stone them.** But they found out about it and **FLED-**". I truly believe there are times when God wants to build Christian character and maturity through suffering and enduring hardship. There is plenty of evidence in the Word that Paul suffered many times, **for the Lord,** and he became stronger and more mature because of it. Like Paul, I have allowed God to do a lot of that in my own life. Again, like Paul and Barnabas, I also know that it is not always God's will for me to submit to harsh cruelty and abuse from someone else. Jesus himself told his disciples in Math. 10:23 "When you are persecuted in one place, **FLEE** to another". Under some circumstances, you present the other cheek. But in other circumstances, you flee, you get away from the danger.

Jesus himself did not allow himself to be persecuted until it was God's time and for God's purpose. He did not do anything according to the will of man or for man's purpose. It was always according to the will of the Father. In John 10:39 he did not submit to the will of man but to the Father's will. It says, "again, they tried to seize him, but he escaped their grasp". He himself did not always present the other cheek. He fled from the persecution and the danger when He knew it was not the Father's will for him to suffer that. We need to follow His example, and Paul and Barnabas' example. We need to be sure what we are suffering is of the Lord and not the will of a man or as the result of biased, partial, perverse teaching. To live healthy Christian lives, we must interpret Scripture in context of the whole Bible. There has to be a good balance, where we weigh one Scripture with other Scripture so that we get a clear understanding of what the Lord would want us to do in each circumstance. To pick out a verse, or even a few verses, build a doctrine on that, then apply it to every like-circumstance, while ignoring balancing Scriptures, is extremely dangerous for any Christian. But when teachers propagate that kind of unbalanced teaching so that great multitudes of women of God endure untold suffering, it is not only dangerous, it is devastating, destructive, and sometimes deadly.

The teaching in many churches today, concerning the submission of women, is far more damaging than the subservient lifestyle forced on Old Testament women. Choice was taken from them, but women of today have the choice because Christ gave them that choice to submit willingly to a loving Christian husband. He redeemed them from that subservient bondage. But men, especially Christian men leaders, have suppressed that freedom through the ages by their false teachings. Women have been denied the freedom that Christ died to give them. Because His Son died for that freedom, is God more upset about the partiality that is taught today then He was with partiality teachings by the Priests of the Old Testament?

Lest the reader get the wrong impression, I want to clarify something before leaving this chapter. Because I have used my personal experiences as a demonstration of the distorted principles of divorce detailed in this chapter, many might think that I hold bitterness toward my ex-husband and that I am still suffering from the wounds from him and pastors. I want you to know, my wounds have been healed. There is no bitterness towards my ex-husband, pastors, lawyers or anyone else. There is no pain when I relate these things. They are just facts. I only shared my experiences to show that when these false principles are put into practice, they do not always produce the effect they are supposed to according to Bill Gothard's teachings. Or any other teacher who is a proponent of these same kinds of false teachings. Gothard often quotes success stories of those who did apply the teachings and got the desired effect. However, those who tell him they applied the teachings, but it didn't work, are told that they didn't try hard enough or long enough or that their attitude or spirit was not right. I am sure he could find areas where I failed, too. I am one who practiced his principles for years before I ever heard his teachings. By nature I have always been a submitted and passive person. After I heard his teachings, I adjusted some things and followed them even closer. As you will see in my personal testimony chapter, I had the right spirit, most of the time. In all, I practiced those principles for 34 years in that marriage. No one can say I did not try hard enough or long enough or that I did not have the right spirit. I chose to share my experiences in this chapter so that others might know that I speak from experience as well as from the Word. I am not just espousing a biased opposing theory. I have lived it both ways. I shared them so that other women might be healed and set free. So that other women might find hope without the guilt and condemnation that comes from these false teachings and teachers.

May God bless His women with hope and freedom!!

# CHAPTER TWELVE
## MY PERSONAL TESTIMONY

Many of Gothard's teachings helped me to mature in Christ so things I have come to understand concerning the particular teachings I shared with you, grieves me. Even though I have been healed of my wounds, it was difficult to write because I know the pain, woundedness, condemnation and guilt I suffered unnecessarily because of it. I know how others have suffered the same things. Much of it is very personal to me and that is why I shared the false principles and their results in my life in the last chapter. Interwoven in my personal testimony, you will see these principles, how they benefited me, how they hurt me, and how some of them had the potential to destroy me.

I came from a home that was good. My parents did not have any major vices. No drinking, smoking, carousing etc. They did not have big anger problems and they did not take out their frustrations on us girls and call it discipline. We were spanked when we deserved it. My parents were married for 57 years. On the day my mother died, my Dad said to me. "I loved her. In all those years I never so much as looked at another woman". How I respect my father for that!!

By nature, I was an introverted and submissive person. I would hide my feelings, bury them. I would not share my feelings because I thought it might hurt the other person's feelings or it would make them angry with me.

At the age of fifteen, I met and started dating the man I would marry. We went steady for a few months, broke up, he served two years in Korea, I finished high-school. He came back, we got together again and got married. I was not yet 19 years old. 14 months later, just a month before my 20th birthday, I had my first daughter.

Starting in the first year of marriage, my husband would threaten me by saying things like,

"If I don't get enough sex at home, I'll go elsewhere to get it". "If I had a wife who did this or that, I'd get rid of her". "I wouldn't have a woman like that". I was always insecure, with of fear of being discarded and replaced. There was fear of not performing good enough or of not being sexually adequate.

The first baby girl was just old enough to sit in a highchair and hold a glass of milk. One day her Dad said to her, "Don't spill your milk". But she did. That is normal. But his reaction was not normal. He backhanded her. He hit her in the forehead so hard that the force of it almost tipped the highchair over. He jumped up and left the room in furious anger. I was stunned and was left with a terrified baby. My mother happened to call when I was still in the shock of this incident. I talked to her about it. He overheard what I said to my mother, became more angry, and refused to talk to me for three days.

From then on, he was able to control me with his threats and his anger.

By 1963, the eighth year of that marriage, we had 3 more little girls. He did not beat the girls daily, as some abusive parents do, but through those years there would be times when his anger would take over and he would lash out at them in a rage. One time I came home from a doctor's appointment and found him kicking one of the girls who was on the floor in a heap. She was only $2\frac{1}{2}$-3 years old. It was occasional things like that. He was harsh and strict with them all the time.

It didn't seem like he was openly disrespectful to me and he taught the girls to respect me as their mother. But he continually undermined my self-esteem and my worth as a person. Nothing was ever quite good enough.

In the spring of 1964, my self esteem was at rock bottom. I did not think I was a good

mother, wife, housekeeper, sex partner or anything.
I felt like I was worthless and my life was a mess.
Then there was a Billy Graham television crusade.
I had never heard of him before. But I listened
and thought he made a lot of sense. The next night
I listened again and said the sinner's prayer with
him. I accepted Christ and made Him Lord of my
life, without even knowing what I was doing. I
said, "God my life is a mess, if you want it you
can do whatever you want with it."

I looked for a church that preached like Billy
Graham did. Even then, I was submitted to spiritual
authority, because he said find a church to attend
and so I looked for one. But I did not find one
that preached like he did in that area. Though
I read the Bible sporadically, I understood what
I read. I bought some Tennessee Ernie Ford gospel
hymn records and learned the words and sang along
with him. I learned to worship God by myself
through that. I would stand ironing all those
little dresses for four girls and sing for hours.
I would rock my little ones and sing the hymns
to them. God took away the sinful desires I had.
He changed me from the inside out. I didn't have
any Christians around to tell me what a Christian
ought to do and what they ought not to do. The
Holy Spirit taught me Himself and changed me
Himself.

About this time my husband began to travel
for his company. He would be gone from 2-3 days
to 2-3 months at a time. He was so strict and
harsh with the girls and there was such an
undercurrent of tension in our home that some of
the girls and I welcomed these times when he left.
I found out much later that some of these trips
provided him occasions to commit adultery. One
time he fell in love with another woman, which
hurt me worse than just the physical adultery.

Also about this time, he began to show a marked
interest in different sexual things and he began

to bring in pornography. I told him that I did not want that stuff in the house for the girls to see, but he brought it in anyway and I feared him too much to throw it away.

Then one day he read an ad in the paper from a couple who lived nearby who wanted to swap mates. For those who are innocent of such things, that means for married couples to exchange mates for a brief sexual encounter. He made an appointment with them and took me to their house. I thank God that He protected me. Nothing happened that night. I had not told my husband about my salvation before, but the next day I told him I had accepted Jesus as my savior and that I could not participate in wife swapping because that was a sin against God. Besides that, it was not in my make-up to do something like that. He was furious with me. He said that if I would not wife swap to please him, if I loved God more than I loved him, and would rather please God than him, then we might as well get a divorce right now.

We did not get a divorce and the issue was dropped. But his sexual appetites for different things accelerated. The angry rages continued.

One day, 10 years into the marriage, in 1965 he told me that he was a transvestite. He had to explain to me that a transvestite is a cross-dresser, a person who wants to dress in the other genders clothing. I had no idea what it was, or that it was a sin. He told me that this had been in his life for as long as he could remember. He had a brief time of freedom from it when he married me. He said that much of his anger was due to the frustration from fighting the desire to cross-dress all the time. This was the time of the beginning of the sexual revolution and even Christians were saying experimenting with new things was good. So that is what I thought this was. Just fun and games. I thought, if I went along with this, then he wouldn't be so angry and we

291

would have more peace in our home. So I bought him some women's clothing, a wig and some make-up. Thank God, He forgives us our sins of ignorance when we come to know what sin is and repent of it!!! I was only a baby Christian of just a little more than a year.

Soon, his dressing up alone was not enough for him. He wanted more. He wanted me to participate in dress up parties with just him and me. His perversion went beyond just dressing up for emotional satisfaction. It included sexual arousal as well. It was a trap and a snare. The beginning of a long road to degradation. I realized that this thing was growing ever stronger and more consuming. It was much more sinister than just fun and games. Then I found Duet. 22:5. "The woman shall not wear that which pertaineth to a man, neither shall a man wear that which pertaineth to a woman, for all that do so are an abomination unto the Lord thy God".(KJV)

His anger had not abated. I knew that I could no longer participate in his dress up parties. They were so shameful and degrading and yet I feared his anger and feared that he would leave me with those four daughters to raise by myself. And so I kept praying for God to put a stop to these awful parties. But God, in His own way, let me know , "this is sin, you are participating in it, you must stop it yourself." Finally, one day when I could handle the degradation no longer, I gathered up my courage and confronted him with the fact that I would not participate any longer. If he had to cross dress, he would have to go to a motel by himself to do it. I would not do it any longer, nor did I want to see him do it ever again. He would have to do it alone. I knew he would leave. He packed his bags and was ready to take them to the car. That ended my participation in those awful dress-up parties. He never dressed up in front of me again. He

292

never went to motels to do it either.

I had witnessed to him many times by this
time. Now I told him that he didn't have to leave.
If God could set a drug addict or alcoholic free,
he could set a transvestite free also. He did
not leave. He eventually accepted Christ. When
he did, he burned all the pornography, all the
women's clothing, make-up and wig. He had some
freedom from transvestitism. He came to know Christ
8 years after I did, in our 16th year of marriage.

It was a period of 7 years from the time
he told me what he was until he accepted Christ.
I never sought or received counseling from anyone
during that time. Shortly after he told me, though,
I developed rhumatoid arthritis. The Dr. asked
if I had had a traumatic experience lately. I
told him what my husband had told me. He asked,
"What did you do about it?" I told him I went
and bought him the clothes, etc. He said "Good
girl". That was the only person I ever shared
my burden with for many years. That was the only
"counseling" I received.

Shortly after he was born again, a very strange
thing happened. We were sitting at a table together
and the subject of Halloween came up. In the early
seventies nobody was talking about Satan worship
and demons like we do today. Christian churches
were holding Halloween parties for the youngsters,
where they would dress up like ghosts and goblins
and devils etc. I was expressing my views that
Halloween was a satanic holiday and that Christian
churches had no business celebrating it in their
buildings that were supposed to be God's houses.
All of a sudden he became furious, he jumped up
and hit me in the face, giving me a black eye and
breaking my glasses. He was mortified that he
had done that. He had never struck me before.
I did not have a great understanding at that point
in time of satanic things, but I knew this was
demonic and it was a reaction to what I had said.

But that was the beginning of God's preparation of what was to come.

Eighteen months after he was born again, he was called into the ministry. He attended a Bible Institute for nine months. God did miracles that I could relate to you, and He answered specific prayers in specific ways, to prove that this was of God. There was no doubt about it. Before he finished nine months at the school, he was called to be a pastor of a church. He served in that church for 18 months. The next pastorate was for $4\frac{1}{2}$ years. The next one was for 4 years. All together he was in the ministry 10 years.

The school that he went to was very strong in the wrong teachings of submission and headship. This fed his tendency to dominate and control, but now it had the sanction of the "Christian" world. These teachings fed into my submissive spirit as well. So the power and control became an even more dominant factor in our marriage. His anger continued to be a major problem also.

About 5 years into the ministry, the anger was fierce and I knew there was something wrong, but I did not know what. Finally he told me that transvestitism was not gone. He had relief from it for a short time, but that it had returned and again he was continually fighting the desire to cross dress. Except, now it was worse, because he already knew Christ and that had not set him free. Now it was more complicated because he was a pastor.

By this time I had acquired a good knowledge of how to do warfare against demons from a seminar that we had attended. He did not like the seminar, so he did not go to as many of the sessions as I did. We moved to the 3rd church. I was continually praying with him to overcome this desire to cross dress, believing that he would be set free from it and overcome it. But as time went on, I began to notice that the seams of my clothing were ripped open. He finally admitted that at times the desire would overtake him and he would put on my clothes. He was much bigger than I. Thus the ripped seams. He said that at times he would not even know what he was doing, but would come out of a trance or whatever it was, and find himself standing in front of the mirror, fully dressed in my clothes. He had not been aware of dressing. Sometimes he would come into the bathroom and watch me put on my make-up. I had the most eerie feeling that it was not my husband who was watching me, but something or someone else looking through his eyes.

Then he began to display other strange sexual behavior. Again, I did not know what this was leading to. Or what it was. But it, too, overtook his life, and mine right along with it.

Finally, I was driven to seek counseling. The man I called was the pastor who had taught the seminar on warfare. I did not identify myself to him. The first question I asked was "could a demon make a man's body do this"? Without knowing me or why I had asked the question, his answer was "Yes, one could do this, but that kind of demon never travels alone, it always travels with the demon of transvestitism and transsexualism." He began to ask me, "Is this happening, is that happening?" and I would have to say yes to every question because it was happening. I was shocked at how demonized my husband was. I was shocked when I understood how I was being used to try to satisfy the demons of lust that were operating in him. It was not a man that I was trying to satisfy sexually. Now this other thing that had taken over our lives had a name -Transsexual. So I told my husband what I had found out and said that if he did not go for counseling and deliverance that I would have to leave him, even though I loved him. We had been married for 26 years by then.

He said he would go for deliverance. That started an 8 year battle for his freedom. I loved him, I supported him, I prayed for him, I held him in my arms for hours at a time to comfort him. I did everything I could think of to do to help him out of the trap he was in. I was willing to die if it would help him be free. Finally, sometimes during the last 3 years of the marriage, I was driven to anger and angry reactions that were very ungodly.

This pastor, who had taught the seminar, agreed to do some deliverance for him. And he did do extensive deliverance. But about the 4th or 5th visit he informed my husband that he was never to set foot on his property again. He said my husband's will was too strong and it was not submitted to God and he must take this to throne room of God for himself.

We had two interviews with another couple for the purpose of having them do deliverance for him. They refused on the same grounds. His will was too strong, it was not submitted to God. Besides that, the woman had the greater gift of discernment and they said that they knew he would never submit to a woman because of his chauvinism.

We did not know anyone else at the time who ministered deliverance. No pastor friend would even listen to such a thing let alone do it. We bought the book "Pigs In The Parlor" by Frank Hammond. I had already sat through all the deliverance sessions with him and a lot of sessions with someone else, so I knew what to do. I also knew that deliverance was a process that had to go along with counseling so that sinful habit patterns could be changed. Otherwise the demons would be able to come back. But he demanded that I do much deliverance immediately. So I did. It did not hold.

His anger grew worse. He became physically violent with me. Many times he'd push me against a wall forcibly, and hold me there, causing bruises and scratches.

He believed he had a hormone imbalance that would make him feel like a woman. So he went to a geneticist, thinking he could be given some male hormone shots that would make him feel more like a man. In relating what the Dr. had said, my husband added some lies to it so that he could manipulate me into doing as he desired. He used that to make me feel sorry for him, and to feel that I was being too hard on him, because after all, he had a physical problem that was partially to blame for all this. The geneticist had told him that physically and emotionally he was a prime candidate for a sex change operation. On the way home from that doctor's office, he nearly committed suicide, but at the last moment pulled the car away from a concrete abutment that he was heading towards at 100 miles per hour. For the next few days, I did not know who I would be talking to from one minute to the next. He would, literally, alternate between the man/pastor who was devastated by this news and the woman within who was elated that he was so much like a woman emotionally and physically. It was a horrible experience.

For months I had been discerning that there was a more powerful demon than transvestite and transsexual in him. But every time I would get close to it, he would get angry. One time though, in a fit of anger, he was storming down the hall after me. He was yelling at me "You think you are so smart, You're so self righteous. I'll show you how wrong you are. If there is any demon like you say, I renounce wo------." That is as far as he got. He was knocked flat on his face from a walking position. Unconscious. The word he was prevented from saying was "woman". That was it's name. I had to pat his face, call his name, shake him, and invoke the name of Jesus many times him before the demon would release it's control over

297

him and let him come back to consciousness. He
had to confess that he had added lies to what
the Dr. had said. When he did that, the demon
had to leave. But he went around with a spirit
of mourning for days after that. I found out later
that it is normal for a person to feel a sense
of loss when a demon has been a part of them for
so long and is no longer there. It is like a part
of their personality is missing.

Many times during those years, he had struggled
so hard and was so weary of it all that he wanted
to commit suicide. One day, I happened to go into
the bedroom, he was sitting on the bed, a loaded
gun and an open Bible beside him. I asked "What
are you doing?" He said he wanted to end it all.
God took over in me. I did not begin to plead
with him or console him. I walked out. He said
"Where are you going?". I said "If you think I'm
going to wait around in this house and wait for
you to kill yourself, you are crazy". I grabbed
my car keys and got in the car. I drove around
for $\frac{1}{2}$ hour, praying and binding the spirit of
suicide all the time. I finally felt a peace
and went home. The gun was put away. He said
the Lord had given him a Scripture that had given
him hope.

After his deliverance began, he stayed in
the pulpit for $2\frac{1}{2}$ more years. Then the Lord removed
him from the ministry. At that point in time, he
gave a public testimony of what had been happening
in his life. He said that God had set him free
from transvestism and transsexualism. He gave God
the Glory for victory. It was a moving testimony.
Very powerful. That was probably the most free
he had ever been. Or ever would be. After six
years of the battle though, he came to a crossroads,
where he was free enough from the demonic influence
over his mind to make a rational decision of which
god he wanted to follow, his god of perversion
or the Living God. He said with his mouth that

he wanted God, but from then on his actions showed that in his heart he had chosen the other way.

During the last 8 years of that marriage, we went to a succession of secular and Christian counselors, deliverance ministers and doctors. During that time his anger continually worsened. I suffered bruises from hits and from being pushed around, and even bites once. I suffered from his verbal, emotional, sexual, and spiritual abuse.

Knowing my heart's desire to please God, he used Scriptures about wives submitting in everything, to manipulate me into doing whatever he desired.

He learned that if he backed me into a small corner or room so that I could not get away from him, he could drive me into hysterics. That became a favorite tactic. The instinct of cornered animals is to fight! Once he cornered me in a bedroom, I jumped on the bed and literally ripped a screen out of the window that was at the head of the bed in an effort to get away. But there were people standing only a few feet away outside the window. So I jumped off the other side of the bed and ran into a bathroom. That was worse, because the bathroom was small and there was no way out. He blocked the door. In my hysteria I raked his arm with my finger nails. Then I saw the blood dripping and I collapsed in a weeping heap on the floor. He told the counselor we were seeing at the time that I was completely irrational at times and that just out of the blue, I had raked his arm like that for no reason at all!! I was wounded to the core to think that I could be driven to do such a thing. I was wounded that he lied to the counselor and that the counselor had believed him. He was an accomplished liar. I was not aware that he was a liar until we had been married for at least 26 years. I trusted him.

After he was removed from the ministry, things were even worse. There was a particular sexual pleasure that he insisted on having me do that was the open door to the demons. He blamed his desire on the hormone imbalance. I fell for his lies once again. Until I talked to the Doctor myself. This was a different doctor, in a different state. He said there was an imbalance because there were more female hormones than normal and less male hormones than normal, but that this was common for obese men. He said that this particular pleasure was not due to hormones at all, but was a matter of sexual preference. He was far more male than female. There was no question about his maleness. When I confronted my husband with that, and said that I would no longer perform those acts for him, he was livid with anger.

Subsequently he committed adultery with a friend. When I confronted both of them with suspicions of what they were doing, I was accused of seeing things that weren't there, and of always making false accusations that he was tired of. (I had never accused him of anything like that before). I ended up apologizing to them both. Later he put his hand on a Bible and said "I swear on the Word that I didn't do anything with her." Another time, he said "God is my witness, I didn't do anything with her." It was months later that he admitted he had sexual relations with her when I suspected it. Knowing how precious the Lord and the Word was to me, he knew he could manipulate me with it, so he used the Bible and the Name of God to substantiate his evil lies.

Though he had not been actively, cross dressing, during those years, there were manifestations of it's influence in his life. Finally, one day he took tricot from my fabric drawers and took it to a tailor to have some night gowns made for himself. They were feminine in design, all they lacked was the lace and ribbons. This happened after seven and one half years of deliverance and counseling. When that happened I knew there was no hope. Then he started coaxing me to go to meetings where transvestites and transsexuals gathered with relatives while they were "dressed". These meetings were designed to help the relatives of such people accept them as they are. I refused to go. It was at this point that God released me, but it took six more months before God worked out the details and I finally left.

A short time before that happened, we went to a couple at a church for counseling. I was determined that I was not going to tell them the problems. Let God tell them. And He did. After a terrible battle, he left me stranded at the church with the couple for a while. He came back and he agreed to give up this pleasure that was the open door to the demons for it was the stumbling block that was destroying the marriage and the ministry that God had planned for him to do. They led him in a prayer to give it up. Within 10 minutes of leaving the church, Satan had already stolen that away from him. For two days he railed at me, claiming that he didn't pray that, saying he would never give that pleasure up. I told him to call the people. I listened on the second phone as he talked to them. The lady told him what he had prayed. He thanked her and hung up. He declared that she was lying too. He never prayed that.

To stay in that marriage I would have had to participate in his ungodly sin. Or else defy the Scripture that says do not defraud your partner of their sexual due. There was no way to live with that kind of reprobation. God released me from that marriage after 34 years. Eight years of them were a living hell, where I felt the filth of demons when I had sexual contact with him. Actually, I had felt that many times before, but didn't know what it was.

I left his house on Jan. 8, 1990. My mother died Jan. 14. My daughter rolled a truck in the California mountains on Jan. 15. I smashed up

a car on Jan. 26. My daughter had another accident
on those same roads a couple of weeks later and
then my youngest daughter said at the end of
Feb. "Mom, I have cancer". The devil tried to
use all of this and the false teachings on submission to say, "See, if you hadn't come out from
under your husband's umbrella of protection none
of this would have happened." My answer to the
Devil was that I had relied on the Lord to tell
me what to do and how to do it everyday and
sometimes every minute for the last eight years.
I knew God had released me from the bondage of
that marriage. And so I told the devil, "I will
say like Job, though he slay me, still I will trust
Him." I know in my heart that the Word of God
is true. He alone is my shield, my buckler, my
refuge, and not a demon controlled man who was
supposed to be my spiritual head.

Within a few weeks after I left his house
my ex-husband had already found a new girlfriend.
Within weeks, he was cross dressing openly and
fully. Something he had never done before, only
in front of me, until I stopped it. He started
a support group for transvestites and transsexuals,
not to help them out of it, but to support and
encourage each other in it. Before our divorce
was final, he and his girlfriend went on TV to
promote this group. The girlfriend accepted all
of that perversion and said it only added a
different dimension to their relationship.

For the first year after I left him, I prayed,
prostrate on my face, for him often. I had others
praying for him. One year later, there was a period
of much concentrated prayer for him and there
was almost a reconciliation. He said he would
go one more time for counseling and deliverance
and that we should set the divorce aside to see
if this would work. He knew his girlfriend would
not be there for him if he went because she did
not want him to do this. So he was willing to

give her up. He said, "If this doesn't work though, I want you to quit praying for me. I don't want your prayers messing up my life anymore." A few days later I felt like someone had kicked me in the stomach. Four words flashed into my mind. DANGER! IRREVOCABLE WRONG DECISION! A deep mourning, grief and fear for him came over me and lasted about two days. No amount of prayer would relieve it. When I spoke to him next, he said at the very time this happened to me he was only inches away from being in a collision with a semi-truck. Then he had immediately made a decision. The decision was that he would not go for deliverance. He would not give up his girlfriend. He wanted to get the divorce over with as soon as possible so I would be out of his life. Since that time the burden to pray for him has been lifted. In fact, the few times I tried to pray for him, it is a though God said don't pray for him anymore. I don't know for sure what the words "irrevocable wrong decision" mean. Perhaps it means that he had crossed a line and God had turned him over to his own reprobate mind forever, because the Word says that God will not always strive with man. But I'm sure it came from God and He knows what it means.

Within 2 months after the divorce was final, he married the woman. He went to counseling for a sex change operation. He was denied the operation, after all of that, because of his age and ill health. He has had his name legally changed to a woman's name. He tricked the pastor who married them into using that name on their marriage certificate even though it was not his legal name then. Though they were legally married as a man and a woman, he denies that he is a man in every way possible. Even their address labels attest to that. They consist of two females names, _____ and _____ and the last name. There is no Mr. and Mrs. He dresses and lives as a woman, including going out in public that way all of the time. Others have told me that his step-grandchildren call him Grandma".

The Word of God is true. Matthew 12:43-45 and Luke 11:24-26 says that when an unclean spirit goes out of a man, it will go back to the "house" it came out of, and if he finds it empty, he will come back in with seven other spirits that are more evil then he is. The final state of that man is worse than before. These passages are found in the context of Christ's own dissertation on Satan and the casting out of demons.

Even though God calls my ex-husband's lifestyle an abomination to Him and even though the Word says anyone doing such things will not enter the kingdom of God, he thinks he is in a perfectly right standing with God. He ignores the warnings of Hebrews 2:2-4, 6:4-8, 10:26-31.

These are just a few of the bad things that I lived through in that marriage.

Many of the things that I learned in all of those seven seminars were good and helpful. But many were very damaging to me and to my children. Had I followed them, some of those false principles could have kept me bound to my husband and would have eventually destroyed me. After God released me from that bond, if I had stayed in the marriage, I would not have had God's protection, because I would have been out of His will. I would have succumbed to the evil ones myself because I would have been clinging to the unclean things, a man, and a marriage, rather than to God.

God forbid that anyone should remain loyal to evil, that they should make excuses and cover up for it for the sake of false principles.

## CHAPTER THIRTEEN
## GLORY TO GOD

Though there are volumes of bad and evil experiences I encountered in my life, those are a few I lived through. I've tried to put 34 years of living in as short a space as possible. There is a point in taking up this much time with all these details. Because now I want to give God the Glory for what He has done. Perhaps this part of my life story will give the reader some insight into my character and who I am. Hopefully, you will see that I am not a radical evangelical feminist. I speak because I have experienced it first hand. I've been down the road of super submission and wrong headship. I know the fruit it produced. Hopefully, you will see were I am coming from and why I am writing this book. Most of all, I pray you will see Christ in it, how He worked all things together for my good because I was called for His purpose and I knew what His purpose for me was.

I thank God that my self esteem hit bottom. If it hadn't hit bottom, I would not have felt the need for Christ when I heard Billy Graham preach. If I had not felt that my life was such a mess, I wouldn't have given it over to God to become the Lord of my life.

Though I love fellowship with other believers now, I thank God that I didn't have Christian friends to rely on to teach me things in the beginning. The Holy Spirit had the time and opportunity to teach me Himself. I learned how to rely on Him to teach me what He wanted me to know.

I thank God for Tennessee Ernie Ford, and his gospel music. I learned how to worship and how to come into the presence of the Lord through his records. I didn't need a church full of people to help me do that. Now, I love to worship in song and music with the brethren, but it was good for me to learn how to do it alone first.

Through all that happened in my life, I learned how sneaky and subtle sin is. It doesn't start out looking bad, but once it gets a foothold it can destroy your life. It starts out small and seemingly insignificant and even innocent, sometimes. But it grows to be a consuming monster.

When I was confronted with wife swapping, I found out what kind of moral character I had. It was a test from God to see if I would put pleasing Him before pleasing a husband. But along with the test came the strength from God to say "NO". Also God protected me because nothing happened the night my husband took me to that couples house for that purpose. From that experience I know that God protected me because of my own personal walk with Him. It was not because I was being obedient to my husband.

Thank God, though I learned it a painful way, I know that you cannot buy peace for your household by compromising with sin. You cannot compromise your walk with Christ expecting that compromise will help to lead someone out of sin. Compromising with sin buys only grief, sorrow, turmoil, trouble, and heartache. It affects you emotionally and physically. It buys guilt and spiritual sorrow because that compromise has grieved the Holy Spirit. It also enables that other person to continue in their sin.

Thank God for teaching me that if I choose to indulge in sin, He will not bail me out of it. I have to determine for myself that what I am doing is sin. I have to repent of it. I have to stop doing it myself. Though I will bear the consequences of it, God will let me sin if I want to. But if I decide I do not want to live in that sin anymore, He gives the power and the strength to stop it, no matter what the cost might be. He taught me that often there is a price to pay for walking in righteousness. I had better be prepared for that and be willing to pay it.

I learned that if I want to be a witness for Christ, my life had better show the fruits of the Spirit. The fragrance of Christ in our lives is beauty to those who are saved and who are walking after the Spirit. But it is the smell of death to the unsaved. The unsaved will hate us, maybe, for the righteousness of Christ that they see in us, but they will respect it. They have to see the difference Christ makes in us if they are to be drawn to God through our witness. One needs to live it as an example. I had to learn when to witness verbally and when to keep my mouth shut. Speaking of Christ at the wrong time and in the wrong way is worse than not speaking at all. I learned to be aware of God's leading when it came to witnessing to my husband.

Because of his life controlling problems, I learned about addictive behavior. What they are, how they develop, and how to break the habits. I also learned about co-dependent behavior. There is a fine line between helping a person to come out of sin through encouragement and support and becoming their "savior" who tries to fix everything. When your whole life becomes centered on that other person and their problem, you have crossed over the line into co-dependency. It becomes an enabling tool for the person with the problem and you become a problem yourself. When you are making excuses for that other person continually, and hiding or concealing the problems from others, and when you keep trying to make the children understand that "Daddy is having a bad day. Just forgive him and go play out of his way." etc., you are into co-dependent behavior. When you minimize or ignore your own hurt and rationalize away the pain, and never confront the person doing that to you, then you have crossed the line. I have lived on both sides of the line. That is one reason why the teachings from Gothard are so damaging. They foster that kind of thing, because there's no balance

307

to prepare a woman to watch out for that. Instead, the teachings suck her and the children right into that kind of behavior. That is why I used the examples from his material that I did. By following his teachings all the way is how I crossed over the line. It took a long time and a lot of healing to come out of that.

Praise God, I finally learned that Agape love is not a sloppy love. It is sometimes tough love. It's knowing when to be soft and when to be tough. That's loving enough to say "I can't let you get by with that behavior. It is ungodly and it is unworthy of a good person like you."

Praise God that submission and headship, the way God intended it to be, is a blessing, and He taught me the difference between the right and the wrong concept of it. He set me free from the bondage of the wrong. Now I am blessed because I experience the right way.

Our God is an all knowing God. He knows what lies ahead for us. If we are open to Him, he will teach us and prepare us for whatever is happening or whatever will happen in our lives. Early in my Christian life, I knew there were demons and that Christians could have severe problems with them. I knew that Christians had authority over them. I don't know how I knew these things except that is what the Word said. I knew that if I encountered a demon all that I would have to do is command it out in the name of Jesus. I had no sense of fear of them. This was 28 years ago, long before the demonic forces in our world became so blatant in their activities. Now everyone is aware of them. Back then, very few Christians acknowledged their activity at all, and especially denied their activities in a Christian's life!! God set up a series of events that gave me much knowledge about the process of warfare and deliverance. He began to sharpen the gift of discernment in me. When my ex-husband hit me in the

face because of the discussion about Halloween,
I knew that the devil was mad at what I had said.
I did nothing about it. That was the beginning
of knowledge. God prepared me step by step for
what was coming. First was the seminar I mentioned
before. Then he taught me that it is expedient
some times to just bind demons in a person rather
than cast them out. I learned to bind the demon
of anger in my ex-husband.

Through the sessions with all of the various
counselors, I learned there are many methods of
warfare. There are no pat formulas in counseling
and deliverance. Every person is an individual
and their needs vary. So I learned how to rely
on the Holy Spirit to be the Counselor in every
situation. Yes, through these experiences, I found
out that in God's economy it would be a waste if
these experiences were for just for my ex-husband
and me. He has used that knowledge in counseling
others.

I know the power of God to set the captive
free. But I also know that the person must change
their life patterns in order to stay free. They
have to be willing to yield to God and allow Him
to transform their minds. They have to be willing
to die to self and the sin that allows demons to
be there in the first place and to keep them out
once they have been cast out. I know that getting
rid of demons is only a small part of freedom.
The bigger part of freedom and staying free comes
from forgiveness, healing of the wounded spirit,
and most of all, being obedient to Christ in all
things. Jesus said "the truth shall set you free"
so discerning the truth sets one free, walking
in that truth keeps one free.

I learned the weapons of warfare and I became
proficient at using them. I also learned when not
to use them. It is not always beneficial to use
Jesus' name to cast demons out of someone. If
they don't walk in the Spirit and in righteousness,

the final state for them is worse than the first, because seven worse demons will come back.

Thank God that in the process of learning, I realized I needed deliverance myself. I needed to be delivered from spirits of despair, rejection, hopelessness, and even death wish.

For quite a while, in about the 32nd–33rd year of that marriage I just had the constant thought that I wanted to die. There was no way out the misery of that hellish marriage. I was not yet released to divorce him and everything was getting worse. I just wanted to die. A friend took us to a mass deliverance meeting. I had never been to one before, I only went to observe. The minister called for death, death wish and suicide to come out. I began to cough violently. That spirit of death wish came out and I never felt that again, even though my circumstances did not change. Later I found that I had two open doors for that death wish to be there. One was that any person with a wounded spirit is vulnerable to it because they are so wounded that they feel the only remedy for their pain is to be dead. So they have an agreement with death. The other open door was that my ex-husband had wished that I was dead. If I was dead, I wouldn't be inter-fering in the pursuit of his perversions anymore. He was not thinking of divorce then either. But his wish was like a curse on me.

Through all the woundedness of that marriage, I had an opportunity to learn about the wounded spirit. This is a wound that goes beyond the physical, beyond the emotional and into the spirit. It is the deepest kind of pain a person can experience, in the very deepest part of their being. When I first learned of the healing of the wounded spirit, I was at a seminar where they needed somebody to be a live example of some of the things they were teaching. My ex-husband volunteered to be the guinea pig. As part of the things they were demonstrating through him, the teacher pointed out how those things must have wounded my spirit. So they prayed for me about them. As they prayed, and God began to heal those wounds, I laughed and cried at the same time. It felt like I was having a heart attack. There was literal pain in my heart. This lasted for a few minutes, while they continued to pray for me that God would heal my wounded spirit. Once the pain was gone, I could remember all those incidences that had caused the pain, but they did not hurt anymore. That night, in the middle of the night, I woke up with laughter just bubbling out of me. It was the joy of the Holy Spirit. I was laughing so hard it shook the bed. That uncontrollable laughter lasted at least a half hour. It was a holy laughter, something I had never heard of before. I didn't know what it was, but it was joyfully good and refreshing.

The very day that I experienced the awesome Grace of the Almighty God that healed my wounded spirit, I began to pray that God would give me that beautiful gift of praying for people with wounded spirits. It is the most precious healing a person can have. When one has a wounded spirit, the pain distorts every perception they have of everything. They view everything through the filter of pain. It's like looking through the wrong colored glasses. When the pain is healed, the distortions are gone. The whole world looks different. And there is hope. Some people do not believe in the healing of the wounded spirit. Many do not like the term "wounded spirit." But it is like salvation, one really doesn't know what it is to be saved until they have truly experienced it. I know that I was full of pain, I was offended easily by little things that someone said or did that were not in the least way intended to hurt at all. I just took it the wrong way because I was seeing or hearing through my filter of pain. There were tears very near the surface all the time. There

311

was a deep sadness in me that would not go away. All of that dramatically changed in a matter of minutes as the Lord healed me. It did not take years of therapy. It only took a touch from the mighty hand of God. Only God can heal a wounded spirit. A therapist can help uncover areas of woundedness. They can help one work through the anger from past wounds. They can help to encourage forgiveness, etc. But only God can heal the wound. That first healing occurred 3½ years before the marriage ended. Periodically, during those years, I would go to have prayer for the new wounds. That gave me hope and courage and the ability to stay in the marriage until God said it was over. After that release came and the marriage was ended, there was more prayer for those final wounds. The people who know me, know that I was remarkably free from bitterness toward my ex-husband. I suffered all the trauma of ending that relationship in divorce, the ripping and tearing apart, like everyone suffers. I suffered the trauma of losing his entire family with whom I had a very close relationship for thirty four years. I especially suffered from losing his mother and mine, both in one week, one through divorce and one through death. I felt he had cheated me out of many things. There was sufficient reason to be angry and bitter. But as the anger would come up, I would deal with it. I would forgive and there would be a healing.

God has graciously answered that prayer for the gift of praying for healing of the wounded spirit in others. He often brings complete freedom from the pain of those old wounds in people as He allows me to pray for them. The Word says that we will be ministers of the comfort we have received from Him. The multitude of counselors my ex-husband I went to provided me with a broad base of wisdom and knowledge. God uses that, combined with His wisdom to counsel and comfort others.

Scriptures for the wounded spirit are: I Sam. 1:15, Hannah is a woman of sorrowful spirit; Job 7:11, Job speaks in the anguish of his spirit; Ps.51:17, the sacrifices of God are a broken spirit; Ps.77:3 "and my spirit was overwhelmed"--all of Ps. 77 is a picture of a wounded spirit. Ps. 142:3 and 143:4 speaks of the spirit overwhelmed with pain and sorrow, both of these psalms picture the wounded spirit and how only God can heal it. Pr. 15:13, "sorrow of heart breaks the spirit"; Pr. 17:22, "a broken spirit dries the bones"; and finally Pr. 18:14, "The spirit of a man can sustain his infirmities, but a WOUNDED SPIRIT, WHO CAN BEAR." All are from KJV.

I learned that forgiveness was not an option, like I had believed for years. It is a command. I have to forgive or God cannot forgive me. (Math.6:14,15). I have to forgive or it opens me up to demonic influences. (Math18:24-35; IICor.2:7-11; Eph.4:26-27,30-32). I have to forgive because if I don't, a root of bitterness will spring up in me and it will consume me and destroy me. (Heb. 12:15). It will prevent anything that God wants to do through me. It will not only defile me, it will defile or contaminate many others who I might come in contact with. I had to learn how to appropriate the Grace of God to forgive that He has already provided for me. He says do not fail of the grace of God lest a root of bitterness spring up. The grace He is referring to is the grace to forgive. Forgiveness of one who has offended me, keeps my channels of communication open to the Lord so that my fellowship with Him is unbroken. This is for my benefit. The other side of forgiveness is that even though I forgive, that will not restore my relationship with my offender unless he repents. But whether he repents or not, whether the relationship is restored or not, I must keep my relationship to the Lord free by forgiving him. My forgiveness cannot depend

313

on his repentance. Perhaps he will never repent. So then I would be stuck in that unforgiveness forever and it would hinder me greatly by causing bitterness in me.

I learned about Agape love, God's love. The words "Agape Love" are tossed about frequently today. But the way many people think agape love works it would better be termed sloppy agape. Meaning that it's a soft love with no discipline and no accountability. By definition from Vine's Expository Dictionary of Old and New Testament Words, agape in the New Testament means "(a) to describe the attitude of God toward His Son, the human race, generally, and to such as believe on the Lord Jesus Christ. (b) to convey His will to His children concerning their attitude one toward another and toward all men. (c) to express the essential nature of God". Love is recognized as love only by the actions it produces or provokes. God's great love is His action of giving mankind the gift of His son. God did not give His Son because mankind deserved it. He chose in His Divine will to send His Son because that is His nature. That act is His expression of love toward us. In a Christian, agape love is the fruit of the Holy Spirit and is the Spirit being expressed through the believer. For the Christian, God becomes the primary focus of their love. That love is expressed by obedience to His commands, which produces death to self in the Christian. Living to please self and to follow one's own will is opposite of loving God. Vine's says "Christian love, whether exercised toward the brethren, or toward men generally is not an impulse from the feelings, it does not always run with the natural inclinations, nor does it spend itself only upon those for whom some infinity is discovered. Love seeks the welfare of all, Rom.15:2, and works no ill to any, 13:8-10; love seeks opportunity to do good to all men and especially toward them that are of the household

314

of faith. Gal 6:10" "In respect to agapoa as used of God, it expresses the deep and constant love and interest of a perfect Being towards entirely unworthy objects, producing and fostering a reverential love in them towards the Giver, and a practical love towards those who are partakers of the same, and a desire to help others to seek the Giver. "

All of that translated itself into my life as I lived out what God wanted me to do in that marriage. I learned, before I knew all the above definitions, that agape love means that you keep loving and giving for the good of the other. You see their woundedness and pain before you see your own. You see where they are and where they are coming from. You help them up when they fall without condemnation. You encourage the good in them and the progress they make. You tell them in love and with gentleness when you see their sin, so that they can recover themselves out of the snare of the devil. You hold them accountable for their actions and behavior. Above all, you love God more than you love the person so that you yourself do not fall into their sins with them or the trap of co-dependency. Agape love is not soft and mushy feelings. Sometimes it's tough. I was not always gentle and kind, especially towards the end of that marriage. But I know that the Holy Spirit loved through me much of the time when my own inclination was to give up and run. But I didn't run until God released me. God loves, but His Word says that he will not always strive with man. He will turn them over to their own reprobate mind and let them go their own way. If He comes to a point in His infinite mercy where He stops striving with them, it is not reasonable to think that He would want one of His children to continue to strive with the person either. He would, and does, release them and call them to peace.

Praise the Lord!! That is one of the greatest things that I learned, Praise the Lord in all things. Be thankful for all things. I came to know that God would work good out of any circumstance, **if I loved Him and was following His will and purpose for me.** I began to look for the good that could come out of a situation and to be expectant that the good would come. I have experienced an exuberant joy at times, from just beginning to praise the Lord with my whole heart in the midst of a most trying situation. I often fail to do that, but I know the heights of Praise when God inhabits it. The Word says that He works all things for the good of **those who love Him and are called according to His purpose.** I learned that means the promise is not for everybody. For the promise to be valid in my life, I had to be loving Him AND I had to know what His will and His purpose for me was. I had to be walking in that, and not walking after my own will for my own purposes in order for it to work.

I learned what a sacrifice of praise was. It's easy to say praise the Lord when every thing is going good, but it is a sacrifice to say "praise you Lord" when everything in your world is falling apart. A sacrifice cost you something. One time when I had left home for a solitary spiritual retreat, I was in such a state that I could not read the Word or pray. I put on a praise tape and walked the floor. Whatever the singers were doing on the tape, that is what I would do. If they were praising God, I would praise Him with them. If they were singing something that I could appropriate as a prayer for my life, then I would sometimes fall on my face before God, asking Him to make that alive in me. I was alone in that motel room, but God had His own way of ministering to me as I brought a sacrifice of praise to Him in the only way I could at the time. Through that I learned that there is sweet peace in the sacrifice of praise. My circumstances did not change, but my spirit was lifted up and I grew spiritually.

I learned when God wanted me to submit, when He wanted me to fight, and when He wanted me to quit. I learned to listen to the still small voice inside that was God giving me direction, day by day, and sometimes minute by minute.

What I am going to share here is a demonstration of that listening. **It is extremely important.** It is based on the story of Samson in Judges Chapters 13-16. Samson always gets a bad rap because people think the bad things he did was because he walked away from God. But Judges 13:25 says the Spirit of the Lord began to move him and then it details what the Spirit moved him to do. Chapter 14:4 affirms it and states that God's purpose for having Samson do these things was because He was going to use them to deal with the Philistines. Verse 6 says the Spirit of the Lord came on him to kill the lion, which was to be used later in another step of God's plan. Verse 19 says the Spirit of the Lord came upon him again and he went and killed 30 men and took their clothes. Though it doesn't say so, the Spirit of the Lord must have been with him through all the bad things he did, because the Lord had not departed from him until verse 20 after all those things were done. If Samson had not done all those bad things, the Philistines would not have paid attention to him. If they had not captured him and felt he was no longer a threat to them because his strength was gone, he would not have been in the position that God wanted him to be in. He would not have been the big attraction that drew so many important people to see their enemy be tortured and tormented. God renewed his strength and he killed all of the lords and all those people for the evil they had done to God's people. **God's purpose for having Samson do the**

317

**wrong that he did was to bring about a way to destroy God's enemies.** I learned that God would protect me in submission to wrong when it was His will for me to do so. **God will NOT protect you in wrong doing unless he has a specific purpose for it and He directs you to do it.** When Abraham asked Sarah to lie, she obeyed, knowing that she would be violated by the king. God did protect her by warning the king about who she really was. One day, early in the eight year battle, I asked God, "do you want me to submit to this filthy stuff that happens in our bedroom?" (This was not cross-dressing. It had to do with the transsexual behavior.) The answer was a definite "Yes". The purpose was so that my ex-husband could be given every possible chance to come out of the trap he was in. God wanted him to be brought to a place where he was free enough from the demonic influence on his mind to be able to make a free choice. He had to have love and support during that time of deliverance and counseling and he had to have time to change his habits. That necessitated a process that would have been cut short if I had not co-operated to a certain extent. After years of it though I complained to God. "God you said to submit to this, I have been obedient. But you did not protect me like you protected Sarah. He is not free. All it has done is brought me more pain." Again that still small voice came, "Yes I did protect you. I love you as much as I loved Sarah. I have honored your obedience to me in this just as I honored and protected her. I have protected you and kept you from being overcome by these same demons that have been in him." I knew from experience that the verse that says bad company corrupts good morals is true. Also I remembered the verse that says "you who are spiritual restore such a one, **but be careful you do not fall into the same sin**" and many other like verses. The closeness of the sexual association of a husband and wife, can transfer demons from one to another. I understood that God had truly protected me from that. But for His grace, I would have succumbed to the evil ones, in search of peace in my home and because of being married to him.

In the last three years of that marriage, we moved around a lot. He was no longer in the ministry. But 5 different times during those 3 years visiting evangelist etc. from different parts of the country, people who had never laid eyes on him before, would pick him out of the crowd and say the same words to him. They would say, "I don't know who you are or what you do, but I see the anointing of God on you. I see you ministering to great crowds of people with mighty power and setting many people free." The word says that in the mouth of two or three witnesses a thing is established. I knew in my heart what God had wanted him to do. I knew the marriage that God wanted us to have. I trusted God that He would do a miracle. God wanted to do a miracle. God is powerful enough to do the miracle. He is all sufficient and all powerful. There was nothing lacking in God. The lack was in my ex-husband.

Finally I learned when it was time to quit. It was hard to quit. It was hard to give up the visions of ministry. At one point, $2\frac{1}{2}$ years before the end, he came to a crossroad in his life. Although he knew the torment I was in, he still insisted on that one sexual forbidden pleasure. I told him that he was at a crossroad and that God was saying he would have to choose between that pleasure and God. He told me that God had been dealing with him for three weeks on that very matter. He said God had told him, he did not need that pleasure. He said with his mouth that he chose God, but his actions steadily worsened after that. It was grievous and hard to believe that he had chosen the wrong path in his heart when he was at the point of the crossroads. I knew that I had done all that any human being could do to help a brother get free. I knew I had been an instrument of God in his life. I knew I had done all that God wanted me to do. I knew I had been a good wife. God gave me the timing and the release when my husband had demonstrated his real heart's desire. God especially hates it when someone uses His name and His Word to substantiate their sin. God will not be mocked, He will not allow anyone to trifle with Him.

Though I said this before, it bears repeating. Had I clung to my ex-husband, and that marriage and that vision of ministry, I would have been out of the will of God and His purpose for me. Had I clung to the false teachings of submission, and divorce, I would have missed God's best blessings for me. All of the counselors we went to in the beginning said, "don't leave him. He won't make it if you do." But the last pastor, even though he is a great proponent of the false teachings we have studied, acknowledged that there was no other way. It had to end. He had witnessed the transvestite, transsexual behavior, and the increasing anger and violence for over a year. He had witnessed the destruction in both my ex-husband and myself in that year. When I told him I was leaving my husband, he believed it was the Lord's will for me to quit. I will always be grateful to that pastor for not clinging to the false teachings, in my case, and for helping me to get out of my husband's house when the time came. That was a traumatic experience for him.

When the others had said "stay" and then for this one to say "it's over", that was the confirmation I needed that this was right and it was God's timing for my release. A stranger gave a word of knowledge confirming it also.

I do understand, thoroughly, what it means to stay in a relationship and suffer for doing

good. I have allowed God to use that to produce
Christian maturity and character. But I also know
that it is balanced with God's mercy and grace
for me. Like Paul said, he knew how to be abased,
but he did not stay in that place of abasement
forever, because he also said he knew how to abound.
It would have been foolish and out of God's will
for him if he had stayed in the place of abasement
so that God could mature him!! The same was true
for me.

If you remember in the last chapter, I said
that my ex-husband had almost decided to go for
one last time for deliverance, but changed his
mind. The words "irrevocable wrong decision"
flashed into my mind at the very moment he made
that decision. When he confessed that decision
to me, that was the final release from him.
God lifted even the burden to pray. It was truly
over.

The very next day I started a new Bible study.
In that study was a young man named Curtis. I
thought this was only a new Bible study, part of
the new adventure of serving the Lord. Little
did I know what God had in store for me next.!!!
It was the beginning of a completely new chapter
in my life, and in this book. He had closed the
door in a final way on one chapter so that He
could begin to open the new one.

I would not trade my life for anything, not
one minute of it. Because of the hardships, I
have to say like Job. "My ears had heard of you,
but now my eyes see you." Job 42:5 . The learning
was hard, but the rewards are great. If I had
not gone through all of that, I would not know,
or be able to share how great our God is.

But I also know, that if I had continued in
that marriage beyond that point, I would have
no longer been in God's will for me. He would
have withdrawn His protection and withheld His
blessings from me. Since being obedient and getting

out of that marriage, the blessings have been multiplied, exceedingly abundantly, above all I could ask or think. So, now, I have even more to share about how great our God is.

I do not believe divorce is the right thing for everyone and I do not believe God will bless everyone who gets a divorce. But I do believe God will bless it if one is following Him with all their heart, and they do it in order to follow in His righteous ways and for His sake. God blesses some with the ability to restore their marriages if both parties throw themselves on His mercy and allow Him to be the Lord of their individual lives. Praise God for those who do this. Their marriages become little bits of heaven on earth. But God also blesses His own with release, refreshing, restoration and brings them to a place of quiet refuge when they walk out of an evil marriage in order to be more obedient to Him. That last statement will be explained and demonstrated in the next few chapters.

# CHAPTER FOURTEEN
## COVENANTS AND DIVORCE

How can I say that God released me from a marriage covenant? Isn't marriage supposed to be a mirror of His everlasting covenant promise? God never breaks His covenant, so the marriage covenant should never be broken either. Doesn't the Word say God hates divorce? Wouldn't God be contradicting His Word if He released one from a marriage covenant?

These are some of the statements, arguments and questions I have heard concerning divorce. I taught that the word "divorce" should never be part of a Christian's vocabulary because that was not an option for Christians. I taught that God has the answer for every problem, if only the two people will apply His answer to their problem. That is what I taught, but the last sentence is the only one I still believe. Now I believe there are exceptions to the first statement.

As I searched the Scriptures for answers, the Lord revealed much to me concerning the whole issue of marriage. He has revealed how it too has become an idol for many Christians. Marriage is a basic, foundational, biblical provision of God. He sanctifies it. That is, He causes the union to be, or pronounces it to be, morally clean. It is consecrated, or set apart by God and it is to be kept pure and holy, as a sacred thing. I believe that with all of my heart. But marriage is not God.

God never intended marriage to be an arena of idol worship where one spouse will bow to the other in a complete sacrifice of self on the alter of marriage. In all relationships, there is a certain amount of sacrificing of one's own agenda, and compromises are made in order to achieve harmony. That is not what I am talking about here. Neither am I talking about the joy that comes from serving one another in love. I am talking about the slavish sacrificing of one's personality in order to maintain a marriage. This kind of behavior turns the marriage into an idol, because one is serving the spouse at the expense of serving God. It is a betrayal of self and God.

A covenant is the confederacy, the alliance, the bargain between God and the people. The word covenant is a strange word. In the original language, there is a sense of cutting, meaning a cutting of flesh. The cutting of flesh, and then passing between the pieces of flesh is what made the compact between the parties of the covenant binding. Shedding of blood occurred when the flesh was cut. God said the sign of His covenant with Abraham would be the circumcision of the flesh. That was a shedding of blood. Under the Old Covenant, animals were cut apart and used for sacrifices, as the sign of agreement between God and the people. The shedding of blood and cutting of the animals was an atonement for the people's sins. Under the New Covenant, Christ's flesh and blood took the place of the animal sacrifices. Christ freed the people from the penalty of sin. Christ's shed blood was the sign of the agreement between God and all who would believe. In a marriage, when the bride is a virgin, there is also a cutting of the flesh, and blood is shed. This is the sign of the covenant between the man and the woman.

A covenant breaker (Rom.1:31) is one who breaks that agreement or is treacherous to the compact between the two people. The word treacherous means to act covertly, to pillage or to rob, to deal deceitfully, to be unfaithful, to offend, and to depart.

It takes at least two parties who agree on something to make a covenant. If one of the two parties of a covenant, breaks that covenant in any way, the covenant is no longer valid. Though God is a faithful God, His faithfulness does not require Him to stay bound by a covenant that the other party has broken. He remains faithful and true to His word, but the other party can renege on their part, so the covenant would no longer be valid and binding.

Let us look hard and long at what God really says about His own covenants and what He does when the other party breaks the covenant.

In Genisis 17:1-14, the Lord made a covenant with Abraham, his seed, and the nations that would come after him, but there were conditions. The covenant made provision for foreign slaves which he either bought or who were born to his household. These were not his seed, but they were covered by the covenant. (It is my opinion this provision for foreigners is a picture of the new covenant, when Gentiles would be grafted in as the Bride of Christ, when there would be no Jew or Gentile.) The sign of the "everlasting" covenant was that every male would be circumcised. That was the cutting of flesh. The conditions of the covenant were the circumcision, walking before God, being perfect, and being obedient. Any male child who was not circumcised **would be cut off because they had broken the covenant.** In verses 15-19 God says the covenant would continue through Isaac, the son of Sarah, and Isaac's seed. "Everlasting" covenant meant it would be perpetual, always continuing. **BUT** to be everlasting BOTH parties are bound by the conditions. Verse 14 says that any male who was not circumcised would be cut off because they had broken the covenant. Cut off means to be destroyed, hewn down, be freed, be loosed, perish. Broken means to break up, to violate, to frustrate, break asunder, cast off, disannul, dissolve, divide, make of no effect, fail, bring to naught, utterly make void.

Isa. 24:5 says that the inhabitants of the earth transgressed the laws, changed the ordinance, and had broken the everlasting covenant.

Jer. 11 speaks of the curse that will come on the people because of the broken covenant.

God says, hear the words of the covenant and do them. In verse 10 God says the people of Israel had turned again to the sins of their forefathers, worshiping and serving idols and had broken His covenant with their fathers.

What did God do about these broken covenants? In Ezekiel 16:59-62, God says that He will deal with them according to how they despised His covenant by breaking it with all their abominations. Even so, later on He will remember His covenant with them, but, vs.61 says, **not by the old covenant He had with them.** In Vs. 62 He says He WILL (future) establish His covenant. If He already had made a covenant with them, why would He have to establish one in the future? Because the old one had been broken and He was no longer bound by it. When the new covenant is established, they shall know he is the Lord. The blindness concerning the Messiah is still upon the Jews, but in Eze. 36, we are told the people will understand that the old covenant was canceled because of their sin. Their hope was lost and they were cut off. God was still faithful and would remain faithful. Vs. 11 says that the new covenant will be better for them than the old one. Vs. 17 says that their defilement was like that of a menstruating woman who was set apart from everyone because of her uncleanness. Vs. 18 and 19 says He judged them, then poured out His fury on them for the innocent blood they had shed on the land and for their idol worship. His fury drove them out of their promised land and scattered them among nations. But vs. 20 says they profaned His holy name further, because everywhere they went, they claimed to be the people of the Lord. Why would that profane His holy name? In their pride, and even in their filthiness, they still believed that they were the people of the covenant! But God said He had sent them away from Him because the covenant was broken, therefore, it was profanity for them to claim to be His people.

Vs.21-23 tells us that He would not establish a
new covenant with them just because they were once
people of the covenant. It wasn't for their sake
at all. When He finally sanctifies the Jews,
causing them to become morally clean, He will
do it so that the inhabitants of all the lands
will know that He is the Lord. That will sanctify
(cleanse and purify) His great and Holy Name.
It is for His name's sake, not for the sake of
the people who broke the covenant. Vs. 25-27,
God says He will bring them back to the promised
land and He will bring them into the New covenant.
In these verses, the process that God uses to
bring them in is the same process He uses for all
believers in Christ. He will take out their old
heart of stone, give them a new heart of flesh,
He will put His Spirit in them so that they can
walk according to His commandments, they will then
be His people and He will be their God. At that
future date He will cause them to loath themselves
for all the iniquities and abominations they had
committed. In vs. 32, He again reminds them that
it is not for their sakes that He will do this,
because they should be ashamed and confounded for
their own doings. So it won't be on the terms of
the old covenant--it will be under the new covenant
of Christ. God stopped working with them as a
nation and began working with them as individuals.
At that future date He will again work with them
as a nation.

Chapter 37 tells how God brings the dead bones
of Israel to new life. To me, the bones represent
the dead old covenant. The bones are not even
a skeleton. They are a heap of disconnected bones,
bones that are utterly separated from original
life, or the original covenant. Vs. 7 says they
come together or are joined together, bone to bone.
Vs. 8 the sinews, flesh and skin, come upon them,
but they still will not have life, for there was
no breath in them. They are back in their land,

327

but they are still dead in the old covenant.
Vs. 10 and 14 represent the Holy Spirit coming
into them to give them new life in the New Covenant
with Christ. I believe this represents the time
of the tribulation when He again works with them
as a nation. Vs. 15-25 shows how they will not
be divided into tribes anymore. All the people
will be just one nation. The mystery of two
becoming one will finally be revealed and completed
for the nation of Israel. Christ will rule over
them as a loving shepherd with only one flock.
Then all nations will know that He has sanctified
Israel and has brought her back to Himself, but
under the new covenant of Christ, not under the
old covenant which the people had broken. This
new covenant under Christ would be much better
for them then the old one. Vs. 24 says that David
would be king over them, they would have one
shepherd. Luke 1:32-33 tells us who the shepherd
is. "The Lord God shall give unto Him (Jesus)
the throne of his father, David, and He shall reign
over the house of Jacob forever and of His kingdom
there shall be no end."

II Chron. 7:12-22, especially verses 17-22,
gives a vivid picture of what God did with Solomon.
"As for thee, IF thou wilt walk before me, as David,
your father, walked AND DO according to all that
I commanded thee, AND SHALL OBSERVE my statutes
and ordinances, THEN will I establish the throne
of the kingdom, according as I have COVENANTED
with David, thy father, saying, 'There shall not
fail thee a man to be ruler in Israel.' **But if
you turn away, and forsake my commandments,** which
I have set before you, **and shall go and serve other
gods, and worship them,** then will I pluck them
up by the roots out of the land which I gave them;
and this house, which I have sanctified for my
name, will I cast out of my sight, and will make
it a proverb and a byword among all nations. And
this house, which is high, shall be an astonishment

to everyone that passes by it; so that he shall say, 'Why hath the Lord done thus unto the land, and unto this house?' And it shall be answered, 'Because they forsook the Lord God of their fathers, who brought them forth from the land of Egypt, and laid hold on other gods and worshiped them, and served them; therefore hath he brought all this evil upon them.' KJV.

God's covenant with David was that there would always be a descendant of David's to rule over Israel. God is speaking to David's son, Solomon. Notice, God gives Solomon conditions that will maintain the covenant. They are "IF you walk before me like David did and DO ALL that I command and OBSERVE all my decrees, THEN I will establish your royal throne as I COVENANTED with your father David. BUT IF you turn away and forsake my decrees and follow other gods and worship and serve them, I will pluck them up out of the land and cast them away from me. I will even reject this temple that I have consecrated for my Name."

The word pluck and roots have the same meaning. They mean to tear away, destroy, forsake, pull up, root out utterly. The covenant that God made with David would be extended to Solomon, but it had conditions that Solomon must fulfill in order for the covenant to remain valid.

I King 11 tells us that Solomon broke the decrees and commands, thus breaking the covenant. God was angry with him, and said He would tear the kingdom away from him. Because of His covenant with David, He would not do it in Solomon's lifetime, but it would be done in Solomon's son's lifetime. Because of God's faithfulness, He would leave the son with only one tribe. The other ten tribes would be given to Jeroboam, so that actually he would be the ruler over Israel. God said He would build Jeroboam a dynasty as enduring as the one He had built for David and He would give Israel to him. He said David's descendants would be

329

humbled, but not forever. The broken covenant did not effect only Solomon, it affected all Israel.

In Jer. 15:1, we read that God told Jeremiah, "Even if Moses or Samuel were to stand before me, my heart would not go out to this people. Send them away from my sight." (NIV). In Jer. 16, He says all the people, including the children, would die of deadly diseases that He would SEND. In vs. 5, God says, "Do not enter a house where there is a funeral meal; do not go to mourn or show sympathy, because I have withdrawn my BLESSING, MY LOVE AND MY PITY from this people" declares the Lord. Vs. 10 says the people will ask Jeremiah why God has done such terrible things to them. Vs. 11-13, God says to tell them "It is because your father's forsook me, and followed other gods and served them and worshiped them. They forsook me and did not keep my law. But you have behaved more wickedly than your fathers. See how each of you is following the stubbornness of his evil heart instead of obeying me. So I will throw you out of this land into a land neither you nor your fathers have known, and there you will serve other gods day and night, for I will show you no favor." He goes on to say that though they will be banished to this land, eventually He would restore them to the land He had given to their forefathers. But for now, He says He would send fishermen to catch them and hunters to hunt them. Vs. 17-18 says, "My eyes are on all their ways; they are not hidden from me, nor is their sin concealed from my eyes. I will repay them double for their wickedness and their sin, because they have defiled my land with the lifeless forms of their vile images and have filled my inheritance with their detestable idols." (NIV)

Jer. 3:1 says "If a man divorces his wife and she leaves him and marries another man, should he return to her again? Would not the land be completely defiled? But you have lived as a prostitute with many lovers---would you now return to me? declares the Lord"

Jer. 3:6-11, the Lord said to Jeremiah, "Have you seen what faithless Israel has done? She has gone up on every high hill and under every spreading tree and has committed adultery there. I thought that after she had done all this she would return to me but she did not, and her unfaithful sister Judah saw it. **I gave faithless Israel HER CERTIFICATE OF DIVORCE and sent her away** because of all of her adulteries." Notice, God did not divorce David, He divorced Israel as a nation.

The word divorce here is the same word as the words cut off that we looked at earlier. It's a primary word that means to cut off, cut down, cut asunder. By implication it means to destroy utterly, to be freed, to be loosed, to perish utterly.

When God said He divorced Israel, it means that He cut the matrimonial bond with her. She had broken her covenant with Him because of her idol worship. When He divorced her, that set Him free and loosed Him from the bond of the covenant with her. The marriage covenant with her was made utterly void. It did not exist anymore, it was dissolved. He was freed from the bonds of that covenant so that He could establish a new covenant through Christ and His shed blood. Through Christ, there is a new Bride. The old wife has been set aside and a new Bride is taken. Christ was a descendant of David, so God kept his word with David, but He ended that old Covenant with Israel. Now the Jews and Gentiles are under the same covenant.

For centuries, there has been no priests, kings, or judges appointed over Israel to rule over her. God stopped appointing and anointing them. There was no nation of Israel, for they were cast out of the land and were scattered to many lands, until 1948 when they became a nation again. Miraculously, many of the Jews had not intermarried with other races, thus they remained a pure race. But God will never again work with them as He did before, by appointing priests and kings and judges. During the great tribulation, He will once again turn His full attention to the Jewish Nation of Israel. He will do that mighty work of removing the veil from their eyes. It will be a special time for them to repent of the past sins and idolatries and to come to know the Messiah. They will not be a separate entity known as "the chosen people" like they once were. The body of Christ, the believers in Him, are now the precious, chosen people of God, the royal priesthood, the Holy nation, according to I Pet. 2:4,9. When the veil is lifted from the eyes of the Jewish people, those who come to the Messiah, will be a part of that chosen generation also. That is when the mystery of two becoming will be complete. There is no Jew or Gentile, in Christ. The divorce between God and Israel was a real ending, or termination, of the special relationship they once had. The relationship, as it was in the beginning, will never again be re-established in the same way. The only covenant that is valid, for now and forever more, is the one established by Christ. He is the only ruler the Jews will have that is anointed of God to be their leader. They will have to come to Him, just as both Jews and Gentiles do today.

God's divorce of Israel has been theologically rationalized so that it is rejected as a real divorce. They say His wife was just set aside for a while, it was not really a divorce, as we know it today. They say the gathering together of believers, known as the body of Christ or the Bride of Christ, is really only an engagement. The marriage of Christ to the Bride won't be consummated until the marriage supper of the Lamb. But however anyone wants to rationalize it, the

332

Bride of Christ, the Church, will be united with Christ BEFORE God turns His full attention back to Israel. In that special time they will have the opportunity to enter into the New Covenant relationship with Christ. It is only through Christ that a new relationship will be established.

God's divorce of Israel was because of unfaithfulness, idolatry, hard heartedness and disobedience. Those things broke the covenant. God set the old wife aside, terminated the relationship He had with her under the old covenant, and took a new Bride with a new covenant.

In our modern day, to say divorce is to be denied because marriage is a picture of the covenant of God is erroneous. God is faithful to His covenants and He does hate divorce. But He hates idol worship even more. When marriage and the preservation of marriage obliges one to be more obedient to the spouse than they are to God, that makes the spouse and the marriage an idol. It leads one away to worship and serve another god.

There is a passage in Deuteronomy that deals with that very thing. Deut. 13:1-11 says that if a false prophet speaks of signs and wonders and they come to pass, they will then entice you to follow and worship other gods. God says don't listen to him, because He (God) is testing you to see if you love HIM with all of your heart and soul. He's saying, walk after the Lord your God, fear Him, keep His commandments, obey His voice, and by doing that, serve Him and cleave to Him. He says the false prophet should be put to death because he has spoken to turn you away from the Lord your God who has redeemed you out of the house of bondage. The false prophet has tried to thrust you out of the way which the Lord your God commanded YOU to walk in. He says, **"Put (purge) the evil away from you." Even if the false prophet is your brother, son, or daughter, or wife (spouse) that you love, or your best friend who entices you to** serve other gods, don't listen to him, don't pity him or spare him, or cover up for him or make excuses for his sin, but rather expose him. You shall kill him (even if it's a loved one). Your hand shall be the first to put him to death because he has tried to lead you away from God. When you stone him to death, all will fear God and will stop doing such evil among you".

This is found in the Old Testament and because we are under the Grace of the New Testament, many will say this is not relevant for today. But our God is a God who never changes. He is still the same God who declared that He was a jealous God, and that no one should have any other gods before Him. He is just as jealous of His people's love and worship now as He was then. He hates any who lead His people away to worship other gods. He still tests His people to see who they really love, to see if they love Him above all others, even a spouse. His principles have not changed.

If we were still under that kind of law that commands stoning to death, it would solve the controversy over divorce and subsequent marriage. The prohibition against marrying again while the spouse lives would be ended. Since we do not stone people to death anymore, what option is there for a spouse when the husband leads a wife away from God to serve him before she serves God? Or, when, through obedience to the false teachings on submission, he becomes her god? In such a case, I believe God's divorcement of the old wife Israel, which ended the old covenant, and then taking a new Bride under the new covenant is a viable picture of divorce and remarriage.

Does the New Testament do away with the principle of Deut. 13?

Two passages in Romans, 1:18-32, and 2:2,5,9, talk about the wrath of God being revealed from heaven against all the godlessness and wickedness of men who suppress the truth, by their godless

334

wickedness. He says, although they knew God, they neither glorified Him or gave thanks to Him. They thought they were wise, but they became fools because they exchanged the glory of God for images of other created beings. They exchanged the truth of God for a lie and worshiped and served created things rather than God, their creator. Remember, these are those who KNEW God it says. Knew means to have a clear understanding and it speaks of an intimate relationship between the one who knows and the one who is known. He says, since they did not think it worthwhile to retain the knowledge of God, he gave them over to their own reprobate minds. They had to have had the knowledge of Him in order to retain it, so they had to have known Him, but chose not to live according to that knowledge. There is a long list of unrighteous deeds they do. They did those detestable things even though they knew God's righteous decrees. He says they deserve death because they not only did those things themselves, but they also approved of those who practice them. In Rom. 2:5, Paul says that because of their unrepentant hearts, they were storing up for themselves the wrath of God's righteous judgment. Vs. 8 says for those who are self-seeking and who reject the truth and follow evil, there will be wrath and anger. Vs. 9 says that God does not show favoritism. He does not recognize Jew or Gentile. The wrath of God came upon the Jew who sinned and did evil first, and it will also come upon the Gentile who sins and does evil. ALL who do evil will be the recipients of His wrath. None will escape. Paul declares here in Rom. 2:13 **" For it is those who obey the LAW who will be declared righteous"** (NIV) Then in Vs. 15-16, he says that it is the ones who show that the requirements of the law are written in their hearts and their conscience bears witness to that by the righteous acts that they do, these are the ones that God will judge as righteous when he judges the secrets of men's hearts **through Jesus Christ**. God has not changed His principles. Even though Christ paid the penalty for sin, each one will be judged according to their obedience to the righteousness that is written in their hearts by God, through knowing Jesus. The truth is, God wants obedience to His just principles, whether they come from the Old Testament or the New. The lie that is exchanged for the truth is that under Grace, we no longer have to be obedient to His commandments, because that would be works. Those who believe and live that way are storing up the wrath of God for themselves, and Christ will judge it! In man's "wisdom" of submission and headship and grace, have they become fools? Have they exchanged the glory of God for the glory of the idols of man and marriage?

II Tim.3:2-5 says that in these latter days, there will be perilous times. Paul says here that "people will be lovers of themselves, lovers of money, boastful, proud, abusive, disobedient to parents, ungrateful, unholy, without love, unforgiving, slanderous, without self-control, brutal, not lovers of good, treacherous, rash, conceited, lovers of pleasure rather than lovers of God. Having a form of godliness, but denying it's power. **Have nothing to do with them.** (NIV) Many of these ungodly things are practiced in many Christian marriages. Under the false teaching of submission for the wife, many women are told to endure an abundance of these things from their husbands. Is the admonition by Paul, to have nothing to do with the people who practice these evil things, not applicable to marriage partners? I do not see any exceptions, exemptions or qualifications in Paul's writing. He does not qualify what he says by saying, "Have nothing to do with them, except if it's your spouse. If it's your spouse, tough luck, live with it."

II Cor. 6:14-17 and 7:1 says "Do not be yoked

336

together with unbelievers. For what do righteousness and wickedness have in common? Or what
fellowship can light have with darkness? What
harmony is there between Christ and Belial? What
agreement is there between the temple of God and
idols? For we are the temple of the living God.
As God said, 'I will live with them and walk among
them, and I will be their God and they will be
my people. Therefore, **come out from among them,
and be separate says the Lord. Touch no unclean
thing, and I will receive you.** I will be a Father
to you, and you will be my sons and daughters,
says the Lord Almighty'. Since we have these
promises, dear friends, **let us purify OURSELVES
from every thing that contaminates body and SPIRIT,
perfecting holiness out of reverence for God.**"
(NIV) The word separate means to exclude, sever,
divide, go away from. Touch not means do not
fasten or attach oneself to. Purify means to purge
or cleanse. Perfecting means to fulfill further
or completely undergo, to make perfect. Holiness
is to bring about a state of piousness.

"Be not unequally yoked" is usually taught
as a rule not to date or marry an unbeliever.
But what does it mean in the light of the passage
we just looked at in II Tim. 3:2-5? In a marriage,
if one claims to be a believer and yet continues
to practice many of those evil things, and the
other is walking in righteousness, are they not
trying to make righteousness and wickedness work
together? Isn't there a conflict between light
and darkness? Is there any harmony when one is
living for God and one is living like the devil?
What agreement can there be if one has consecrated
oneself to be a temple of the living God, but the
other one wants to be served like an idol? God
says it cannot be so. He says to "come out" and
sever or separate yourself from that. Don't fasten
or attach yourself to that unclean thing. IF you
separate yourself from it, THEN I will receive

you. He is saying, by severing or separating yourself from all unclean alliances is the way to purify or purge yourself from that person who is contaminating your body and your Spirit. The alliance with that person is what is keeping us from fulfilling or completing the state of purity, or holiness that God wants us to strive to achieve here on earth. This is done out of fear or reverence for God. In other words, any relationship that prevents us from perfecting holiness is a compromise. It is a test to see if we prefer to compromise for the sake of the relationship or are we willing to separate ourselves from that person in order to revere God. Do we love the one we are in the relationship with more than we love God? If we are not willing to separate ourselves from that person, then He said He will not receive us. How does this Scripture fit with the one in Deut. 13? Does it not say the same thing?

It is always taught that the passage in II Corinthians does not mean that one should separate from a marriage partner because I Cor. 7:12-16 says if one is married to an unbeliever they should not seek a divorce, because the believer sanctifies the unbeliever. Also, how do you know that the believer won't save the unbeliever. This is used as the proof text for the philosophy that teaches that no matter what a spouse is or does, one must endure it. It doesn't matter what compromise one has to make in their walk with Christ to achieve it, they are to stay with the spouse, because the word says "do not seek divorce". The part of these verses that is totally ignored in that philosophy is the phrase about IF the unbeliever is **willing** to live with them, they must not seek divorce. But if the unbeliever wants to leave, let them go. The believing spouse is no longer bound to them, for God has called them to peace.

What does "willing to live with them" mean? That answer is found in I Cor. 7:27-35. Vs. 27 says, "Are you married? do not seek divorce. Are you unmarried? Do not look for a wife." (NIV) Paul says he is saying that because those who are married will face many troubles in this life and he wanted to spare them that. Then in vs. 29-31 he says, "What I mean brothers, the time is short. From now on, **those who have wives should live as if they had none;** those who mourn, as if they did not; those who are happy, as if they were not; those who buy something, as if it were not theirs to keep; those who use things of the world, as if not engrossed in them. For this world in it's present form will pass away." (NIV) Did Paul mean that only men should live as if they didn't have a wife or that all those who are married should live as if they weren't? Is he saying to ignore your spouse? No, that is not what he means. He says that marriage is just like mourning, being happy, buying things and using things. They are all in the same category. They are things of the world that people get engrossed in. I was shocked when I finally saw and understood what that meant. **Marriage is a thing of this world only.** It passes away, like all other things of this world. Therefore, do not get overly engrossed in it. Don't let it take the place of God in your life. Don't let it prevent you from fulfilling God's purposes for you. While I always knew that there was no marriage in heaven, it hurt to realize that actually, marriage is something that passes with this world. My own marriage is something very precious to me. I don't like to think of it as an affair of this world only. I want it to be in a more elevated place than just being happy or sad or something I buy in the store. But in eternity's economy, they are all on the same level. It isn't that marriage is not important to God, He invented it! But even marriage passes away.

Paul goes on to say in vs. 32-34 that unmarried people will concern themselves with how they can please God. Married people are concerned with how they can please the spouse and so their interests are divided. He calls these concerns about pleasing the spouse "affairs of this world". Vs. 35 says, "I am saying this for your own good, not to restrict you, but that you may live in a right way in undivided devotion to the Lord". (NIV) So what does he mean when he said those who are married should live as if they were not? He means that they should not let their devotion to God be compromised by their love and devotion to their spouse. They should never compromise pleasing God in favor of pleasing the spouse. In the marriage, if they come to a place where they would have to compromise their walk with God, then act as though they were not married. Please God with undivided devotion.

In the light of these truths, what does the earlier passage mean when it says, if the unbeliever is willing to live with the believer, don't seek divorce, but if the unbeliever wants to depart, let them depart. It means that the believer should be living such an undivided, uncompromised walk with God that the unbeliever is put in a position where they must make a choice. They have three options. One is that they will want what the spouse has and will convert also. Two, they will like this believer's lifestyle but will not accept it for themselves. But they willingly allow the believing spouse to continue to grow in the Lord with no hindrances from them. Third, they won't like the believer's lifestyle at all, they refuse to allow growth in the believer, and the believer will not compromise their walk with the Lord to please the spouse, so he leaves. In that case, the believer is to let them go. They are not bound to that person any more. God has called them to peace means that he does not bind them to that covenant with that person any longer either. This word "called" means bid or commanded. The word "peace" means to set at one **again.** Since complete opposites cannot be set at one, in context, it means they are bidden to be, or commanded by God to be, single again as though they had never been married. The bonds of the marriage are dissolved as though the spouse was dead. The relationship no longer exists. Some argue that the unbelieving spouse must literally leave, in order for this to be a valid grounds for divorce. But a spouse can cruelly leave emotionally, spiritually and in every other way, but stay physically, just out of pure spite or meanness. The word for leave is actually the word depart and that comes from an obsolete root word that means a chasm, or vacancy, or impassable interval. The spouse has already left the relationship, there is an impassable vacancy of emotional and spiritual communication. There is a broken covenant in every way except the physical presence. I believe in such a case, it is valid for one to ask the unbelieving spouse to leave, or to leave the situation themselves. Whatever it takes, do not compromise devotion to God in order to hang on to the spouse or the marriage.

Many, in fact, most people will take exception to what I have just written. The more marriage is an idol to them, the more angry they will be about it, even if the Word is clear. So let's look at what Jesus himself says about it.

Luke 14:25, Jesus is talking to a large crowd of people who were following him. In vs. 26 he says, "If anyone comes to me and does not hate his father and mother, his wife (spouse) and children, his brothers and sisters--yes even his own life--he cannot be my disciple. And anyone who does not carry his cross and follow me cannot be my disciple." Does Jesus mean that we are to hate all of those people we are supposed to love?

341

Hate means to detest, especially to persecute; by extension it means to love less, hateful. What He means is that the cost of discipleship, or of truly following Him, may involve severing some relationships, even with your spouse, if necessary. The cost is definitely high!! A person dies on a cross. So self must die also, along with relationship, in order to follow Him. If one is not willing to give up every relationship, and self, in order to follow Him, then He says they cannot be His disciple. He may never ask a person to leave their loved ones, but they had better be willing to if He asks it. They must love Him more than the spouse, the family, and self. Jesus is saying that no person, even a spouse, should prevent you from following Him to the fullest. He is saying that is the cost of discipleship. This is opposite of what we hear today. I have heard it said that the spouse and family come **before** service to God. They say, "After all, God gave that responsibility of spouse and family, so that should be #1 on the priority list." It has been said many times that if a person feels that God called them to preach or to be a missionary, and the spouse does not agree, then one either must wait for the Lord to get through to the spouse so they will change their mind, or don't do the ministry at all. What happens if the spouse does not want to walk in the will of the Lord? What happens if they refuse the call of God? Should the spouse then be obedient to the call of God or to the will of the spouse? Today's teaching would say cater to the will of the spouse. They must wait for the spouse to catch the vision also. If they don't, God will not bless the ministry, because the person has left their first obligation, which is the spouse and family. This is a way of the world, it is not what Jesus said at all.

Jesus continued to illustrate the cost of discipleship with verses 28-35. He gives three parables. One is about the builder who does not count the cost of the tower he is building. Part way through, he runs out of money and cannot finish the tower. Everyone laughs at him. The point here is that there is a cost of discipleship. Be sure to count it. Know in your heart if you are willing to pay the cost, no matter what it is, so that you won't have to quit half way through your walk with Him. People will laugh at your witness to them about following Jesus, or "accepting Jesus into your heart". They will laugh at you and say Jesus isn't real. Jesus is the foundation of the tower. Do you have what it a takes to continue building on Him, or will you cut and run when you find you can't pay the cost? Will you find the cost too high and you can't pay it, because you thought salvation was a free ride with no cost attached?

The second parable is about the king who is confronted with an army that out numbers his army two to one. The king must decide if he wants to fight it out or does he want to bargain, making concessions and compromises to make peace. In other words, he decides if the battle is worth losing everything for, or is it better to compromise to make peace at all cost. What would he have to give up to make a compromise? Integrity? Slavery for some of his people? etc. etc. Or does he fight to the finish to maintain integrity or whatever? Obviously, Jesus means that he should fight rather than compromise, for He says, "In the same way, any of you who does not give everything he has cannot follow me?" He is saying, are you willing to lay everything on the line to follow me or will you compromise along the way to gain peace here on earth for yourself. Will you fight for His cause or compromise for your own cause?

The third parable is about salt. If it looses it's flavor it is no good for anything. We are to be the salt of the world. Our life testimony for Him must count for something. If we cannot even bring salt to our loved ones, but compromise our walk with God in order to please them rather than God, how can we be of any value to the world?

Finally he says. "Hear what I say". He says following me is not a free ride. The cost is very high. Are you willing to pay it? The cost may be severed relationships with people you love.

Jesus is saying exactly what God said. I am a jealous God, Thou shall have no other gods before me. Not your mother, father, children, spouse or good friend.

Matthew 10:34-39 says more of the same. "Do not think that I have come to bring peace to the earth. I did not come to bring peace, but a **sword**. For I have come to turn a man against his father; a daughter against her mother, a daughter-in-law against her mother-in-law, a man's enemies will be members of his own household. Anyone who loves his father and mother more than me is not worthy of me; he who loves his son or daughter more than me is not worthy of me; and he who does not take up his cross and follow me is not worthy of me. Whoever finds his life will lose it, and whoever loses his life for my sake will find it." The word peace here means to set a one, rest, quietness, and by implication, prosperity. The word sword means judicial punishment, which comes from a root word that means a battle, controversy, fighting and striving.

Does this sound too harsh? Am I reading too much into these parables and words of Jesus? Is that truly what He means? Is He saying the same thing to us that God said to Abraham when He asked Abraham to sacrifice his son Issac on the alter? God said that sacrifice of his son was a test to prove that Abraham loved God with all of his heart, all of his mind, and all of his soul. Abraham passed the test. God said, "Now I know that you

344

fear God, because you have not withheld from me
your only son." (Gen.22:1-12) Some people have
claimed that Abraham knew all the time that God
would provide a sacrifice. People just do not take
God seriously when they cannot accept what God
really meant in some of this sticky issues. They
want to make excuses and say that's not really
what it means. Our understanding of these things
and our willingness to do them as Abraham did,
if we are called on to do so, will determine whether
or not we can pass God's proof test. Most people
do not want to understand that. It goes against
the theology of today, which is that grace does
not require any sacrifice from us. Jesus paid
it all, He was the sacrifice. Any kind of sacrifice
on our part is works, and there are no works
involved in being saved by grace. The words of
my Bible teach me differently. It is true that
Jesus paid the price for my salvation and I can
do no work to add to that, but if I have truly
been saved by Grace, THROUGH FAITH, my life will
be a life of obedience at any cost, in reverence
to my God. The very Grace that provides salvation
is the same grace that will not allow me to have
any other gods before Him, not even spouse or
family.

Let's look at some more of God's covenants.

I Sam. 2:27-30. The Lord says how He had
established Eli's priesthood with a covenant He
made with Eli's father. He said in vs. 30 "I said,
indeed, that thy house, and the house of thy father
would walk before me FOREVER; BUT NOW the Lord
saith, be it far from me; for them who honor me
will I honor, and they who despise me, shall be
lightly esteemed" (KJV) Lightly esteemed means
accursed or despised. Even though God said the
priesthood of Eli's father would last forever,
the covenant was broken by Eli's sons because of
their evil corruption. They profaned the sacrifices
that God had ordained the priests to make, they

caused the people to sin, and they were immoral.
God was not bound to maintain a covenant which
the second party had broken. The covenant was
established with one who honored God. But God was
released from that covenant when He was despised
by the priest's sons. They were the ones who broke
the covenant. God's promise was that He would
**end the covenant** by killing the two sons in the
same day. Vs. 3:14 says they had sinned against
God so grievously that there was no way for them
to repent and there was no way that God would
reverse the penalty for their sin. They broke the
covenant and it could never be re-established.
Vs. 35 says that God chose another to take the
place of the priests for He said, "I will raise
up for myself a faithful priest who shall do
according to that which is in mine heart and in
my mind; I will build him a sure house, and he
shall walk before mine anointed forever." (KJV)

I Sam. 2:25, Eli says to his sons, "If a man
sin against another man, God may mediate for him;
but if a man sin against the Lord, who will
intercede for him?" (NIV) In the Old Testament,
the priests interceded or mediated with God for
the sins of the people. When Christ was crucified,
died, was resurrected, and ascended to the right
hand of God, He became the mediator for His people.
But even under the new covenant, established by
Christ, there is an unpardonable sin of blaspheming
the Holy Spirit for which even Christ cannot
intercede with God.

God held Eli accountable for his sons because
he was too lenient in training them. He spoiled
them. I Sam. 3:12-14, God says, "I will perform
against Eli all the things that I spoke concerning
his house; when I begin, I will also make an end.
For I have told him that I will judge his house
forever for the iniquity which he knoweth, because
his sons made themselves vile and he restrained
them not. And therefore I have sworn unto the

house of Eli that the iniquity of Eli's house shall
not be purged with sacrifice nor offering forever".
Eli's sin was not only that he did not train his
sons well, but, even worse, he knew of their evilness but he did not restrain them from performing
their priestly duties. By not restraining them,
he allowed them to profane the Holy God and the
priesthood. He was choosing his relationship with
his sons above his relationship with God, and
above his obligation to God to keep the priesthood
pure. His sons were more important to him than
God and the priesthood were because God said in
I Sam. 2:25 "you honor your sons more than me".
   Before leaving this passage, I would like to
make a few observations about honor. The covenant
with Eli's father was based on how he honored God.
But when Eli and his sons did not honor God, they
broke the covenant. Honor is not an unmerited
respect that is granted indiscriminately. It is
something that is earned. Honor is repaid with
honor, and conversely, if one is not worthy of
honor, then honor is not due them. God changed
a covenant on the principle of honor. In the
marriage covenant, how important is honor? I Pet.
3:7 says it is important enough that if a man does
not honor his wife, it will hinder his prayers.
He is to honor her because of Christ in her, because
she is a joint heir with him. This is speaking
of people who have life through Christ. Romans
12:10 says "in honor preferring one another".
This is also based on Christ in the believers.
The two verses together mean one needs to esteem
the value of Christ in a spouse as a fellow
believer. The honor due them is honor due to the
worthiness of Christ in them as temples of the
Holy Spirit. It is in honor of His priesthood in
them. So it is not unmerited honor.
   Going back to the subject of covenants, the
last aspect of God's covenants that I want to look
at is in Lev. 26:40. God gives conditions that

347

the people had to meet in order for Him to maintain the covenant he had made with Jacob, Isaac and Abraham. The conditions were, 1) They must confess both their own and their father's iniquity done against God. Why did they have to confess their father's sin? Did that mean they had to take responsibility for their father's sin? No. By confessing that their fathers had sinned, they were renouncing a loyalty to their fathers who had sinned before them. They were putting their loyalty to God above their loyalty to a man. By doing this, they were breaking the fetters and chains of the father's sin that bound them, because the Word says that the sins of the fathers are passed down to the third and fourth generation. So they were breaking the generational curse brought about by the father's sin. That sin would have no power over their lives anymore. By confessing the sins of the father, it also breaks the familial pride, therefore, it is an act of humility before God. 2) They must confess that they had walked contrary to God. In other words they had to admit that they knew God's ways but had deliberately chosen to walk in disobedience to them. They had to "own" their own acts of disobedience. 3) They must confess that God had walked contrary to them because of their sin and that God himself had brought them into the land of their enemies. Notice, they had to understand that their sin had caused God to turn His back on them and that He did not **just allow them to fall into the hands of their enemies, but He actually gave them over to, or deliberately delivered them into the hands of the enemies.** They had to recognize that they were being held accountable for their sin, and that they were experiencing God's just wrath for their sin against Him. 4) By understanding and acknowledging these things, they would allow their their uncircumcised hearts to be humbled. 5) They had to accept the punishment for their sin, knowing that they were deserving of that punishment. They were also recognizing that He is a just God, that He will do what is right.

The greatest lack in many of today's Christians is that they do not believe God is holding them accountable for sin anymore. They believe Jesus paid the price for sin, therefore, they will not be accountable for it. **They do not believe they deserve punishment.** All they have to do is say "Sorry Lord" and then rest in I John 1:9 that all is forgiven and cleansed. **There is no real repentance.** They do not believe God would send anything hurtful to them as a form of discipline because they do not understand His justice and His wrath. They say a God of love would never deliberately **send** anything hurtful, He might **allow** it to happen but He would never **send** it. They say the Old Testament doesn't apply to us today. They forget how often Jesus said, after healing or delivering someone, "Go and **sin no more,** lest something worse happen to you." It sounds like worse things would happen because of sinning more. I wonder where the "something worse" would come from and why would it come?

In verse 44 God said if they did these things, if they took these steps of repentance, He would not destroy them or break covenant with them. So we see that if they did not meet these conditions, He was not obligated to, nor would He, maintain His covenant with them. God always provided Himself with a faithful remnant who would repent and turn back to Him so that through that remnant the promised Messiah would come. Jesus was the ful-fillment of the covenant to Abraham and to David. But from the time of Jesus on, the old covenant has not been maintained. It was replaced with the new and lasting covenant that is not for the Jews only as the old covenant was. The nation of Israel was set aside as a whole nation. God did not work with a chosen people as a nation anymore, but with individuals who believe in Christ.

Now that we understand a little about the covenants I want to pose a question. Did God ever command divorce?

The following commentary from Ezra 9 and 10 is an Old Testament version of the passage we have just looked at that says "be not unequally yoked".

The priests, king, leaders and officials of the Israelites married foreign wives. By their example, they led the people into marrying the polluted, corrupted people of the land. Their detestable practices filled the land with impurity. Ezra says because of this intermarrying, they deserved to be completely annihilated by God. But God was gracious and left a pure remnant. The faithful ones repented, confessed their sin and wept bitterly over it. Keep in mind that the word repent does not mean just a deep sorrow for sin, it means a complete turning away from that sin. It was not enough to say, "O God, this was sin, I am sorry, forgive me", they were required to do something more. Ezra 10:11 says that in spite of their unfaithfulness, there was still hope for Israel. Their hope was in confessing their sin to God and then **doing His will by separating or divorcing themselves from their foreign wives and children.** These were their loved ones. I am sure they loved them deeply. But their only hope to escape the wrath of God was to leave those loved ones and turn back to God. I think they wept bitterly, not only because they had offended God so seriously, but that in the repentance they knew the pain that would come to them from separating themselves from the spouses and families. This is pain they brought on themselves, because of their own disobedience, but it was none-the-less grievous to them.

Ezra 10:9 says that God was gracious to them because He left them a remnant and he gave them a firm place in his sanctuary. He gave light to their eyes and **relief from their bondage.** He did not desert them in their bondage. He granted them new life to rebuild the house of God and to repair it's ruins. He gave them a wall of protection in Judah and Jerusalem.

When the Israelites went into a foreign land, God always commanded them not marry inhabitants of that land because that would corrupt them. But they disobeyed God. Their only way to correct that was to confess their disobedience and leave those corrupt relationships.

Even though I have just written some of the following things, I am going to repeat myself to show how this passage in the Old Testament, relates to the ones we were just looking at in the New Testament.

God had commanded those people not to marry the impure and corrupt people of the land. Is that not the same thing that we are commanded in the New Testament when it says "be not unequally yoked"? Unequal means to join together with someone different, associate discordantly in servitude, by law or obligation with someone strange. Discordant means there is a lack of agreement, there is conflict. Servitude means the condition of being a slave, slavery, bondage. Strange means foreign to the family of God, in this instance. Also, in the passages from the book of Corinthians, New Testament believers are told to separate themselves from those who practice evil, those who are unclean. A Christian is the temple of God and there can be no agreement between the temple of God and idols. He says separate yourself from them and touch not those unclean things because they will pollute you, who are the temple of the living God. I Cor. 7:1 says purify yourselves from these contaminating relationships so that you can be perfected in holiness out of reverence for God.

To stay in a marriage that defiles and pollutes the temple of God is a far greater sin of unfaithfulness to Him, than it is to break a marriage vow. That is what God told Ezra.

Many Christian marriages are polluted and perverse. A person who chooses to come out from that kind of marriage in order to follow God, can be called a remnant who remains obedient to Christ. When they do that, God brings them into a firm place in His sanctuary. He gives them relief from their bondage and then He rebuilds their house. They are wounded and damaged temples of God, but He restores the ruins of their lives. He gives them a wall of protection from the enemy, the devil. This is a promise for one who will not put other gods before him--even a spouse or children. Is this not what Paul meant when he said "God has called them to peace"?

The truth about divorce is revealed here. It is not true that God holds marriage SO sacred that it must be maintained at all costs. It is not true, that a woman who walks out of a perverse marriage, is walking out from under her "umbrella of protection" (her husband) and is therefore subjecting herself to the enemy. The truth is, if she comes out from that unclean alliance, **in order to be more obedient to God, THEN** God will be her wall of protection, her refuge. He will give her relief from that bondage she was in. He will bring her into a firm sanctuary with Him. Rather then the woman tearing down her own house, as these false teachers preach, God will rebuild her house. He will restore the ruins of her life. This is truth. As long as the woman clings to her "pharaoh", wanting his protection more than God's, God will let her dwell in the shadow of the man. As long as God's protection is not wanted, and she prefers the man over God, God will not protect her. It is opposite of what we have been taught!! It is only when she recognizes what she has done, repents of it like Ezra and the faithful ones did, and leaves that discordant servitude, that God will protect her and rebuild her ruined life for her. That is when she will find safety in God's sanctuary.

This is not the milk of the Word. This is what Paul called strong meat in Heb. 5:11-14. It is difficult for a teacher to explain because it is grievous to hear and to live by. It does not tickle one's ears. People who are immature in the Word, are not skilled in the Word of righteousness. This belongs to the mature believer whose senses have been developed enough to be strong in discerning good from evil. Two other passages that address this area of things hard to teach and hard to understand are John 6:60 and II Pet. 3:10-18.

Many will not accept this as truth. Many will call it heresy, because it goes against their theology. Many will say that I am promoting divorce. In reality, the way that marriage is upheld today is the real heresy. The false teaching on submission and headship is the real reason for many divorces. These teachings are contrary to God, for they make men and marriages idols. It is the ancient practice of Baal worship, except it comes in a dressed up, pretty package, so that it appears to be godly. It is part of the apostasy of the last days. Apostasy is the deliberate act of rejecting God's revealed truth. Paul says in II Tim 3:5, apostates have a form of godliness, but deny the power of it. In other words, they have all the outward expressions of godliness, but they have departed from the truth of God. They forget that Jesus said, "Love the Lord your God with all your heart and with all your soul and with all your mind. This is the first and greatest commandment. And the second is like it: Love your neighbor as yourself. All of the Law and the Prophets hang on these two commandments."(Mt.22:37-40.) One cannot love God with all of their heart, mind, and soul, if they are loving a human with all their

353

heart, mind and soul. If they are bowing to the
wish and whim of a spouse, they cannot bow to the
will of God. The truth is, that what I have written
goes against man's theology, but it lifts up and
exalts God and puts Him on the throne where He
belongs. When the idols of man and marriage are
torn down, God is lifted up to His rightful place.
Then, the love for God will produce a healthy love
for self. That will work itself out in the love
of spouse in the right way. There will be no need
for the man to be the idol in his home, because
he won't need that to prop up his pride. He will
already have that healthy love of self because,
as he loves God with all that is in him, God will
give him his sense of worth. When he is not
struggling with issues of pride and ego and worth,
he will not have the need for pre-eminence in his
home. He lets go of selfishness. He will be able
to love his wife. She will be able to reverence
him, because she, also, is making the love of God
her first priority. She too will have a healthy
love of herself. She will not have to turn to her
husband for that. The fallen state of woman is
what gave the woman the desire to turn to her
husband instead of God. That turning to man often
includes the desire to let him take responsibility
for her spiritual condition. She uses the false
concept of "headship" as an excuse to abdicate
her responsibility for herself before God. That
is a perversion of the protection aspect of
headship. It is as distorted as the rulership aspect
of headship is for the men. When God is her first
priority, she will assume responsibility for herself and her relationship to God. There is no longer
an expectation for the husband to bear this responsibility for her. It takes the burden off of him.

The love we have **for** God, produces the love
**of** God in us. That love flows out to others.
It brings us into a right relationship to God,
and through that, right relationships to people.

That is what Jesus meant when He said that all
of the Law and the Prophets hangs on the first
commandment of love the Lord your God with all
your heart, mind and soul. Then you can love your
neighbor as yourself. Then you can love your
spouse.

Contrary to what many might think about what
I have written about divorce, I am not promoting
divorce. The teachings I have written here will
not cause divorce, unless the couple's relationship
with God is not right. Rather, they will produce
strong, healthy, truly, Christ centered marriages.
As the idols come down, there will be a whole new
perspective on marriage. The foundation will be
right and strong. The love of God will reproduce
itself in that marriage. The marriage will then
be a real picture of God's covenant. Both parties
will be responsible to God for themselves and
their covenant with Him first, then they will be
responsible to each other in their marriage covenant. They will willing submit to one another
out of reverence for God.

It is the Love of God, working itself out
in a marriage that will keep it together, not the
control and domination of false submission and
headship. Love is the way of the Lord. False submission and headship produces control and domination
which is the way of the devil. You choose who
you will follow. Like the people of Ezra's day,
there is hope for you, if you recognize your sin
of unfaithfulness to God because you have made
spouse and marriage your idol. You can repent of
that. Weep before God for having idols in your
life. God may rebuild your marriage on His right
foundation, or, in some cases, He may ask you to
leave that marriage. Which ever way He leads
you, if you are in His will, He will repair the
ruins of your life. Either way, He will set you
free from harmful bondages that have been inflicted
upon you by the doctrines of demons, taught by

man. Doctrines that have led you away to other gods, gods of spouses and marriages.

Today, the view on marriage in Christian circles, promotes it as the highest calling there is in a Christian's life. Marriage, in the right way, is a very high calling because it will be a witness of the love of God as it manifests itself to everyone watching that couple. It will be a powerful weapon against Satan as the union and unity of the couple portrays the union God has made between Israel and the Gentiles. It will remind Satan that Jesus has triumphed over him. When marriage becomes the idol of a person's life, when that marriage is full of dominance, control and subservience, it is neither a witness to others nor to Satan. It **must** be brought into it's proper perspective, which is to view it for it's eternal value, rather than just for it's temporal value to the couple while they are here on earth. It has got to be viewed as an arena where love is the supreme demonstration and where unity produces power against Satan. It is a very high calling. But the high calling is not just to maintain a marriage, it is to overcome the earthly desires and selfish purposes of the couple in the marriage. To see just how high this calling is, we must understand some other Scriptures. These are a few more of those things that are hard to teach and hard to understand.

In Matthew 19:3-26 Jesus speaks about marriage first. The pharisees were trying to trick him by asking about divorce. Jesus tells them that God made male and female and that He joined them together as one and no man should tear that asunder. That was God's original plan. Again, trying to trick Him, they asked then why did Moses permit it. He answered, because of the hardness of men's hearts Moses allowed it. I believe the hardness of men's hearts has a twofold meaning. One was that their hard hearts did not want to obey God.

Two, was that their hard hearts made them selfish, unkind, unloving and abusive towards their wives. It was not like that with Adam and Eve before the fall. It was not God's plan for marriage to be like that. It was hard for the disciples to comprehend how the man could overcome his disobedience to God and his hardness of heart towards his wife. If he couldn't do that, how could he be saved?

Next Jesus goes into the short little verses about the children and allowing them to come to him. He says unless a person has the innocent, trusting, belief in Him like a child has, they can't be one of His. It is the pride of the intellect and worldly wisdom of man that will keep them from believing in Him for salvation. That pride in those things has to be overcome. Again they were exceedingly amazed at his teaching and wondered how could anyone overcome the pride of intellect and be saved.

The third thing Jesus brings up is the rich young ruler, who was unwilling to part with his possessions in order to follow Christ. Jesus said it was not easy for a rich man to enter into the kingdom of God. Again the disciples wondered how could anyone overcome their desire for riches and be saved.

Verse 26 ties it all together. In man the ability to overcome the problems in marriage, the pride in intellect, and the possession of riches is impossible. He cannot overcome them by himself. It is only through making Christ their Lord and making God absolute number one in their life, by exalting Him above all else, can He make it possible for them to overcome and be saved.

Mark 10:1-31 is one parallel to Matthew 19:3-26. Except in Mark, Peter carries the conversation with Christ further. He says we have left all to follow you. Jesus answers him by saying, "Verily I say unto you, there is no man that has left

357

house, or brethren, or sisters, or father, or mother, or wife (spouse), or children, and lands, **for my sake and the gospel's,** but he shall receive an hundredfold now in this time, houses, and brethren, and sisters, and mothers, and children, and lands, with persecutions; and in the World to come, eternal life"(KJV) Mark says the disciples were "astonished out of measure" and asked who could be saved. Verse 27 says man does not have the ability to leave these things in himself. It is only through God that it is possible. Jesus would not have spoken about leaving family etc. if there was no possibility of that being a requirement of following Him sometimes. The disciples understood him only too well.

The third parallel is in Luke 18. Marriage is not mentioned in this gospel, but the faith as a child and the rich young ruler is. Again we see that they understand the high calling but are shocked by the hardness of it. What they are really wondering is, this is so hard, how can anyone be saved. But Jesus says in verse 27 that it is impossible with man but it is possible with God. In this gospel, Peter's continued conversation is recorded where Jesus answers the remark that Peter makes in both gospels. Peter says, "We have left all and followed you.", to which Jesus replies, "Verily I say unto you There is no man that has left house or parents or brethren or wife, or children, **for the kingdom of God's sake** who shall not receive manifold in this present time, and in the world to come life everlasting."

There are so many riches to uncover in these gospel accounts.

One jewel is that there an eternal purpose for all of this. These things are to be overcome for the primary reason of promoting Jesus, and the kingdom of God here on earth.

Another treasure is that when we give up all to follow Christ, there is an earthly reward, because those things we give up are replaced with more and better than what we give up. In other words, when we hang on to some of these things of earth with a tight fist, we may be hanging onto an imitation pearl when God wants to give us a Pearl of great price.

The gold in all of this is life everlasting.

Notice how the emphasis is on eternal values or the life to come. The next chapter in the book will help to focus on those eternal values.

Only through God being number one in our life can He make it possible for us to have the courage and strength to put Him before spouses, families, riches, and pride in ourselves and our intellect. The disciples knew and understood the hard things that Christ had to say. But, they were given the blessed hope that in God it is possible to do whatever He called on them to do.

Ezra and the faithful remnant were given hope. The disciples were given hope. We are given hope. But the hope lies in a complete turning to God where He is lifted up as King and Lord. With man, it is impossible, only with God is it possible.

This chapter on divorce and covenants is not to discredit God's faithfulness, or to promote divorce. It's purpose is to present a balanced truth about God's covenants and how He dealt with covenant breakers. These understandings will bring balance to the myth that God does not allow divorce under any circumstances for a Christian because that would go against His covenants. Many divorced Christians who suffer under the condemnation of other Christians, because of false views about covenants and divorce, will have their painful burden lifted. New understanding of truth will set them free. Perhaps even some of those who condemn will be set free also. My prayer is that the idols would come down in every Christian marriage and that God would be exalted. That every marriage would be restored and rebuilt on that basis. But I know that there are those who will not abide by these hard things that Jesus himself said. So I also pray for wisdom for people to know when the god in their life is more important to them than God is and what to do about it. Jesus said that Moses allowed divorce because of the hardness of people's hearts. The condition of hardness of heart still exists in mankind. I need to expand on that before leaving this chapter.

In Matthew 19:8 Jesus said, "Moses, because of the hardness of your hearts, permitted you to put away your wives, but from the beginning it was not so." Mark 10:2-12 is the same story. Both accounts say that God did not intend marriage to end in divorce, but because of the hardness of the MEN'S hearts, Moses permitted it.

In these accounts, **Jesus did not condemn Moses for allowing it, nor did he say anything to reverse what Moses had permitted!** He stated that it was not God's original intention for there to be divorce. This statement of God's original intent has become the focal point of the passage. It has been used as the proof text concerning divorce. Jesus' statement that it was not so in the beginning, coupled with God's statement in Malachi that He hates divorce has become the iron clad rule. NO DIVORCE. The real meaning of the message delivered by Christ is missed. And that is that Moses permitted it because of the hardness of heart.

A word study shows that the words heart, soul and life are interchangeable. Heart and soul especially have the same meaning. They encompass the mind, will, emotions, intellect, and feelings. According to Strong's Concordance the Greek word for hardness of heart is aklerokardia. It means a "destitution of spiritual perception." Destitute means to be completely lacking in something--extreme poverty. Perception means consciousness, awareness, knowledge, and insight. In reality what Jesus was saying was that men had become so completely lacking of spiritual consciousness and awareness that they were devoid of spiritual knowledge and insight. They could no longer perceive spiritual things, the things of God. What I believe he was saying was that before the fall of Adam and Eve, man had the spiritual perception of what God had intended for marriage. God created Adam with the spiritual perception of the value of the woman. But after the fall, that spiritual perception was lost. As man's heart grew harder and became void of spiritual understanding of marriage, it affected how he viewed and treated his wife, until finally, Moses allowed them to divorce their wives. I believe he allowed it to protect the women from abuse, that resulted from the hardness of men's hearts.

Remember in earlier chapters I talked much about the misinterpretations of Gen. 3:16 and how the real meaning is "You will turn to your husband and it will cause him to dominate you'? I believe that as the woman lost her spiritual perception she turned away from God to man. She began to look to her husband for everything. As he lost his spiritual perception, he lorded it over her in domination and cruelty. I believe that it finally got so bad that Moses permitted divorce to end the cruelty and dominance. I believe that all of this was incorporated in God's statement in Malachi that he hates divorce AND he hates the men's violence against their wives. The spirit of the woman still belongs to God and the man is violating it with his violence. This is what Jesus was referring to when he said in the beginning it was not so but Moses permitted it because of your hardness of heart. Women had turned to men, making them their idol. Men had made themselves idols to their wives by accepting their worship rather than turning them back to God. Then they dominated them and expected their wives to turn

361

to them even more. Divorce ended that form of idol worship for both the man and the woman. As I stated before, **Jesus never stated that what Moses permitted was contrary to what God permitted now. He did not refute, revoke or reverse Moses' permission.** By the time of Moses, the prophetic utterance of God that woman would turn to man and he would rule over her was fulfilled to the fullest. His earliest intentions for man and woman had been completely corrupted. He still hates divorce and he still hates the violence committed against the woman. He will hold man accountable for that. As head, the man should be turning his wife back to God rather than pridefully demanding that she submit even more to himself as her idol.

This should shed some light on the answer for abuse in Christian marriages. It should remove the guilt that women feel when they cannot endure abuse from their husbands. It should help pastors to counsel women who come to them for help when the husbands are abusing them. It should end the shame and stigma of divorce for a Christian. As I said before, the condition of hardness of hearts exists today. Perhaps even worse than then.

God, deliver us from this faulty view on covenants and divorce. Help us to see how you responded to broken covenants and covenant breakers, give us the wisdom to know how and when to do likewise.

CHAPTER FIFTEEN
EPHESIANS:PORTRAIT OF GOD'S COVENANT

Is marriage ever a real portrait of God's true covenant? Yes it is. But it is not a portrait of God's covenant when one spouse becomes an idol to the other because of false teachings of headship and submission.

What is God's best covenant? He established His everlasting covenant when He divorced Israel, setting her aside so that He could make a new covenant through Jesus Christ.

Israel was God's chosen people. He worked through them only and His covenant was with them only. He set up a line of priests who were the mediators between God and man. God's Spirit dwelt in the Holy of Holies, in the Temple. The Holy of Holies was separated from everything by a thick veil. No man could go into that place unless God bid him to go there at specific times and under specific conditions. Even the priests went into the Holy of Holies with a rope tied to their foot, so that if God was displeased with them and struck them dead while they were there, they could be pulled out without anyone going in to get them. That is how separated all people were from God. The priests made sacrifices and said prayers for the people's sins. There was an elaborate system of prescribed sacrifices that God required to be made at the hands of the priests. Though there are many incidences recorded in the Old Testament of God speaking to different people, the people did not have access to God the way we do. The Word says God spoke to His people through the Prophets.

A study in Ephesians is valuable in gaining an understanding of what the old and new covenants meant. This understanding is necessary in order to understand how marriage can be a picture of the true everlasting covenant. It shows how two become one.

363

Ephesians 2:11-13, Paul says the Gentiles did not have the covenant of promise that was given to Abraham. Therefore, they were without hope and without God. But now they were brought into the new covenant through the blood of Christ.

Verse 14: "For He is our peace, He has made the two nations into one and has broken down the wall of partition between us, (Jews and Gentiles)" In other words the wall of hostility that was between the two nations was abolished. When Christ died on the cross, the veil in the temple was torn in two. The veil represented the separation between God and man, and between the nations. When the veil was torn asunder, this represented the end of the old covenant. This was His divorce of Israel. Henceforth God would be dealing with all people, not just the Jews. He would be dealing with them in a new and different way. The new covenant was established through Christ's shed blood and His death. Now all people, Jews and Gentiles alike, had access to God himself. There was no longer a need for priests to mediate for the people. There was no longer a need for animal sacrifices. Christ was the sacrifice that ended the need for the sacrifices. His shed blood was sufficient in God's eyes for all sin, for all time. He alone became the mediator between God and man. Salvation and redemption came to all who would believe in Christ Jesus. This salvation through Christ was for Jews and Gentiles alike. Through Christ, we have all become the seed of Abraham, joint heirs of salvation. There are no longer separations between Jew and Gentile.

Gal. 3:26-29 says: "For you are all the children of God by faith in Christ Jesus. For as many of you as have been baptized into Christ have put on Christ. There is neither Jew nor Greek, there is neither bond nor free, there is neither male nor female, for you are all one in Christ Jesus. And if you be Christ's, then you are Abraham's

seed, and heirs according to the promise." (KJV)
By this we know that the wall of hostility between
the Jews and Gentiles was broken down. We know
the same wall of hostility that separated male
and female is broken down also. There is no longer
a separation they, too, are one in Christ.

Does that mean that all the hostility between
the nations ceased? NO!! It means, although the
carnal nature of man would keep the hostility going,
the provision for peace was there. All they have
to do is appropriate that peace through Christ
Jesus. All are heirs according to the promise
of Christ. The male and female issue is the same.
The carnal nature would keep the hostility going,
but the provision for unity and peace must be
understood and appropriated.

Going back to Ephesians 2:15, His purpose
in abolishing the old covenant was so He could
create in himself one body out of two. He joined
the two nations into one, thus making peace between
them. He did the same for male and female, for
all people of all races.

Eph. 2:16, by Christ's body he reconciled both
of them to God through the cross. Through that
act he put to death the hostility between the two.

Verse 18 says that through Christ both have
access to God the Father. Because of Christ,
neither Jew nor Greek, neither male nor female
has more access to God. Neither male nor female
has more ability to hear from God or to receive
direction and leading from the Holy Spirit.

Why did God want to do this?

Verses 20-22 says He did it because He made
Christ the cornerstone so He could use ALL
Christians as building blocks to build himself
a new temple. He joined them together in Christ
to raise up a Holy Temple for Himself, one dwelling
in which God lives by His Spirit. Since the veil
was destroyed, there was no longer a Holy of Holies.
Subsequently, the Temple itself was destroyed.

He chose a new temple in which to dwell.

Eph. 3:3-6, Paul says that by God's grace he was given this revelation knowledge that had been hidden from man through out the past ages. This is a mystery of two becoming one. He says he wants all to understand this mystery of how the Jews and the Gentiles became fellow partakers and heirs and are now of the same body. How they became joint partakers of salvation through Christ. He again emphasizes how he wants all to understand the mystery of how two become one in verse 9.

I, too, want to make it plain to everyone how this same mystery makes two become one in a marriage. It is the same principle.

Why is it so important for all to understand this mystery?

Eph 3:10 says it is because He wanted to demon-strate His wisdom and power to the principalities and powers in heavenly places. The two nations becoming one united force in one body was a demonstration to Satan and all demons and all angels that His eternal purpose was accomplished through Christ Jesus. God's prophetic utterance to Satan, at the time of the fall in the Garden of Eden, was fulfilled. The seed of the woman, whom Satan had deceived, had finally come. In His death, Satan had bruised Christ's heal, but in His res-urrection, Christ had forever crushed Satan and his power. Now there was one united force. There was no longer a divided body of people. They were all one. All differences of race and gender were wiped out so that they could unite their energies against the common enemy, Satan. The common de-nominator that made them into one force was Christ Jesus. It will forever be Christ. We know in the natural, nations and man and woman continue the hostility between themselves, but it ought not to be so. When a Jewish person comes to know the Messiah, they understand and they do become one with the Gentile brothers and sisters. They no longer cling to the barrier that has separated the nations. It should be the same for two people in a marriage. This is the mystery of two becoming one.

God intended the two nations to come together under one Spiritual bond. Jesus is that bonding agent. If male and female could understand that if there was a spiritual bonding between them in a marriage, as God intended, the spiritual power that would be demonstrated in that marriage would be a mighty weapon against Satan. But if the hostility between male and female still rages, then the house is divided and it cannot stand. That is the reason Satan has deceived and distracted people with false teachings on headship and submission. That is why the cunning deceiver has made good people believe maintaining a marriage is more important than maintaining an obedient relationship with God. That is why he has caused marriage and spouses to become idols.

The mystery of two becoming one IS spiritual and it must be spiritually discerned. Spiritual bonding for a couple is essential in order for a Christian couple to have the mystery of two becoming one operative in their lives. Spiritual bonding is understood through the Spirit.

Two becoming one is God's purpose of the ages. It is not just for our own comfort and a way for us to have our needs met. Those are the benefits, not the purpose. We need to get our eyes off of self, each other and the marriage and look at the whole picture of marriage in the light of eternal values. There is a much higher spiritual purpose for a person to be equally yoked with another believer. Equally yoked does not mean just uniting with another believer. It also means that they are spiritually equal in God's eyes and they should be equal in each other's eyes. This equality gives the needed power to each one to pull together in the yoke so that the load is evenly

367

distributed. They can work together as a well precisioned team to accomplish what God has set for them to do as a couple. Imagine a yoke of oxen. One is very big and strong and dominate. The other is much smaller and weak and puny. The small one is subservient and does not know what to do. Can't you just see the pair in harness going zig-zag, up and down, unevenly, the stronger one pulling ahead of the other? They are so unequal that no work can be done. But if the oxen are equal in size and strength, they work together in harmony. They are able to do a superb job and accomplish their purpose.

Eph. 4 gives all Christians instruction about works of service they are to do for Him. Each one, individually, is to mature until they attain the full measure of what God has for them in Christ. This will then produce the unity of faith.

With Christ as the head, they are joined together, built up in love, **every** part working together. They are like the equally matched yoke of oxen.

We are created to become like God in holiness and righteousness. Now, Christ in us makes that possible.

Eph. 5 goes on with the instructions of how to attain this holiness and righteousness. Read these chapters of Ephesians and apply them to your marriage. I'll take a few verses to show you what I mean by applying them to your marriage.

Vs. 3-4 speaks of fornication, uncleaness and filthiness. This is immorality of any kind. Some erring teachers will teach the verse that says the marriage bed is undefiled, means that a married couple can do anything they want to sexually, as long as both partners are comfortable with it and no one gets hurt by it. This is a lie. If God says something is a sin outside of marriage, it is sin in His eyes in a marriage as well. A sin does not stop being a sin just because there is a marriage ceremony. If it is called sin elsewhere in the Bible, it is sin in a marriage, too. I am referring to such things as sodomy, for instance. Sodomy, according to the dictionary, means any unnatural sexual practice. The usual definition says it can be between two males, or a person and an animal. But it can include anal intercourse between a husband and wife. God sanctifies the marriage union so that the couple are not committing fornication. That is what God means when He says the marriage bed is undefiled. It is not a license to commit all kinds of ungodly, unclean acts. A good rule of thumb to judge whether an act is unclean or not is to ask, "Is this a natural use of the body. Is this what God intended this part of the body to be used for?" In other words, don't leave the natural use of the body parts as God created them to be used for, for that which is unnatural. Many godly couples have brought their marriage into defilement, because they became ensnared with a filthy unnatural use of the body. The word filthy means lewd, or obscene.

Verse 4 talks about obscene talking and foolish jesting. This is "dirty" talk concerning sexual things, course remarks about, or to, your partner, perverse terms to describe sex acts or body parts. Dirty stories and off-color jokes, jokes that tear down, cut down, or put down your partner, these are all foolish talk and jesting. They defile and demean the partner and the marriage. Rather than use these kinds of words, give words of praise and thanksgiving. Speak words that uplift, encourage and build up your partner. Use terms that make the sex act sound beautiful rather than dirty.

Don't use vain words to deceive one another and don't be deceived by flattering, vain words that lead you to be disobedient to God.

Understand what the will of God is for each one of you. Help each other to attain that.

Vs. 18 says each one is to be filled with

the Holy Spirit. Vs. 19 tells us how to do that. We do it by filling our hearts, minds and mouths with psalms, and hymns, and spiritual songs (PRAISE) and by making melody in our hearts to God. If a married couple were to speak those things to each other, rather than the obscene sexual words and the course jesting that tears down and demeans, they would bring each other into the presence of the Lord. They would be keeping the marriage on a spiritual level.

Vs.20: To be filled with the Holy Spirit, one must have a grateful attitude so they can fill their heart and mind with thanksgiving for all things. I would add that if you say with your mouth, "I thank God for you. You are a blessing to me. You are a gift from God, sent by Him especially for me", your mate will be blessed and lifted up. If you fill your heart and mind with the good things about that mate, you won't be dwelling on the negatives that can destroy your marriage. Thanking God for your mate is a spiritual exercise, tearing them down for their short comings is an exercise of the flesh.

Vs.21 says this is how you submit to ONE ANOTHER IN THE FEAR OF GOD. This is spiritual reverence for our awesome God. It is a recognition and a reverence for who Christ is in your partner. This takes it out of the mere physical realms and brings it into the spiritual realms. It elevates the marriage from the flesh to the spirit.

Vs. 22: When the husband is doing this, the wife is persuaded to submit to him because she knows he is first submitted to God. She feels safe in spiritually bonding with him. When the husband is not doing well spiritually, a wife does not feel safe with him.

Vs. 23: The husband is the head of the wife just as Christ is the head of the Church. How was Christ the head of the church?

1. Christ was head of the church spiritually.

2. He was the source or birth place of the church.

Man was created first, woman was taken out of him, therefore, he was the source or birth-place for the woman.

3. Christ demonstrated his headship by lovingly teaching man spiritual things. As they learned from him, their temporal life came into alignment with holiness and righteousness.

Man teaches the wife spiritual things and demonstrates godliness to her as her head. When she sees that his godly behavior is in alignment with what he is teaching her, she is persuaded to follow him as her head.

4. Christ died for His church in order to become it's head.

Man must die to his own selfish, fleshly desires and his own carnal nature in order to demonstrate his worthiness to be the spiritual head of his wife.

5. Christ was a servant and He condemned the "lordship" of anyone over anyone else. That kind of thing was a thing of the flesh, a thing of the world, and He said it would not be like that for anyone following Him. He forbade it in any rel-ationship. He did away with that when He said "It won't be like that with you".

Therefore, as "head", the man must follow Christ's teaching and **put away the concept of his lordship over the woman in the flesh and assume Christ's example of headship in the spirit.**

Vs. 24, So just as the church is subject to Christ, so let the woman be subject to her husband in everything. This verse is so crucial that I will devote the next chapter to it. But for now, I will say Christ was obedient to the Father in holiness and righteousness.

So should the church be obedient to Christ in all holiness and righteousness.

ALL OF THIS OBEDIENCE IS A SPIRITUAL SUBMISSION

Vs.25, Husbands love your wives, even as Christ loved the church and died for it.

Not many husbands are called upon to literally die for their wives in the flesh. So what does that mean? I believe it means he is to love her with such a selfless love he will die to his own natural, carnal, selfish desires. He builds her up in love by living what is spiritual. All Christians are to die to self. His dying to self is the example for her to die to herself.

Vs. 26, Christ sanctified and cleansed the church through washing by the water of the Word. He taught them spiritual things in order to cleanse them from the old nature of the flesh. This cleansing from the old nature is what set them apart.

Vs.27, Through this cleansing by the word, Jesus perfects His bride so she can be presented to Him without spot or wrinkle. It makes her holy and without blemish, or any such thing.

Vs.28, This is what a husband should do to show his love for his wife, so he can be her head as Christ was head of the church. He brings her to holiness through washing her with the Word, as he lives out his walk with God as her example.

Vs.29-30, As he washes her with the Word and cares for her spiritual welfare, she will become spiritually bonded with him. Together they are the spiritually united members of one body.

Vs.31, Because of the need for a spiritual mate, a man will leave his father and mother and cleave to his wife. Because of God's desire for a united body, they must be one in the spirit, just as the church is one, united by the Holy Spirit, so it can be one body that is separated from all other humanity. This united body cannot allow even the natural relationship of children and parents to interfere with this union. The husband and wife are one in body and in spirit.

Vs.32-33, Though Paul was speaking of the

372

mystery of the Church becoming one out of two
nations, He says in verse 34 that in the same way
this is the kind of love and spiritual bonding
that enables a man to love his wife as he loves
himself and for her to be able to respect him.
This can only happen in the spirit when God is
#1 for both parties.

If God joins two together in a spiritual bonding
that He has chosen, and He joins them together
as He did the Jews and the Gentiles, they should
be able to stand through anything.

From the time of Christ until the end of the
age, His church has been coming together in one
body. It will be one body throughout eternity.
But it won't be a body in the flesh. It will be
a body in the spirit. Nobody can change that.
The earthly marriage bond, as we know it, is not
eternal. It ends when the flesh dies. But the
eternal spiritual bond in Christ, that makes a
couple one in the spirit, will make them a part
of the eternal body forever.

In our humanity, one of a spiritual partnership
can walk away from the Lord. When that happens
the spiritual bond is broken between the man and
woman. Then the marriage can be in trouble. When
the marriage is dealt with in the natural, or in
the flesh, it is in trouble. The two becoming
one is spiritual in nature, just as the two nations
becoming one is spiritual in nature.

So the key to a beautiful marriage is that
each individual must maintain a 100% commitment
to love and obey God first and always. When God
is kept #1 in the eyes of the couple, they will
not become idols to each other. Marriage is viewed
in it's proper perspective and it does not become
an idol either. There will be no power struggle
between them. They will think in harmony. Mal.
2:15 says that God joined them together, yet He
retained their spirits for himself. This means
they are individuals, separate, and independent

of each other because their spirits belong to God. Yet, because their spirits are bonded to each other, they are interdependent. As they join together in harmony and unity, deep satisfaction comes to both. Their spirits are in one accord, so when they submit to one another they are submitting to God.

When there is a bonding in the spirit of two people who are sold out to God, it produces a Song of Solomon kind of love. Their love of God will produce a kind of love that will bind them together like super-glue. This is the kind of marriage that is a true representation of the love Christ has for the church. This is the kind man cannot put asunder. In this kind of marriage, that is based on the spirit, there is no rebellion in either party over their roles in life. Headship and submission becomes so natural it produces I Corinthians 13 kind of love. There is perfect contentment, joy, unity, satisfaction and happiness like God intended in the beginning, before Satan came between Adam and Eve with his war between genders. Christ ended that war, just as he ended the hostility, the wall, between the two nations. Together, Jew and Gentile have become one united force, forming the body of Christ. The gates of hell shall not prevail against that united force. Together, man and woman have become a united force, one in the body of Christ. The gates of hell shall not prevail against a marriage that is taken out of the physical realms, where the wiles of Satan can flourish, and is brought into the spiritual realms to form one body.

Every time Satan witnesses that kind of marriage, he sees that the war he started between Adam and Eve is really over. The man and the woman are now one, like Adam and Eve were. That reminds him that Christ truly did triumph over him. He is reminded he is the loser, he is already defeated. This couple is living proof of that. He cannot stand it, because he sees how his plan to destroy mankind, God's most precious creation, has been completely foiled. His plan of destruction by dividing the nucleus of the family, the foundation of society, has been forever interrupted by the unifier of all mankind, Christ. The broken down wall of hostility has broken his power. Oh, people, do you see the higher calling that marriage SHOULD be? It is the eternal value that counts. It cannot count for anything if the marriage and the spouse are taking the place of God, if God is not lifted up higher than the marriage and the spouse. Yes, marriage should be maintained, and every effort should be put forth to maintain it in the most God honoring way possible. But it cannot be maintained if the price of it is for one mate to sell out to the other in idol worship. Satan laughs with glee when he sees how effective the false teaching of submission and headship has been as Christian marriages crumble because of them.

Christians, give up these false concepts of headship and submission. Repent and be free from these spots and wrinkles before it's too late.

# CHAPTER SIXTEEN
## EPHESIANS 5:24
### SUBMIT TO YOUR HUSBAND IN EVERYTHING

The previous chapters have given us a good basic understanding of some of the Scriptures that have been perverted, misinterpreted, distorted, and used abusively to make Scripture say what it does not.

Other than Genisis 3:16, I believe this one verse, Eph. 5:24 has been the most abused Scripture of all. It is the basis for untold suffering for women through the ages. The very best preachers all interpret the verse the same way. They will preach a beautiful sermon on how women and men were created equal. Both in God's image. They were given equal, co-regency over living things. Both male and female are of equal value or worth to God. **B U T** because Eve's sin caused the fall, even though they still have equal value and worth, God commanded the woman to be subject to the husband as the "federal" head. She is commanded to submit in **E V E R Y T H I N G**. Though there is no such word in Scripture that says man is the federal head of the woman the word "federal" has been added by many men. It means the governing ruler.

It has been explained by the best theologians that the "head" has been given the authority over every function of the wife's life. The "head", as it's function in the physical, natural body tells the rest of the body what to do. It sends signals to the rest of the body to walk, to breathe, to eat, etc. The foot, or the respiratory system, or the digestive system does not tell the head what to do. The head controls everything the body does. Because the Bible uses the analogy of the physical body to show how the church has many members, but one body, they believe that the analogy is continued when it says the man is the head over the wife. Therefore, the man has a right, indeed, an obligation, to tell his wife what to do. He has the right to expect that his wife will obey him in everything. They believe that God has given all right of decision in every matter to the husband, because the foot can never tell the head what to do. The head must control every situation. Most preachers will say, "Folks, I didn't say that. I didn't put that in the Bible. It is the Word of God! I know that today it is much abused, but the Bible says 'wives submit to your husband in everything'. There is no getting around it. Husbands are commanded to govern and wives are commanded to submit. Everything means everything. No matter what he says or does, you are to submit. If you don't willingly submit to him in everything, you are rebelling against God himself because you are going against God's word and His established order." They **might** add, "if your husband tells you to sin, then you don't have to do that on the grounds that you must obey God rather than man, when it comes to sin. But biblically speaking, in **everything else** you must submit." Sometimes, some will concede that much.

    **"Everything"** is **always** associated with the physical world. That is, the right of the man to tell the woman how to dress, where to go, when to do something or not to do something, etc. The right of decision in all matters of the home and family are his. He is the boss, he's in control. It's always in the realms of the physical world of the flesh. Then the words "spiritual head" are sometimes added in an off-handed, almost unimportant, meaningless way. Like submitting in spiritual things is required, but that is not the main issue. The main issue seems to be, obey in all physical things. If there is a difference of opinion in a decision, the final word is his because God made him the head.

    I often prayed, "Lord, that IS what the word says, submit in everything, but what does it really mean to you? We know you don't want your women to be abused, in the name of submission, for that is contrary to your nature. So what is the answer for this? I need a concrete, biblically sound answer that will refute, beyond any shadow of doubt, what we have been taught it means.

One day, the Lord kept prompting me to look up the word "everything" in Eph. 5:24. I thought I knew what it meant. Like most of us, that does not seem like a word that would be necessary to look up. After all, we all know what "everything" means, don't we? So at first I resisted, but finally, when the nagging thoughts would not go away, I was obedient. That was the key God used to unlock the truth and understanding of that verse. I pray it will be as freeing to you, the reader, as it was to me.

There is an absolutely astounding, revolutionary, truth found in the definitions of the words **"EVERYTHING** as it is used in Eph. 5:24!!

According to Strong's Concordance the word "every" is number 3956, a Greek word, pas; includes all forms of declension; appar. a prim. word; all, any, every, the whole: all (manor of, means), alway(s), any(one), x daily, +ever, every (one, way), as many as + no (thing) x throughly, whatso-ever, whole, whosoever.

That definition was as I expected it to be. It means all inclusive. Nothing is excluded.

But the word "thing" as used in Eph. 5:24 was not what I expected at all, in the light of how it has always been translated, by almost every theologian since the church began, probably. Again, I will give the direct quote from Strong's Concordance, so there can be no misunderstanding or bias on my part. The number is 5313, the Greek word "hupsoma"; from 5312; an elevated place or thing, i.e. (abstr) altitude, or (by impl.) a barrier (fig.): height, high thing.

5312, hupso; from 5311; to elevate (lit. or fig.):

exalt, lift up.
5311, hupsos; from a der. of 5228; elevation, i.e.
(abst.)altitude, (spec.) the sky, or (fig.) dignity:
be exalted ,height, (on) high.
5228, huper; a prim. prep.; "over" i.e. (with the
gen.) of place, above, beyond, across, or casual,
for the sake of, instead, regarding; with the acc.
superior to, more than: ( + exceeding abundantly)
above, in (on)behalf of, beyond, by,+ very chiefest,
concerning, exceeding (above, -ly), for, + very
highly, more(than), of, over, on the part of, for
sake of, in stead, than, to (-ward), very.   In
comp. it retains many of the above applications.
     Though it is not mentioned in this list, there
is one final word  that is connected.  It is 5310,
hupsistos;  superl. from the base of 5311; highest,
i.e. (masc.sing.) the Supreme (God), or (neut.
plur.) the heavens: most high, highest.
     As I read the first four meanings for "thing"
**there was an awesome comprehension that the
"thing" in "every thing" had nothing to do with
physical matters at all!!! "Thing" here means
the high, exalted things of God. The spiritual
things. "Thing" is an elevated, heavenly spiritual
thing that transcends the mundane, physical things
of this world. These high spiritual things are
the "thing" women are to be obedient to their
husbands in!! The impact of this discovery is
enormous!!!**
     To make sure I was not reading into those
meanings what I wanted to see, I did a small survey
amongst a number of good solid Christians.  I did
not tell them what word I was defining,  or what
verse it came from.  I just gave  the definitions
from Strong's.  First I gave them the definition
for "every".  It was  unanimous  the  meaning was
"all inclusive, nothing excluded."  Then I gave
them the first four meanings of "thing".  The
meanings they gave to these four definitions were:
1. God, heaven, something high up, something on

a higher plane.

2. Worship, God, lift up, raise or exalt, idolize, and speaking of the Lord Himself.

3. Heavens, heavenly, lifted up, it would be idolatry if anyone but God was lifted up like that.

4. God, The Lord, The Supreme Authority, and, relationship between God and his people.

Of all the people I asked, it was unanimous that the word meant God and high, godly, spiritual things.

When the words were defined, with no distortion or pre-conceived ideas from knowing what verse it came from, their conclusions were all the same. They were the same as mine. **We are looking at the spiritual truth that women are being instructed to submit to their husbands in the high spiritual things of God, NOT the things of the world and the flesh.** Couple this with the usage of the middle voice principle that we learned earlier. The woman is not being instructed to blindly submit to her husband in every mundane physical thing, she is being instructed to willingly submit to the high exalted spiritual things he would teach her **ONLY**. According to what he is teaching, she has a choice to submit or not!!

Let us look again at a loose paraphrase and my commentary of Eph. 5 while keeping in mind the thought that the meaning of the word "thing" is spiritual only, not physical.

Verse 1: Be followers of God.

Verse 2: Walk in love. The same kind of sacrificial love that Christ showed us when He died for us.

Verse 6: Don't let any man deceive you with vain words. Not a spouse, pastor, teacher or any one.

Verse 8: You once walked in darkness, but now you are children of light, so walk in the light.

Verse 9: The fruit of the Spirit is goodness and righteousness and truth.

Verse 11: Reprove or expose the works of darkness. As we read in another chapter, there are no exceptions to this admonishment. It includes spouses, best friends, relatives, pastors and Bible teachers. Verse 13: Those dark things that are exposed and made known by the light, are then light. Verse 14: Wake up, Christian, and let Christ give you light. Verse 15: Walk carefully and not as a fool, but as a wise person. Verse 17: Be wise and know what the will of the Lord is. The will of the Lord is that you be filled with Spirit, that you walk totally in the Spirit and the light of His Word, and don't be deceived.

In context, the next verses all deal with things of the Spirit. These are high, exalted, spiritual things. Verse 18: Be not drunk with wine, but be filled with Holy Spirit. Verse 19: (Because you are filled with the Spirit) speak to yourselves in psalms, hymns, and spiritual songs, singing and making melody in your heart to the Lord. (Without the Spirit, can anyone do this? This is a thing of the spirit, not the flesh.) Verse 20: (Because you are filled with the Spirit) give thanks to God, always, for all things, in the name of the Lord Jesus Christ. Verse 21 (Because you are filled with the spirit and others are filled with the Spirit) submit yourselves one to another in the fear of God. (Notice, we do not submit to one another of the world or in the flesh, but to other Spirit filled Christians, in the awesome reverence of God. This is a highly spiritual exercise. Notice, also, when there is submission one to another, no one is assigned the position of "boss", or the "one in control", or the "one who is given right of decision". There is equality in mutual submission. No one is "over" the other and no one is "under" the other. This mutual submission is out of respect for God, who He is, and how He is manifested, in

381

the other person.)

Verse 22 (Because you are filled with the Spirit) you wives submit to your own husbands, (who are also filled with the Spirit) in the same way you would submit unto the Lord (The Lord is not standing over us dictating what we are to do in the flesh, we submit to Him in the Spirit).

Verse 23: For the husband (who is filled with the Spirit) is the head of the wife, (who is filled with the Spirit) just like Christ (in the Spirit) is head of the church (because He) is the savior of the body.

In the Old Testament there is no reference to man being the head of the woman. The majority of the time, the head is talking about the chief representative or spokesman for a tribe of Israel. Sometimes it meant king, governor or ruler. There are only two places in all of Scripture where it says specifically the husband is head of the wife. One is here, the other is II Cor. 11:3. There is a key word in these verses. Both times it says "husband is head OF the wife". OF is the Greek prefix apo, it means derived from, coming from, resulting from, caused by. This most assuredly means we are talking about man as the source of woman. If the word "over" had been used rather than "of", then there could be a possibility that it could mean dominion, because over means above in position or superior. Please remember this is a word we saw before. It is the same word that described how Jesus, the human, was derived from, or was caused to come into being, by God the Father.

Verse 24: Therefore-----(Because Christians are filled with the Spirit) they will be subject to Christ. Therefore (because the husband and the wife are filled with the Spirit) **the wife will be subject to her husband in every high, exalted, lifted up, Spirit filled, thing of God he shares with her.** (We willingly submit to Christ in the

Spirit, and wives are to willingly submit to the spiritual things in the husband in the same way that they would submit to the spiritual things of Christ, because her husband is representing Christ to her as he walks in the Spirit.)

Verse 25: Husbands (who are filled with the Spirit) love your wives (who are filled with the Spirit) just like Christ loved the Church and died for her.

Verse 26: He died for her so that He might sanctify, or set her apart, so that He could cleanse her with the washing of water by the Word.

Verse 27: So that He can present it to Himself as a glorious Church without spot or wrinkle or blemish, or any such thing, that she might be holy.

Verse 28: In this same way men should love their wives. (They love their wives by being so filled with the Spirit that they are able to wash her and cleanse her with the Word. The high spiritual things that he has learned and practiced will be the things that he washes her with. They will make her glorious, without spot or wrinkle or blemish or any such thing. They will make her holy. He can present his spiritual work in her to the Lord.) He who loves his wife in this way, loves himself. (It is a Spirit filled love and has to do with spiritual obedience that is far above and beyond any mere act of obedience to the lower flesh nature. Controlling her in the fleshly way that has been taught does not produce a spirit filled wife who is without spot, wrinkle, or any such thing. Controlling in the flesh has nothing whatsoever to do with washing her with the water of the Word. Controlling her in the flesh does not produce holiness in her.)

Verse 29: No man hates his own flesh, (the wife is flesh of his flesh and bone of his bone. The man needs to have the same spiritual awareness of her value that Adam had for Eve before the fall because she came out of his body.). When he cherishes and nourishes his wife in spiritual things, He is nourishing and cherishing himself. Just as Christ is preparing the church to be presented to Himself, because He loves the church as He loves himself, so the man should be preparing his wife in the same way, which is in the Spirit.

Verse 30: The man must do this in the Spirit and through the Spirit because we are all flesh of Christ's flesh, and bone of His bone, both the Spirit filled man and the Spirit filled woman are part of His body.

Verse 31: For this reason the two have become one. In the flesh and in the Spirit.

Verse 32: The great mystery of two nations becoming one united body in Christ is the same mystery that makes a man and a woman one. Both, nations and couples, need to understand the implications of what Christ has done to form this one body. They need to appropriate it and make it alive in their unions. It is accomplished in the Spirit and through the power of the Spirit. It is a high spiritual thing, far above the flesh nature. This kind of high spiritual union demonstrates the high spiritual power of God, through Christ, to all principalities and powers in high places, both in heaven and on earth.

Verse 33: They are both filled with the Holy Spirit and that is why the man can, and should, love his wife in the Spirit. That is why the woman can, and should, revere her husband in the Spirit. That is why Christians are admonished not to be unequally yoked to an unbeliever. An unbeliever cannot be filled with the Spirit and they cannot accomplish the oneness of spirit that brings about the Spirit kind of love and obedience.

In the order of creation, Adam was made the "head", because he was the source or origin of Eve, just as Christ is the head of the church, and God is head of Christ. But, no one seems to consider that this spiritual headship was given

to Adam, by God, **BEFORE** the fall. **The "headship"
of man was not a result of the fall.** In the
beginning Adam was given the command from God not
to eat of the tree. As "head", he told Eve. This
was a high spiritual thing from God that he was
passing on to her. Eve needed to be obedient to
this spiritual thing he had told her. But Eve
was beguiled and deceived and disobeyed. Adam told
her the word, but he did not wash her and cleanse
her with it, because he did not protect her from
the spiritual power of Satan. He did not confirm
the word to her with action by intervening. He
allowed her to be spotted and wrinkled and blemished
by a high, spiritual, evil "thing", Satan. He
failed in acting out the headship responsibilities
God had given him. Now through Christ, "Adam" has
a chance to redeem himself. He is given the
directive to wash his wife with these high spiritual
things of God. Except that now he has the Holy
Spirit's indwelling power to help him live up
to that spiritual responsibility. As he demonstrates
how the Living Water has impacted him, and has
cleansed him, he can wash his wife with the cleansing Word, and it will be meaningful to her. It
will persuade her to follow him in spiritual things.

Lest men come under a burden of condemnation
here, let me explain something. "Washing her with
the Word" does not necessarily mean that a man
must routinely read 2 chapters and a Psalm a day
to her. He washes her with the Word by living
out the principles of the Word before her as a
living example. Washing by the Word is not to
become a burdensome chore that sends him on a guilt
trip if he does not read so much a day. Just
sharing a thought from the Word, or a verse or
even a part of a verse, or singing or humming
a hymn etc. expresses that the desire of his heart
is to share God with her. I feel "washed" when
my husband does these things. I especially feel
"washed" when he hugs me and prays out loud for

me. It is a most beautiful experience. There is a cleansing. The minor irritations that I might be feeling towards him vanish. Washing her with the word is just a part of his living witness to her, it is not a loathsome burden.

People, the submission that Paul is trying to get across to us is far above anything that we have ever heard from theologians who always bring this spiritual truth down to the level of a worldly, carnal, male supremacy issue. When this truth is removed from the carnal worldly realms, and is practiced in the spiritual realms, we will see an unprecedented healing in marriages. Marriage will again be what God intended for Adam and Eve. Couples will be joined together by God, in a spiritual "weld" that flesh cannot break apart.

I can hear the wheels turning in many people's minds as they think on these things. Some will say the meaning of "things" goes right along with the theology of the centuries, which means that the man has been given the place of high priest in his home. God said so in Gen. 3:16. He is supposed to be lifted up and elevated to a place where he is revered as the ruler of the family. But then we would have to make some excuse for I Peter 2:9 that says **every** believer in Christ is now a chosen generation, a royal **priesthood,** a holy nation. Women are chosen, they are royal priests and a holy nation. If God ever really established a patriarchal priesthood of the family, it was done away with when the Law was given and God set up the the priesthood of Aaron and Levi, etc. That priesthood ended when Christ rent the veil. The priest's job was to say prayers and make sacrifices for the people's sin. When Christ rent the veil, every one who believes in Him has access to God through Him. Every believer makes their own sacrifices, which are their own bodies as a living sacrifice. The fruit of their lips is a sacrifice of praise. Monetary giving is a

sacrifice. Doing good work or service is a sacrifice. And there is a sacrifice of prayer. This
is for every believer, not just men as head of
the household. Therefore, the man cannot be lifted
up as priest anymore. Christ did away with that.

There are 11 places in the Bible where this
translation of "thing" is used. In II Cor. 10:5
it is referring to high spiritual things or beings,
but they are evil and they exalt themselves above
the knowledge of God. They form evil spiritual
strongholds in men's minds to keep God and His
Truth from being known and exalted in them. In
II Cor. 11:15, this is another evil being or thing,
a messenger of Satan that was sent by God to buffet
Paul. Gal.5:6 says that circumcision or uncircum-
cision means nothing in the high exalted spiritual
things of God. Jesus, lifted up and exalted, does
away with that sign of the chosen race. There is
no sign of the chosen race anymore except Christ
crucified and resurrected. Gal. 6:15 says the
same thing. Eph.5:27 was quoted several times
earlier because the word "thing" is in that verse.
It also refers to evil, high spiritual things that
cause spot and blemish and wrinkle in the believer.
Phil.1:6 says be confident of this very thing,
meaning a very high spiritual truth, that He who
began a good work in you will finish it. The
other four times, the word "thing" is related to
spiritual good works and spiritual well doing which
a Christian operating in the Spirit does.

If one wants to say that the husband is the
high, exalted, head of his home and that is what
"submit in EVERYTHING" means, then the man **is**
being put in the place of God. To lift him up
like that is idol worship. Then it does have the
stamp of evil on it. It is a high, lifted up,
exalted place, but it is an evil place and not
of God. The way submission is taught today, imposes
a control over a wife that brings some high, lifted
up, spiritual thing on her that gives her spots

and wrinkles and blemishes. They are evil. Rather than washing her with the water of the Word, this washes her with the stain of idolatry.

Some may say in the list of definitions, there are words like, "barrier" "instead of", "over", etc. To use these definitions, it would be placing the man over her, instead of, or in the place of God. Can anyone really think that is what it means? Since God Himself said He was a jealous God and there should be no other god's before Him and this was His greatest commandment, would God later say, "but I put the husband in My place over the woman"? Would He say "wife, lift up and exalt your husband in my stead"? Or would He say "woman, I have placed your husband over you as a barrier between you and me. I will work on your behalf only through your husband, who will stand between you and me"? How absurd!!

If one wanted to say that the husband has been placed over the woman as a barrier, that cannot be, because there are no barriers between any believer and God or Christ. However, the man could be a barrier between her and evil IF he was washing himself and her with the water of the Word. IF he was living the Spirit filled life before her. IF he was teaching her how to use her armor of God against Satan and his messengers and his wiles. IF he himself was waging a war against Satan, on her behalf, with weapons that are not carnal. In that case, he would be doing what Adam failed to do. He would be providing a protective barrier for her. But he can never be a barrier between her and God.

The misinterpretation of Gen.3:16, of the Old Testament, "your desire will be for your husband, and he will rule over you", is coupled with the misinterpretation of the New Testament in Eph. 5:24 "submit to your husband in everything". Satan has used that to dupe and deceive God's people into practicing idolatry. This deception has caused

men far more harm then they could ever imagine.
While they may enjoy the carnal pleasure of being
the "boss" and having their ego pumped up because
they have so much control over someone, they need
to remember that there is pleasure in sin only
for a season. Sin's pleasure will one day extract
it's price. Breaking down this deception and
exposing it to the light of what "everything" really
means, is for man's benefit as much as it is for
woman's benefit. Both need to be set free from
Satan's well hidden trap.

This is the truth and the light of what it
means to "submit to your husband in every 'THING'".
It has **absolutely nothing** to do with who makes
the final decisions in the marriage concerning
worldly things. Or how the wife is to submit to
every worldly thing he commands her to obey. It
has everything to do with the submission of the
woman to the high, exalted, spiritual, things of
God in her husband. Let the darkness be exposed.
Let it be light to you. Let this truth set you
free and illumine your marriage with the glory
of God. Let the heavy burden of headship be rolled
off of men and let the bondage of submission be
broken off of women. Renounce the darkness and
walk in the glorious light. Then your marriage
will reflect the glory of God, rather than the
spirit of the world. It will be the high spiritual
union that God gave to Adam and Eve. It will
be a powerful weapon against Satan, as others DO
see the everlasting covenant of God, through Christ,
manifesting itself through that kind of marriage.
The marriage with the Lamb is a spiritual marriage.
That is the picture we need to paint for others
in our earthly marriages. We need to take our
eyes off the world view of marriage and focus them
on the eternal view of marriage. Walk as wise
men, not as fools. May God grant that men would
become convicted and be willing to lay down these
false concepts that allows them to be idols to

their wives. Please, Lord, let repentance come to men and women.

## CHAPTER SEVENTEEN
## PARTIALITY AND THE UNITY OF FAITH

Malachi 2 has already been referred to several times in this book. But we need to go into greater detail on this important passage. It is extremely relevant for us today for it shows how perverted submission affects women and the church as a whole.

For the most part, the following is my paraphrase and commentary. I invite you to follow along in your Bible as an accuracy check.

Malachi 2:2 God speaks to the priests who have turned away from Him and He says He would curse their blessings and had already cursed them. The word for blessing here means their benediction or the divine blessings from God on their lives, and their prosperity. But this word comes from another primary word that means adoration and worship of God. So it has a twofold meaning. 1) God had removed His benevolent and bountiful blessings from their lives in every way. 2) He refused, and even cursed their worship of Him. Their worship was no longer acceptable to Him. The word curse here means that He called down a bitter evil against them. He judged them as people to be loathed, detested and abhorred. They were an abomination to Him. Yet these were the men He himself had set apart, anointed, and appointed to be His priests, His ministers. We see that He did not rescind His calling on them, but even while they were in the position of priests, He called down evil on them, He removed His blessing from them, He refused and cursed their worship of Him. Do you think He blessed and received worship from the people who followed in the corrupt ways of the priests?

Malachi 2:5-6 God says He made a covenant with Levi to give him life and peace because of how Levi feared or revered and worshipped God. He said the law of truth was in Levi's mouth and iniquity was not found in his lips. It is important

391

to see that iniquity was not found in his lips and the law of truth was in his mouth. The fear of God resulted in something he would speak in truth. He walked with God in peace and in straightness, in righteousness, and justice. He was a just man. He used those qualities in himself, along with his knowledge of the truth that he spoke, to turn many from sin.

Malachi 2:7-8, God says the priests had not received that knowledge from Levi's lips or the law from his mouth. He spoke it, but they did not receive or accept it. They did not teach or practice it. The priest's had turned from God's ways of righteousness and justice and had caused the people to stumble, or to sin, because of their own corrupt way of interpreting and teaching the Law. They had corrupted the covenant God had made with Levi.

Many preachers of today have caused people to stumble too, because they have followed the Jewish traditions and other historical traditions rather than God's Word. These men, too, have been called by God and have been entrusted with knowledge and truth, but they have corrupted it. Because of that, they have perverted the new covenant of grace through Christ Jesus and the freedom for ALL believers from the law. Men are deceived and caught in the trap of male superiority and dominance and women are the victims of the trap. Some women use it as an excuse to shift responsibility for their own spiritual growth and works to their husbands. So both stumble. The New Covenant in Christ has been corrupted, just as the covenant with Levi had been corrupted.

Malachi 2:9, God said the priests were more contemptible then all the other people because they had been entrusted with His Word and His ways but they had not kept them. Their main offense was that they were **partial in the law.** The leaders, who had more knowledge of God, were more contemptible in His sight because of that fact.

In the list of many applications the word partial can have, the following seem to best fit what God wants to convey here. The meanings are, exalt self, lift self up, lofty. He is saying the priests have set themselves above the people. They had exalted themselves because of who they were and the positions they held. As we will see later, their teachings exalted men above women also. Today, men, as "head", have also lifted themselves up and exalted themselves above women because of the position they hold in the family. Pastors have done the same thing because of the position they hold in the Church.

Here we will take a little detour to see what the New Testament has to say about this same matter of partiality.

In James 2:4 we have the same word, "partial", but here it means to separate thoroughly, to withdraw from, by implication, to oppose, and figuratively, to discriminate. In James 2:1, James says that in the Lord Jesus Christ, the Lord of Glory, there is no respect for persons. Which means the Lord himself shows no favoritism nor makes earthly distinctions for any one. Position, calling, giftedness, gender, race etc. mean nothing to Him. In 2:4 he says if the brethren show favoritism and are partial in themselves, they are judges with evil thoughts and in verse 9, if they do this they are committing sin. Verse 8 says that the royal law of Christ is to love your neighbor as yourself.

This passage refers to a specific form of partiality, because it speaks of discrimination between the poor and rich. The rich are treated with deference, the poor are despised.

The principle is much broader than that. Partiality in any form, whether it's shown on the basis of gender, race, position in the church, economic status. etc. is not of God or of Christ

in either law or grace. Verse 7 says that practicing
partiality is blaspheming the Name of Christ, by
which we are called. The practice of partiality
on any basis, seems to be a far more serious sin
than most people think. This is actually saying
that to be partial is to revile Christ's name.

What we have just learned in James is
consistent with what God said in Malachi 2:10
about being partial. It is also consistent with
what I wrote in Chapter 6 about how the veil of
Christ, that covers the woman, was being blasphemed
because of the partiality shown toward men, both
in the home and in the Church. The man of the
house is held in much higher esteem than the woman
is. Men in ministry are treated with deference.
Women in ministry, for the most part, are not
accepted, therefore, they are despised.

Malachi 2:10 says we are all one in the Father
who created all of us. Partiality is treachery
against the brothers. It profanes the covenant
of the Father. In the age of the Church, this
partiality is against the whole body of Christ.
It does not just wound women, it wounds the whole
church. It has a malignant affect on all.

Old Testament partiality profaned the old
covenant between God and Israel. New Testament,
partiality profanes the new Covenant with Christ,
which provides grace and freedom for all believers.
That grace and freedom includes the freedom from
partiality of gender discrimination. The word
"profane" means to wound, to dissolve, to break
one's word, to defile, to pollute, to prostitute,
to stain. It's a strong word.

In verse 11, it says that partiality profanes
the very holiness of God!! To practice partiality
on any basis is to dissolve and break His word,
that is, to make it meaningless and powerless.
It defiles, pollutes, and stains His holiness.
What a serious offense this is against God! It
is an insult to God because it prostitutes His

Holy nature. Partiality dilutes, dissolves, and neutralizes Christ's sacrifice until it is meaningless. It defiles, pollutes and stains the covenant He paid for with His blood. What an insult partiality is to Jesus Christ!!

Malachi 2:10 spoke of the treachery against the brethren. But in Malachi 2:11-17 God is dealing specifically with the treachery of the man against his wife. God says He will not accept the offerings from men who profane His holiness by dealing treacherously with their wives. God has witnessed the covenant between the man and his wife. The word "treacherously" means to be deceitful, to be unfaithful, to treat her offensively, to transgress, and to depart. The word has a much broader meaning than just "divorce".

God says in verse 15, that He has made them one, but He has kept the residue of their individual spirits for himself. He made them one so that the offspring would be sanctified and holy and not illegitimate children. But their spirits are His. Therefore, the man needs to be very careful about what he does against this woman whose spirit still belongs to God. He needs to recognize that even though they are one, he does not "own" her spirit. It does not belong to him.

Verse 16 says that God hates divorce, AND He hates it when a man covers his violence with his garment. There are several words we need to understand here. The word "cover" means to cover with clothing in order to hide, to keep secret or to conceal the violence. It's like putting on a garment of respectability in front of other people in order to cover up the violence done in secret. The word "violence" means wrong. It implies cruelty, damage, false, unjust, oppressive, unrighteous, violent dealing against. It comes from a root word that means to be violent, to maltreat, to violate, to make bare, to take away violently, and to imagine wrongfully. The word "garment"

395

means clothing, something to wrap around a person. But there is also a curious euphemism that is associated with this particular word in Malachi. It is "wife". A euphemism means to use a good or favorable word for an evil or unfavorable one. It substitutes a word that is less expressive, but is not as distasteful as another. In this particular case, it sounds less offensive to say a man covers his violence with his garment then it does to say a man covers his wife with violence. One means the man is wrapping up his violence in his cloak so that it is hidden. The other says he is covering up, or wrapping up, his wife with violence!!

This one passage tells us very clearly that God hates any kind of abuse that a man will perpetrate on His wife. This does not mean just physical abuse, like beating. It also means emotional abuse and cruelty. It means treatment that is unjust, unfair and unrighteous. It means oppressive behavior that stifles her spirit and her personality. Many of these kinds of things happen in a Christian marriage, because of the false teachings that man is the head and the woman is subject to him in every thing, even if it's cruel and oppressive. Some have gone so far in this teaching that they will actually say if the abusive husband kills her, while she is being obedient to submit in everything, then she will die for the glory of God! In this book we have already seen some of the sick, distorted reasoning and teaching on the subject of headship and submission. Husbands who use headship as a license for that kind of behavior, and teachers who teach this kind of distortion of Scripture, will be held accountable by God for it because this is partiality of the worst kind. Such teaching is completely opposite of the admonition for men to love their wives as Christ loved the church and gave Himself for her.

# PARTIALITY AND THE UNITY OF FAITH

Much of what is happening to women through the false teaching on submission, both in marriages and in the church, is partiality, and God says He hates it. He cannot bless a man who deals with his wife that way. He cannot bless a church who holds it's women in oppressive bondage either. This is a major reason why many Christian marriages are falling apart and why many churches are power-less and irrelevant.

Malachi 2:17 says that all of this has wearied God. He is tired of all the words of His people, who speak that the woman is of equal value and worth, but then, by their actions, flaunt their partiality. The partiality is blatant when Bible teachers and preachers say a woman must endure all kinds of abuse because she is to be subject to her husband in every thing. God says this is an evil in His sight, but it is called "good", biblically sound teaching by man. He does not delight in this kind of teaching or this kind of abuse, just because man calls it "good". The partiality that is shown when a man is given this kind of power over his wife is evil in His sight. God says there is no justice in it. It defiles His holy justice. It defiles His name. It profanes His holiness. It profanes and blasphemes Christ and his shed blood that removed the differences of Jew and Gentile, male and female, bondslave and freeman. He made them one in Him because of that shed blood.

Malachi 3 speaks about the Lord Jesus coming like a refining fire, a fuller's soap, a refiner and purifier of silver, to purge His people like gold and silver so that they can offer themselves to the Lord in righteousness. He will come in judgment of those who oppress other people by their partiality, because that partiality shows they do not fear God. That partiality includes the oppressive domination of husbands over their wives. It includes the way women have been excluded from ministry in the church.

The verses in Malachi speak of Levi and then the priests who followed him. In the New Testament, there is Christ and then the men who fill the offices of apostle, prophet, pastor, teacher and evangelist. The priests spoke things that were corrupt because of the partiality it promoted. They were holding up themselves and some elite group of people, especially men, as special people. They were condemned by God for it. He withheld His blessings from them and refused their worship. Under Christ, those who are in Him, are all priests. They are ALL royal heirs. There are no special people who God holds in higher regard then others. Many people in the office of pastor follow the example of the priests. They also speak corrupt things that promote partiality.

The New Testament sequel to Malachi is I Tim. 5:17-21. It says the elders who rule well, especially those who labor in word and doctrine are worthy of double honor. Notice several things here. The word "rule" means to preside, or to stand before. It does not mean "lord over", "govern", "be boss". "Word" means to say or to speak, as a speaker. "Doctrine" is instruction, teaching. "Well" means with honesty. Elder means older, senior, and presbyter. It is sometimes interchangeable with pastor/minister. "Honor" does NOT mean higher esteem then someone else because of what God has called and gifted them to do. It means money, pay, or monetary reward. So, this is a person who presides over a meeting, speaking and teaching the truth in honesty, one who is worthy of being paid for his labor. It does not mean one who is to "lord" it over anyone.

No one should bring an accusation against this kind of person, **unless** there are two or three witnesses to substantiate the accusation.

If they **are** guilty of sin, then even as an elder, they should be exposed and rebuked openly, so that others will learn  to fear God.

Verse 21 says: "I charge you before God, and the Lord Jesus Christ, and the elect angels, that you observe these things without preferring one before another, doing nothing by partiality."

What this is teaching is that just as the priests were not above anyone else, nor were they exempted from censure because of their position, neither is the person filling a ministry office above anyone else, and neither are they to be exempt from censure. The hierarchy that exists in churches today where a pastor and his board are set above any other Christian, and where he feels he is immune from censure, or even questioning, because he is the pastor, is partiality. God hates it. It profanes Him and Christ. In this passage we see that partiality even offends the elect angels!!

In view of all of this, can we justify the partiality that exists in today's church concerning women?  The teachings of today are based on old Jewish and historic traditions that prefer and exalt men over women, both in the home and in the place of leadership in the church. Again, I say, the mouths of men speak that women are of equal value and worth, but their actions speak louder than their words. Their actions prove over and over again that men are preferred far above women. Their mouths are corrupt and they speak perverse things. It's a corruption, an evil, that men call good. God hates it.

I'll ask another question. In view of all this, can the hierarchy that is practiced in local churches and in denominations be justified?

Keeping all of this in mind, let's look at something in Galatians 3:26-29. It says we are all children of God because of our faith in Christ Jesus. We have all put on Christ. There is neither Jew nor Greek, neither bond or free, neither male nor female; for we are all one in Christ Jesus. Because we are all Christ's, we are Abraham's seed and heirs according to the promise. Chapter 4:1-7 says the heir, when he was a child had the same standing, or position, as a servant, even though he was the heir. He needed to be under tutors and governors until the appointed time of the father. Before Christ, we were immature children, we were in bondage to the elements of the world, that is, we were under the world system. But once Christ came, we were redeemed from that bondage. We became adopted sons of the Father so we no longer had the standing of a slave, but the position of a son, an heir of God through Christ. The world system was no longer our governor, meaning the "lord" and "slave" relationships ended. There was no longer a "lord" who was the boss, who could command that his slave obey him. The "lordship" of husband over the wife of the Old Testament also ended with Christ. That is a system of the world that does not exist any longer in a Christian marriage. It is only the world system that demands there be a "boss" in a relationship. As far as I know, there is no Scripture that countermands Christ's command that it would not be so in His Church.

Twenty years ago, I memorized Gal. 2:20. "I am crucified with Christ: nevertheless I live; yet not I, but Christ who lives in me; and the life I now live in the flesh I live by the faith of the Son of God, who loved me and gave himself for me." But on Easter Sunday, 1995 the truth of that verse penetrated my soul. I saw it in context of how there are no more distinctions for those who are in Christ Jesus. This is how it translated itself to me. I have been crucified with Christ. It is no longer I who live, but Christ Jesus who lives in me. Therefore, I am not a Jew, I am not a Gentile, I am not black, I am not white, I am not male, I am not female, I am not a pastor, I am not a layman, I am not a Pentecostal, I am not a Baptist, I am not "me". The distinctions

of white, Pentecostal, female live no more. Though
I still live in the flesh, I am only Christ, who
lives in me. You are none of those things either.
You are only Christ who lives in you. The great
equalizer is Christ Jesus. He levels every distinction to nothingness so there is no partiality.
No one can claim any special place or privilege
for who they are, what they do, or what race or
gender they are. His purpose for this is Eph.
4:13 "Till we all come into the unity of the faith,
and of the knowledge of the Son of God, unto a
perfect man, unto the measure of the stature of
the fullness of Christ." Verses 14-16 says we
are no more like children who are led astray with
every wind of doctrine, taught by men who deceive
with cunning craftiness. But we will all speak
the truth in love, so that we can all grow up into
our head, Christ Jesus. We are all joined together
as a tight unit, each one supplying whatever it
is that God gave us to do. So that we edify the
whole body with love. That is why God is not
a respecter of persons and neither can we be.
No one can be better than anyone else. **There can
be no unity of faith as long as men do not grasp
the truth of Gal. 2:20. There is no unity of
faith as long as men hold to the fact of the flesh
that says there is Jew and Gentile, male and female,
black and white, pastor and laymen, and so on.
As long as they do not understand the spiritual
truth that everyone is nothing but Christ living
in them, they cannot come to a oneness or a unity
of faith. There are too many man made and man
honored distinctions amongst God's people for there
to be any kind of unity of faith.** The unity of
faith is when we all come to see we are all one
in Christ, regardless of whether we have white
or black skin or female or male bodies.

As long as man persists with the concept of
distinctions between male and female, color or
race, rich and poor, the elite "in" groups or

cliques in a church, the separateness of the clergy from the laity, and the separated denominations, there can be no unity of faith. That is what Paul was saying in I Corinthians 1:10-17. He was not saying everybody had to think and speak alike, as though they were a bunch of robots. He was saying, concerning the body of Christ, there are no distinctions. All are one. If we are not all one, then Christ dying on the cross was not effective, it means nothing. The wall of hostility was never broken down between Jew and Gentile or male and female.

All of I Corinthians 12 is a strong appeal to believers to recognize the equal status of all believers, and to understand how important each person is. No one is more important than another. Verse 25 says that there should be no "schism" in the body. That means there should be no division, no gap, because of more or less honor given to more or less noble parts. God has put each part in the place that He wants it, and has given honor to all.

Females and males exist in different bodies in the flesh, have different temperaments, and have different roles in the natural physical functions. But in the spirit there are no such distinctions. Man does not separate the physical differences from the spiritual differences, thus confusion and partiality reigns. The body of Christ is in the spirit. There is no difference between male and female there. There is no difference in function, such as a female role and a male role, because God has chosen which part of His body will have what function and He makes no distinctions between male and female or any of the rest of the distinctions man makes. God is no discerner of persons when it comes to giving out His gifts. He gives them to whoever He wants to have them. The Bible says He gives them as He wills. And He gives them in the amount He wills. The Bible has no verses that say, "These are gifts to be given to males only and these are gifts to be given to women only." In the several lists of gifts in Scripture, there is not one word to indicate that God had any intentions of segregating them into male and female gifts. Who is man, then, to be a discerner of persons and a discerner of who has what gifts and of how and where they should be administered in the body!!??? The childishness of the Corinthians exists now, even stronger than it did then. Partiality amongst the brethren is a major ingredient of the apostasy of the last days. How would Paul admonish the church of today? What is God saying to the church of today.!?

I believe the partiality that He hated, and rebuked the priests for in Malachi's day, is the same partiality that He hates and is rebuking the leadership of the Church today for. I believe the spots and wrinkles and such things must be recognized and repented of, so that God can pour out His Spirit on all mankind, but especially on the Church. Revival cannot happen until the spots and wrinkles and blemishes are washed clean with repentance.

Through the teachings of Promise Keepers and others, the race barriers are beginning to crumble. Caucasians are repenting and asking forgiveness from African and Native Americans. They are beginning to understand the hurt that has been inflicted on humans and the damage that has been done to the church through racial discrimination.

When will people begin to understand that the prejudice and discrimination against women is of an even greater magnitude than those others all put together? When will men of all races begin to repent of that? That wall of hostility, that particular gender partiality, that God said He hated in Malachi, when will that come tumbling down so there will be unity in the body of Christ on all fronts? I see small cracks in the wall,

403

but it will be the last one to come down. Until then, there cannot be a complete unity of faith.

The feminist movement has been blamed for a confusion that has arisen in what men perceive as their role in life. It is said that the rise in male abuse of women and the rise in homosexuality is caused by this confusion that men feel. Could I be so bold as to suggest that maybe God is behind this? Is He using this to shake up, uproot and tear down traditional male dominant roles. Is it bringing men to a point where they will begin to question and examine those traditional roles and finally discover the impartiality of God? Could God be using this to bring about the unity of faith in genders?

I pray, oh God, that your Holy Spirit would accompany this book and use it as a mighty tool to smash that monstrous wall. May people everywhere be struck with an overwhelming mourning and repentance, so you can cleanse the Bride and make her ready for the coming of the Bridegroom!

# CHAPTER EIGHTEEN
## WHAT ABOUT THE GIRLS?

Many times I have been asked, "What about the girls? How did all of this affect them?" I feel it is appropriate for the readers to have the answer to that question also. I asked all four of them if they would like to contribute something in their own words.

### LORI

The first response came from the youngest daughter, Lori. She accepted Christ when she was quite young. She is currently a missionary in a very difficult foreign country, which cannot be named. She is married and has two sons.

Just to give a little insight into her background, she was the only baby who was not a planned pregnancy. Her father was very upset when I became pregnant. He was angry about it for three or four months. During that time, I would speak to that baby in the womb, telling it I loved it and I wanted it, even if daddy was upset. After he got over his anger, he wanted, and looked forward to having, this baby as much as he did the others. From the time she was born, she was afraid of men. When she was old enough to notice someone enter a room, she would scream if it was a man. Sometimes, if he had been away on a trip and she hadn't seen him for a while, she would scream when her father came into the room. She was a mama's girl. I do not have any specific, vivid memories of her being abused by her father as a child, other than the strict harshness and anger that was always present. The following is her letter.

"I guess, upon thinking about it, my thoughts of Dad and the affects the years have had on me I really think that the situation didn't affect me as much as Lynn, Mary and Renee. I was such a 'mama's girl'. That was either because of Dad, or that was my natural constitution. I've never put a lot of pondering into my growing up years.

I really don't remember a lot. I have a few happy memories. The only 'sad' ones are when you were going somewhere and I had to stay home, I was very sad, which is a normal childhood emotion. Being the 'baby' of the family also was a shelter in itself. I do remember having to do a good job of cleaning the lodge. I'm glad for that because it helped --helps me now in my own housekeeping.

As far as how this affected my relationships now, I really don't know. If there would have been any bad things, the memory has **graciously**, by the Lord, been taken away. Occasionally something will pop up, like Dad being a strict disciplinarian. For example, I've now learned, with two boys of our own, that training and disciplining children is to be done by love through the rod of correction, not through frustration or anger with a belt. When I write that, I don't mean it sarcastically or saying it from a bad experience, but rather from learning this through my own experiences in child training 2 children.

I've always felt extremely secure with you. You bore whatever burdens and sorrows in your own life. I remember you always loving and caring for me with joy and happiness. I do remember when we were in Cambridge and we (you and I) were riding our bikes. You began to cry, weep for sorrow of heart. You began to speak some, but really no details, other than it was about Dad. I remember being somewhat confused because I'd not known anything was wrong between you and Dad. So, in reality I believe through your total dependency upon God to get you through, HE only let me see your love for God, and your love and joy in caring for me.

Now, only because I've been told some of the bitter details, and have seen only a very little of what all this has done to Lynn, and Dad's 'giving up the fight' concerning his sin of the flesh, it just kind of puts a numbness in my emotions for what I'd known as my Dad. I'll speak with him on the telephone--but mostly as I would an acquaintance, not as one would talk to their Dad. I do love him--because he is in the position of my earthly Dad. Being separated in distance also, for the present, sets me apart somewhat. Perhaps that's a blessing from the Lord." That was all she wrote.

From my own perspectives about Lori, I had just become a Christian about the time she was born. She was the one who was rocked and had hymns sung to her most. Renee was only 17 months older than Lori and she benefited from that too. Both of them had the benefit of a Christian mother earlier in their lives than the other two did. She was already gone from home, except for a few months, when the worst battles with my ex-husband were going on.

The most painful experience I suffered with Lori and her Dad came when she was around nineteen. She had just returned from a year at Bible School. I took her to Minneapolis for a week of nursing assistants training. It was during that week I contacted the pastor who had conducted the deliverance seminar about my ex-husband's problems. What he told me made me understand how demonized my husband was. After she completed her training, her Dad took her to the Twin Cities to find a job. She found one in a nursing home. Then she needed a place to live. As he was driving around in the area, he happened to see a man outside working in his yard. He stopped and talked to the man, and found out he was a policeman. The man said he had a son who had a spare room to rent in a house he was remodeling. So without seeing the house, or the son and without knowing anything about him, arrangements were made for Lori to rent this room. The son had another male friend living with him. The house was supposed to be finished by the time she was to move in. So he packed up her things and had a parishioner with a truck,

407

take her stuff to this house. I could not believe he thought it was all right for her to live in a house alone with two men. When we got there, the house was in shambles, a total mess. It would be months before it was livable. Then we discovered that the owner and his live-in friend were homosexuals. But my husband started unloading Lori's things and he was going to leave her there in that situation. My stomach was sick. I couldn't believe he intended to leave her there in such a godless situation. She kept assuring her father, "it's okay Dad, if you want me to stay I will." But you could see by the look on her face she was feeling abandoned and scared, but if it would please Dad, it didn't matter what she felt. I said "If you leave her here, you will leave me too. I will not allow this to happen. What is wrong with you that you would leave your own daughter in a horrible situation like this?" He was absolutely furious with me. I was so ashamed for all this to be happening in front of the parishioner who had brought her stuff. The most embarrassing thing was that he could see that his pastor's morals were such that he was willing to leave his young daughter in such an ungodly atmosphere. What I truly believe, he was under a demonic influence that was not letting him think straight. We finally went to a nearby church of our denomination and spoke to someone there who had told me about a room that was for rent with four other girls. We took her to that place, unloaded her stuff, and left her there. No one was home. It was a strange city to her, a strange house, with people she had never met. She was a very naive girl. We did not help her to get settled or anything. We got in the car, and left her, standing in the street with tears in her eyes, waving good-bye to us. That day and that scene are forever burned into my memory. I was helpless to do anything about it except what I had already done. It appears the memory is far more painful for me than it was for her. She would do anything to please her father.

Lori had a couple of relationships with men before she got married. They were very dominant men. Her husband is extremely dominant, more than her father was. She acquiesces to his every wish. She is a sweet, beautiful young lady. Through her sweet spirit, many young women have come to know the Lord. But she is convinced they are on the mission field **only** because her husband has a ministry. She's been taught that men alone have ministries. A woman's only place is to play a supporting role for their husbands. Her name is not even mentioned on missionary news letters from them.

## RENEE

Renee is next to the youngest. She was our last planned baby. Her father said since this was going to be the last one, he wanted it to have a French name, whether it was a boy or a girl. He was very proud of his French nationality. The fact that Renee was definitely planned is important.

As a child, Renee had a flair for drama and fantasy. She could make people laugh. As a young adult, she wrote and directed the most outstanding church Christmas program I have ever seen. It started with the Christmas birth of Christ story, but went on to the crucifixion of Christ, with a real person acting as Christ on the cross. Then in complete darkness, the tape by Don Francisco "He's Alive" played. At the crescendo of the tape, the spotlight lit up the empty cross. She said without the crucifixion and resurrection, the birth would mean nothing. The Christmas story is only complete with the resurrection. It was magnificent. She has great talent.

She came to know the Lord when she was ten.

When I asked Renee if she would like to write her thoughts for the book, she was willing to do that. But as time went on, she found she couldn't do it. She has given me permission to write in some things she has shared with me verbally and some things I remember.

The first really bad thing I remember was one day when we owned a resort. We had a mini-store for the guests. Renee's father caught her taking a candy bar from the store shelf. The punishment for that was far greater than the offense deserved. She was a small girl in size, about 12 years old. There was a landing going into the house by the store. He caught her there, threw her down on the landing and proceeded to pound her with his fists. When I saw what he was doing, I stopped him, but it was too late. She was not hurt badly, but she told me years later she had dissociated. She imagined herself down in the basement, standing under the place where she was laying, looking up and and wondering what it would look like if her bones came poking through the floor. She was being hit hard enough she felt that could happen.

She remembers often as a young teen, she wanted to kill herself because life was so confusing and hurtful.

She felt she was never good enough for her father. No matter what she did or how hard she tried, she could never please him. She felt worthless. She wanted to run away and be a prostitute. She thought that would be an honest thing for her to do, because she felt a prostitute was the dregs of the earth, and that was what she felt she was. The dregs of the earth.

During her high school years, she was active in the church. She would help the youth leader with activities for the youth etc. But her father, who was pastoring the church at the time, would yell at her about everything. Even when she had nothing to do with something, he would yell at her that everything that went wrong was her fault. His behavior towards her was so bad and so obvious

an elder, who was also a good friend, confronted
him about it one day. He said what my husband
was doing to her was very wrong and it was
especially wrong for a pastor to behave that way.
This man knew Renee very well and he knew she
did not deserve any of this treatment. It was
totally unwarranted. She was a wonderful girl.

After she graduated from high school, she went
to Bible school for a year. At Christmas time
she came home on vacation. She did not even have
her suitcases in the house yet when her father
back-handed her across the face for some very
trivial matter. She had just turned nineteen.

After her year at Bible School, she stayed
at home for a couple of years. This was the
beginning of the 8 years of battle for my husband's
freedom. She suffered through those first years.
These are some of her memories of that time. There
was violence in the home. She said she never knew
when she went off to work if I would be there when
she got back. She thought I might be dead. Or
that we might both be dead. One from murder and
one from suicide. She was there the day my husband
came home from the geneticist office. She heard
his lies then. She too, felt sorry for him and
believed him.

She did come home one day and I wasn't there.
I had packed a few things and left. I went to
my sister's house. He made her promise she would
not let me back in the house or give me anything
from the house if I should happen to ask her for
anything. Or if I should happen to go there when
she was home and he was not. He put her in the
position of being in the middle. He had always
told all the girls they were to obey his rules
or they would be kicked out of the house. Though
she never had to make a choice, she felt he had
put her in a position of choosing between us and
perhaps betraying her loyalty to one parent. That
rule of unconditional obedience caused all the

girls to have a sense of insecurity, just as his
threats when we were first married, that he would
find sex elsewhere etc., did to me. Their performance must meet his standards or he would get
rid of them!!

I was gone only a few days. After I came home,
the battles still raged. She told me years later,
all that time she feared for her life as well
as mine and his. She said she always slept with
her car keys under her pillow with the window
slightly open so she could grab the keys, jump
out the window to get out of the house and away
in a hurry if she needed to.

As I said, for years, he would yell at her
about things she had nothing to do with. He
treated her terribly. Just before the time he
started to go for deliverance, we all went to a
Bill Gothard Basic Youth Seminar. During that
seminar, he became convicted about the way he
treated her. So one night after the seminar, he
took her out in the car for a little drive. He
stopped and talked to her. He told her he treated
her so badly because he did not think she was
his child.!! Her coloring was different from her
sisters, and her temperament was different he
said. Remember, I wrote earlier the fact that
she was a planned child with the French name to
carry on his French heritage was important.

The first time I talked to that pastor about
deliverance, the last thing I said to him was,
"I don't suppose it has anything to do with what
we've been talking about, but my husband treats
this one daughter so badly, it's a shame. Is that
demonic?" I was shocked at his answer. He said,
"Yes it is and it is directly related to these
problems. The demons in him want her to do the
same sexual things that you are doing. To be mean
to her is his defense against that happening."
After his confession to Renee that he did not
believe she was his daughter, and after getting

412

this information, I went to the Lord in fasting and prayer about it. The answer came back to me. Of all the perversions that were in my husband's life, the one thing he abhorred and detested was incest. He hated that. So his defense against what the demons were wanting, was to be mean to her. But the demons knew of his stand against incest. So they convinced him that even though this was the most planned child of all, she was not his. That way, if they could get their own way, which was for him to molest her, it would not be incest, because she was not his. This was confirmed at the deliverance seminar where my husband volunteered to be the guinea pig to demonstrate what they were teaching. When he confessed his anger and meanness to this daughter they immediately discerned it was incest. I had said absolutely nothing to them about anything. So it had to be God who gave them that word of knowledge. They pointed out how that must have wounded me because if he thought she was not his child then he thought I had committed adultery. He confessed that, and asked forgiveness. That was one of the things they prayed about when they prayed for the healing of my wounded spirit. **Though it never happened in the physical,** in the spirit realms there was incest going on his mind. Renee knew and felt this in her spirit, although she was not conscious of it in her mind. Later, it came up in her counseling sessions. There was a strong sense that she had been sexually abused, but there was no memory of it ever happening in the physical. I explained to her what the Lord and two different counselors had told me about it.

After a couple of years, she decided to go Trinity Bible College in Deerfield Ill. to get a degree in psychology. While she was there she saw one of the psychology professors as a client for over $2\frac{1}{2}$ years. For one year she saw him once

a week for counseling sessions. Then she saw
him two and three times a week for a period of
time. Then went back to once a week for the rest
of the time. She said it took three months of
counseling about it, before she could bring herself
to the point where she could admit she had been
physically abused by her father. At that point,
she could not admit yet that she had also been
emotionally and mentally abused. The sexual abuse
that happened in the spirit, had to be faced yet.

After college, she worked in the Chicago area
for a while and then she joined the Navy. She
was in the navy for six years. She got married
to a fellow Navy man in Dec. of 92. Then she
transferred from the Navy to the Coast Guard.

She says this whole thing has hindered her
as an adult. She says there are many times in her
work when she has to stand up to men. She finds
that very difficult and intimidating. Once, she
realized being around a certain superior officer
caused her great fear. Unconsciously the man was
causing her to relive her childhood. His demeanor
was the same as her fathers. She felt worthless
and completely incompetent and unable to please
the man, just like she felt growing up.

She has a very difficult time trusting people.
Especially pastors and Bible teachers.

She says she hates surprising things. She
only feels comfortable when she knows what is
going on all the time. She needs to be prepared
for every situation so she can control it. Part
of this comes from officer training in the military,
but a greater part comes from her childhood fears.

As I said, when I first asked her if she wanted
to write anything for the book, she said she would.
But when the time came, she found she could not
do it. Even after all the counseling and the ensuing
years, she realized she could not delve into her
memory of these things. It would be too painful
for her. She said she had no counselor, no pastor

414

and no very close friend who could help her walk through it. Though he is a great guy, her husband has a difficult time understanding her family. She felt she would be overwhelmed by the pain of the memories.

She has some good memories of her father, she appreciates the way he instilled in her that she can do anything she sets her heart to do. She is not afraid to venture out into new territory and conquer it. He instilled in her a love for reading and a desire to seek knowledge. One thing she shares with her Dad is a fondness for Zane Grey books.

She is the only one of the four who communicates with him. He and his wife went to visit her and her husband a while back. I think that is one of the reasons she came to the point where she could not handle digging around in memories. I think the present was enough. She said the visit was very good in some ways, and she enjoyed it. But it was traumatic in other ways, because she saw him living as a woman all the while he was there, even when they went out in public.

This daughter is more assertive. She is beautiful, too. She loves the Lord. She has lead people to the Lord. I know the influence of Jesus in her life has touched people through the years. Though the fruition of it has been delayed, I know her heart's desire was to one day minister her psychology and her God to troubled women. She is wonderful with children.

In the past she found it difficult to develop relationships because she did not fit in with the southern lifestyle. She is in the military and had no children. Those things are not compatible with the women she knew from her church, as their life consisted of getting married, having babies and home-schooling those children. While she and her husband had friends, they were not the close kind that could help someone through what she feels she would be going through if she opened up the past memories.

Like all my daughters, she has been a blessing to me through the years. I am very proud of her, as I am of all my girls. She lives so far from me the intimacy of relationship we used to have is difficult to maintain. We miss that.

Since the writing of this section, Renee found a church and friends that were more compatible. She has also had a son. We had a chance to renew our relationship through spending some time together when he was born.

## MARY

Mary is the next oldest daughter. It only takes an hour and fifteen minutes to get to her house. She is married and has two sons and two daughters. She and her husband have worked with youth for about 20 years and are youth pastors at their church. She accepted Christ when she was young, 8 or 9 years old. He changed her, and was so real in her life I believe that is one reason she was least affected by her upbringing. She had a sunny disposition. She would spend a lot of time alone in her room drawing or learning how to play a guitar and singing and writing songs as a teen.

This is the daughter that was huddled on the floor as her father kicked her, when I came home from the Dr. office. She does not remember it. She was $2\frac{1}{2}$ or 3 years old.

This is her letter.

"Living with my Dad was like 'walking on egg shells'. I never knew when he would blow up over the littlest things. I remember walking across the living room on my way outside to play. He was reading the newspaper and as I passed through he yelled at me for shaking the paper. These are the types of things that were common occurrences. His anger was always uppermost in my mind when I was around him--at the dinner table-working out

416

in the yard--as he passed through the kitchen as we were doing dishes. I never knew if a fist would slam down on the table and scare the wits out of me or if he'd yell at my mother because the soup was too hot, or skid a chair across the floor because it wasn't aligned with the table, or kick the dog down the stairs because it was in his way. Anger ruled our home. Out of fear I learned to keep my mouth shut and to stay out of his way.

I also learned what made him happy, so I catered to his every whim, like a puppy dog, willing to do anything just to get a pat on the head.

There was very little touching that took place between my Dad and I. Unless it was a slap or a spanking with a belt. I remember getting hugs when he came home from long trips over seas.

The first compliment I remember receiving was when I was in Junior High as I played my guitar.

Even as a grown adult, with children of my own, I was always concerned about how 'crabby' Dad was going to be around the kids if they (my parents) stayed for a couple of days.

I guess if I were to express my Dad in five words, it would be: 'He was an angry man'.

Not all was bad though. There were many good things in my childhood that I remember. Dad always used a nickname for me--it was 'Muffet'. I think it came from the nursery rhyme 'Little Miss Muffet'. It pleased me when he used the nickname because I knew he was feeling kindly toward me. I remember Christmas and him passing out gifts and how he insisted that only one person open one gift at a time. It made me feel singled out and special, to be made the center of attention like that.

I enjoyed watching him play on his knees with our German Shepherd, Pepper. He would get on his knees, with a leather glove on and he would wrestle with him.

He was always my hero. Kind of like my knight in shining armor that I bragged about to all the

kids at school. I would tell of the trips he'd
go on and the times we'd all celebrate by going
out to dinner when he returned home. The home
movies of the places he had traveled to were great.
The souvenirs he gave me, I will always cherish.
They have been used time and again, by myself for
school projects, and now by my own children for
show and tell or something similar.

As I grew older, there were two things that
I appreciated most about my Dad. His love of
reading and his love of a good discussion. As
an older teen and young adult, I always enjoyed
our talks into the night. When we came together
as a family to visit, that was one of the things
I looked forward to most.

I think that now as an adult, I see how he
shaped my life for good and bad.

I know I learned early that I would never allow
any man-husband or not, to talk to me and treat
me as he did my mother. My Dad taught me to stand
up for what I believed in, and that is what I have
done when it comes to male pride and egotism.
Yet, on the other hand, I became an adult who had
a problem with having confidence in myself and
believing that I was worth something. But where
my earthly father failed, my heavenly Father
fulfilled.

As I look back in relation to my Dad, my
greatest joy was when he trusted Christ and served
Him. Yet, my greatest sorrow was when he turned
away from Christ to follow the flesh. I still
don't understand it, and it has brought our family
a lot of heartbreak. The hardest part of all is
the fact that I love him very much, but cannot
be with him like we used to. Yet he thinks we
hate him. Nothing could be further from the truth.
Sin brings sadness, death and separation and that
is what I have felt towards my Dad. Sadness that
he is hurting and we are hurting. Death to a hope
that my children would know the grandfather who

418

had said 'no' to sin and 'yes' to God. And
separation in a father-daughter relationship.

One thing is sure though--God is good!! He
has given me a step-dad who has a lot of love and
support to give to me--and a lot of wisdom and
direction to give my children. For this I am
thankful.

As I close these paragraphs, somewhere toward
the end of this book, I would lastly like to say,
the number one influence in my life was my mother.
She asked me to write about what it was like to
live with my Dad, and I did that. However, the
things that I learned from my Mom are eternal.
I learned what not to be--that is a 'doormat'.
I've learned I'm special because God said so and
I believe Him. However, I would never have found
Him had it not been for my Mom taking me by the
hand and kneeling with me in our family room as
we prayed along with hundreds of other people at
a Billy Graham crusade we watched on TV.

From her I learned perseverance--that no matter
how bad things are--God is greater than all of
it. My Mom is an example of the woman of Proverbs
31. It promises that the woman who follows God
will have children who will grow up and call her
blessed. So I honor my Mother for her undying
love for Jesus Christ and the pursuit of His truth.
My prayer is that I could become like her." That
was her contribution.

This one, too, is a beautiful daughter. She
is like a solid rock. Her wisdom and faithfulness
has reached many with the love of Christ. She
is a very special person.

By her own words, she said that she learned
to shut her mouth and to stay out of her father's
way. Because of that and her deep commitment
to Christ at such an early age, and because there
weren't as many trauma's to her, I believe she
was the least affected. I thank God that at
least one was spared the suffering that some of

the others have experienced.

At this point, before going to the oldest daughter, I would like to share a few quotes with you from the book "If Only He Knew" by Gary Smalley. The book reveals the serious consequences that occur when a man does not love his wife the way Christ loved the church. 1. A woman who is not properly loved by her husband can develop any number of serious diseases, (Dr. Ed Wheat) 2. Every aspect of a woman's emotional and physical existence depends on the romantic love she receives from her husband, (Dr. James Dobson). 3. A husband's lack of love for his wife can drastically affect their children's emotional development, (John Drescher in 'Seven Things Children Need). 4. A rebellious wife and children are more likely to be found in the home of a man who does not know how to lovingly support his family. 5. A man forfeits his good reputation by refusing to love his wife as he should. It tells the world he is self-centered and unreliable. 6. The son of an unloving husband will learn to treat his wife the same way his father treated his mother. 7. The last, but most important one that concerns my family saga, is that **improper love increases the possibility of mental illness requiring psychiatric treatment of family members.** According to an article written by Dr. Nathan Ackerman, mental illness is passed on within a family from generation to generation. In the same article Dr. Salvador Minuchin, a psychiatrist, said family members get caught in a groove of mental illness by putting undue stress on each other.

## LYNN

Lynn was the first born. The pages she wrote will be in the next chapter. What she heard me say was I would like her views on how the perversion of submission has affected her, rather than how living with her father affected her. But what she wrote is very pertinent to the book because it gives a victim's view of how the perversion of submission works in the church to inhibit, undermine and destroy the works of women in ministry.

Because of the hurtful place where she is, Lynn can not deal with writing about her father yet. She has given me permission to write her story.

Lynn was the little one who was hit for spilling her milk.

One day, when she was about 13 months old, I had the Asian flu. I was in bed all day, delirious with fever. Her father was taking care of her. He bragged from then on how he had potty trained her in one day. We had an old fashioned potty chair that had one strap that went around the tummy and one that went down between the legs to keep the child from getting up. What he did to potty train her was to spank her very hard, sit her on the potty chair and strap her in. He did this over and over for hours, hardly letting her out of the chair all day. He was proud of his accomplishment.

These are only a couple of vivid memories. There are many more.

One day when she was about five years old, she decided she wanted to take her little sister, who was only 3, and run away from home. I thought this was amusing at the time and that it was just a childhood whim, perhaps mimicking something she had seen on TV. I remember every detail of that incident as though they were etched into my mind. I just stood back and observed everything that happened.

Lynn always had a mind of her own. She was bright, intelligent and had an extraordinary ability to reason things out at a very early age. When she was around six, I had a new baby and was in poor health. She had swept the kitchen floor for me one day. When I asked her to do it again, she was not rebellious or anything like that, but just matter-of-factly said "no". I said, "You did such

421

a good job for me before, why don't you want to do it again?" She said, "The more things I can do good, the more things you will want me to do, so I don't want to do it."

She was such a capable child, I did expect too much out of her. At times, I was short tempered with her. I felt I treated her differently from the other children. One day I attended a PTA meeting whose guest speaker was a child psychologist. During the question and answer time I asked this question. "I have four daughters. I can understand and give the three younger ones room to be children and can acknowledge their childish behavior, but I expect so much more from the oldest and cannot do the same for her. Why is that?" She answered it would not be fair to my husband for her to answer that question in public, but she urged me strongly to get that child in for counseling immediately. I did not think she had enough information to make that kind of judgment. I did not know about my husband's perversions yet. But I wish with all my heart I would have listened to her and followed her advice!

It was only a couple of years after this when my husband began to bring pornography into the house. I told him I didn't want it in the house so the girls could get hold of and see it. I did manage to get him to keep it out of sight, but it was easily accessible.

My husband was Catholic when I married him, although he did not follow it and rarely went to church. I converted to Catholicism for a short time. At one point in time, we lived across the street from a Catholic church. Even though the two oldest girls had their "first communion" in that church, I was no longer following those beliefs, and did not attend church. But Lynn would get herself to church every Sunday. She would help out in any way they would let her help. I had just become a Christian a few months before moving

422

to that neighborhood. She watched the same Billy Graham TV Crusade that Mary and I watched when Mary accepted Christ. But Lynn would not accept Him.

Around age 12, a neighbor lady caught Lynn in a very compromising sexual situation with her son. As Lynn ran out of her house, the woman chased her, followed her into our house and all the way upstairs to Lynn's room. All the while delivering a barrage of berating words at her. I was not home at the time this started, but came in as this irate mother was storming out of my house.

You will see in the next few pages how important these details are in Lynn's life.

She grew to be very independent and rebellious.

We left the Milwaukee area and moved to a resort on a reservation in Minnesota, May 1, 1970. Lynn was 13. There was only 3-4 weeks left of the school year. My children had a lady bus driver who was a witnessing Christian. She talked to Lynn about the Lord and wrote long letters about Him. I didn't know this woman was a Christian and I didn't know what these letters were about. One day, as Lynn was devouring one of these letters, I asked what was going on. Lynn thought I might get mad at her and she said she thought I would not understand it, but she had accepted Christ and this woman was writing her instructions from the Bible. She turned 14 the following November and was a 9th grade student.

In the spring of her 10th grade, when she was 15, she met a 20 year old young man. He was a nephew of the lady who had led Lynn to the Lord. He hung around the school a lot, because he was a bus driver and did some mechanical work etc. in the school garage. Soon after she met him, he got a job at a paper mill. That spring, he came and asked if he could date her. He was very polite and seemed very nice. We let her go with him.

423

She turned 16 in November and married him in February. There was nothing we could do to prevent that marriage. She would have run away to marry him if we hadn't permitted it.

In the early fall, before Lynn's 16th birthday, her father accepted the Lord. He was the last of our family to become a Christian. He talked to Lynn's boyfriend about the Lord, and as a reslut, the boyfriend said he accepted Christ, too.

After they were married, he did not want her to come to see us very often. He had money for all kinds of expensive "toys" that he wanted, like guns and boats. But he did not have money to buy her necessities. She rebelled at that and eventually became a spendaholic. He had a tremendous anger problem. He acted out his anger by grabbing a gun and going out to shoot. This frightened her terribly. After they were married, she finished high school and one year of legal secretarial training. After 4 years of marriage they got a divorce.

One major contributing factor to their problems, was his parents had given him a plot of land, which he built a house on, right next to their own. Physically and emotionally, he never left his parents. He did not communicate with Lynn, but she would find out things he was planning to do through her in-laws. However, he never confided anything that had to do with problems or feelings with them. They never discussed problems or feelings either. Those were things one did not talk about to anyone.

They were divorced for 15 months. Lynn went to Bible school. While there, she met some teachers who had been on the mission field and who had first-hand knowledge of demon warfare. Lynn had an acutely keen sense of discernment, in both realms of the spirit, the Godly and the ungodly. Even though that school frowned on such things at the time, incidents occurred where Lynn began to use the gift of discernment. She learned all she could from those knowledgeable teachers.

The Bible school always required the students to practice what they had learned through the week by sending them to neighboring cities and churches to do ministry on the weekends. Lynn's assignment was to work in evangelism in the worst part of Manhatten. So every weekend for at least 8 months, she worked and gained more knowledge from the evil abounding in that place, and God's power to overcome evil. She worked under an excellent pastor who had been saved and had come up out of that environment. He had much knowledge and wisdom to share and she absorbed it.

After her year at Bible school she came home. She had a beautifully meek and quiet spirit. Her ex-husband said he had suffered many hardships during that time which drew him close to the Lord. He promised Lynn if she would marry him again, he would sell the house that was next door to his parents, and he would go to Bible school himself, because he felt drawn to ministry, too. He seemed very sincere and humble. They got remarried. They became pregnant. When they were married about 8½ months, he told her he was not going to sell the house, he did not want to read the Word or pray with her the way she wanted him to. He wasn't going to Bible school. He had places to go, things to do, and people to see and they did not all include her or her kind of God. However, he continued to go to church and to take an active part in it. He allowed her to take an active part in ministry work of any kind the pastors would let her do. They started a church in their home with a presiding pastor, which grew into a regular church. She had a vision for the church, for a school in the church, and the exact floor plan of the church and school. She never told anyone of the vision of the floor plan. When the church was built, it was the exact vision she had seen.

She worked hard to get the required corporation papers, licenses and other ground work done for the school. She had a good reputation in the town and many business people committed to help financially because of her. But the church hired another woman, from outside the church, as administrator of the school. Much of the support that had been promised because of Lynn was withheld because of this other woman's bad reputation. The woman embezzled money from the school, among other things. The church fired her, then asked Lynn to take the administrator job. She did it for five months without pay and got the school out of the mess the woman had gotten it into. She did a great job. But, sadly, she had a "nervous breakdown" because of some of the things that happened at the church and school. They left the church.

During all these years, her husband would say he was behind her endeavors, but often when a crisis would come, he would leave her hanging out on a limb with no support from him. He rarely protected her from anyone. He rarely ever stood up for her.

While some of these things were going on, my ex-husband told the whole family that he was a transvestite-transsexual and he was going for counseling and deliverance. By this time Lynn knew she needed deliverance too. She went for extensive deliverance. I went to every session with her but one. She was going through tremendous pressures from all sides.

They started attending another church. She became the church secretary. She went for some training to start a ministry center, which she started with the church's blessing. The stresses in the family were intense, and she confided in the pastor. Then she took further training and the tests to obtain an Exhorter's license in that denomination. She earned her license. But due to her emerging mental and emotional condition, and her failed marriage, they withheld the license. She had left her husband around that time. About that time, she knew she should not be active in ministry and voluntarily withdrew from everything she had been involved in.

She had gone back to college. That spring she received her A.A. degree. While in college, she began to have some confusing problems. She realized there were blocks of time she could not recall or account for. The time just disappeared. In February of 1993, she went to the hospital for the first time. She was diagnosed with major depression, Post Traumatic Stress Disorder, and finally, with Multiple Personality Disorder. (MPD)

For those who don't know what that mental illness is, it is a coping mechanism of the mind some people develop when the hurts and traumas of their life become unbearable. They dissociate themselves from the pain by developing another personality to bear the pain for them. They are not conscious of doing this. Nobody knows why children can be raised in the same home environment, suffer some of the same traumas, but only one child will begin to develop these other personalities, which are called alter ego states or just plain alters. One person can develop many alters. The alters hold the memory and the hurt of the past traumatic experiences. The person is not cognizant of these past things. But at some point in time the mechanism breaks down. It is almost like the system goes into overload and then the fuse blows. They can no longer cope.

Of all mental illnesses, MPD can have the best rate of recovery. For the average person, it takes about seven years of therapy to be healed. The person usually must recall most of the traumatic experiences, including reliving the pain and hurt of it. Then that personality can be merged or integrated with the core or birth personality.

427

It is an extremely painful and arduous process.
They may have weeks of intense anxiety before a
memory comes to the surface to be dealt with.
When one of the alter personalities is present,
the voice can change, the handwriting can change,
the behavior will change. There have been studies
done of the brain that shows even brain scans
change. A great many MPDs will cut, burn or
otherwise abuse themselves when an alter is present.
Many MPDs want to commit suicide. About 90 % of
them are women. Most have been sexually abused
and a great many of them have been satanically
ritualistically abused. They isolate themselves
because it is such a bizarre disease they are
embarrassed and ashamed. They never know when something will trigger an alter to the surface and
they might act weird in front of people. It's
a hellish existence. Most of them have their
children taken away by the courts. Most of their
families abandon them because they do not understand
what is happening. They are often rejected by
friends and family because of fear and ignorance.
They feel so alone in their battle, because they
are not supported like people with a terminal
illness might be. Sometimes this is a terminal
disease because some do succeed in committing
suicide. The road to wholeness and health is a
daily battle. Many times the battle is so hard
fought they want to give up and just die. There
seems to be no R. and R for these warriors though.
There is no rotation for rest and recuperation.
Many of them fight on through the nights. Because
of nightmares that come with sleep, many suffer
from sleep deprivation as well, making matters
worse.

This is where my beloved daughter is.

Her alters began to be created as early as
7 months of age. There was an alter created when
her father hit her for spilling her milk. When
that memory surfaced, and she verbalized it, she

even described the layout of the kitchen where
it happened. There is no way she could have remembered that in the natural. She was too young
when it happened. We did not live in that house
very long so she did not grow up knowing the place.
I had no pictures of it either.

There was an alter created who had to live
through the pain of the potty training day. The
therapist literally had to re-enact the scene and
undo the straps of the potty chair for that little
13 month old alter child so it could be free. She
had to encourage her that it was all right to get
up off the chair.

I, and my present husband, have helped her
to go through a memory process several times.
One time it was the brave little five year old
who wanted to run away with her little sister.
She wanted to bring her to a safe place. This
incident was connected to the incident of the daddy
kicking Mary on the floor. He had spanked them
and then told them to stop crying. Have you ever
heard a parent say to a child, after they had
punished them, "Shut up or I will really give
you something to cry about"? This is what happened.
Suddenly, the incident that seemed amusing to me
years ago, was no longer amusing. For the first
time, I saw the connection between my husband
kicking one child and the running away incident.
When the memory came for her, I wept and held her
while the little five year old alter relived the
whole experience. Every detail was exactly how
I remembered it! With the voice of a five year
old, Lynn tried to tell Mary, "Don't cry, he'll
hurt you more". But Mary didn't stop crying so
he kicked her. I wept as she pleaded with Mary
not to cry anymore. And I wept as she watched
her little sister being kicked by her daddy. I
wept as the five year old desperately tried to
get her sister to safety. I wept as she explained
to her sister that she couldn't pack very much

in her little toy suitcase. I wept when she helped her three year old sister put on her snow suit and told her she had to wear a hat and mittens and boots because it was cold outside. I wept as the suitcase popped open on their journey across the street to the neighbors, and things fell out in the snow and she scrambled to retrieve them. And I wept because she cried when she decided there really was no place to go and she would have to bring her sister back home. She cried because she had failed to protect and rescue her sister. There is nothing amusing about that incident in my mind anymore. It was tragic. I had witnessed all of that in the natural when they were five and three. Now I witnessed it through the pain of a five year old alter personality who could not bear the pain of seeing her sister being kicked.

The pornography in our house was another factor in her MPD. Because of those, Lynn knew what a playboy bunny was. An alter named Bunny was created to combat rejection, because if that was what her father liked, if she was a bunny she might be able to please him. Remember I wrote that Renee had been sexually molested **in the spirit** by her father? Well Lynn was too. I believe in his mind there was incest going on. Years later, Lynn confronted her father and asked if he would have been pleased with her if she had been a playboy bunny. Though he denies it now, at the time she asked, he admitted that was true, way back then, when that alter was created.

Lynn had an alter named Prostitute. It was created partially from the pornography and the spiritual sexual abuse. She thought that was what would please her father and also that was all she was worth. Both Lynn and Renee felt the same things concerning the spiritual incest abuse, both thought prostitution was all they were worth. Only one created an alter personality and one did not. The alter, Prostitute, wanted to carry out the

function it was created for. Thus the incident
with the neighbor boy. However, it has been discovered that Lynn had the actual experience of
sexual abuse from a great uncle, an uncle and a
satanic ritual abuser, among others.

Lynn was introduced to satanic ritualistic abuse
by going to a girl friends house early one evening
when a satanic meeting was going on. She did not
remember this, or anything else that happened after
that, until the memories began to surface during
therapy. We had no idea anything was happening
at all. At that time we never knew such a thing
existed.

Through facts I cannot share, I know my ex-
husband's acts of adultery and his sexual lusts
and perversions opened her up to these abusers.
I believe when Lynn married so young and left home,
those evil desires on his part, his anger and
harshness were all transferred to Renee. That
is when he began to treat her so badly.

At the time the alters Bunny and Prostitute
were created, another one named Nun was also
created. This is why Lynn went to church and did
all she could there. Somehow she knew the sexual
things were wrong, even though she thought it would
please her father. Somehow she was aware that
one needed to please God too. Perhaps that came
from the influence of Christ that was beginning
to show in my life, the Christian music I played,
and Billy Graham's TV crusades.

When Lynn was married at 16 and her new husband
began acting out his anger with guns, she became
so frightened her emotional growth stopped developing. The newly born again Christian Lynn began
to develop on the principles of the Lord. That
was what her life was based on. There was great
spiritual growth throughout the years. She ministered to many people. But those hidden things
of the past were lurking under the surface. Finally
when the system began to break down, she voluntarily

stopped all ministry work.

Since the first time she went to the hospital, there have been many suicide attempts. She has scars up an down her legs and arms and some on the chest from cutting. Some of the alters were occult alters that were formed from involvement with the occult and occult type religions. Because of the MPD, her 2 sons mostly lived with their father while they were younger. Much of the time, her relationship with them is painful. In the past, even though they viewed a video of what happens to MPDs, there has been very little support, understanding, comprehension, or compassion for what their mother is going through. Even though they were old enough for some of that to be happening, their father and grand parents say these are attention getting devices. They continually debunked psychology, therapy, and everything that happens, in front of the boys. The boys mimic their father. Remember the seven points I quoted from Gary Smalley's book? Every one of those points is manifesting itself in that family. Boys will treat their mother, and every other woman, the same way the father treats his wife. At the time of this writing, the boys are 16 and 18. One of them lives with her now. They are struggling to overcome some of the bad influences in their lives. It is a hard time for them.

Lynn's life is a painful existence. Yet she clings to her belief in God. It is strong. It is the only thing she has to hang on to. She believes she is going through a Job experience. But she wonders if it will ever end. When the memories come, she must feel the pain, acknowledge that it happened to her, own it as her own pain. Then she must forgive the perpetrator. The alter personality then must come into agreement with God because Lynn is a Christian. That may sound strange, but it really isn't. The alter personality is a part of her old nature, just as we all have

432

an old nature. Except hers is more intense than
most people's old nature's are. We all have to
fight to bring the old nature under the control
of God. We all have little rooms of sin etc. where
we try to keep God out, but we have to bring that
into agreement with God and His principles. So
it is with the alter egos, because they are part
of her.

There is a terrific battle for her soul. Because of all her experiences and knowledge in both
spheres of the spirit realms, she is an invaluable
tool for God, and will be more so, once she is
healed and free. She will have a mighty testimony
to share because it is only by the blood of the
Lamb that she will be set free. That testimony
and the blood of the Lamb will be a mighty weapon
against Satan and the forces of evil. She often
tells of how she has reached out to other patients
in the hospital, but she doesn't realize, even
in her sorrowful circumstances, she is doing God's
work. She feels ashamed because she feels her
life is not a good witness for Christ.

As the abuse of women has become an epidemic
over the past few decades, so has the incidences
of MPD. It is a comparatively new diagnosis in
the mental health field. There is controversy
over it. But there can be no doubt about it when
one experiences it or lives through it with a loved
one. It is a most horrendous life. No one could
ever imagine it or act it out. It is real. It
is painful. It is draining. It consumes their
lives. But it can be cured.

This daughter is like the other 3. She is
a beautiful woman. She loves the Lord. She is
a valiant fighter. I am proud of her.

This is the story of how living in our dysfunctional home affected her. The sins of the
father have truly impacted her life. That does
not negate my own dysfunctions which fed into
his, and their impact on her or my other daughters.

PERVERSION OF SUBMISSION

This is why I must expose the false teachings that allow these kinds of things to happen in a home under the name of "submission to your head" and "staying under the umbrella of protection" at all costs.

All of my daughters have been affected by those false teachings. Some are suffering more than others. My grand children are affected. Their greatest disappointment is that the older ones looked up to their grandpa who was a minister. They do not understand how he could be a minister and yet do the things he did. They say he blew it. They remember the good things of Christmases and other family gatherings and they miss that. Only God knows the long-term, deep effects of it on their lives.

B U T --- All my girls know Jesus. They are fighters because they know Him. In spite of the circumstances they are in or the afflictions they are suffering, they have learned, or are learning, what Jesus meant when He said to Paul in II Cor. 12:7-10, "My grace is sufficient for you". No matter what the thorn in the flesh is, His grace will see, and is seeing, them through it. When they are weak and can't carry on, His strength carries them and is abundant and sufficient for them. Even in the suicide attempts, His Grace brought Lynn back. In her weakness, God proved himself strong. Verse 9 says when a Christian is in that kind of desperate place, Christ shows His sufficiency in power, therefore the power of Christ rests on them. The word rest here means to abide with, to tent upon, it comes from another word that means to be superimposed over. So Paul was saying that at those awful low times when we are so weak we cannot stand, the miraculous Jesus builds a tent over us, he lives with us, He is superimposed over all those infirmities and weaknesses and that is what carries us through. No matter what the thorn in the flesh is or what it's source is,

434

Christ's strength is stronger.

A N D ---thank God for II Cor. 4:8,9 and 16-18
where it says, we are hard pressed from every side.
But we are not crushed. We are perplexed but we
are not in despair. We are persecuted but not
forsaken. We are struck down, but not destroyed.
We may feel crushed and we may experience despair
and we may be struck down at times, but those things
are not the final place. Because Jesus is there
He lifts us up out of those things. Even though
the outward body is perishing under the afflictions,
the inward man is being renewed everyday by the
Lord. The afflictions are not going to last forever.
Compared to the exceedingly, eternal weight of
Glory they are producing for us, they are light.
The word eternal means perpetual, for ever, everlasting. So though we may suffer for months or
even years, it is short compared to perpetual and
everlasting. The word light means easy, less.
In the natural, afflictions do not seem light or
easy, but compared to the weight of Glory they
will produce, they are light and easy. The weight
of Glory means a load, abundance, authority, a
burdensome weight. So what our suffering produces
is an abundant load of authority and Glory that
will be used in eternity for God's purpose, it
is preparation for reigning with Christ. The word
exceeding means a point reached or entered of place,
time, or purpose. It means abundant, far more,
and continual. It comes from another word that
means a throwing beyond others, a super-eminence,
far more, excellency, beyond measure.

What all this means is, even though we do not
deny we are afflicted, and we feel the affliction,
we recognize these afflictions only last for a
little while. But in eternity, the kingdom of God,
they are bringing us to a place of everlasting,
abundant, pre-eminent, excellent authority that
God will use for His purpose. That will go on
forever and forever. That is the hope we have.

That is the reward for not giving up in defeat when these afflictions strike. That is why Paul said we could be thankful in our infirmities. That is why he said in II Cor. 4:19, we don't look at things that are seen but at things that are unseen. The things that are seen are only temporal, while the unseen things are eternal. We must keep our eyes on the eternal value of our suffering, otherwise we will be overwhelmed with the afflictions. Keeping our eyes on the eternal value of our suffering somehow helps us to bear it now. I think that is the key of the martyrs that gives them courage to go through what they do.

It is not wise to deliberately seek situations that will cause us to suffer thinking it will bring us eternal Glory. We must be wise to know if our suffering is of God's choosing, or God's will for us. But, no matter what suffering we encounter, if we love Him and know His purpose for us, He will make all things work together for our good. The key is that we love Him and know His purpose for us.

I pray this chapter about my daughters will help readers to see how the false principles of other chapters sets children up for destruction. I pray women might be encouraged to be more bold in protecting their children, even from their own fathers if necessary. May God give them wisdom to know when it is necessary.

I pray God's blessings on my daughters.

CHAPTER NINETEEN
A VICTIM'S VIEW

Much of this chapter is written by Lynn-Marie.
At the time of her divorce, Lynn changed her name
from just Lynn to Lynn-Marie, a combination of
her first and second name. She said she chose
that name because it represents the new person
she is becoming, through healing and combining
all the alter personalities. Because of the nature
of her mental illness, Lynn-Marie has not read
the book. She has no idea of the things I have
written, so what she wrote was not influenced by
me. These are all her own thoughts, feelings,
and perspectives.

"My mother has asked each of us, her daughters,
to submit a piece for this book. We were asked
to share the impact of the perversion of submission
on our individual lives. Each of the four of us
has lived, or is living through, our own private
hell to one degree or another.

I am Lynn-Marie, the eldest daughter. It will
be five years in February, 1998 since my first
visit to a psychiatric ward for what was thought
to be Major Depression. I spent 11 days in that
unit, only to be diagnosed with Post Traumatic
Stress Disorder"(PTSD) as well. Several weeks later,
while participating in a Partial Hospitalization
program, I was diagnosed with Multiple Personality
Disorder. (MPD, now called DID-Dissociative Identity
Disorder.)

Largely due to my father's pervered view of
submission, I was raised with the dual message
that women were cute "playthings" AND that **anyone**
--man or woman--could do whatever they chose and
set their mind to do. He raised us in his extreme
perfectionistic and narcissistic lifestyle. He
opened the doors wide open to the occult for me
by encouraging me to get into ESP and mind control,
etc. At the ripe old age of nine, I sold my soul
to the devil, in order to have power over other

people so I wouldn't be hurt anymore. I decided
to become a playboy bunny so that my Daddy would
love me, and also to be a nun so that God would
love me. I was raising myself Catholic at the time.
Thus began a lifetime journey of being a people
pleaser and of being caught in "the perversion
of submission trap".

Our family became a "Christian" family, when
my Dad accepted Christ when I was 16.

At 16, I married a man who said he was a
Christian. Both my father and my husband abused
me under the name of "submission". Whatever the
man said to do, or to accept, was the law. Their
law was backed up by twisted Scripture and teaching
from well-meaning men. Sadly it was teaching that
**did not** agree with the Word of God. I could not
say or do anything that was contrary to my father,
my husband, or even most of the pastors I served
under. Without the consent of at least one or two
of those men, I could do nothing.

A time came when, because of my deep involvement
in cult and occult activities, I knew I needed
some extra spiritual help. I had to ask, and wait
for their permission, to go to see a Berean Baptist
Pastor for this help. This pastor was trusted
and was well known in our state as a man who helped
Christians come out of the occult. Even though
I had my father's, my husband's, and even my
pastor's permission to go to him, I had to fight
tooth and nail **against them** in order to get to
the pastor's place to receive his much needed help.

The submission deepened daily. I was forced
to resign all positions in the church, even though
I was no different when I was asked to step down
from these positions of service as I was when
I took those positions. Eventually, I was extended
the left-foot of fellowship, biblically of course,
because what I had lived through did not match
up with any of their "theology". Though many of
these men were not formally trained--they stood

in judgment over me.

This is only one example of how unquestioning obedience and submission to authority can get perverted. If I dared to question that authority, I was told by my father, husband, pastor and board members, that I was rebellious. I was told, "Rebellion is as the sin of witchcraft"— SIN in capital letters. Since I was constantly, usually legitimately, questioning my authority figures because their theology didn't match the Word, **according to their standards, I was constantly living in sin.**

This kind of submission decries ungodliness. It **assumes** the woman is not as intelligent as the man, and that the woman cannot learn how to discern the Word of God—using the exact same Bible tools a man uses. Last, but not least, it assumes that the woman could not actually have such a close personal relationship with her Heavenly Father and His Son that she could possibly hear His voice for herself.

Before all this church activity began, I had been to a Bible school that taught only the Word of God. It was intense Bible study. My three sisters and my father attended the same school. The school gave the students every opportunity for ministry on the weekends. Application of the Word that had been absorbed during the week was given out to others on the weekend. My weekend experiences were in Manhattan—where you either learned to walk by God's Spirit leading you, or you literally could be beaten or killed on the streets.

Because of this Bible background, each pastor in each of the churches (there were several of them over a period of almost 20 years) was glad to have "help" with ministry labors. The hardest lesson I ever learned was in the last two churches that I worked in. Both have the same scenario. There was an insidious type of control that produced one of two things.  Either there was a power struggle to maintain one's Biblical convictions or one ends up working for God out of fear that he/she might come out from under "the pastor's umbrella of authority".  This kind of perversion of submission wended it's way through me like an unseen spider web.

At one church, I asked if I could begin to organize a Christian school.  True, I was never TOLD that I would be made administrator of that school, but neither was I discouraged in any way by them when I said I felt that God was leading me in that direction.  Two months before the school opened, the church board hired a woman with previous experience.  This woman had a bad reputation in our small community.  Through various activities I had unknowingly built a good rapport with community members, including the business people in town.  When the town people and business people heard who the new administrator was, they began to back out of the promises and financial commitments they had made to the school because they had trusted me.

I was weary and very hurt.

To make a long story short, three months later this woman was suing the church and had stolen hundreds of dollars of all the children's book money.  Those of us parents who were not her immediate friends had unwittingly signed a contract saying WE as parents would be liable for any lawsuits brought against the school.  The pastor had just told all of the parents this news and then he asked me to step into this mess as a temporary administrator.  Because I did not want the school to close, leaving my children as well other people's children without a school, I accepted---under my husband's urging.  I had to answer to both the church board and the school board, yet I had no voice or vote on either board.  All matters were conducted through one member of the church board who acted as a liaison man between the two boards. When the school term ended in June we had a grand and happy school picnic to celebrate all that we had accomplished together those last $5\frac{1}{2}$ months of school!!

I wish that I could say the story ended there on that happy note. NOT SO. The two boards convened, and asked me to be present. I wish I could tell you what happened at those meetings-- but I cannot tell you. Why? Just as some trauma at nine years old caused the alter personalities of "Witch", "Bunny", and "Nun" to be created, so the trauma of that night caused another personality called "Professional" to be created. Professional holds the memories of what happened that night, but I am not yet ready to face the hurt of what happened. The only thing I can tell you, is that I had been given a position of responsibility without the necessary authority to carry out what needed to be done. I had labored under those conditions for $5\frac{1}{2}$ months. I had my first "breakdown" shortly after.

The last church in which I was able to consistently minister had a vision for a ministry center. Their mission was to heal broken people. The pastor repeatedly said that a woman in God's ministry was equal to a man in God's ministry. I believed him. I believed that HE believed that. One day, after struggling for months with a male trainee for the center, I went to the pastor and told him about the struggle I was having with this trainee. Pastor set up a time for both of us to meet with him. I had told the pastor that I really believed this man had a problem with women in leadership positions. The pastor pooh-poohed me, but assured me that if that really was so, he would stand behind me 100%. As the trainee and I walked into the pastor's office, the first words out of the trainee's mouth was that he did not believe in serving under women in leadership positions.

He said that he would not now, or ever, serve under a woman's direction.

Sadly, in the end, the pastor showed, and gave, his allegiance to this one year old baby Christian because he was a male. The pastor stood against me, because I was a woman. He never really got beyond his own bias and fears. I never was given the authority necessary to bring this brother to a place of unity or anything else, that I, as a co-minister should have had the authority to do.

These are incidents of abuse of authority and misuse of leadership and submission. I won't deny that they were very hurtful to me. I have experienced some things that weren't so bad and yet, on the other hand, things that were even more deeply hurtful.

The thread these incidents all have in common is the perversion of submission. None of the men could get beyond their own insecurities, fears, and biases. I believe all these men mentioned here have a warped view of submission and authority which warps their view of women and thus of themselves. It is a never-ending circle that most men are unsuccessful in breaking.

I believe some of these men had a true desire to serve God. They were sincere. Again, sad to say, sincerity is no excuse for spiritual abuse or for the perversion of submission.

Today, I am psychologically disabled. Though there are many other forms of abuse that I have suffered, none has been more insidious and more harmful than the spiritual abuse.

Five years toward healing is just a start for me. I've been told by several reliable authorities that it will take at least two or three more years of the healing process before I will be able to go back to college, with one class or on a part time level. I am told that it will be another 5 to 7 years before I am healed enough to mainstream back into society and support myself again. This will happen IF I don't give up on myself and quit the journey altogether.

Spiritual abuse is the ultimate of abuses. It goes beyond physical, beyond the intellectual, beyond the psychological, straight to the **spirit** of a person. Who will help to heal those spiritual wounds?

I don't stand in judgment of any of these men. That is God's department. But I do hold them accountable for their words, behaviors and actions. They are forgiven by me through the grace, power, and blood of Jesus Christ. But by the same channel they are forgiven, they are also held accountable."

That ended her letter.

As I read my daughter's words, I could not help but think back on chapter six of this book. I think of the veil that is Christ, that is over the woman as well as the man. I think of how that veil of Christ is trampled under foot by men, both for women as a gender and women as ministers of the gospel.

My daughter's writing brought to mind how similar the hurts and wounds are for my daughters and myself. We are only one family, yet there are four examples of the results of spiritual abuse from males, in just this one family.

Lori, the youngest, is suffering the rigors of missionary life in an awful country. She leads people to the Lord. Her life demonstrates Christ and humility. She has much to share and to give of Christ in her. Yet when she was home on furlough, the men of her denomination would not ask her to speak to their women at missionary conferences. She was totally ignored except by a few women who asked a few questions after the services. One church outside of her denomination asked her to speak to their women. She did a terrific job, women were touched, the cause of the gospel was proclaimed and some funds were pledged to their missionary endeavor. Yet, as I said before, she has been taught and believes that only men have ministries. She is not afforded the dignity of having her name on the missionary news letters. Perhaps this is a safety measure for her. She does struggle with depression, but she attributes it to the conditions in the foreign field. What do you think? Is it possible that she, too, is suffering from the dual spiritual wounds that come from being denied the dignity of personhood and of Christ in her being denied?

Renee, the next youngest has escaped the spiritual abuse and discrimination that the rest of us have experienced. She has been allowed to do what ever she felt God was calling her to do. In her current situation though, she would not be allowed to teach a mixed couples class for instance, regardless of her one year at Bible School and her 3 years at Bible College. It is not a matter of training, it is a matter of the old "usurp the man's authority" issue. They might allow her to teach women. In her work in the military, her knowledge and expertise has been shunted aside and her officer's training negated by some men of inferior rank. They can get by with it because she is a woman. On the other hand, she works three times as hard as a man, but when there is recognition of that, some men will say she only got it because she's a woman, not because she worked so hard for it. That is a secular thing, not a spiritual thing. But it is very painful.

Mary, who has devoted her life to youth work, has also experienced the negative effects of men and submission. Tom, her husband, works at a full time, shift work, job. So Mary is the one who does a majority of the youth work. Mary had her year of Bible school and the weekend ministries to prepare her. Tom had no training except what the Lord taught him and his experience. I am in no

444

way putting down Tom and his training, I am merely
drawing a comparison. They work together beautifully
as a team. But they were allowed to do it because
of Tom.

Tom and Mary and a couple of other men from
their church all went through training in their
denomination for what is known as an Exhorter's
License. That license says they are qualified to
be next to the pastor in spiritual leadership.
Women are allowed that much, but only the men can
take further steps to become ordained. The ceremony
to celebrate the receiving of the license is called
"Being set forth". It is the same as being
commissioned, with the laying on of hands. It
is a recognition of the call on their lives. Tom
and the other men were called forward one Sunday
for their "setting forth". But Mary, who had gone
through the same course at the same time, and
had passed the same tests and had received her
license, was ignored. When the pastor was asked
later, why he had not called Mary forward with
the men, he simply said he had forgotten that she
had obtained her license, too. The next Sunday
he mentioned his error and mentioned her name.
I don't remember if she was called forward or
not. It was a significant accomplishment for the
men, but her setting forth was just an after
thought. Mary is patient. Now after 15 years of
faithful work in that church, a different pastor,
and a lot of new people in the church, she is
being given her rightful place and now has the
dignity afforded by the title of youth pastor.
Mary was never looking for recognition, she just
wanted to do the job God called her to do. That
was her joy. She had that joy without the title.
She would have continued her work without any title.
That is not the point. The point is that without
Tom being called into that ministry as well, Mary
would never have been given the opportunity to
do it. Because they worked as a team, the door

445

was opened for her to be given the place of leadership. Yet that authority is limited because, as a woman, she cannot be on any board. So she has no vote etc. Tom often has to do the speaking for her in meetings of the men etc. because she is a woman and a woman's voice is not heard.

How many thousands of women are there who have been called into a specific ministry by God, but are denied the opportunity of service, because they had no husband to open the door of opportunity for them? How many have accomplished all the requirements of education, training, and experience and a maturity in Christ that far surpasses the man in the pulpit or the men on the board, but they are denied the privilege of serving their God with all of that? Their calling is as definite and as valid as the man's, but the door of service is closed because they are mere women. How much spiritual pain have these women endured? It is not just her human spirit that is grieved, the Spirit of God in her is grieved too, for the veil of Christ in her and on her is being trampled underfoot.

Lynn-Marie's experiences speak for themselves. Those were only a few of her disappointments concerning ministry.

My own disappointments in ministry are many. In my Christian walk, I eventually found a church where the Bible was preached like Billy Graham preached it. I sat in that little church many times and my heart would cry out in response to a message to give your all to Christ. I would say. "God, I will go any where and do anything you want me to do, only my husband isn't even saved yet. Save him Lord, so that together we can do a work for you." There was a most definite call on my life for ministry before he was ever saved. He got saved, he received the call, he went into the ministry. I was overjoyed that the ministry would begin. I loved being a pastor's wife. But

in the first church, the men were afraid that some
woman might lead some of the other women astray
with this wild new charismatic teaching, so they
would not allow even a pastor's wife to teach their
women. I was not a Pentecostal then. In the next
church, for one reason or another the opportunity
was also denied me, except for a handful of women
at a Bible study once a month. The third church,
I did teach some women sometimes. I had a weekly
Bible study with some women outside the church
for several years, and I taught the teens Sunday
School class. All the while I was learning the
Word. And all the while, I was racking up
experience after experience where the power of
God and the wisdom of God was being grafted into
my soul and spirit. Whatever God opened the doors
for me to do was a joy. But my ex-husband let
me know that people did not want to hear a pastor's
wife, they wanted to hear the pastor, so in joint
Bible studies, for the most part I kept my mouth
shut. Then my ex-husband was removed from the
ministry and the church he was pastoring. I
mourned not having the opportunity to teach. Or
to pray for people or to counsel them. Then God
gave my ex-husband one last chance at ministry.
He still held a ministerial license and a pastor
allowed us to begin to team counsel and he let
us teach some Sunday school classes. That license
opened the door in that church. Because I was
a minister's wife, I was accepted. The Lord had
shown me the needs of the women in that church.
He gave me the vision of ministry to them.
I began to feel that God was telling me to
take some Bible courses in preparation for a license
of my own. I was in that process when God released
me from that marriage. God had made me aware
of the women's needs before this happened though.
I went to the board and presented what I felt God
was calling me to do, specifically that I was to
get licensed and become a women's pastor. If the

ministry was not to be in that church, then at least it was to start there, because God had shown me the needs and gave me the burden for the women in that particular church. That board listened, anointed me with oil for that ministry, prayed with me about it. They said that if it was of God, God would prove it by granting me a license. Then they would see how God would lead. Like the men at Lynn-Marie's church, they never said they would consider giving me a position like that. They, in fact, said they had never heard of a women's pastor. But they never discouraged me in anyway from thinking that it might come about either. The pastor said several times that he would love to have me on staff to work with him. God did His part. He miraculously granted me a license in pastoral care. I had to fill out the written exams, and go through an oral interview with the men at the district headquarters, just like any other pastor. They recognized the call of God on my life and they felt I was sufficiently qualified so they issued a specialized ministry license in pastoral care. That license even gave me the right to marry people legally. But the church, even though they prayed with me again about it, never did anything with it. Eventually God showed me His plan would never work in that church because of the prejudice against women in ministry that existed in the leadership. There had been no ministry for women in the church for almost twenty years, in spite of the fact at times there were three married pastors on staff. That denomination is very strong in women's ministries. The pastor said it was not his responsibility to provide something for the women. His other remark in an annual business meeting of the whole congregation, was even though the denomination had issued me a license, he, personally, could never sit under a woman. He did not believe women should be in any kind of pastoral position. He

had signed a statement of recommendation for me
to get that license, but by his statement to the
congregation, he undermined anything God would
want to do through me. God had already shown me
nothing was going to happen at that church and
He was weaning me away from it. The burden for
the women had lifted and I mourned over it. I
mourned over the fact I would be leaving the church
in the near future. Before I left there, the women
rose up and had a meeting with the pastor. They
confronted him with all of the prejudice they had
felt concerning women and the use of their gifts
and callings. They discussed all their needs, and
those needs were exactly what I had presented
to the board months before. But I had nothing
to do with organizing the meeting, nor had I ever
spoken to any woman there about how I was feeling.
By that time I was no more than an interested
by-stander. I found out several years later,
though, that I had been blamed for inciting the
women against the pastor, and that I had been
disciplined by the board and pastor for it. I
had NEVER been disciplined by any board or any
pastor for anything, ever.

The next church I went to, my new husband and
I were getting along great. The pastor there was
open to women in ministry. But then he began to
change. He had been calling my husband and myself
to come forward to minister to people at the alter
calls etc. But all of a sudden he began to pull
away from me for no apparent reason. I had started
a women's ministry, but had not taught anything.
The meetings were just getting acquainted testimony
times where other women shared. But he began
sending spies in to see what I was teaching.
Later, these people confessed this and asked my
forgiveness for allowing themselves to be manipulated by the pastor into doing such a thing.
Through a series of circumstances, we found out
the former pastor had told this one that I had

incited the women against him and I would do the same to him and the women of his church if I was allowed to continue. He was told I was a troublemaker. That ended my ministry in that church. It was all based on untruths and slander, for my loyalty to pastors was such at the time that I never spoke a word against them. I would in fact defend them. But the bad reputation, based on absolutely nothing but gossip and slander was spread throughout our church community, as well as to the District Headquarters of the denomination I had been a part of, up until the time of my resignation because of their policy about divorce and remarriage.

The next church, was a new church. I was not looking for any kind of ministry. The pastor and board began to call for women to come forward to minister to other women. They made a big deal out of saying they wanted to let the women of the congregation know who they could go to for ministry. Five women, including myself, were interviewed, but then the whole matter was dropped. There was no acknowledgment by the pastor or board of who the women were even. Without the pastor or board's recommendation, the women of the church had no idea who they could trust. To me, that was like a carrot dangling on a stick. Because my heart is in ministry, I looked forward to a door opening through that, but it did not. Not for me and not for those other four women. I discovered much later this third pastor had also been the recipient of the slanderous report from the first pastor.

Like Lynn-Marie, there have been worse things that were even more hurtful that have happened to me concerning women in ministry. I, too, have felt that same piercing spiritual hurt that because I am a woman, all the training, all the knowledge, all the maturity in Christ, everything He has invested in me through all these thirty plus years of walking with Him, means nothing. A newly born again Christian male is preferred over that. They can, and do, stand in judgment of me, who I am in Christ, what Christ has endowed me with and what God has called me to do. I agree, that of all the kinds of abuse I have endured, that kind is the worst. I am not a pushy, aggressive type person who would force myself on church leadership. It has taken me a long time to get to the point where I feel what God has called me to do is His valid ministry. Like Deborah, I am more worthy than any man is to do what He has called and equipped ME to do. No one can do my job. What He anoints me to do does not depend on the approval of man.

I also have forgiven these men. But that does not stop new wounds from being inflicted time and again by other men. Again, I say like Lynn-Marie, the channel of Grace through which I am able to forgive, is the same channel by which they will be held accountable for their own actions.

I'm sure there are many women who will identify with us and who echo our sentiments. They know the pain of this form of spiritual abuse, too.

I pray that God would reveal to men how they are cheating God, cheating the body of Christ and how they are inflicting so much pain on women. I pray they would see the damage they are doing to the cause of Christ. I pray these things, not in a vindictive way, but so that they might repent before it is too late, for they will be held accountable for it before God.

# CHAPTER TWENTY
## BEAUTY FOR ASHES

Although part of Isaiah 61:1-3 is speaking of the return of Christ and His millennial reign, it is a precious verse for believers now, as well. The whole passage is a beautiful promise. Verses 1-3 read, "The Spirit of the Lord God is upon me, because the Lord hath anointed me to preach good tidings unto the meek; he hath sent me to bind up the brokenhearted, to proclaim liberty to the captives, and the opening of the prison to those who are bound; to proclaim the acceptable year of the Lord, and the day of vengeance of our God; to comfort all that mourn; to appoint unto those who mourn in Zion, to give unto them beauty for ashes, the oil of joy for mourning, the garment of praise for the spirit of heaviness, that they might be called trees of righteousness, the planting of the Lord, that He might be glorified. " (KJV) Those words brought tears of gratitude because I see how much of what is written there has been fulfilled in my life. It is a complete picture for me.

Our God is a most faithful God. His Word is there for us to appropriate, to bring healing, comfort, promise. Because verse 2 speaks of both the first and second coming of Christ, I believe I can appropriate these verses for myself, because I live in the interim between those two advents.

For all my Christian life, with all my heart, I wanted to follow God and do His will for me. I wanted to be everything a godly Christian woman should be to bring honor and glory to God. In that 34 year marriage, I tried to do that. I thought submission to my husband was godly. As a pastor's wife, I wanted to demonstrate what I had been taught a godly woman was supposed to be. But I was in a prison, a bound captive. I was in mourning most of the time. I was perpetually brokenhearted. I felt God was not being glorified in me or my life.

452

life. I often bowed to the man and man's traditions rather than to God. When I was first baptized in the Spirit, I was forbidden to speak of it, because my pastor husband didn't believe in it. He preached against it. I thought my first priority was to be obedient to him because he was a pastor. The reasoning was if he, as the pastor, did not believe in the baptism of the Spirit, then what credibility would he have with his congregation if his own wife did not agree with him? What if she practiced something different from what he preached? How would that look? I was in mourning because the Holy Spirit in me was in mourning--He was deeply grieved!! I was not a tree of righteousness, a planting of the Lord. In spite of what I **wanted** to be in the Lord, after my husband came to the Lord, and accepted the call to ministry, I became a tree of tradition, a planting of my husband. It took years to break out of those traditions and to uproot that tree.

God opened the prison door, just a crack at a time. He began by binding up the broken heart. He proclaimed liberty to this captive. Finally, He flung that prison door wide open and I walked out of my prison. He comforted my mourning. He gave me beauty for ashes and He lifted that spirit of heaviness off of me. He brought joy and laughter into my life. In spite of the fact most of the Christian community thinks divorce and remarriage is almost the unpardonable sin, I am now a tree of righteousness, a planting of the Lord. I no longer bow to idols of men. Because of Him, I have an anointing to preach good tidings to the poor imprisoned captives, specifically, to those captive women who are now living what I used to live. I have news to set them free. I can tell them how God heals the wounded spirit, the broken heart. I can say, "turn from your idols that hold you captive and God will bring you the oil of joy and He will build something beautiful out of the

453

ashes of your brokenness. He will bring praises
of Him to your heart and to your lips. You will
wear a garment of praise, as the heaviness of spirit
is lifted from you."

There are many pastors who say one of their
biggest problems concerning divorces in their congregations, is if one who is divorced, marries
another, and it turns out to be very good, then
they have trouble convincing others it is not of
God and it is not good. This is true especially
if the divorced one gives God the glory for their
new life with the new partner. The divorced one
is supposed to say, "I was very wrong to get a
divorce, but I have asked God's forgiveness for
this awful sin. Now He is rebuilding my life.
But I'm sorry I sinned against Him, and you, by
getting a divorce. Don't follow my example, stay
married. That is the very best thing you can do."
We are supposed to repeat this over and over, lest
we lead others astray. We are supposed to deny
the merciful way God worked for us and we are to
deny we are blessed by God with a new mate and/or
a new ministry. Divorced persons are looked upon
as being less "spiritual" than others. Services
to the Lord are often denied to them because this
almost unforgivable sin is supposedly tainting
their life and their service. It is as though
God's gifts and anointings end when a divorce
occurs, but even more so if there is a marriage
to a new partner, because many feel the rest of
those lives are being spent in the sin of adultery.

I want to say I AM deeply sorry for the hurt
I caused people in the process, and I AM sorry
I was forced to go through a divorce in order to
keep my integrity in the Lord. My original desire
was for God to do a miracle in my ex-husband's
life. That did not happen because he refused to
die to his perversions. But I will never deny the
gracious mercy of God when He opened the prison
door for me. How could I ever say what I believe

was a merciful act on God's part, was a sin on my part? That would be like saying, "God, in your mercy, you caused me to sin". I will never apologize to anyone for the blessings He has bestowed on me, both in the release from that marriage and in the new path He chose for me to walk in. Nor will I ever say those things are anything but blessings. Beautiful gifts of God. They are not God's second best choice for me, they are the absolute best!! I further believe they are earthly rewards for my faithfulness in wanting to please God, rather than man, no matter what the cost was. I will not belittle the greatness of God or his blessings by apologizing to anyone for them.

As I wrote earlier, there was a concentrated time of prayer for my ex-husband. He almost turned back to God. But he didn't. At the very moment he made his decision, God spoke the words, "DANGER, IRREVOCABLE WRONG DECISION" into my head and my spirit. When my ex-husband confirmed that decision to me, God lifted even the burden to pray for him. This was according to my ex-husband's last request that I stop praying for him because he didn't want my prayers messing up his life anymore. God gave him the desire of his heart. He ended the relationship in every way.

This is also a repeat of what was written in the last chapter, but I want to bring these events into proper sequence. A year before the marriage ended, I had the vision for ministry to the women in the church we were attending. The ministry was to be a women's pastor. The Lord led me to take some Bible correspondent courses in preparation for becoming licensed in pastoral care in that denomination. This vision had been shared with the pastor and board of the church. They had anointed me with oil and had prayed with me about it. They said if it was of the Lord, I would get the license and then they would see what to do after that. I left my husband in January, 1990, and was granted the license in March. I worked many volunteer hours a week in ministry of various sorts in the church. Then I took 18 weeks of training in preparation for a broader ministry. I felt God was going to develop a ministry for me in that church. I was extremely happy and content there. I thought I would just spend the rest of my life, alone, in ministry. It would start in that church, and perhaps at some point in time, it would take me elsewhere. I thought my life was set for the time being. But doubts began to creep in that any of that vision for the women's pastoral ministry would ever come about.

In January, 1991, I was ready to start the new ministry I had prepared for. This was the time I referred to before, when there was almost a reconciliation with my ex-husband and then God spoke those words to me. He definitely ended that relationship, before He opened the door for a new one. At the same time, He was beginning to close the door for ministry in the church. A couple of months later I knew He was weaning me away from my home church because the prejudice against women in ministry would prevent it from happening. I wept brokenheartedly at the alter, but then I told God that I would be like Abraham. I didn't know where He would lead me, but I would go without fear to where ever He sent me. I knew it was going to be a weaning process, I was not supposed to just stop going there, but at some point in time God would say to leave.

In the new ministry class there ona a young man named Curtis. Because of the trust factor that must be established in the group, the groups are supposed to be limited in number and after the second week, no new members can join. Our group started out with the right number, but for one reason or another only two people stayed with it. Curtis was one of them. Because I had a limited income, I moved the meetings from the church to my house, in order to save gas money.

For the first nine weeks of the study we had a wonderful time with the two students and myself. The three of us got to know each other quite well. But the second week of the next nine week session, the third party left town. So then there was only Curtis and I. We continued the study with just two of us for 7 weeks. Because we were not limited timewise by church hours, after we had covered the regular study material, we would go on for hours, just discussing and sharing the Word. It was marvelous. Because of our mutual love of God and love of the Word, our spirits bonded together. God began to teach me about spiritual bonding. He began to show me, through the relationship with Curtis, He has a far superior plan for a married couple than anything I had ever known. It was something He wanted me to know and to teach.

One day, I got a call from a woman who wanted counseling for herself and her husband. After hanging up, I realized I needed a partner for this kind of ministry. I asked God to bring me a partner. At that moment I did not know God already had a ministry partner planned for me.

As the oneness of spirit grew between Curtis and I, a very deep respect for him developed. I loved him dearly as a brother in Christ. I admired him greatly. His hunger for the Lord impressed me very much. I began to perceive there was a call to ministry on his life. I asked him if he knew there was a call on his life. He said yes, he knew that. Within a few days, we felt God was calling us to work in some kind of ministry together. We would wait on the Lord to show us what kind. We agreed we would seek the Lord to know what study He wanted us to do in preparation for this ministry after the last weeks of the study was over.

At this point, in mid April, God had said He was weaning me away from the church. I said

I would trust Him and go where He sent without fear. Less than a week later I awoke to the realization I was deeply in love with Curtis. Not just as a brother in Christ, but as a man. I admitted this to God. (As though He didn't know!) When I admitted this to God, there was an immediate partial revelation of the ministry God was calling us to. It would be a ministry that exemplified God's kind of love, and how His kind of love is first built in the spirits of two people who are spiritually committed to Him above all else. I could teach the concept of spiritual bonding alone, but it would take a married couple to demonstrate it!

Along with the admission, and in spite of the revelation, there was a barrage of self-condemnation and doubt. How ridiculous to think a young man like Curtis would ever be interested in an older woman like me!! It was out of the question!! I was 2 years short of being twice his age!!! How could I have ever let this happen??? I asked God for a sign to confirm this was of Him or get Curtis out of my life, quick.

Two days later, we took my car to my daughter and son-in-law's house so the men could work on the car together. This was planned before my revelation. It was a Sunday. They worked on the car in the afternoon, and we all went to church in the evening. I was not thinking of how I had asked for a sign. I was lost in worship. I was kneeling in the aisle a few feet away from Curtis, who was sitting in the pew. All of a sudden I saw a vision. There was an extremely pure, white, light that seemed to be going up to, and down from, the throne room of God. The pure dazzling, light was a holy love. It was our love going up to God individually and His love coming down to us individually. But then it swirled around us, wrapping the two of us together in holy, pure love. It enveloped us and bound us together. The love was

458

so pure, so radiant, the power of it was almost tangible and overwhelming. God made sure I knew this was not a figment of my imagination. After the worship time finished, one of the worship team said that she had seen a vision that was so lovely she had to speak of it. She described seeing the roof of the church rolled back and a pure, beautiful white light was streaming up and down to the throne room of God. She felt like she was basking in the warmth of beautiful sunlight. Then, to confirm it even more, after church another lady came to me saying, "There is so much love all over you, I want a hug so some of it might rub off on me." This confirmed that not only was the love I had for Curtis of God, but God would visibly manifest that love to others, thus confirming the ministry would be a ministry of love.

A couple of weeks later, I was with two people at a prayer meeting. I said Curtis and I felt we were being called into a ministry together. I asked if they would pray to see if this was of God or not. That is all I said. As they prayed, the man began to chuckle. When he was through praying he said the Lord had given him a beautiful vision. He saw a brilliant, pure, white light going up to, and coming down from, the throne room of God. He said the ministry was from God, it would be far reaching and fruitful. Then, curiously, he asked if my divorce was final yet, cautioned me about guarding my heart, but said God would meet those needs as well. Also, he said to avoid the appearance of evil. But the ministry was of God. It wasn't until then that I shared God had given me the same vision of the beautiful white light streaming up and down to heaven. I did not share that the light was a holy love and how it had wrapped Curtis and I together. Nor did I share with anyone that I was in love with Curtis or that the ministry God was calling us to would require that we be married. I felt God was saying not to speak to anyone about this, not even Curtis.

At the time all this was happening, I was doing a lot of journaling. I would like to share a page out of that journal with you.

April 19, 1991: The ministry together will be to exemplify God's love in a Song of Solomon kind of love. Love--real love--is ageless.

April 26,1991, 5 A.M.: God revealed a blindingly beautiful ministry that I had never heard of before. We would teach seminars about love. The love people would see in us would flow out from us and touch lives. It would anoint them with this kind of love for each other and would restore marriages by the power and love of the Holy Spirit. This would be a mighty weapon formed against satan and his attack on marriages and the home. It would be mighty to the pulling down of strongholds of all that is against God's people in marriage. Love is the supreme attribute of God. Why should God not bring a couple together in this kind of love and then use them to baptize other couples with the same kind of Love? (Later I read in Derek and Ruth Prince's book, "God is a Matchmaker", they are a couple who God uses to anoint couples and pray for them in that very way.)

April 26, 1991, 6 A.M.: This kind of love cannot be taught and it cannot be strived for in the flesh. It can only come when two people have individually committed themselves to God and have cried in their hearts, "create in me a clean heart oh, God. Renew a right spirit in me." His Spirit is a Spirit of pure love. The teaching is in conjunction with the touch of God that transforms.

April 26, 1991, 6:45 A.M. Love transcends ages. It took God 27 to prepare me for Curtis and this ministry, it took Him 3 years to prepare Curtis for me. We delight ourselves in the Lord and His Word first, therefore we can delight in each other. (God is so faithful. In spite of all His confirmations, I still had bouts with self condemnation and doubt. Once I asked God, "Did you ever do this to any other woman? Did you ever put an older woman together in marriage with a younger man to accomplish your purposes?" Not two days later a friend said "Have you heard of Derek Prince?" I answered in the affirmative. She proceeded to say, "Did you know God gave him a vision and he married a woman who was almost twice his age? They had a long ministry until she died. Then God gave him another vision and he married a divorced woman 18 years younger than he was. Now they have a world wide ministry too." This came out of nowhere!! God just wanted to affirm this in every way for me. Though I had heard a lot of Derek Prince tapes, I never knew anything about his personal life.)

April 27,1991, 6 A.M.:It seems God is saying, "This is of me. Do not torment yourself with doubt. Be patient and enjoy this. It is a beautiful thing I have created in both of you. It is a part of your reward for these earthly times for your faith- fulness to Me. I restored everything double to Job in his earthly life and I will do the same for you. Curtis is my appointed one, too. I have great and mighty things for him to do for me. I have put holiness and a desire for holiness, into both of you. I have put purity and the desire for purity into both of you. This has a mighty purpose and in due time the 2 of you will reap a harvest for me because of it. But for now do not doubt. Just bask in the sunshine of my love for you as it becomes more and more expressed through Curtis. Enjoy and cherish each moment as it comes. I am opening up a new world for both of you as you grow together. Don't tarnish the wonder of it all with your doubts. Put your MIND at ease, stop think- ing and analyzing each thing and letting all these doubts in. Just relax and let things happen the way I have planned them. Trust what I speak to your spirit, not what you THINK with your mind.

461

Curtis will tell you when I tell him, when the time is right."

The following is what I felt as God showed me what His kind of headship was through Curtis. You may feel the words are too strong for feelings towards another human being. But for me, it was a revelation of God's nature in a man. It was a demonstration of how God is head of Christ and Christ is head of the church. It was something I never knew existed. After 34 years of the other kind of "love", false headship and false submission, it was almost overwhelming in it's purity and loveliness. Remember, I loved Curtis, but he did not know it yet. He did not know he loved me in any way except as a sister in Christ. But this reveals WHY I loved him!

May 9, 1991: Last night we talked to the pastor about our feelings that God was calling us together in a ministry and about my discipiling Curtis further. It went well. But afterwards I asked Curtis if I had talked too much. He gently said that I had not talked too much, but that he would have talked more. He said he needs to be allowed more time to say what he wants to say. I felt bad that I had been insensitive to his need. He so gently leads me in the right way. I don't want to be the leader--in my heart, I AM sitting at his feet. In my spirit, I am totally submitted to him because he is so submitted to God. God, help me to get my head and my tongue into the right position, too. God, I kneel and weep before you in awe at how big you live in him, and how your love and gentleness comes through him to me. God, I am humbled by his beautiful spirit. He lets me be me, with all my faults. He patiently waits for me to see for myself, what I have done. Then when I ask him about it, he gently talks to me. God, there is no one else like him. I see you in him, Jesus. Even in this discipleship training for ministry, I know in my spirit he is to be the leader and already is head of this ministry team. I am only imparting what I know to him. I am already basking in his leadership. What a comfort! What a blessing! I trust him so completely. I feel humbled before you God because of the purity and beauty of it. I am in awe of You, and him. But there is an exhilaration and a singing in my heart and I am lifted up in the humbleness. God, words fail me." (End of journal entry.)

For the first time, because of the way Curtis was, I truly felt God's love and acceptance of me. All the years of being a Christian in that other marriage, God's love and acceptance was hidden and buried under pain and perversion. When I left my ex-husband's prison, I felt freedom and peace and joy in being myself, a person in her own right. But I never experienced God's love until Curtis demonstrated it to me through the Spirit's working in him. It was a spiritual thing, not a thing of the flesh. For the first time, I felt in awe of God's love for me, so why should I not be in awe of the demonstrator of that love also?

Our studies continued. In May some time, as part of the material we were studying, there was a section on marriage. Since he was a handsome single guy, and I was a single woman, we teased each other about finding a suitable partner out there in the world. I said there where no men like him out there. A week or two later, Curtis pressed me to admit what I was feeling for him. I told him I loved him as a man and respected him very much. But I did not say what I had felt God was saying concerning marriage and ministry. I thought when I admitted I loved him, he would end the relationship. But he didn't. It had cleared the air, so to speak. We continued our study.

Over Memorial day, I was out of town for the weekend. I had given my house key to Curtis because there were a few certain Christian programs he wanted to watch on Trinity Broadcasting Network.

He could not get TBN at his house. When I got back, he had left me a note. The note talked about an unusual experience of feeling an overwhelming love of God that came upon him. I think it was the same kind of love from God that I had felt when I had the vision. It was a baptism of love for each other and for the ministry.

In June he pressed me again to say what I felt for him. Again, my expectation that the relationship would end didn't happen.

In July, we, and some other friends from church, went to a distant town for a Mike Williams crusade. After one of the first evening meetings, Curtis again pursued the issue of my love for him, but this time, he admitted he had deep feelings for me too. Sunday afternoon, just before the last meeting, we were walking around a little park. There was a park building with an outdoor stage. We sat down at center stage to talk. God was really touching both of us with the love we had for each other. This time, he also pressed me to tell him what all of the vision of ministry was. So we finally confessed to each other what God was doing in each of us. Curtis said, "We are already so much one in the spirit and one in the emotions, all there is left is for us to be married in the flesh." I cried and demanded, "How could you ever handle being married to an older woman like me?" He answered honestly, "I don't know how I would handle that, but God does." We walked some more, arm in arm. I cried a lot and he assured and comforted me. Our questions to each other were, "Is this truly of God?", "Does He really want us to be married?", "What will people say and think?", "Who will accept us and this marriage?", "What will parents and family say?".

In the evening session, one of the friends who was with us had a message from the Lord burning inside, but there was no opportunity to speak it and she didn't know who it was for. After the

meeting, she and her husband and Curtis and I
were walking around that same park. We sat down
to pray. As we prayed God spoke these words through
Karen. She knew nothing of our relationship except
that we thought God was calling us together as
a ministry team. She did not know what had trans-
pired earlier in that same park. These were the
words that came forth. "The Lord would say unto
you, you are vessels, set apart, holy and pure.
Purified gold as tried by fire. I will protect
you from harmful words of people. And I would
say unto you what God has joined together, let
not man put asunder." She said she didn't know
why that Scripture was given because she had always
understood that to be part of a marriage ceremony,
but she guessed God could apply it to a ministry
as well. She and Ray didn't understand our tears
and our praises of God. They had no way of knowing
God had just answered the questions of our hearts.
They did not know until a week later what God was
really doing.

So, we planned to be married. My children
did not object. They had their own private thoughts
about it. But the two daughters and families who
live in the area did everything possible to make
our wedding day a success. My sisters and families
did not know Curtis or his sweet spirit and so
there was some opposition from them for fear I
was setting myself up for hurt. But the one who
lives closest, attended the wedding. My Dad took
me down the aisle. I had been married before,
but my beloved had not been married before. He
wanted a nice wedding with the tuxedo and all.
I felt he should not be denied his wish. And
besides, I felt like I had never been married
before. I felt like a virgin because of the purity
of this relationship. My dress was not a dress
with a sweeping train, but it was white lace, with
a touch of pink and silver thread through it.
We had two matrons of honor and two best men. It

was a gorgeous wedding, all done in teal and white, with Christmas greens, silver and teal decoration, even teal and white poinsettias and birch logs with cedar bough candle holders. It was especially meaningful because it was performed in the very church were I had that beautiful vision. We had a regular worship time instead of traditional wedding music. A friend had written a special song that he sang. A daughter and son-in-law sang another special song, another daughter read our unusual story. The worship team and the ladies of the church helped with the reception and refused to take honorariums for it. A grand daughter and grandson insisted on being a flower girl and a ring bearer. And two more insisted on being ushers.

Those of Curtis's family who lived close enough, attended the wedding. His parents, who travel full time, did not get the invitation. They were wounded that we didn't invite them. We felt hurt that they didn't come. But months later, when we discovered they hadn't received the invitation, we both expressed our sorrow about it. We have a very close and wonderful relationship with them, as well as with my two sisters and all of their families, my Dad and Curtis's brothers and sisters.

God did shield us from much hurt and pain from wagging tongues though. The pastor of the church where I had the vision of ministry to women, opposed the marriage. He and his board chose to discuss us and determine what they should do about it, without even talking to us. They had decided if we would wait at least six months, but preferably a year, if we would encourage Curtis's parents to talk to the pastor, to be sure they approved, then they would feel we were in our right minds and we were submitted to their authority. Then the pastor would marry us in the church and things would be done right. We had not asked him to marry us. But we stayed in the church for a while.

466

No one spoke to me about anything, not the pastor or anyone, but I was excluded from being asked to pray for people or from doing anything else I had previously been doing in the church. Weeks later, one of the elders came to me with a smitten conscience. He said he could not let me go on thinking everything was all right and I would be allowed to minister in that church again if I married Curtis. He said even if we abided by all of the things they had dictated to us, they would still not permit me to do anything there again. He said all support of our marriage had been stricken from the records. Without talking to us to get the facts, they judged and convicted us. I had broken their rules by falling in love with a student for one thing. Though we felt it was God's sovereign will for us, because He had a purpose in it, they thought it was unethical on my part. I was never truly "on staff". And then for Curtis to be so young was another. And then to break the taboos of marrying somebody else after divorce, well that would just be the end of ministry. They never extended the courtesy of speaking to us personally about any of this. Not one of them had any idea of what God was saying to us. The pastor thought he had a revelation from the Lord that he was not to marry us, we were not then, or ever, to be married. He conveyed that to Curtis's parents, causing a great deal of trouble. But when the elder told me what had been decided, I walked out of the church and never went back. God had said 4 months earlier, before Curtis, he was weaning me away and I would know the time to leave. I knew that was the time. We wrote a letter to the pastors and each member of the board of the church explaining our position. We did not receive a reply from any of them. A year or more later, the pastor met us for coffee to say he forgave us. Through this and other things we have heard since, we know that God, indeed,

467

was faithful to protect us and shield us from many hurtful wagging tongues.

The blessings for me and my family that have come from our marriage cannot be counted. One of the things I thought God was saying to me was that through Curtis He would restore the things the locust had stolen from my children and grand-children through their natural father and grand-father. Curtis has never had a child of his own to raise, yet he has a father's heart. He makes sacrifices of time, energy, and money, to accom-modate the kids and the needs that they might have. Like all parents, sometimes our plans are interrupted by some crisis for Lynn-Marie or one of the other children or grand-children. He's never upset or angry about that. He says "that's what parents are for. That's what being a parent is all about." He gets insulted sometimes if I say "my kids" instead of "our kids." He delights in doing thoughtful or fun things with them and for them. He teases them about buying him presents all the time, but he loves spontaneously buying them little things. He instinctively knows when one of them is hurting and is in need of en-couragement or help and he is quick to give it. He's remarkable. They love him.

My Dad is 86, but Curtis loves to be with him and would do anything he could for Dad. He is very sensitive to my Dad's feelings.

My sister, in particular, has said more than once, that though she thought in the beginning I was going to get hurt, she is so thankful I have him in my life. She sees how he loves me and takes care of me. They all do. He is helpful to all of them in whatever way he can be of help.

He is very witty and makes us all laugh. Yet he can come up with the most profound insights and wisdom. His wisdom and maturity was one of the things that attracted me to him.

We were married December 14,1991. In March

of 1992, I was having some pains in my throat.
I realized these pains started if I walked only
a block on the level at a moderate speed. If
I walked a slight incline, the pain would start
within a half block. I saw my Dr. and in May had
the first angiogram, followed by the first angioplasty. By November 1992, I had 9 more angiograms
and 2 more angioplasties. So for the first year,
Curtis was really tested. I agonized and grieved
that my beautiful young husband was married to
a "sick old woman". That is how I perceived it.
God had to deal with me about that wrong perception. I began to notice how many young couples
had to deal with serious sicknesses in one partner
or the other. He showed me that my age was not
a major factor. I had to stand up against satan,
who wanted to destroy the beautiful love God had
given us. God had to show me how merciful He was
to have given me such a loving, strong young man
to take care of me. Anyone who has had angiograms
knows they do not incapacitate a person from having
them done, unless some complication arises. So
Curtis didn't really have to deal with an invalid
type situation. But there were so many of them
and the angina never did go away. In March of
1995, I had the twelfth angiogram and found out
there were some more serious blockages. So some
of our activities are limited because of the angina.
Through it all, Curtis demonstrated the most loving,
caring, tenderness any woman could ask for. He
takes care that I don't lift and carry too much.
He watches so I'm not out in a cold wind. etc.
He knows what I can handle and what I can't. He
watches over and protects me, but he doesn't go
too far in that either, so that I feel smothered.
He instinctively knows when I have pain. After
3 more angioplasty type procedures, I finally had
bypass surgery in August of 97. Still there is
some angina.

Because he was here with me, I didn't have

to go through all of this alone. My children would have been with me if I needed them, and some of them have been with us at various times when I went to the hospital. The 3 that are in states were with us for the bypass. But it is not an obligation for them to be there so I'm not alone. I feel it has been less of a burden for them because I had Curtis.

He is the most romantic man. He brings me flowers frequently. Once he didn't bring one bouquet, but three of them. Sometimes he brings me wild flowers, or first flowers of the spring. He makes up songs and sings them to me. He knows when I am down or discouraged. He gently prompts me to tell him what's bugging me. He never condemns or gets irritated or angry with me, even if what I'm upset about is rather silly. At really serious times, he has even stayed home from work to comfort me and to talk it out. He is my greatest encourager in every aspect of my life. But especially he encourages me to be the very best I can be for the Lord. He is not threatened by my knowledge of the Word. He glories in it. Yet, he can and does teach me, too. I feel as though I am the most loved, most special woman in all the world to him. I feel so protected. He truly "knows" me and is sensitive to my every need or desire. He is far more sensitive to my needs than I am to his.

The protection that I feel in our relationship is something I have spoken of in seminars. There are women who have actually been jealously angry with me about it. I understand that. They are like I was before. They do not know such a thing exists in marriage. They can't feel or experience it in their own marriages. Like me, they may know a type of bullying protection. It's as though the man is forcing some protection on his wife because she doesn't know what is good for her. The result of that is not a feeling of protection, but a feeling of being bullied. What I experience from Curtis is the gentle caring protection that I think God gives us as His children.

Curtis makes my daughters feel like they are special and loved also. He will buy them flowers sometimes too. He goes out of his way to do special things for them.

There is no way of accounting for the father's heart he has demonstrated for Lynn-Marie through these years as she has suffered through her healing process. It is a supernatural fathering gift of God for him to step in and act like a nurturing father to one who is older than he is. Yet that is exactly what he does. Sometimes she has been taken to a hospital somewhere and we will have to go retrieve her car. He is tall and so when he drives her car the seat has to be moved back. When she gets in the car, she says "Daddy long-legs has been in here". So at times, she fondly calls him Daddy long-legs.

The Grand kids think he's great. He's helped the boys build a fort and he built a club house for the girls. He goes hunting with the boys or takes them on little camping trips for hunting. He writes them hilarious letters. When the boys call, if I answer the phone, they say "Hi. Is Curtis there." They rarely call to talk to me.

He has fulfilled many of the things God said were reasons for putting Curtis and I together. He has restored to my children and grandchildren some of what they were robbed of.

I could go on and on about Curtis. But I'll stop.

How could I ever say to anyone God's real choice, His true will, was for me to stay in the first marriage, in order to accommodate the twisted, demonic, perversions of what a marriage and a man should be? How could I believe God would want me to stay there and cater to the unclean spirits my ex-husband was not willing to give up? He chose his own way. When he did, God, in His love and

mercy for me, released me. In actuality, the divorce
just ended the relationship, because biblically
speaking, the marriage vows had already been broken
many times, in many ways, by my ex-husband, long
before God released me. The release did not break
any vows, for one cannot break something that is
already broken! I can say I am sorry that it ended
the way it did. But I cannot say in my heart that
I sinned against God by leaving. Rather than
compromise myself in my walk with Him, I chose
to leave. I feel that is according to Deut. 13:1-11,
especially verses 5,6,8, and 10. He led me to
the god of self and demon controlled perversion.
These verses show there are things that supersede
marriage vows, even though God was a witness to
them. Because of that, I believe I left him for
God's sake. I believe it was God's will for me
to leave him. Jonah 2:8 speaks to my soul and
spirit. It says those who observe lying vanities
forsake their own mercy. I believe if I had stayed
in that marriage because of all the vane and false
things that are preached, I would have forsaken
the mercy God wanted to abundantly pour out on
me. I would have forfeited that mercy.

I did forsake my ex-husband, his house, his
land, his brothers and sister and their mates,
his mother and his father for His name's sake.
I could have chosen to keep all of those relationships, because they were dear to me. I could
have chosen to succumb to the perversions of demons
so that my ex-husband would be free to live with
me AND the demons. It would have given him peace
with me and we could have stayed together. I chose
to forsake all of that and go with God. I believe
Curtis is part of the hundredfold God promises
to those who forsake ALL to follow Him. I believe
I did what God wanted me to do in the ex-husband's
family and in his life. I was the first one to
be born again in that family, now many of them
are too. I was faithful until He said it was over.

The Scripture I stand on here is Math. 19:29 and Mark 10:29-30. How could I ever say that by leaving that marriage, I sinned against God? How could I ever apologize for the beautiful husband God has given me, when He restored to me a hundredfold? I can't apologize, I can only say how blessed I am of God and bow to Him in awe. Because Mark 10:30 says that we will receive an hundredfold NOW IN THIS TIME--I believe the prophetic things concerning Curtis, that God spoke to my spirit, truly means Curtis is an earthly reward for my faithfulness to God. He is gentle, sweet, kind, never angry with me, has never raised his voice to me. He watches over me, he protects me. He's romantic. He builds me up emotionally and spiritually. He always says the right thing at the right time. He's a miracle of love. He's a gift from God. I am blessed beyond measure.

Thank you, Lord, for your infinite grace and mercy that you have given to me in the gift of Curtis.

I pray that some people, who have been tormented in spirit and by other Christians concerning divorce, might find hope, inspiration and freedom from those things through this testimony. God, heal the broken hearted and set the captives free!

## CHAPTER TWENTY ONE
## BEHOLD MY LOVE

Hi! I am Curtis. I'm Joan's husband. Every story has two sides, so this is my side of our story.

In January of 1991, some friends encouraged me to start going to a new bible study group that was starting in the church I was going to. I was at a place in my Christian life where I was very discouraged with Christians that I knew. I didn't see much fruit in their lives and some of them, including pastors, had hurt me pretty badly. I was ready to hang it up as far as going to church was concerned. I wasn't so sure I even wanted to be a Christian, either. But I started going to this group. I thought it would be okay, because it was a small group.

The leader of the study was a woman, which I was glad of, because it was easier for me to talk to women than it was for me to talk to guys. I had some ideas of what a Christian was supposed to be like from what I read in the Bible and from what God was teaching me. I noticed the teacher had all of these characteristics that Jesus has, and it was real. **I really, really needed to see that in a person** and it helped me to open up and be honest with God and her.

The first couple of classes where at the church. For some reason of their own, others had dropped out so there was only myself and another girl left in the group. So we switched the meetings to the leader's house. The room the church had given us to meet in was not a very cheerful room. It was in a sub-basement and it was gloomy. I didn't feel comfortable there. I was glad to meet at the leader's house. It was a homey atmosphere that made me feel comfortable and more at ease. I could concentrate more on God instead of Church. I felt God's presence and love in her house.

As the weeks went by, I learned about things

that went beyond the material we were supposed to be studying. Like forgiveness and healing of the wounded spirit. I got healed from some of the hurts of the past. I loved, and sucked up everything that God was teaching me, and everything we were learning together.

The young woman stopped coming to the classes after the 10th or 11th week of the Bible studies, but I wanted to continue the studies anyway. Our focus was on God. It didn't matter whether there was two or three of us. I never gave the matter of how many we were a thought. I just wanted to learn more about God. So we went on with the studies. But now, God led us even further beyond the regular study materials, and we would talk about the Word and the Lord for hours.

I had a deep love and respect for Joan, for her character and her wisdom in the Lord.

One day Joanie asked me if I felt that God was calling me into a ministry of some kind. I said yes. I had known for about a year before the classes began, that God had something for me to do. A lot of people had told me that also. I knew it would be a ministry with men somehow. I did not like that because men didn't seem to acknowledge that they had emotions, and they didn't know how to express feelings or understand them. Shortly after Joanie asked me that question, I began to feel that we would be able to counsel and pray for others together. I felt that I would be blessed if we worked together, and that those we worked with would be more blessed. The Lord did lead us into counseling with people. He touched quite a few lives through that. Their lives changed because of it. And we were blessed, too. Somewhere along the line, I began to feel that the ministry would be bigger than just counseling together.

One day in May, Joanie was showing all the signs of a love sick puppy and I knew this was an issue that had to be confronted. I was very

surprised by what I was seeing. Up until this time
our total focus was on the Lord, now it seemed
to be us and the Lord. I wasn't worried about it,
because of Joanie's character and habit of following
the Lord. But I wondered what was happening.
I believe now that it was God's way of gradually
bringing us to a point where we could accept where
He was leading us. At any rate, I didn't feel
like it was something that I wanted to run away
from. So I confronted her about it. I plainly asked
what her feelings for me were. She was nervous
and almost in tears, but she told me she was in
love with me. I knew she was serious, she was
in love and she meant it. When she told me the
truth, I wasn't mad, and I wasn't jumping up and
down with joy either. I just thought that once
it was out in the open, we could deal with it.
I thought our relationship in the Lord and with
each other was strong enough that we could deal
with it. The method of dealing with it would be
that we would both follow the Lord. I was relieved
it was out in the open. We agreed that for the
time being, there would be no more brother/sister
in the Lord hugs.

We continued with the studies. There was no
further personal discussion.

On Memorial weekend, Joanie went away. She
gave me a key to her house so I could watch some
programs on TBN. While I was watching, I was
very much touched with God's love, for me and for
others. It was overwhelming. I was weeping and
crying and God's love just flowed over me and
through me. It felt so warm. I wished Joanie
was with me to share God's blessing of love.
I couldn't wait to tell her what happened.

In June, I confronted her again about her
feelings for me. I felt like she needed to verb-
alize her feelings. She did. Nothing had changed.

Later in June, without my permission, God began
to change my feelings for her. At first I thought

God was crazy and I didn't understand what He was doing. But the more I fought the feelings, the more God made my feelings for her turn into more of a husband/wife kind of love. I wanted to be with her all the time. I wanted to honor and cherish her, so that she would feel it. I wanted to take care of her, I wanted to make her laugh. I wanted to be there for her. I wasn't afraid to meet her relatives. That was a biggy for me! I wanted to share everything that God had for us together. God gave me the desire and the boldness to follow Him and to do what God wanted me to do, even if it went against public opinion or church opinion.

We heard that there was going to be a Mike Williams crusade in a town that was about a six hour drive from us. When I heard about it, I just knew that we were supposed to go to it. Joan knew a friend there that we could stay with. So in July, we went to the crusade. It was a great experience. God really moved and healed us in many ways. We were blessed in more ways than we could even know.

By this time, God had been doing so much in both of us, and touching us so deeply that we could not contain it. I felt so close to her that I just wanted to touch her or hold her hand. So I followed my feelings and did hold her hand during the services. By the second night, I knew the direction that God was leading, I felt like I needed to talk to her about it. We went for a short drive. We came to a place where we could park that was a beautiful scene. There was a church on a hill, in front of the church stood three crosses. There were lights spotlighting the crosses that made them look golden in the night. Where I parked, we could gaze at that beautiful scene. Somehow, it seemed like it was a holy place. But even that didn't make it any easier for me to talk. I wanted to have a confirmation, for the third time, of what Joan was feeling. She was still feeling the

same thing. After she told me she was still in
love with me, I felt I had to tell her what was
going on in me. So, reluctantly, I admitted to
her that I had strong feelings for her too. At
that point, I could not yet say to her that I
loved her or make a commitment by asking her to
marry me. God still had a little bit of work to
do in me. Two days later, before the evening
service, we were walking around a little park.
It was God's timing and God's place. We sat on
center stage of a building in the park. At this
time I **knew** God was telling me to marry her and
that the ministry would be a ministry of love.
Again I wanted confirmation. So I really pressed
her hard to tell me **everything** that God had shown
her in the vision of ministry and how it related
to us. She started crying and admitted that we
were not only supposed to be in a ministry together,
but that the ministry would require a married
couple. And that the Lord had told her in April
that we were to married. Then I said that the
Lord was telling me the same thing. Then I finally
said that we were so one in the spirit, and one
in the emotions, that to be married in the flesh
was the only thing left to do. She cried harder
and asked "How could you handle being married
to an older woman like me?" I had to be honest.
I didn't know, but God did. So that was what I
told her. So we walked around some more, hand
in hand, asking questions about what people would
say and how would this marriage be accepted, and
was it really God's will?

That night we were praying with friends in
the same park. One of them had a message from the
Lord that answered all of our questions. It was
very meaningful for us and we believed it was from
the Lord because we knew our friend's character
and her love for God. She knew nothing of our
relationship together, other than God was leading
us into some kind of ministry. The whole message

was confirming, but the most confirming of all was that God said, through her, that what God joined together, let no man put asunder. I knew that was a confirmation directly from Him that we were to be married.

One thing that God has never stopped teaching me, is how He is so sovereign. He told us to be married six years ago. Trusting Him was hard because it wasn't common or culturally acceptable for a man to marry an older woman. I trusted God and He has rewarded me to overflowing with the best wife and family in the world.

Their were some people, Christians, who thought I was crazy. They said God would never do anything like that. I was taught that you were to tell Christians by their fruit. People seemed to want to get to know me because of the fruit in my life, but I wasn't seeing much of the fruit or Godly character that I was looking for in their lives. So it was hard to listen to the Lord's soft voice over some people's loud voices. The few people that did seem to have good fruit in their lives, and that we talked to, agreed that this marriage was of God. So in the end, my trust in the Lord and my love for Joanie helped me through this growing period in the Lord.

I love Joanie. Our spirits are one. I believe and have said many times that our spirits loved each other before we did!! In our love we are one, and in truth we are honest with each other. She loves me the same way I love her. We have never argued about anything. We have never raised our voices to each other or did anything bad to each other. Not that either one of us is perfect. But it's like Jesus. He loves the sinner and accepts them. Then they make the choice to follow Him.

I love Joanie and her uniqueness that makes her her, even her snoring that I can tell 3 houses away. Just kidding.

I will serve her before I will serve guests

because I feel that is more right than "proper
etiquette" that is man's traditions.

I will spend time talking with her, taking
any amount of time she needs. I praise the Lord
that I am self-employed because when something
really serious happens in the family, I will stay
with her to comfort her.

When she is in the hospital, I'm not out working somewhere or going fishing or something, I'm
with her.

We hate being apart from each other. If we
feel this way and we are only humans, imagine being
apart from the Lord!! Often I hear, "wouldn't
it be great to be in heaven with Jesus". I feel
that we have some of that kind of oneness all of
the time. The eagerness to hold each other again
and to physically feel the love, support, and
protection we draw from each other is wonderful
and it is missed when we are apart.

The Bible says to speak what is good and
edifying. It is not what goes into a man that
defiles him, it is what comes out. It is very
commonly accepted in our culture to degrade women
and girls by teasing them, cutting them down, and
making them feel worthless. All these things will
totally destroy a woman. When kids are growing
up, you know how important it is to encourage them
and lift them up in what they do. As they grow
into maturity, it really shapes their life, personality, character, and their outlook on life.
So in the same way, a man should encourage and
uplift his wife with edifying words. We have seen
a woman get married who was full of joy, happy,
life of the party, and totally at peace. But
after three years of being teased, cut down, and
not being encouraged, and lifted up by her Christian
husband, she was depressed, suicidal, never smiling.
She can't smile sometimes. Husbands and wives
have a great responsibility to each other. The
vows they made were before God, you know.

Besides my wife, I have children and grand-children. Do you want to know what I think about having four daughters older than me? And 9 grand-children younger than me? Sometimes it's tough! But listen to this!!

One of my daughters has a car that I sometimes have to go get and deliver to her. For obvious reasons, she has the seat all the way forward so she can reach the peddles. I have to move the seat back as far as it goes, like it should be. So to her, my name is Daddy-longlegs.

Since they were already grown when I inherited them, I didn't worry about fathering, but just being friends. That was easy. But as the Lord said, I have been helpful in their lives as a father. Also I have learned so much from them!! I grew up in a dysfunctional family. When I met and spent time with Joan's family, I saw love in a family like I had never seen before. I didn't know it existed.

The grandkids were something else. They all wanted all of my time. They didn't want to share me with anyone and would fight over who got to sit next to me at the dinner table. Christmas is great!! I get a bunch of presents!!

I feel a great responsibility as step-grand father, and step-father. I really want to help them when they need help. Sometimes I want to say things, but I'm not sure how it will be taken. I am not loud or aggressive. The Lord has to be in it. Praying about it and waiting for the Lord's timing is essential if what I want to say is to help them.

I feel that kids are family and they deserve to take priority over most things. There have been many times when Joanie and I have planned some-thing or my work is scheduled. But something happens and we will go to help in what ever way we can. Sometimes just a hug can do so much for a person in need. Knowing that they can call, talk, ask of me, is a privilege and an honorable responsibility. I feel that's part of being a Daddy.

Loving Joanie is the most easiest thing I have ever done!! God is #1, Joanie is #2. I worship God because I love Him, not because the Bible says to. I submit to the Lord, learn from the Lord, go through trials with the Lord, die to the flesh and the lusts of the world to please the Lord because I love Him. He is an awesome God that I proudly serve. It is not just because it's in the Bible, it's not a matter of works. It's a matter of love. Jesus gave of himself as an example and gave honor to those who gave to Him sacrificially. The same is true in my relationship to Joanie. I love pleasing her, putting her first. Even if it's raining, I'll open the car door for her. When we come home from a walk, I will serve her a drink of water first, not ignore her and guzzle the water myself, while standing in her way. When we come home from a long drive-- I'll let her use our one throne room first. When we go grocery shopping, I carry the bags into the house. I love to tell her how beautiful she is, how great the food tastes, how the house looks good. I try to get up first and make breakfast for her sometimes, but she always gets up too. I do the heavier work around the house, like vacuuming. I help her to change the sheets on the bed, because I know the bending over while tugging and stretching on the sheets makes the angina start sometimes. Sometimes, when she's working on the book, I will cook and do dishes so she can continue working.

I love explaining how special she is to me, encouraging her, making her laugh and giggle. When she wants something done around the house, I want to do it. I would never think of whining about it or making excuses not to do it either.

She deserves to be loved the way I love the Lord, in spirit and in truth. I make Joanie feel special. I want her to be able to think of me and

get warm and snuggly inside. I want her to be the
best godly woman she can be. I am a big part of
God's plan for her life. God is using me to help
Joanie reach God's goals for her life.

*******

This man is truly the head of our house. Every
day he demonstrates how God is head over Christ,
and how Christ is head over the Church. He demonstrates the servanthood of the head. In the same
way that I honor Christ as my head, I honor my
husband as my head. There is no battle in our
home over who is the head, the "boss". There is
no chaos in our home because no one is acting
like the "boss". There is no one who is in command
or in charge. I asked him one day, "do you feel
like the head of our home?". His reply was a
classic. He said, "I don't even think about the
term "head". We are so one in the spirit and in
our hearts that we think alike and want the same
things. As long as it is what God wants, that's
what we want." Jesus loved the father so much
that everything He said and did and taught, was
what the Father wanted. That is the kind of love
God has given us to share with each other and to
share with anyone we come in contact with. It
is directly opposite of the current teaching on
submission. The fruit of it is love, joy, peace,
honor and respect. There is a mutual submission
because of the love of God. We serve one another
because of that love. We have a deep gratitude
for what God has given us in each other. We are
a gift from God to each other, and each day we
have together is a gift from God. This is the
way God intended marriage, headship and submission
to be.

# CHAPTER TWENTY TWO
## MIRACLE OF LOVE

What is headship? It is a miracle of love!

This short chapter is the recap of the other chapters, so there will be some repetition.

God, the "Head", loved so much that he **GAVE** His only begotten Son. Jesus, the "Head", loved so much he **GAVE** His life as a ransom for many. The headship of Father and Son is demonstrated only by loving and by giving. This is to be the model of "headship" of man and woman. The word does not say head **over** but head **of**. God the Father and Jesus the Son only blessed those that they were truly head of. There is no element whatsoever of control, domination, or ruling over the will of those who are under their headship. Jesus himself said anyone who was His follower would not have dominion or lord it over **anyone.**

As the Father demonstrates His love, and as the Son demonstrates His love, it inspires those who have come under that "headship" to fall on their faces in awesome reverence. They are in awe of the sense of being loved and protected and provided for. They feel free to come into the arms of refuge of the Father and to be cuddled there and comforted there. They feel that there is no condemnation from the Father. There is a joy and a peace. They respond to the love of the "head". They worship Him and follow Him with a joy of obedience. Their hearts are so turned toward the Father that it grieves them deeply to even think of doing something that would offend Him. Their desire is to please Him. They willingly submit to His love and His desires. They know that the Father will not ask them to do things that are beyond their capability of doing, or that are harmful for them. He'll not demand that they serve him. He'll not act out of selfishness, He'll only act out love for them and what is best for them. They can rest in the goodness of Him. That is headship. He created us to respond to that Headship by returning love and worship to Him.

He created the man as the "head" of the woman so that she could respond to his love and protection and provision for her. God created or formed her out of the man. He created her as a weaker vessel physically so that she would need his strength. At the same time, He created her in a position of strength because she was the final touch that made all of His creation exceedingly whole. She was created to rescue the man from his aloneness.

While the woman was created to be the nurturing mother of children, the husband was given the ability to nurture his wife and his children. Therefore they both have the nurturing qualities of God the Father and Jesus the Son. Jesus, demonstrating His character as head of the church, said to Jerusalem, "How I wanted to gather you under my wings like a mother hen gathers her chicks, but you would not". This demonstrates a nurturing headship. "Let me cuddle you in my arms of safety. Let me protect you and nurture you there." This is the essence of headship. This is the head of the household of God. This is how God is the Head of the Son and the Son is Head of the church. This is how the man should be the head of his household.

As I said before, my husband is the head of our household. I write this section of this final chapter with tears of gratefulness in my eyes, as I reflect on the blessings that God has bestowed on me in the man He gave to me to be the head of me. There is so much of Jesus in him. He is so strong and so masculine and yet the gentleness and meekness of Jesus is there. I know his protection. I can feel him acting as a shield between me and things of this world that would want to hurt me emotionally or physically. I feel that shield even more from spiritual wounds. He knows my moods and he takes me in his arms and holds me and comforts me with the love of God. He doesn't condemn or scold or demand. He just loves. He demonstrates to me the love that I never knew in all of my life. His demonstration of love taught me what the love of God is. I do not worship him in the same way I worship God, but I reverence him with everything that is within me. It is as God said it should be. Husbands, love your wives as Christ loved the Church and gave Himself for her. Wives reverence your husbands. I willingly submit to my husband.

As God and Jesus demonstrate their headship by loving and giving, so he wants man to demonstrate to his wife that same loving and giving. I believe that because God gave the headship to man, He will bestow on the man a special grace to fulfill what God has designed him to be as head. He will restore to the Christian man the spiritual perception concerning his wife that was lost when Adam and Eve sinned. He will again be able to see his wife as a precious part of himself that was a gift from God to rescue him from his aloneness. The man has to tap into that source of Grace. My husband has somehow done that.

As my head, the love of God flows through him and out over me. So his banner over me is love. I sit at his feet and bask in his love. While I do that, I am sitting at the feet of both my Jesus and God my Father. I am submitting to their love as they demonstrate it through my husband. He brings me into God's presence. To stand beside my husband and behold his face while his eyes are closed and he is lost in worship, to see him kneel in prayer, for him to take my hand and say "Let's pray about it",

486

these are some of the things that inspire an awesome reverence and trust in me for my "head". I respond to him with my respect and love and reverence for him. Because, just like submitting to my Father, by submitting to him, I am only submitting to what is best for me. I am submitting to God, through him, because he is submitted to God first.

As I love and revere him, I bring him into God's presence, because that demonstrates God's love for him, through me, his wife.

The union of a man and woman is supposed to be a demonstration of God's love in human form. There is no place for domination and control or lordship over anybody in God's plan of headship and submission. What is taught today about headship and submission is a gross perversion of God's plan, perpetrated and perpetuated by Satan since the time of Adam and Eve. The "chain of command" type headship is an exact replica of the world's system that Christ forbade. It is the exact opposite of His teaching that the head would be the servant. Today's teaching makes the man a lord who is bowed to, and served, by the wife and children. He is not last, as Jesus said, he is pre-eminent and first. There is not a hint of that kind of thing in God or in Christ as Head. Their pattern is the one we should be following in our marriages.

For 34 years, I lived in a marriage where Satan's perverse plan of submission and headship was practiced. I thought it was God's way. The reinforcement from so-called "Christian perspectives" was even more torturous to live by than the secular world's perspectives. But in that marriage I tried to live out those principles, thinking they were God's plan. I bowed to, and served the man, the created rather than the Creator. All of my efforts were in vain. It was not in the heart of my ex-husband to be submitted enough to God so God could transmit love through him. He never demonstrated headship in accordance with God's demonstration of headship. So no matter how much I submitted, with a sweet spirit or not, it produced only misery and failure. It was not my spirit, or my submission, or lack of it, that determined the outcome. It was what was in the man's heart.

I praise God I suffered through all of that. In His wisdom and in His time, he released me from that marriage bond. I never dreamed I would ever marry again. I did not know that I had no idea of what real love and real headship and real submission was. He brought Curtis into my life. Through Curtis, He taught me what love was, He taught me what He means by submission and headship in the home. Through Curtis, He taught me what being one in the spirit is all about. Through Curtis, He taught me how two become one. He taught me what "submit one to another in the fear of the Lord" truly means. If I had not known the wrong and the perverted way, I would not know the glorious blessings of the true way. I **know** what God has given me in the headship of this husband is a rare jewel to be treasured. I praise and thank my God for my husband and for His blessing of headship.

I thank God that I have been given a view from both sides of the fence. Because I have walked both paths, perhaps that will validate some of the things I've written for people who would doubt.

My prayer for this book is that it will somehow reach God's people with the truth of what submission and headship is. It is a most beautiful blessing from the Father. It's a spiritual thing. It is not God's plan for the man to take rule over his wife's will in the flesh, for that is contrary to the very nature of God and Christ. It is the heart of the Father for His children to walk in blessings, not this man-made curse of false headship and false submission that is the doctrine of demons. Jesus Christ gave His life to set us all free from all such curses.

My prayer is that this book will be used of God to take out one more spot, stain, wrinkle, and evil thing, from the Bride. I pray that it will be a tool that Jesus would be able to use it to set many captives free from the principles of false headship and false submission that makes men idols and women idol worshipers. I also pray that many pastors and laymen will be set free from the false headship and false submission that makes pastors idols and congregations idol worshipers.

GOD, SET US ALL FREE FROM THE APOSTASY OF THE PERVERSION OF SUBMISSION!!

**REFERENCE RESOURCES**

The New Scofield Reference Bible; Authorized King James Version; Editor, C.I. Scofield, D.D.; Copyright, 1967, by Oxford University Press, Inc., New York

Oxford NIV Scofield Study Bible; Editor C.I. Scofield, D.D.; Copyright 1967 by Oxford University Press, Inc., New York

The Septuagint Version, Greek and English; Zondervan Publishing House of the Zondervan Corp., Grand Rapids, Michigan 49506

Strong's Exhaustive Concordance of the Bible; James Strong, S.T.D.,LL.D.; Published by MacDonald Publishing Co., McLean, Virginia 22101

An Expository Dictionary of New Testament Words; W.E.Vine, M.A.; Published by Fleming H. Revell Company, Old Tappan, New Jersey.
\*\*\*\*\*

To order copies of The Perversion of Submission write to:

The Perversion of Submission

**Joan Erickson**
**4365 Elmwood Lane**

Or telephone    **Hermantown, MN  55811**
(218) 722-4695